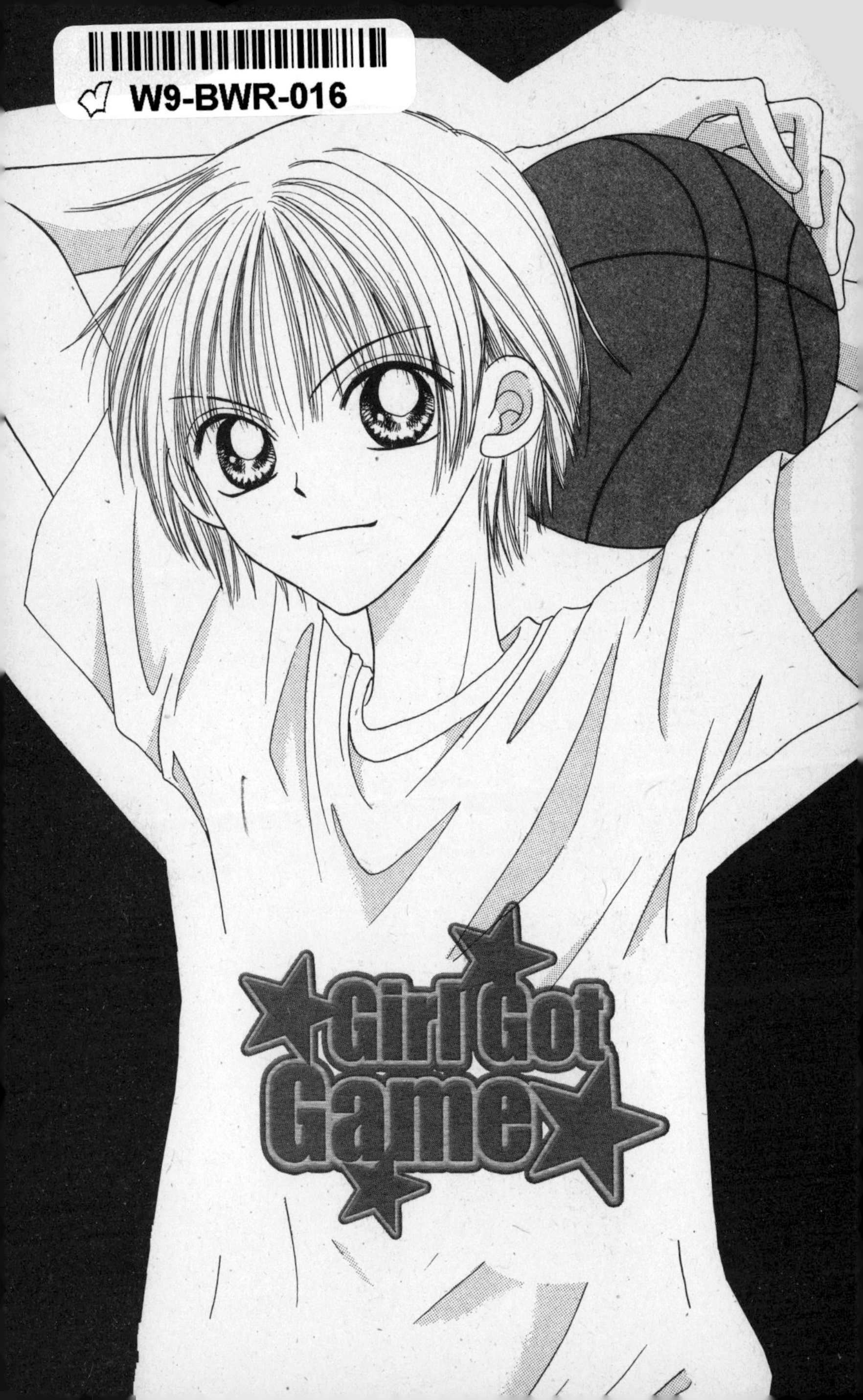
Girl Got Game

## *Girl Got Game Vol. 7*
## created by Shizuru Seino

Translation - Aya Matsunaga
English Adaptation - Kelly Sue DeConnick
Copy Editor - Suzanne Waldman
Retouch and Lettering - Benchcomix
Production Artist - Vicente Rivera, Jr.
Cover Design - Christian Lownds

Editor - Rob Tokar
Digital Imaging Manager - Chris Buford
Pre-Press Manager - Antonio DePietro
Production Managers - Jennifer Miller and Mutsumi Miyazaki
Art Director - Matt Alford
Managing Editor - Jill Freshney
VP of Production - Ron Klamert
President and C.O.O. - John Parker
Publisher and C.E.O. - Stuart Levy

A  Manga

TOKYOPOP Inc.
5900 Wilshire Blvd. Suite 2000
Los Angeles, CA 90036

E-mail: info@TOKYOPOP.com
Come visit us online at www.TOKYOPOP.com

ISBN: 1-59182-986-0

First TOKYOPOP printing: January 2005

10 9 8 7 6 5 4 3 2
Printed in the USA

by Shizuru Seino
Volume 7

HAMBURG // LONDON // LOS ANGELES // TOKYO

# The Story So Far

Some people will do anything to realize their dreams...even if it means disguising a girl as a boy so she can play on a famous boys' basketball team. If you don't believe it, just imagine how Kyo Aizawa feels--her dad's the one who cooked up this crazy scheme!

Kyo's father was once a great basketball player who aspired to play for the NBA. Unfortunately, an injury ended his career before it even started. Despite his disappointment, he passed his love of the game--and his moves--to his daughter.

Kyo wanted to date a boy, not become one, and she was not happy about her father's kooky plan...until she met Chiharu Eniwa, the boy who was to be her teammate on the court...and her roommate in the dorms!

As luck would have it, Kyo and Chiharu got on each other's nerves right from the start, but Kyo's attempts to get past Chiharu's gruff, sullen exterior eventually made the two of them friends. In turn, Chiharu's thoughtful kindness also swept Kyo off her feet...and she wondered if she might have some serious feelings for him.

Kyo and Chiharu's peaceful coexistence was cut painfully short when an old friend of Kyo's named Tsuyaka Himejima arrived on the scene. Tsuyaka knew Kyo from her previous school and transferred to Seisyu so they could play on the same team again. When Tsuyaka learned Kyo was masquerading as a boy, she was willing to protect Kyo's secret...until Kyo proved she was unwilling to leave the boys' team. Attempting to force the issue, Tsuyaka tore open Kyo's shirt in front of Chiharu, revealing Kyo's breasts! Though Chiharu didn't tell Kyo's secret, he did have a tough time adjusting to the idea of a female roommate.

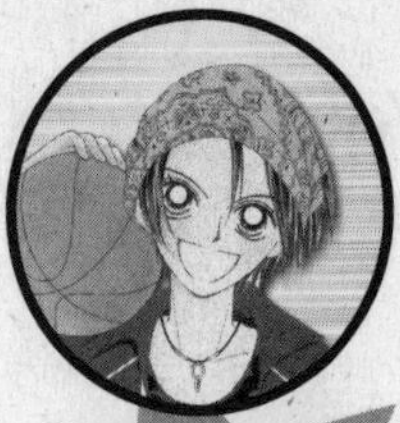

Kyo Aizawa

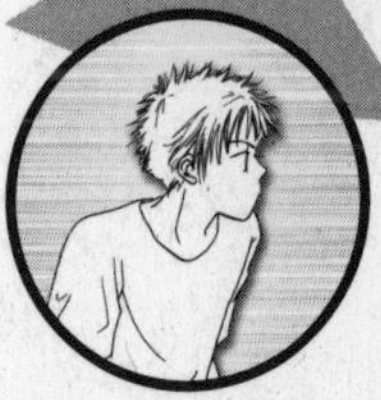

Chiharu Eniwa

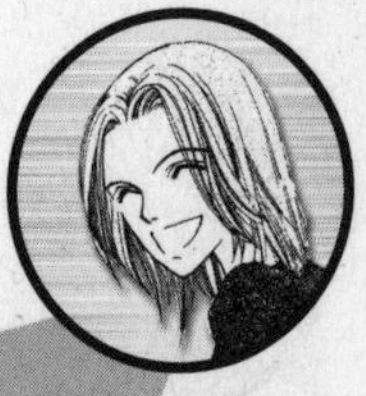

Hisashi Imai

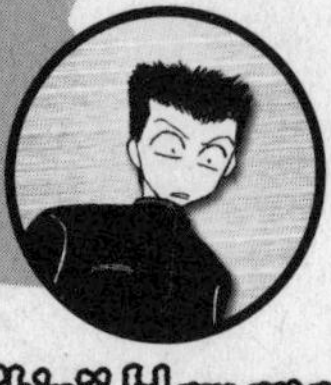

Shinji Hamaya

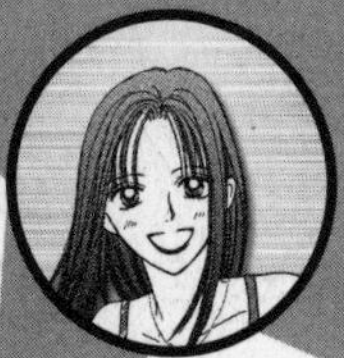

Ayaha

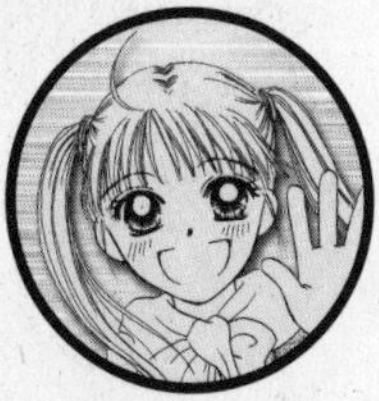

Akari Tojo

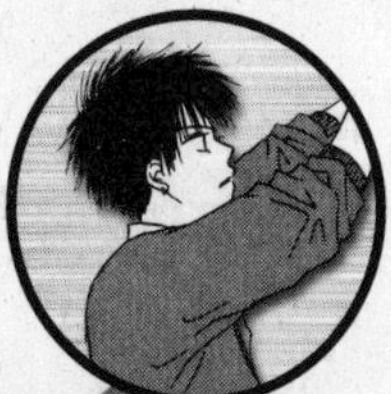

Kensuke Yura

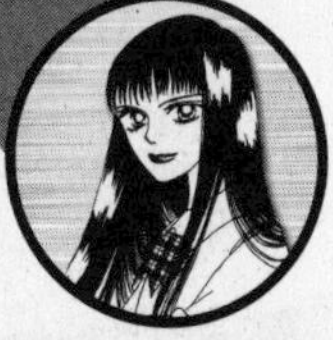

Tsuyaka Himejima

Just as life seemed like it was going to return to "normal," Kyo literally stumbled across Kensuke Yura on her way to practice. Yura, it turns out, is one of the best players on the Seisyu High basketball team, but he hadn't shown up for practice or any games since before Kyo became a member. However, once Yura met Kyo, he started showing up for practice again...though none of the other boys seemed happy about it.

Though Yura's skills on the court are impressive, he was a very poor team player whose steadfast refusal to rely on others alienated his teammates. Unfortunately, Yura's "loner" behavior also extends to his personal life, and it's in large part due to his photographic memory. Yura's perfect, unfailing memory makes school a breeze...and life a pain. He remembers every detail about every bad thing that's ever been said or done to him, and it's left the gifted young man bitter, angry, untrusting, and friendless.

Recently, Kyo's attempts to help Yura led the disturbed young man to kidnap her and take her to an abandoned building which was rigged to explode and burn with both of them inside it. In order to regain Yura's trust, Kyo told him that she's really a girl. As the building burned around them, Chiharu forced his way through the flames to rescue Kyo. Unwilling to give up on Yura, Kyo enlisted Chiharu's aid to rescue Yura as well, despite Yura's desire to die. Confused and touched by their act of kindness, Yura seemed to finally form a bond of trust with his two teammates as they helped him limp away from the burning wreckage.

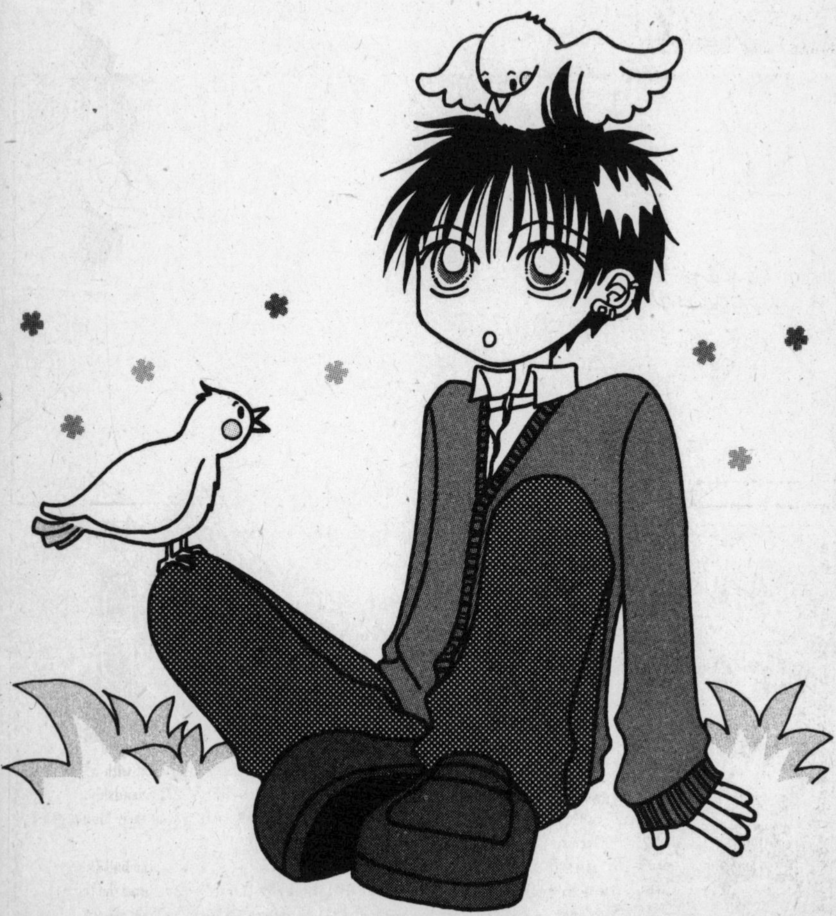

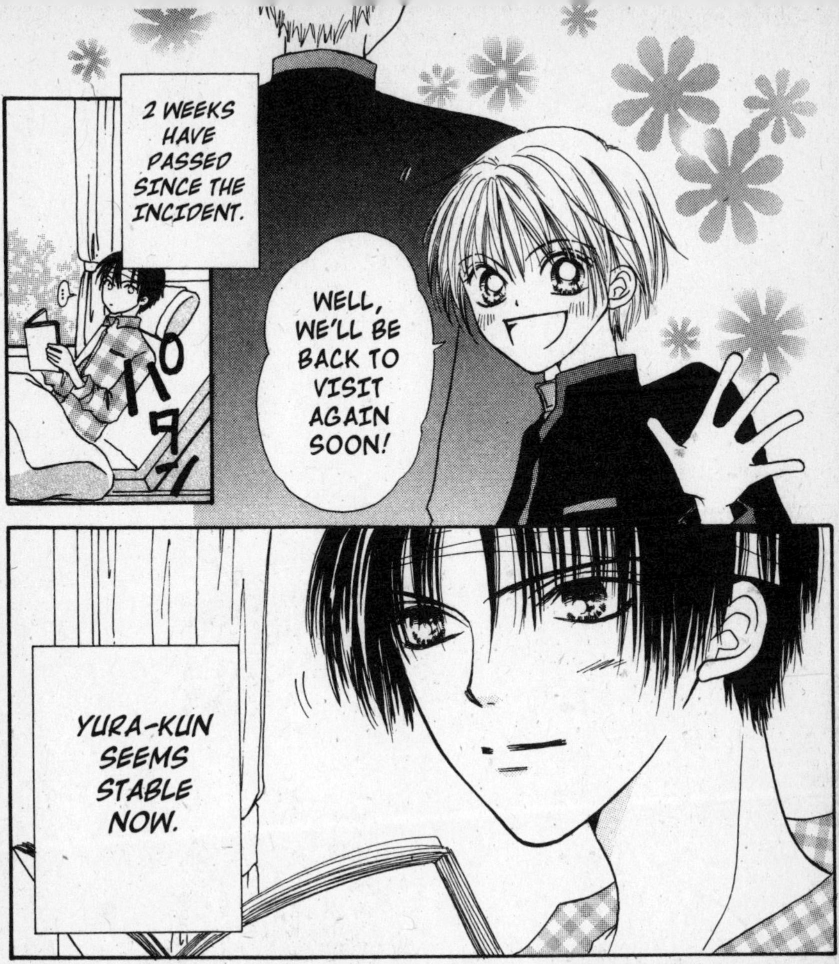
WELL, WE'LL BE BACK TO VISIT AGAIN SOON!
2 WEEKS HAVE PASSED SINCE THE INCIDENT.
パタン
YURA-KUN SEEMS STABLE NOW.

**Girl Got Game**

## Our story so far...

KYO AIZAWA transferred to Seisyu High and dressed like a guy in order to join the men's basketball team and realize her father's dreams.

* Her teammate and roommate, CHIHARU, discovered her secret but kept it to himself. The two became very close, then...
* KYO befriended YURA, a super-good-looking scholarship student with a genius IQ and an attitude problem. YURA, suspicious of KYO's friendship, kidnapped her and, in a suicidal plot to prove she was untrue, rigged their hiding place to explode.
* Their teammates went looking for them, but when they found them, the building was already on fire. CHIHARU braved the flames to rescue them, and the three escaped by jumping from the roof. YURA was moved to tears by their efforts.

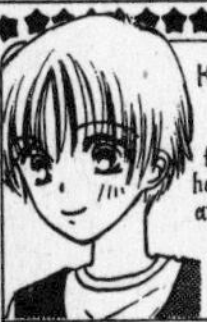

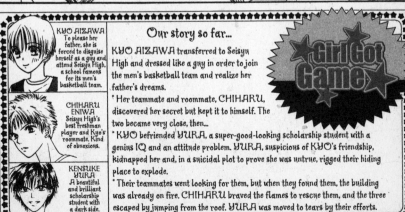

**KYO AIZAWA**
To please her father, she is forced to disguise herself as a guy and attend Seisyu High, a school famous for its men's basketball team.

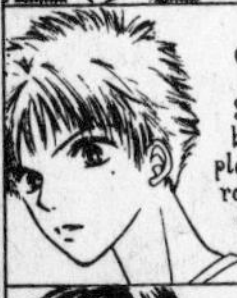

**CHIHARU ENIWA**
Seisyu High's best freshman player and Kyo's roommate. Kind of obnoxious.

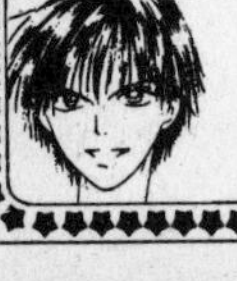

**KENSUKE YURA**
A beautiful and brilliant scholarship student with a dark side.

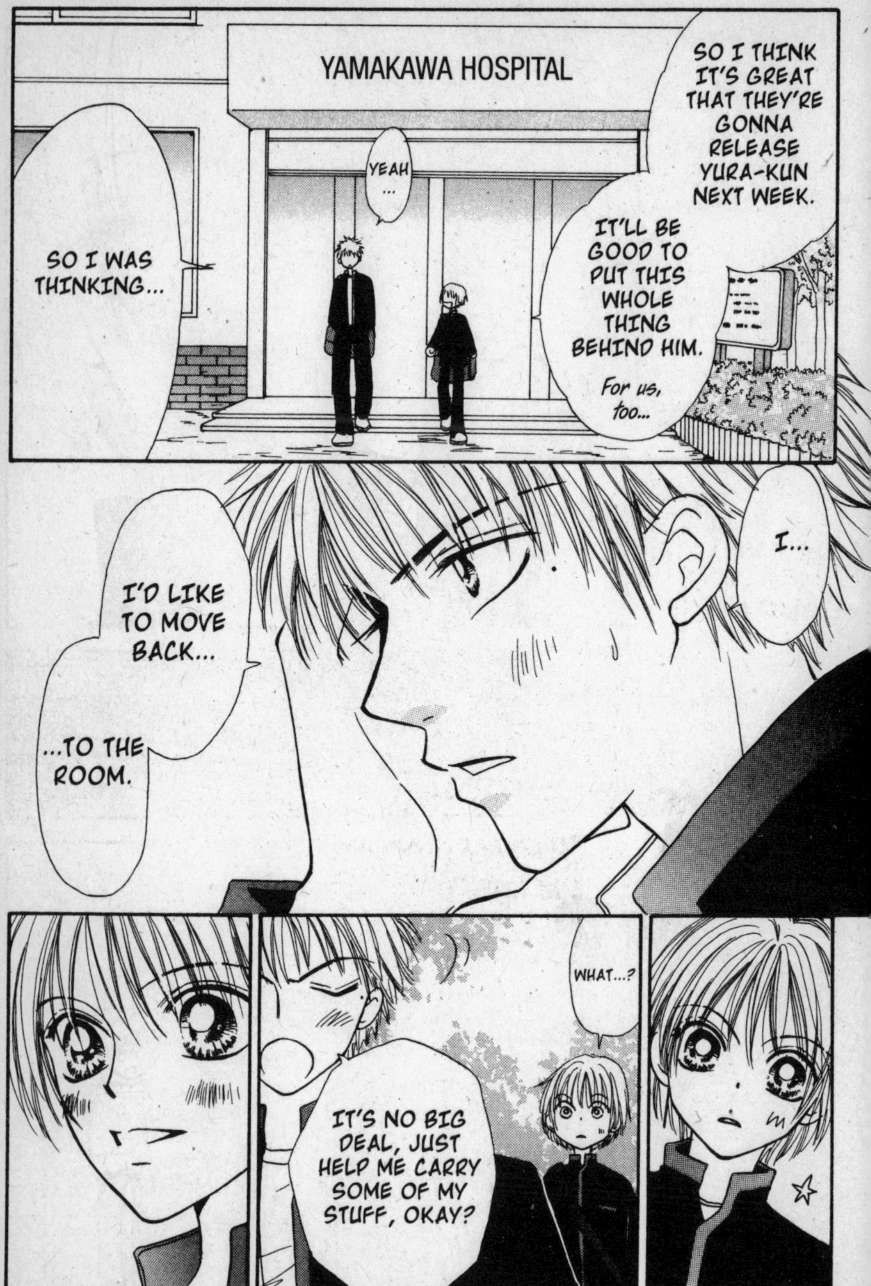
YAMAKAWA HOSPITAL
SO I THINK IT'S GREAT THAT THEY'RE GONNA RELEASE YURA-KUN NEXT WEEK.
IT'LL BE GOOD TO PUT THIS WHOLE THING BEHIND HIM.
For us, too...
YEAH ...
SO I WAS THINKING...
I...
I'D LIKE TO MOVE BACK...
...TO THE ROOM.
WHAT...?
IT'S NO BIG DEAL, JUST HELP ME CARRY SOME OF MY STUFF, OKAY?

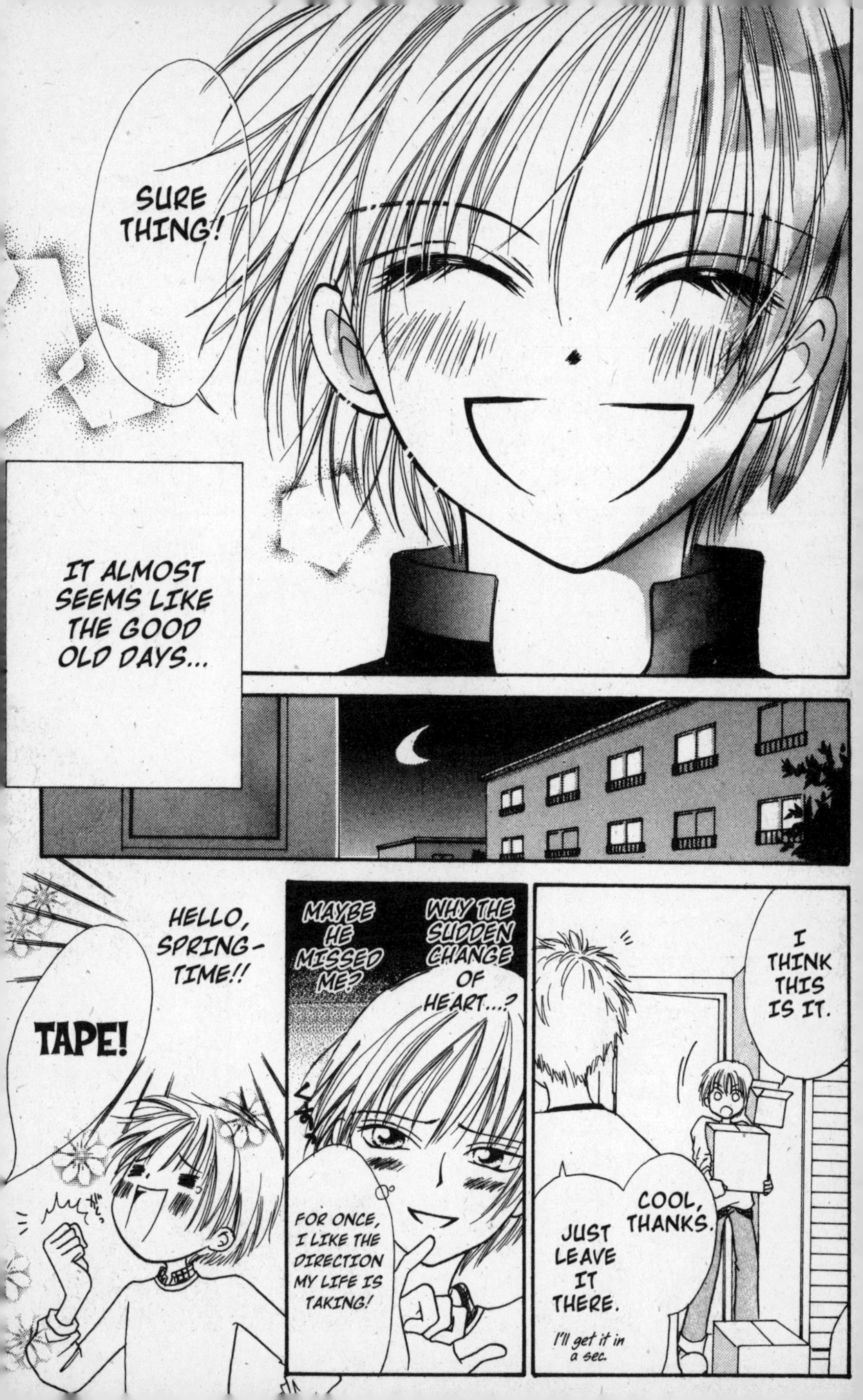
SURE THING!
IT ALMOST SEEMS LIKE THE GOOD OLD DAYS...
I THINK THIS IS IT.
COOL, THANKS.
JUST LEAVE IT THERE.
I'll get it in a sec.
WHY THE SUDDEN CHANGE OF HEART...?
MAYBE HE MISSED ME?
FOR ONCE, I LIKE THE DIRECTION MY LIFE IS TAKING!
HELLO, SPRING-TIME!!
TAPE!

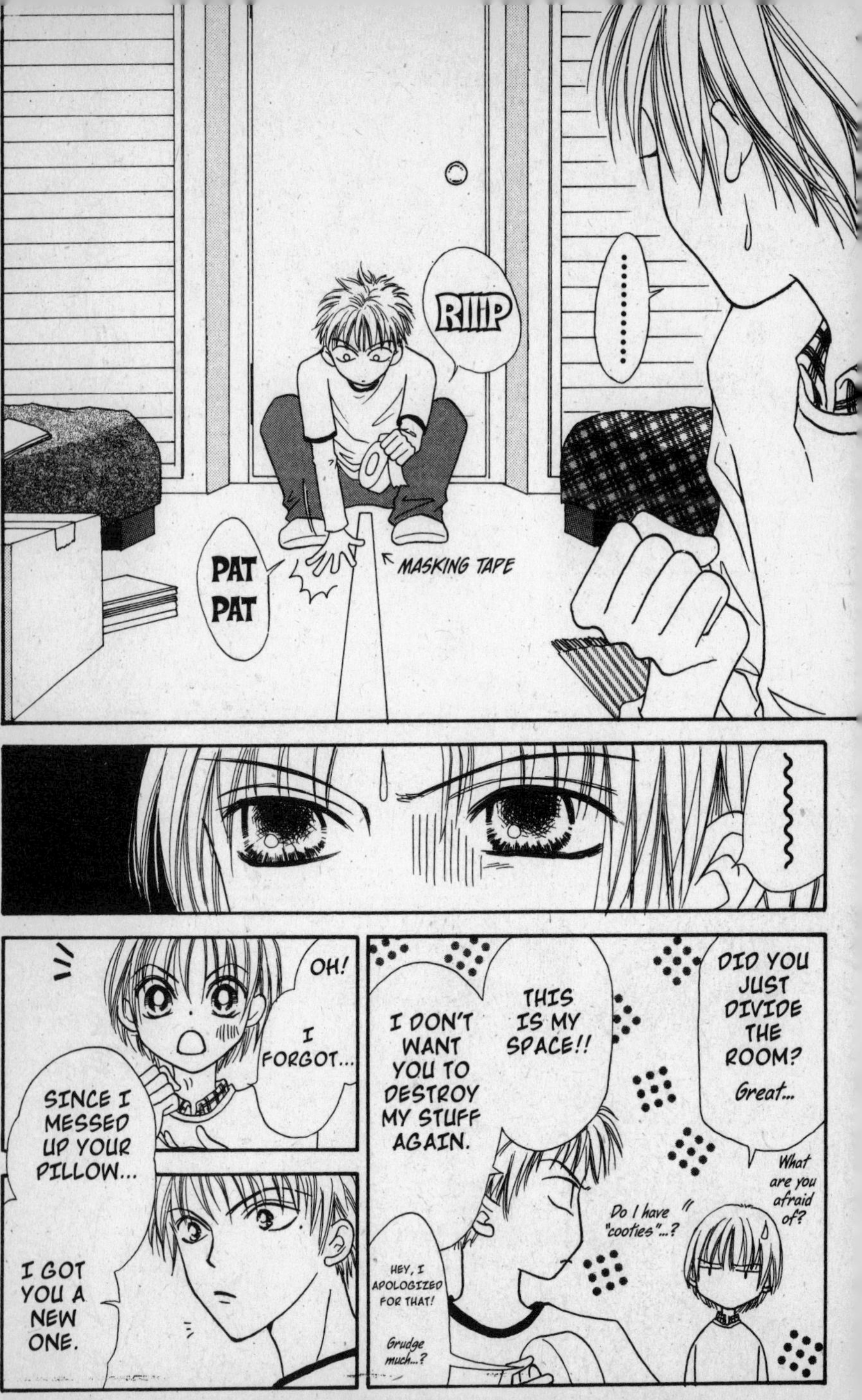
......
RIIIP
MASKING TAPE
PAT PAT
DID YOU JUST DIVIDE THE ROOM? Great...
What are you afraid of?
THIS IS MY SPACE!!
I DON'T WANT YOU TO DESTROY MY STUFF AGAIN.
Do I have "cooties"...?
HEY, I APOLOGIZED FOR THAT!
Grudge much...?
OH!
I FORGOT...
SINCE I MESSED UP YOUR PILLOW...
I GOT YOU A NEW ONE.

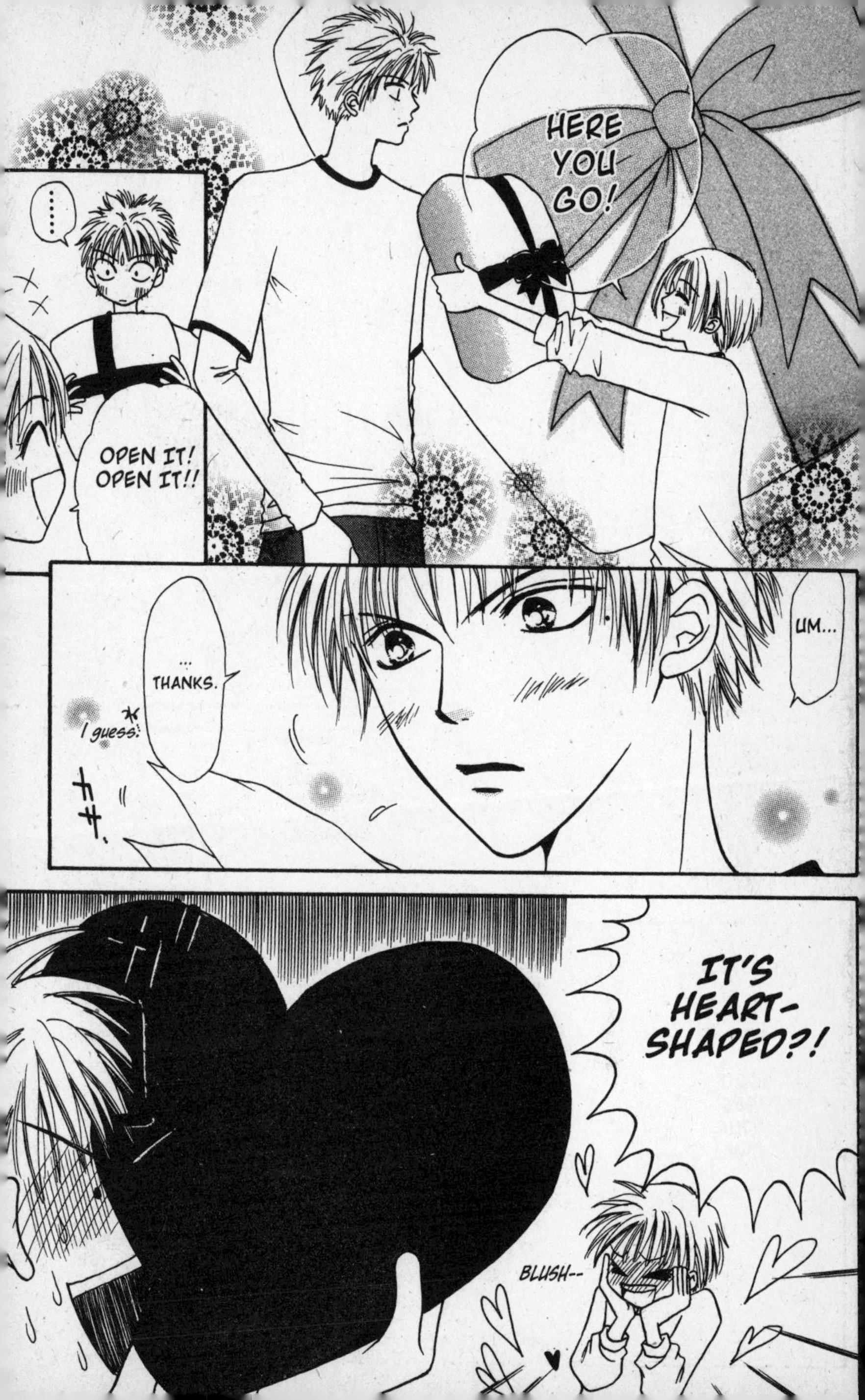
HERE YOU GO!
......
OPEN IT! OPEN IT!!
UM...
... THANKS.
I guess.
IT'S HEART-SHAPED?!
BLUSH--

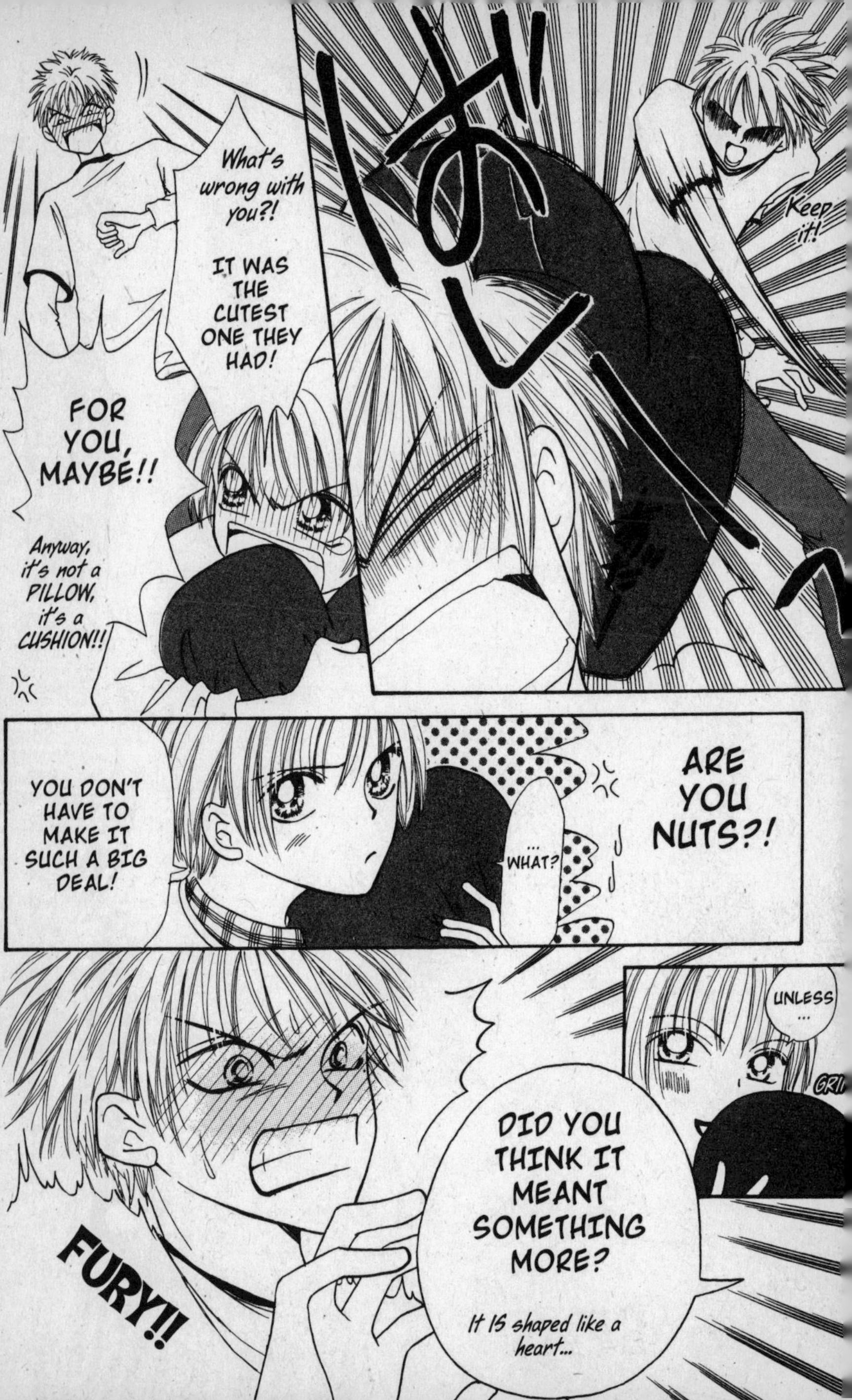

Keep it!
What's wrong with you?!
IT WAS THE CUTEST ONE THEY HAD!
FOR YOU, MAYBE!!
Anyway, it's not a PILLOW, it's a CUSHION!!
ARE YOU NUTS?!
...WHAT?
YOU DON'T HAVE TO MAKE IT SUCH A BIG DEAL!
UNLESS...
GRI
DID YOU THINK IT MEANT SOMETHING MORE?
It IS shaped like a heart...
FURY!!

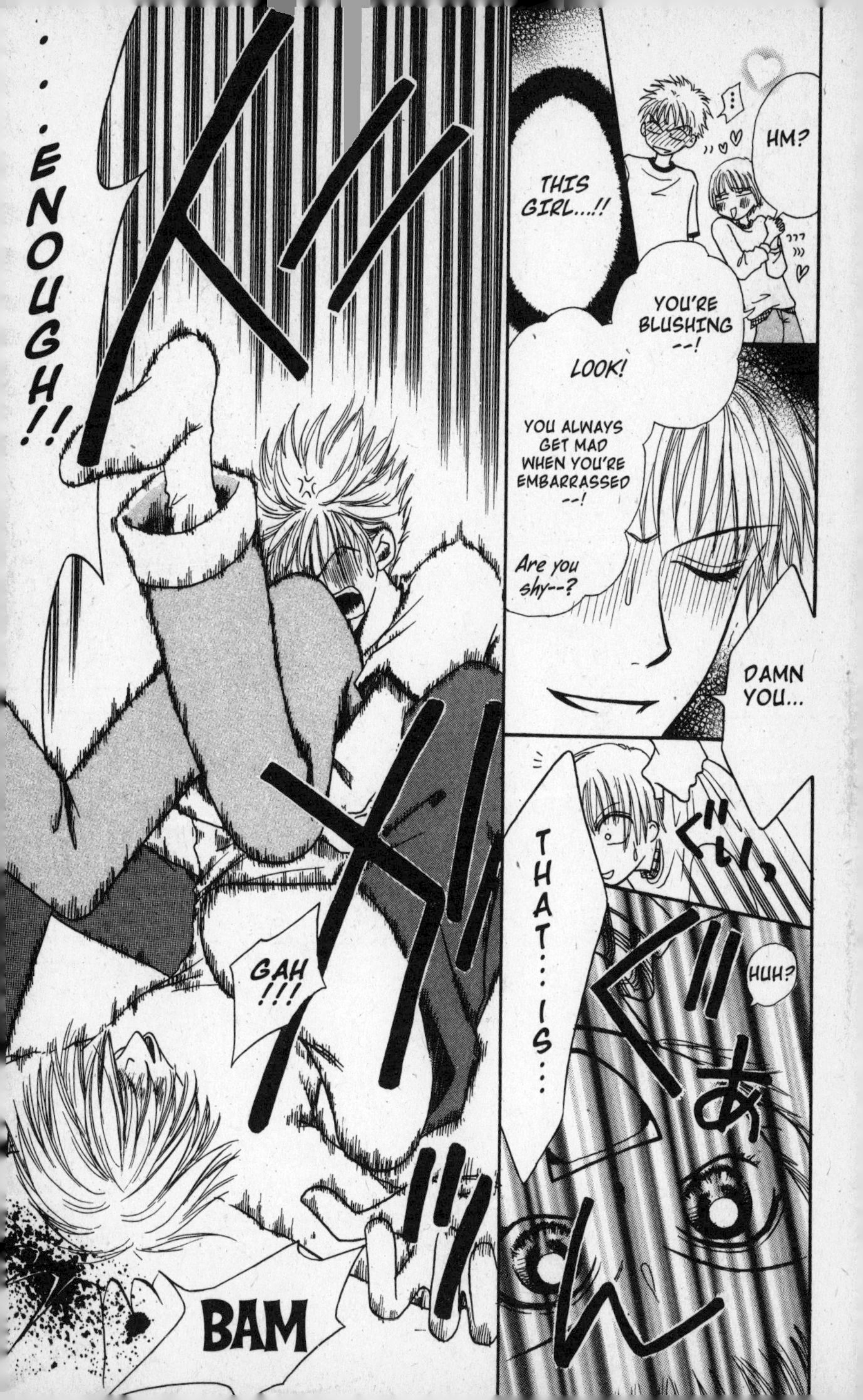
HM?
...!
THIS GIRL...!!
YOU'RE BLUSHING --!
LOOK!
YOU ALWAYS GET MAD WHEN YOU'RE EMBARRASSED --!
Are you shy--?
DAMN YOU...
THAT... IS...
ぐいっ
HUH?
ぐあん
...ENOUGH!!
GAH !!!
BAM

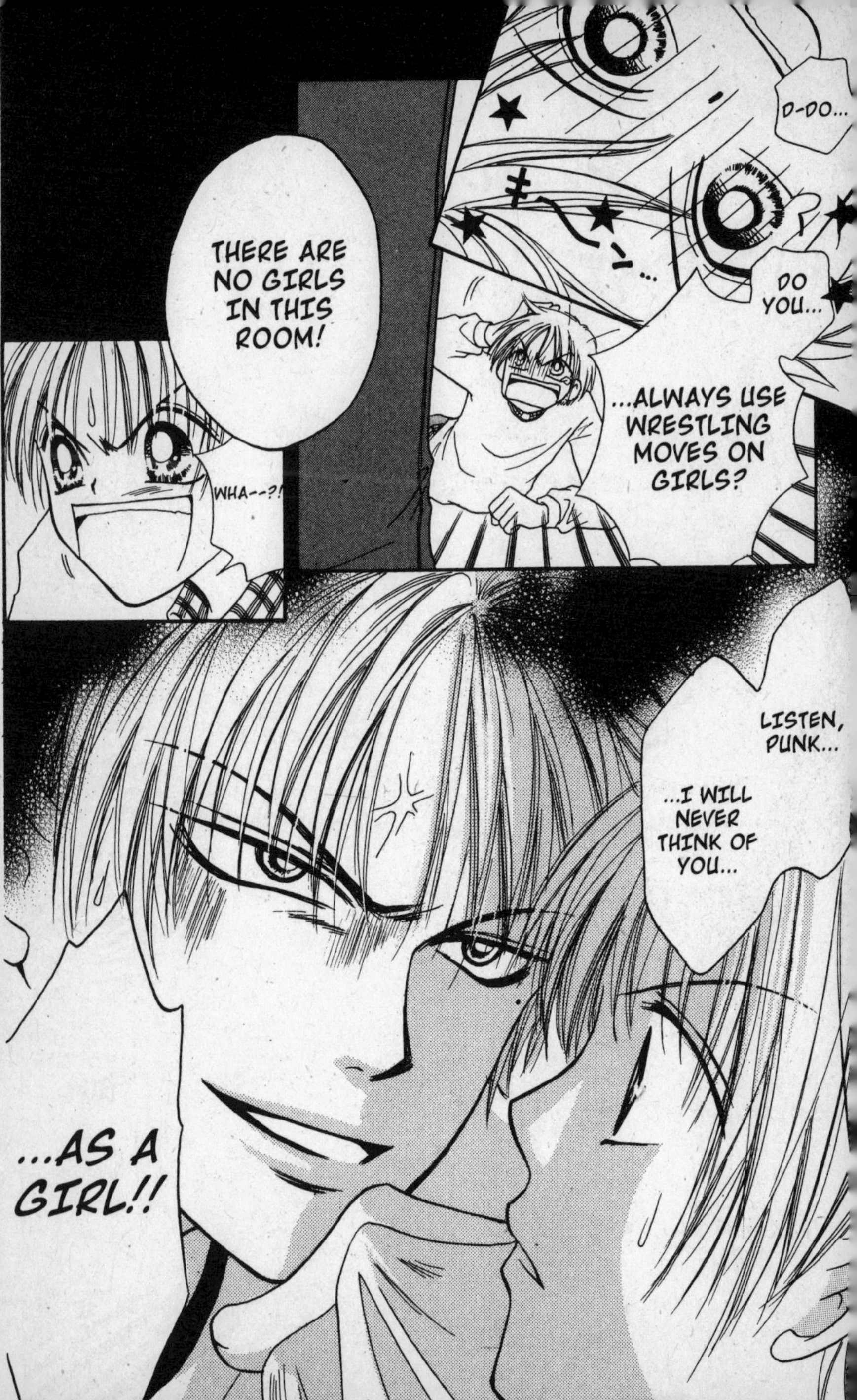
D-DO...
DO YOU...
...ALWAYS USE WRESTLING MOVES ON GIRLS?
THERE ARE NO GIRLS IN THIS ROOM!
WHA--?!
LISTEN, PUNK...
...I WILL NEVER THINK OF YOU...
...AS A GIRL!!

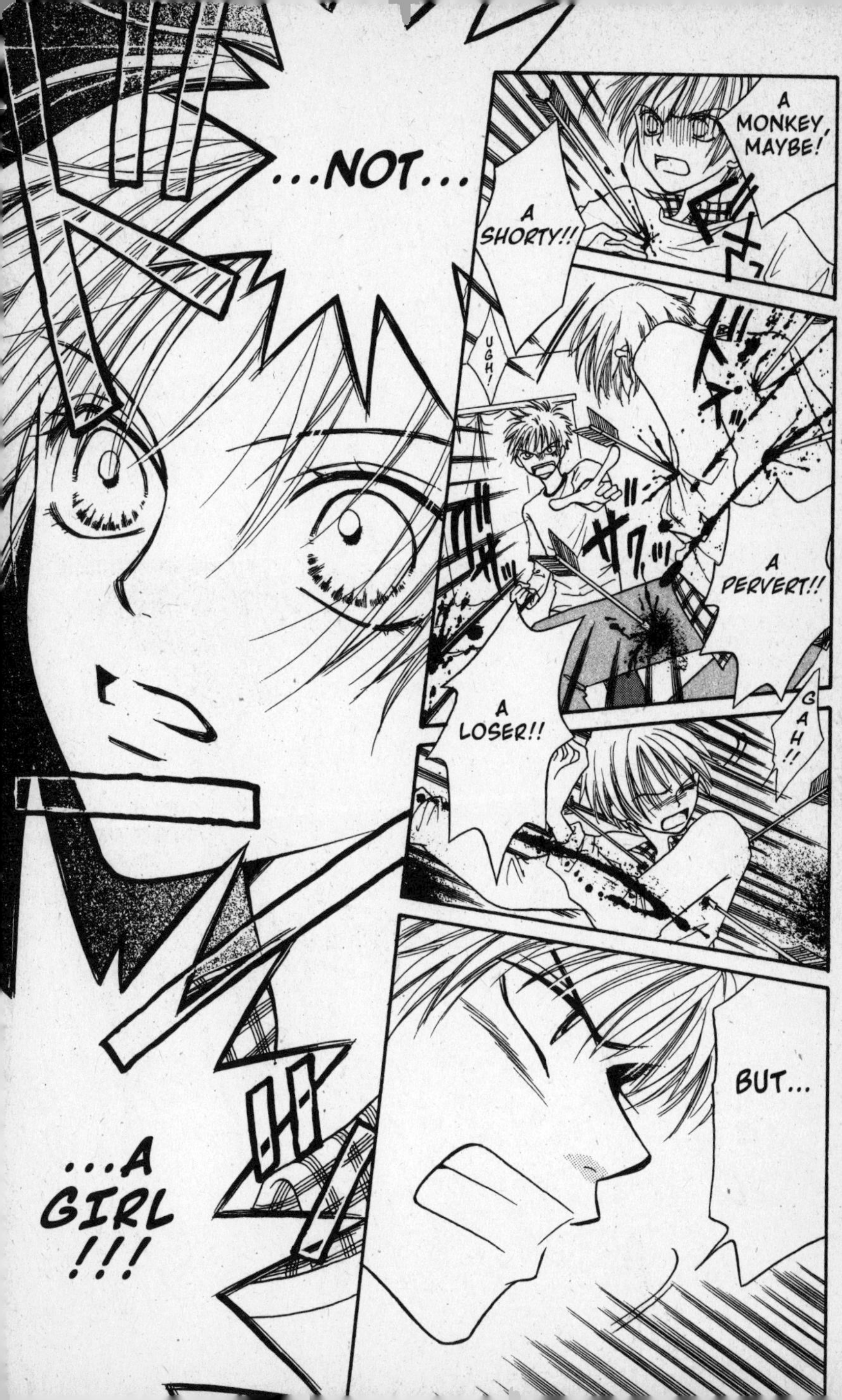
A MONKEY, MAYBE!
A SHORTY!!!
UGH!
A PERVERT!!
A LOSER!!
GAH!!
BUT...
...NOT...
...A GIRL!!!

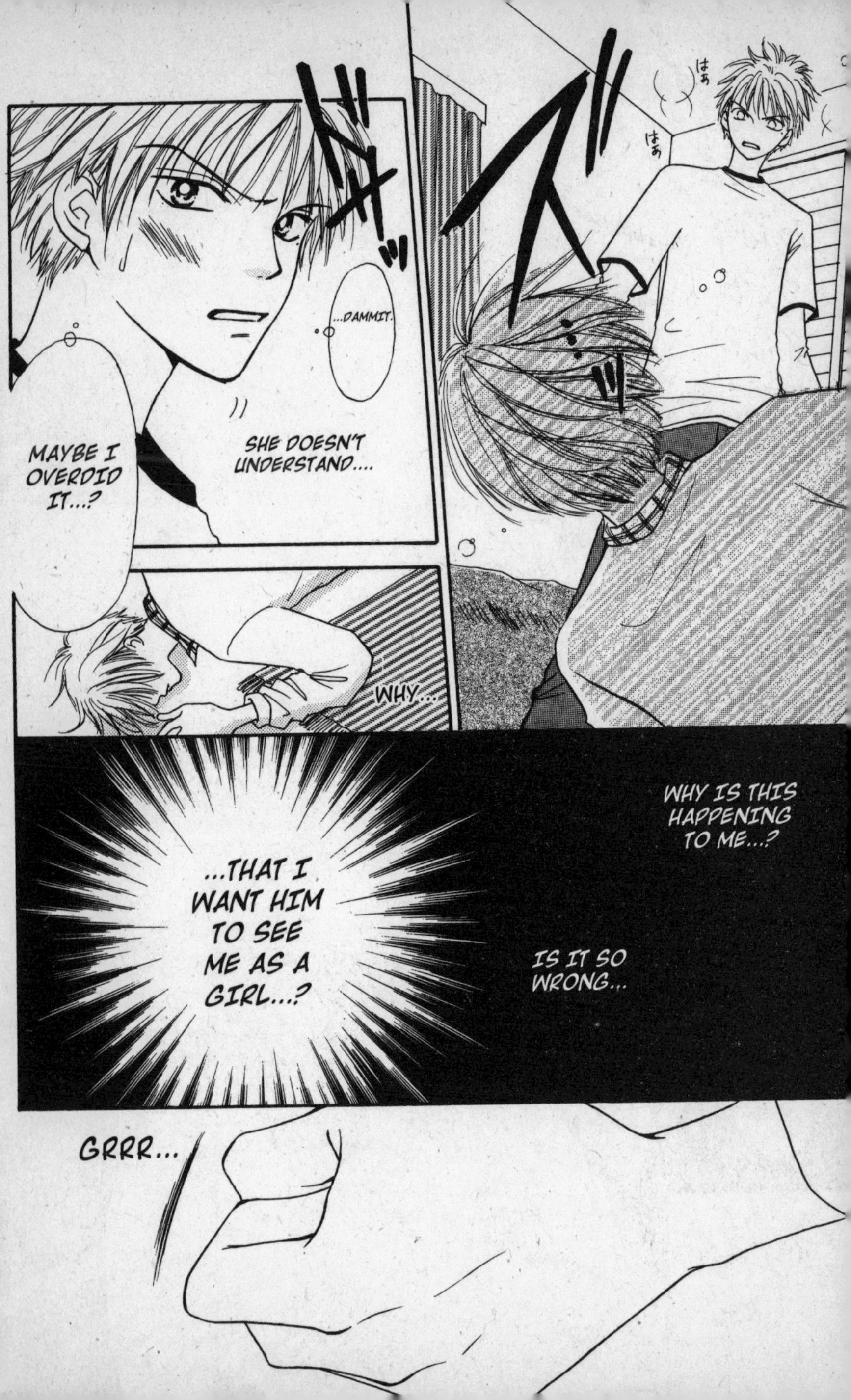
はぁ
はぁ
...DAMMIT.
SHE DOESN'T UNDERSTAND....
MAYBE I OVERDID IT...?
WHY...
WHY IS THIS HAPPENING TO ME...?
IS IT SO WRONG...
...THAT I WANT HIM TO SEE ME AS A GIRL...?
GRRR...

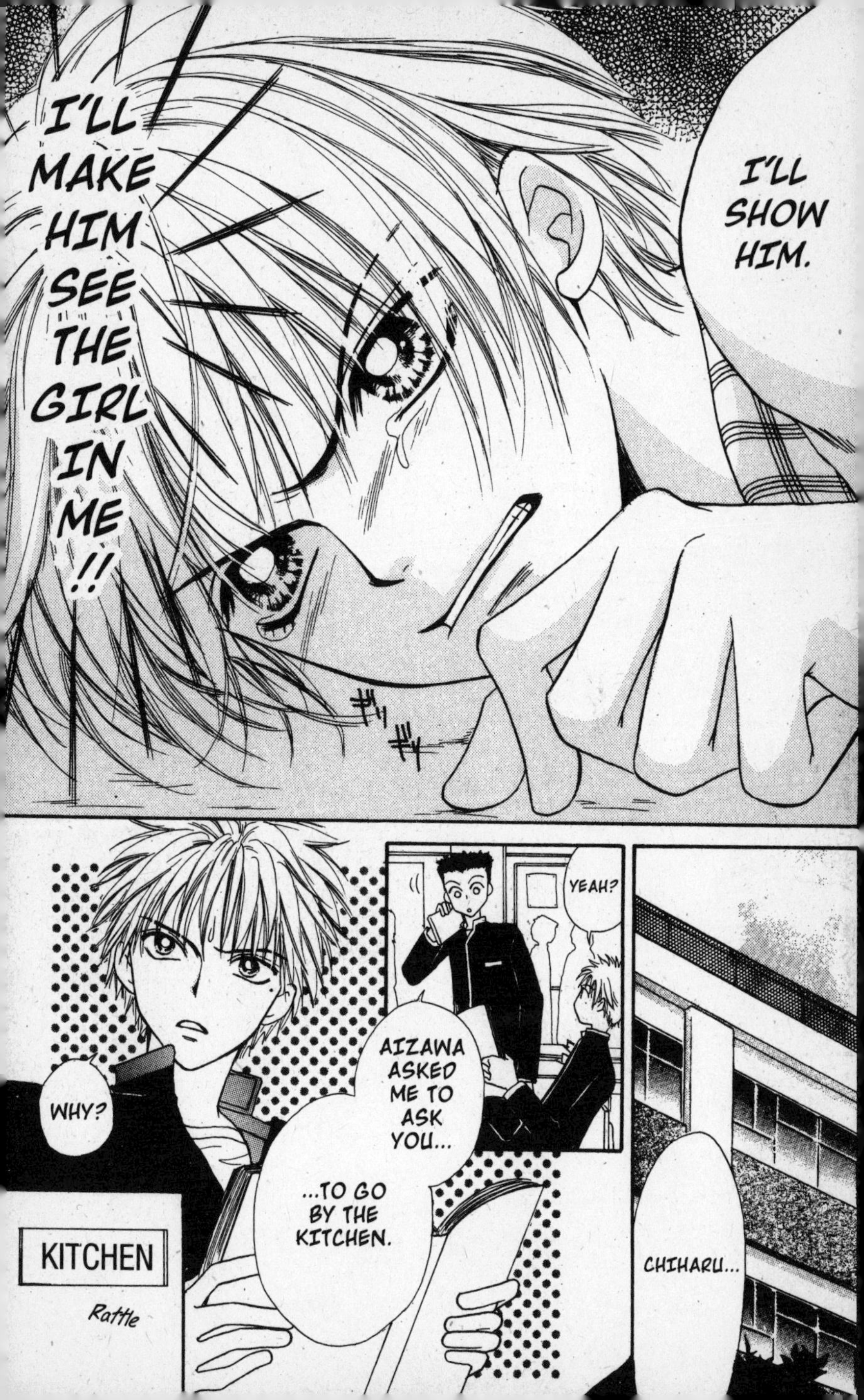
I'LL SHOW HIM.
I'LL MAKE HIM SEE THE GIRL IN ME!!
CHIHARU...
YEAH?
AIZAWA ASKED ME TO ASK YOU...
...TO GO BY THE KITCHEN.
WHY?
KITCHEN
Rattle

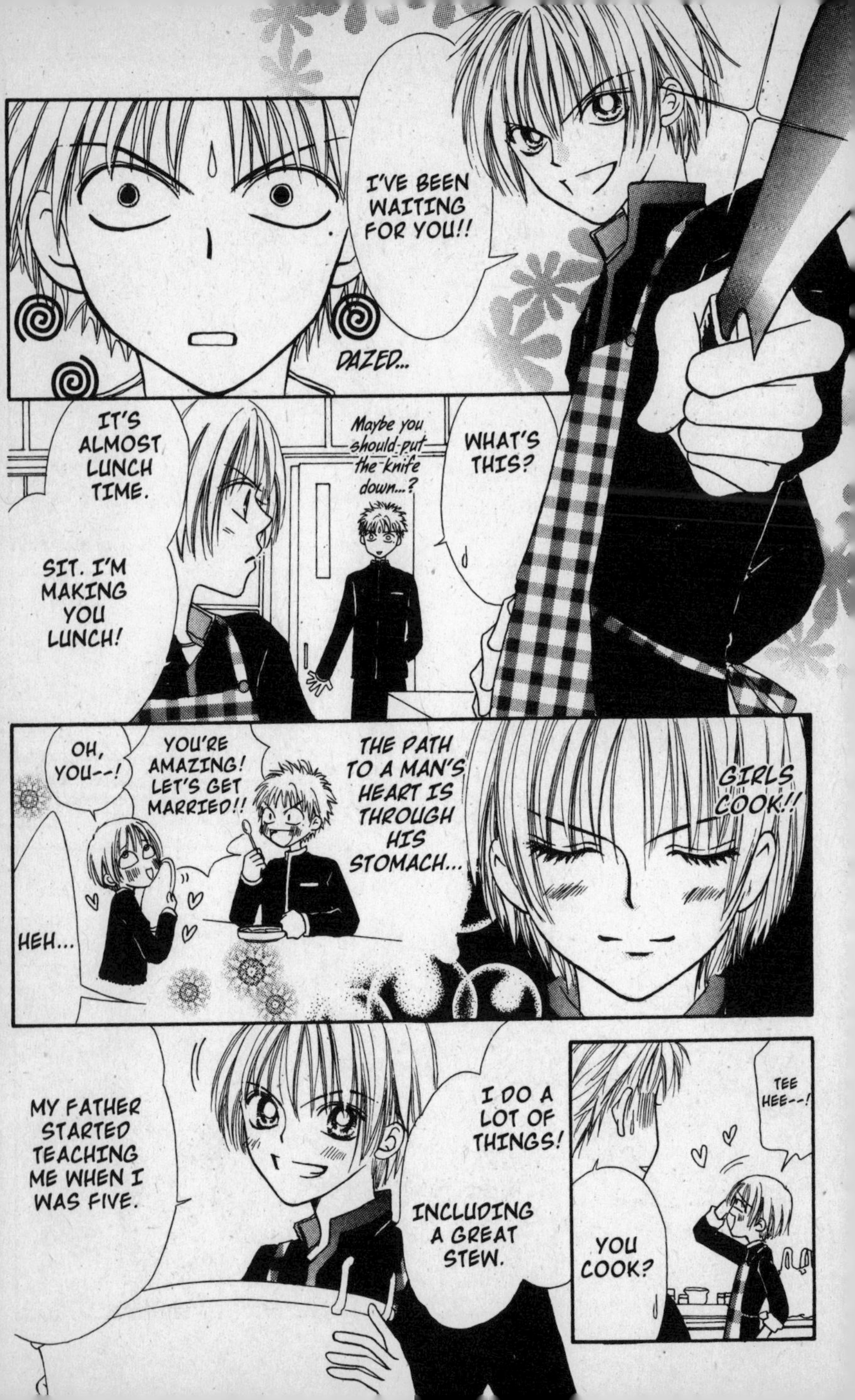
I'VE BEEN WAITING FOR YOU!!
DAZED...
WHAT'S THIS?
Maybe you should put the knife down...?
IT'S ALMOST LUNCH TIME.
SIT. I'M MAKING YOU LUNCH!
GIRLS COOK!!
THE PATH TO A MAN'S HEART IS THROUGH HIS STOMACH...
YOU'RE AMAZING! LET'S GET MARRIED!!
OH, YOU--!
HEH...
TEE HEE--!
YOU COOK?
I DO A LOT OF THINGS!
INCLUDING A GREAT STEW.
MY FATHER STARTED TEACHING ME WHEN I WAS FIVE.

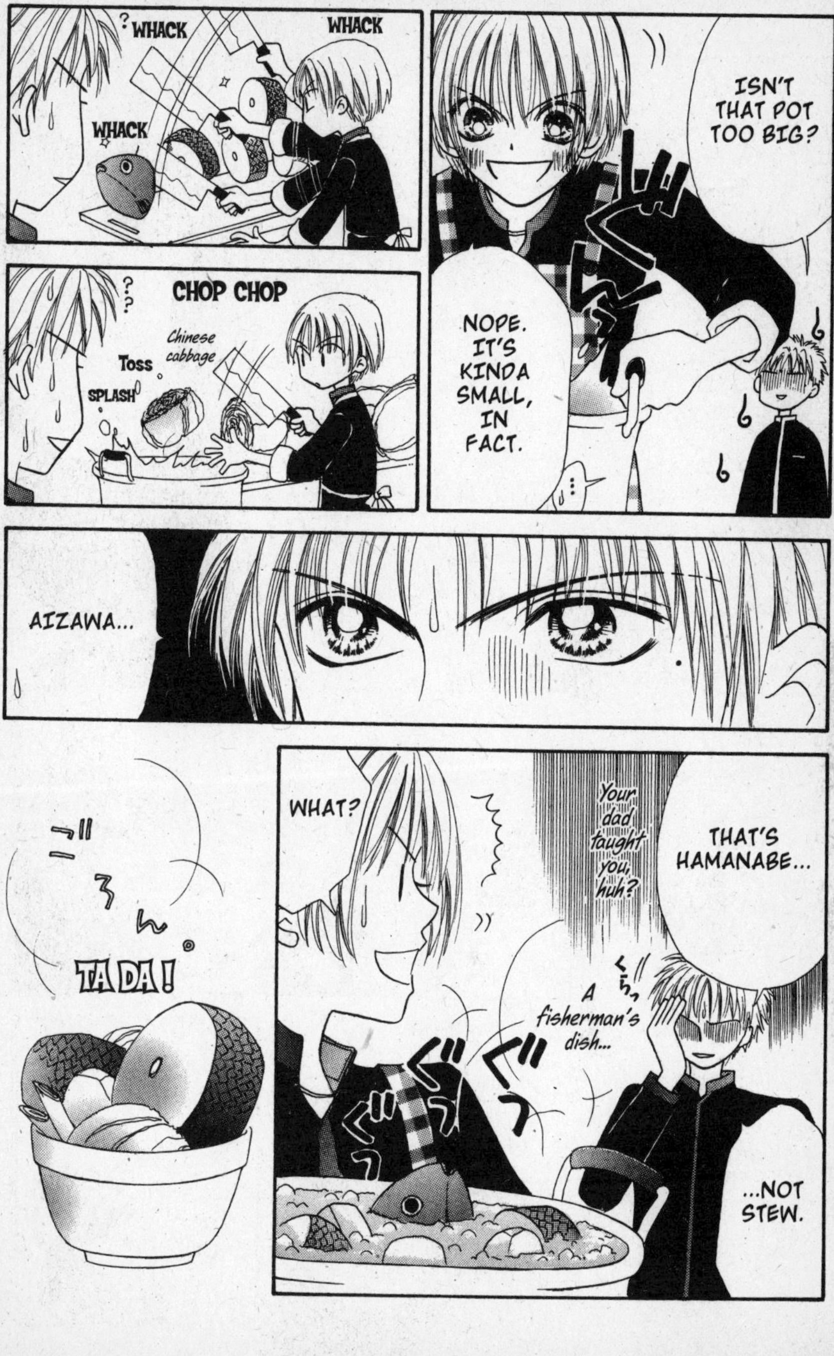
ISN'T THAT POT TOO BIG?
NOPE. IT'S KINDA SMALL, IN FACT.
...
WHACK
WHACK
WHACK
CHOP CHOP
Chinese cabbage
Toss
SPLASH
AIZAWA...
THAT'S HAMANABE...
Your dad taught you, huh?
WHAT?
A fisherman's dish...
...NOT STEW.
TA DA!

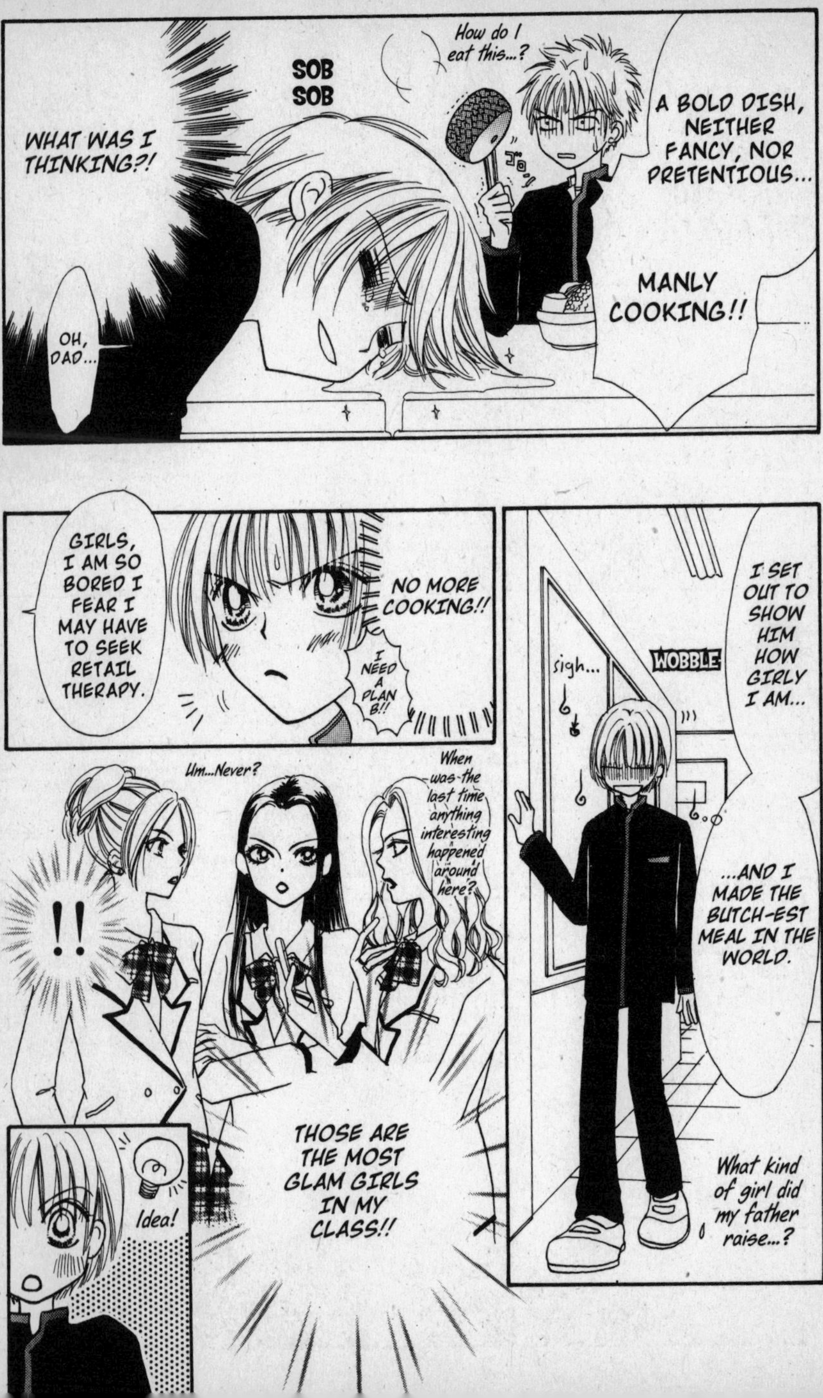
A BOLD DISH, NEITHER FANCY, NOR PRETENTIOUS...
MANLY COOKING!!
How do I eat this...?
SOB SOB
WHAT WAS I THINKING?!
OH, DAD...
I SET OUT TO SHOW HIM HOW GIRLY I AM...
WOBBLE
sigh...
...AND I MADE THE BUTCH-EST MEAL IN THE WORLD.
What kind of girl did my father raise...?
NO MORE COOKING!!
I NEED A PLAN B!!
GIRLS, I AM SO BORED I FEAR I MAY HAVE TO SEEK RETAIL THERAPY.
When was the last time anything interesting happened around here?
Um...Never?
!!
THOSE ARE THE MOST GLAM GIRLS IN MY CLASS!!
Idea!

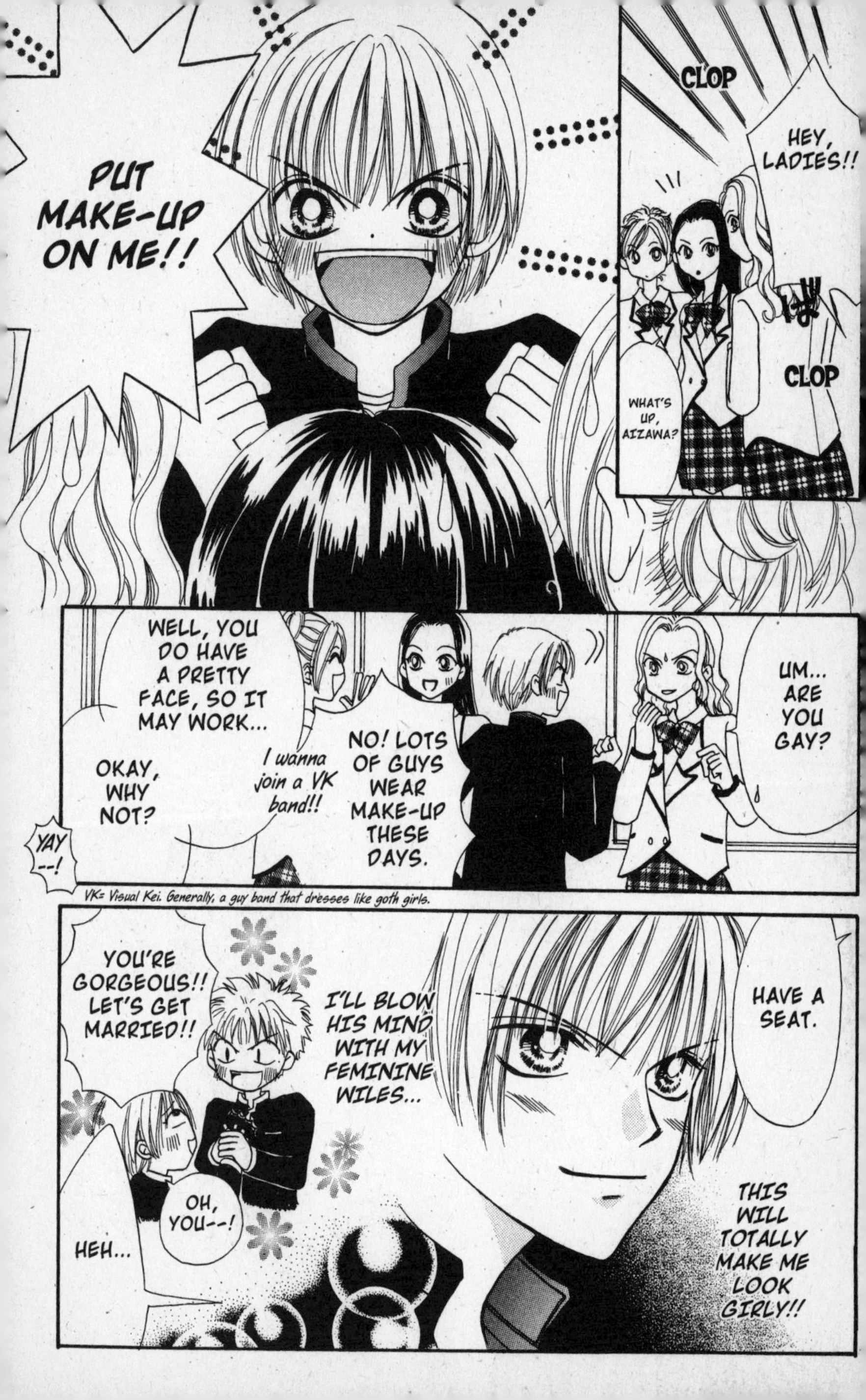
CLOP
HEY, LADIES!!
WHAT'S UP, AIZAWA?
CLOP
PUT MAKE-UP ON ME!!
UM... ARE YOU GAY?
NO! LOTS OF GUYS WEAR MAKE-UP THESE DAYS.
I wanna join a VK band!!
WELL, YOU DO HAVE A PRETTY FACE, SO IT MAY WORK...
OKAY, WHY NOT?
YAY--!
HAVE A SEAT.
THIS WILL TOTALLY MAKE ME LOOK GIRLY!!
I'LL BLOW HIS MIND WITH MY FEMININE WILES...
YOU'RE GORGEOUS!! LET'S GET MARRIED!!
OH, YOU--!
HEH...
VK= Visual Kei. Generally, a guy band that dresses like goth girls.

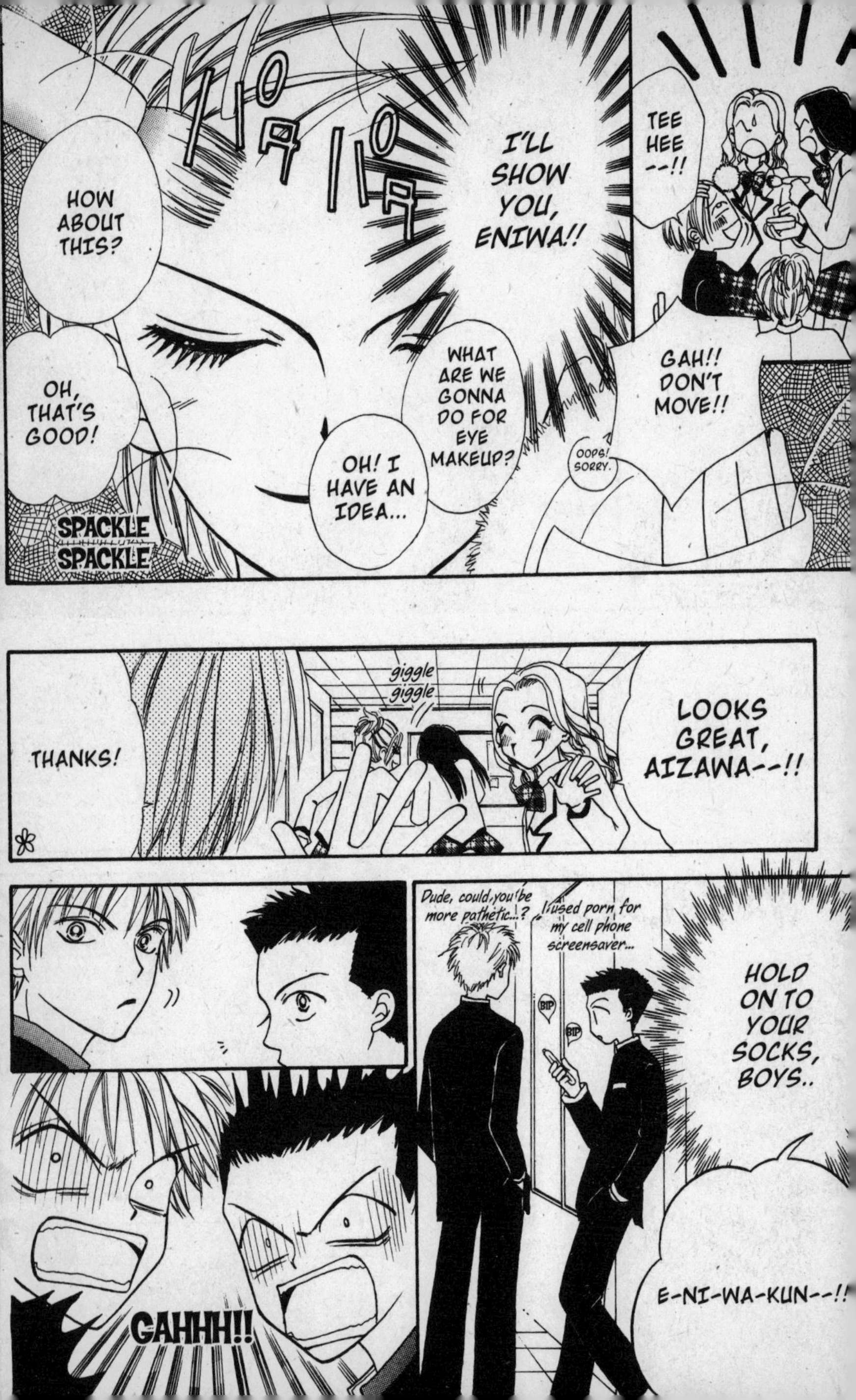
TEE HEE --!!
GAH!! DON'T MOVE!!
OOPS! SORRY.
I'LL SHOW YOU, ENIWA!!
WHAT ARE WE GONNA DO FOR EYE MAKEUP?
OH! I HAVE AN IDEA...
HOW ABOUT THIS?
OH, THAT'S GOOD!
SPACKLE SPACKLE
LOOKS GREAT, AIZAWA--!!
giggle giggle
THANKS!
HOLD ON TO YOUR SOCKS, BOYS..
I used porn for my cell phone screensaver...
Dude, could you be more pathetic...?
BIP
BIP
E-NI-WA-KUN--!!
GAHHH!!

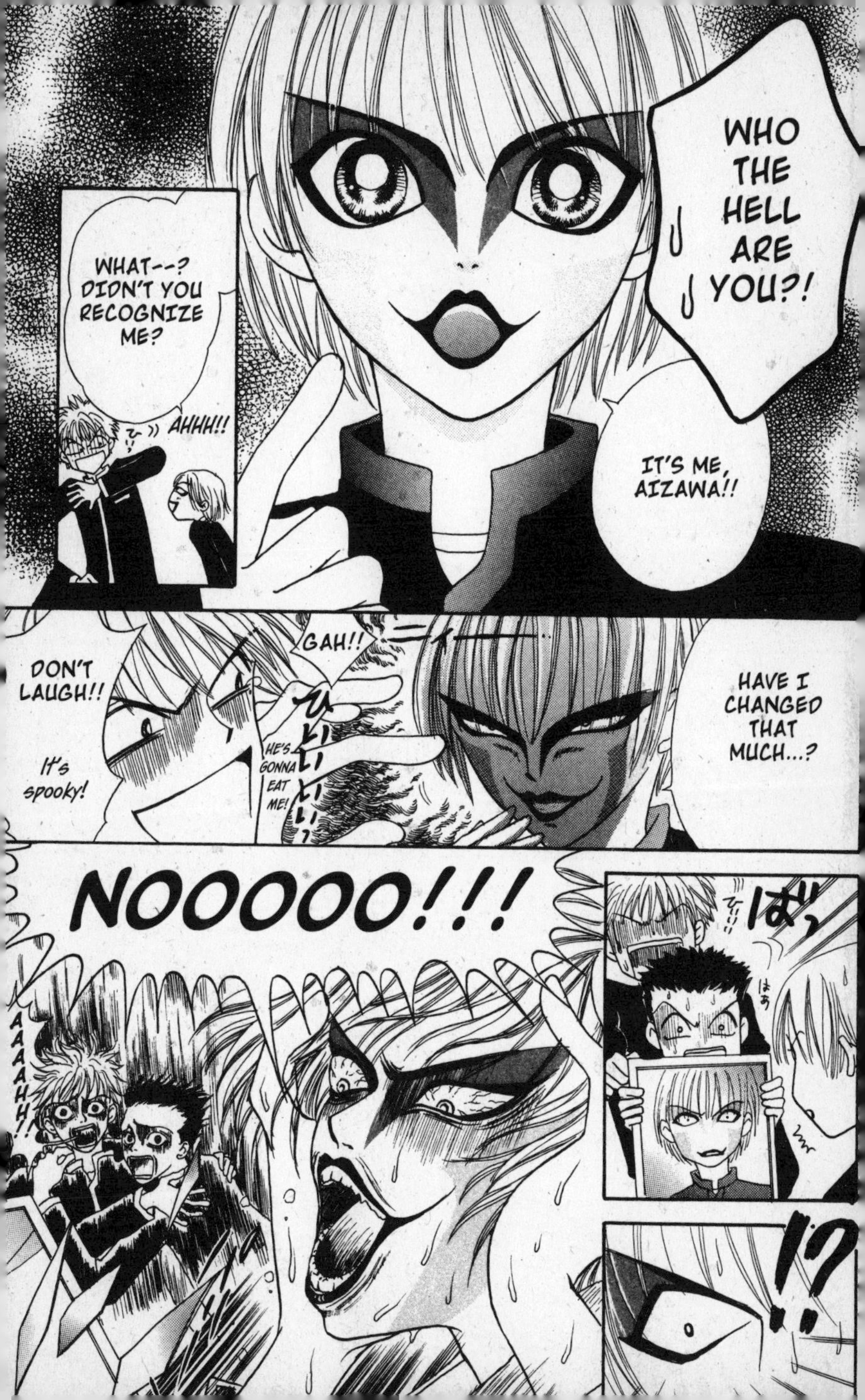
WHO THE HELL ARE YOU?!
IT'S ME, AIZAWA!!
WHAT--? DIDN'T YOU RECOGNIZE ME?
AHHH!!
HAVE I CHANGED THAT MUCH...?
GAH!!
HE'S GONNA EAT ME!
DON'T LAUGH!!
It's spooky!
ぱっ
!?
NOOOOO!!!
AAAAAHH!!

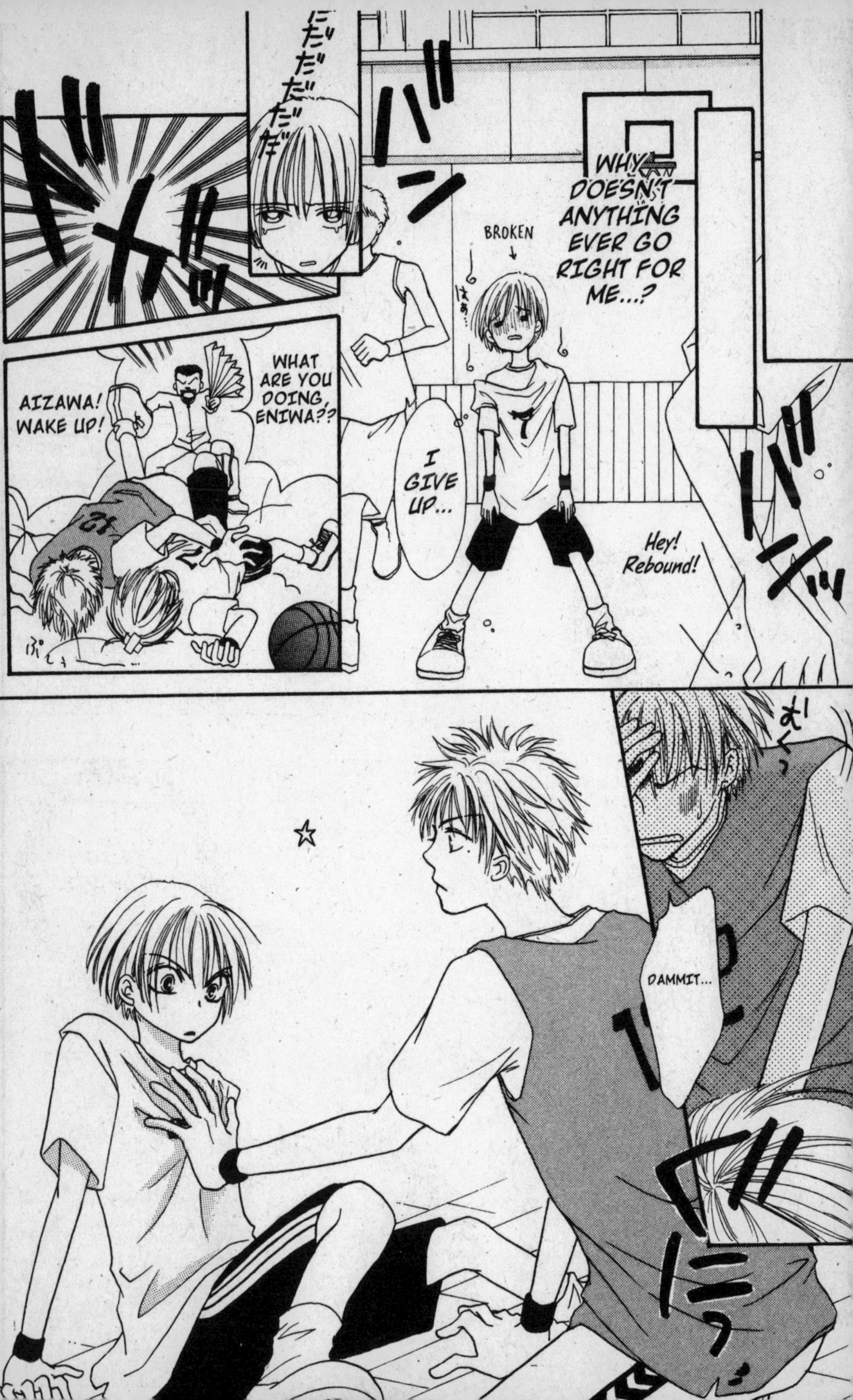
WHY DOESN'T ANYTHING EVER GO RIGHT FOR ME...?
BROKEN
I GIVE UP...
Hey! Rebound!
WHAT ARE YOU DOING, ENIWA??
AIZAWA! WAKE UP!
DAMMIT...

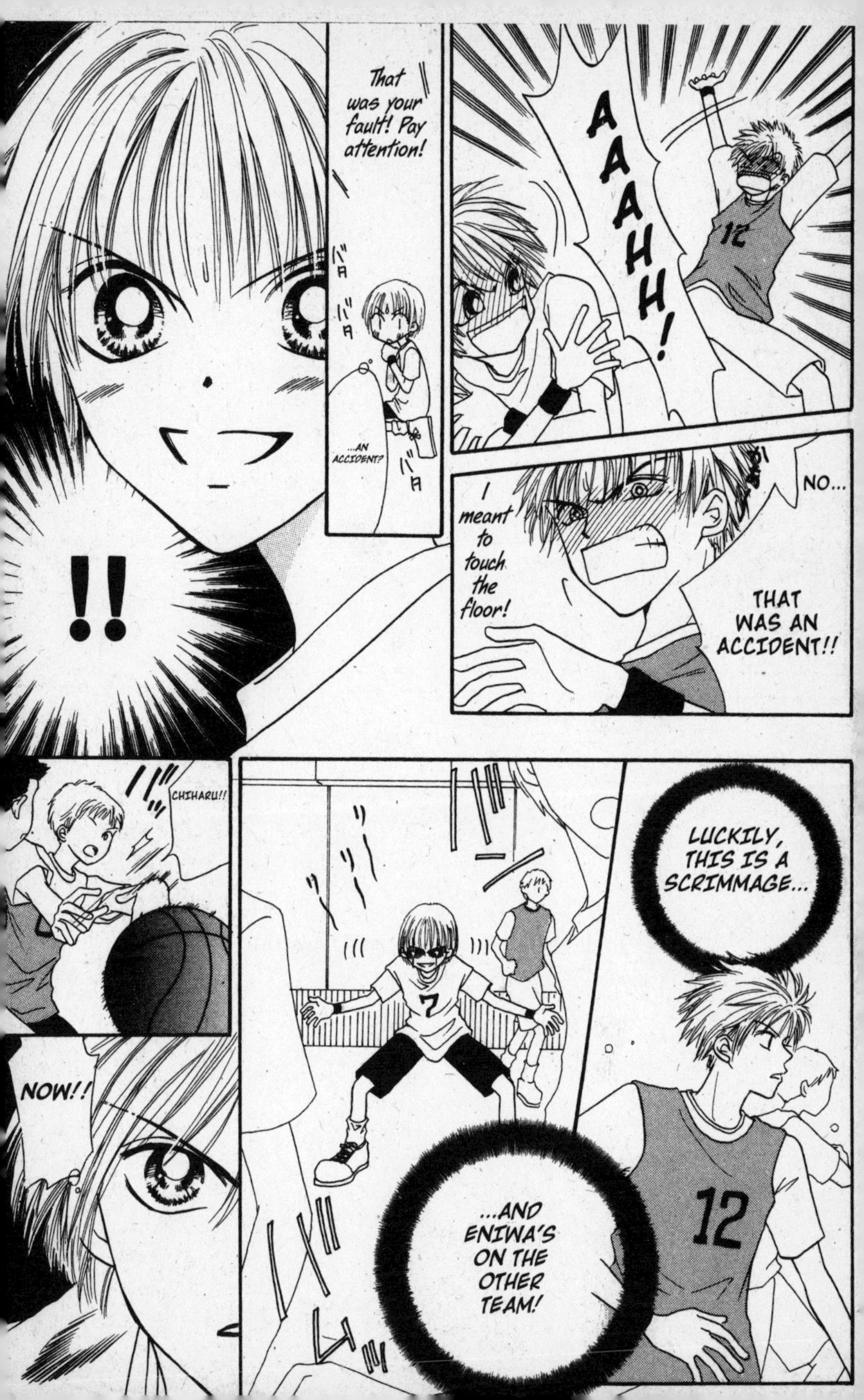
AAAHH!
That was your fault! Pay attention!
バタ バタ バタ
...AN ACCIDENT?
NO...
I meant to touch the floor!
THAT WAS AN ACCIDENT!!
!!
LUCKILY, THIS IS A SCRIMMAGE...
...AND ENIWA'S ON THE OTHER TEAM!
CHIHARU!!
NOW!!

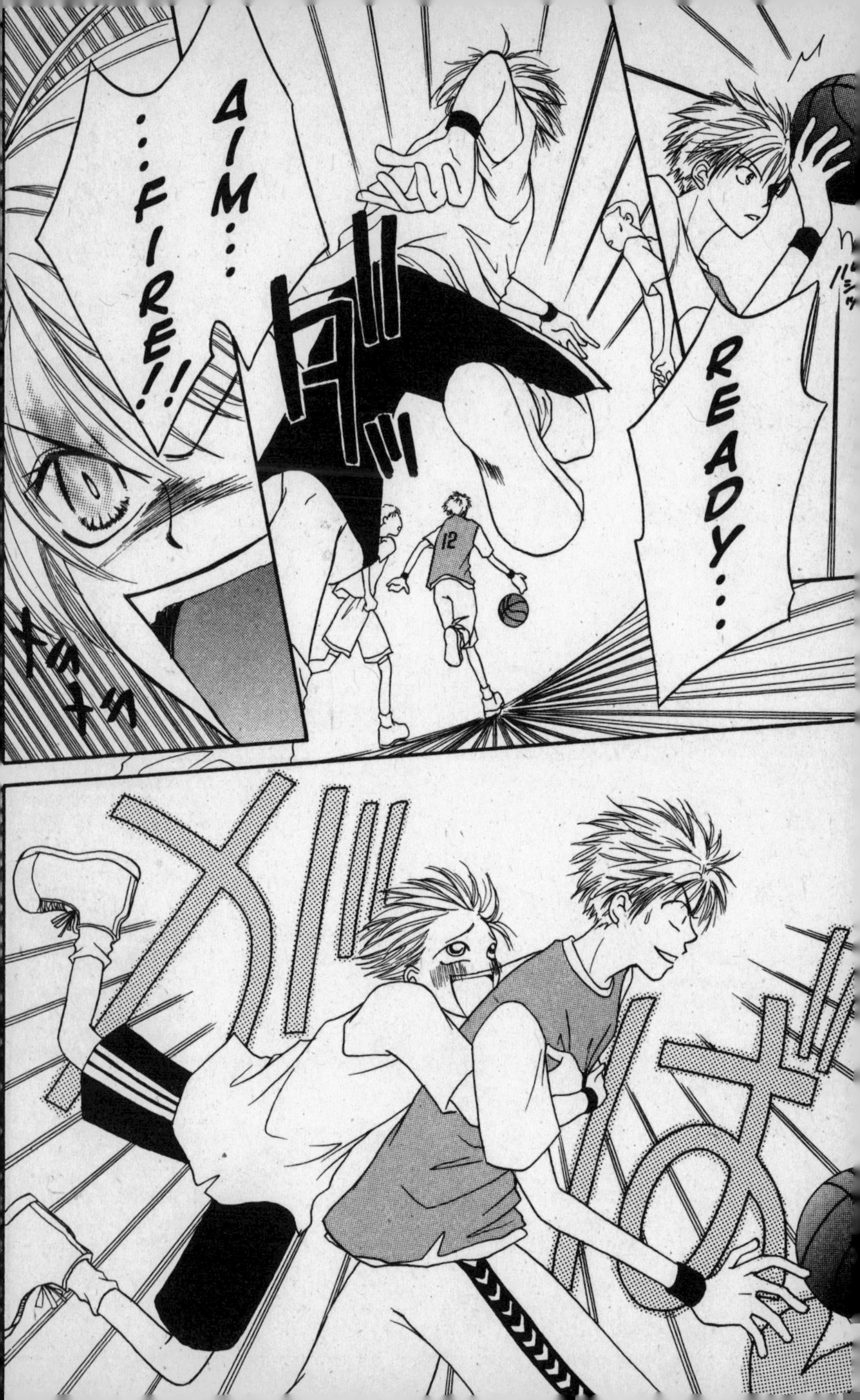
READY...
AIM...
...FIRE!!

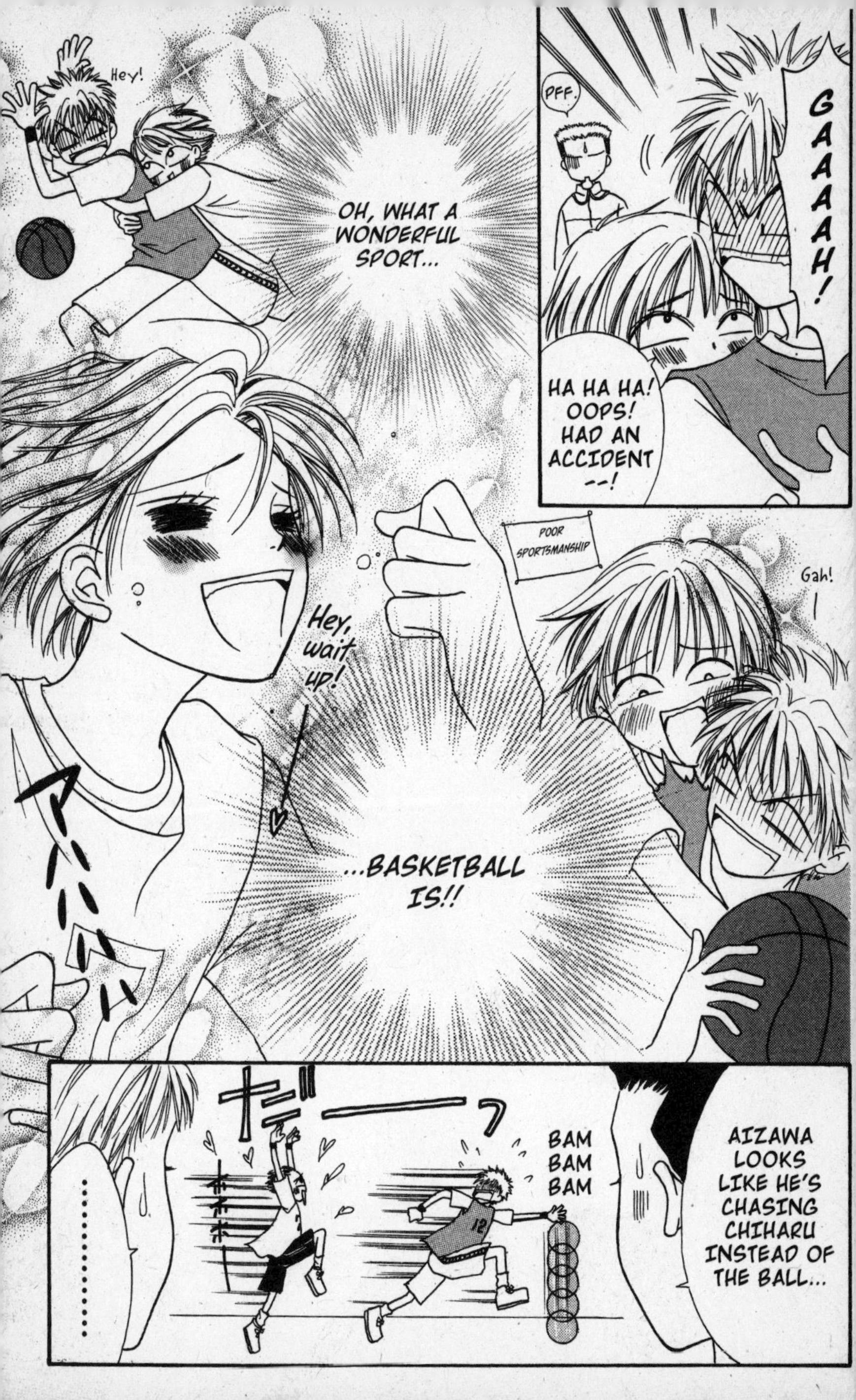
PFF.
GAAAAAH!
HA HA HA! OOPS! HAD AN ACCIDENT --!
OH, WHAT A WONDERFUL SPORT...
Hey!
POOR SPORTSMANSHIP
Gah!
Hey, wait up!
...BASKETBALL IS!!
AIZAWA LOOKS LIKE HE'S CHASING CHIHARU INSTEAD OF THE BALL...
BAM BAM BAM
........

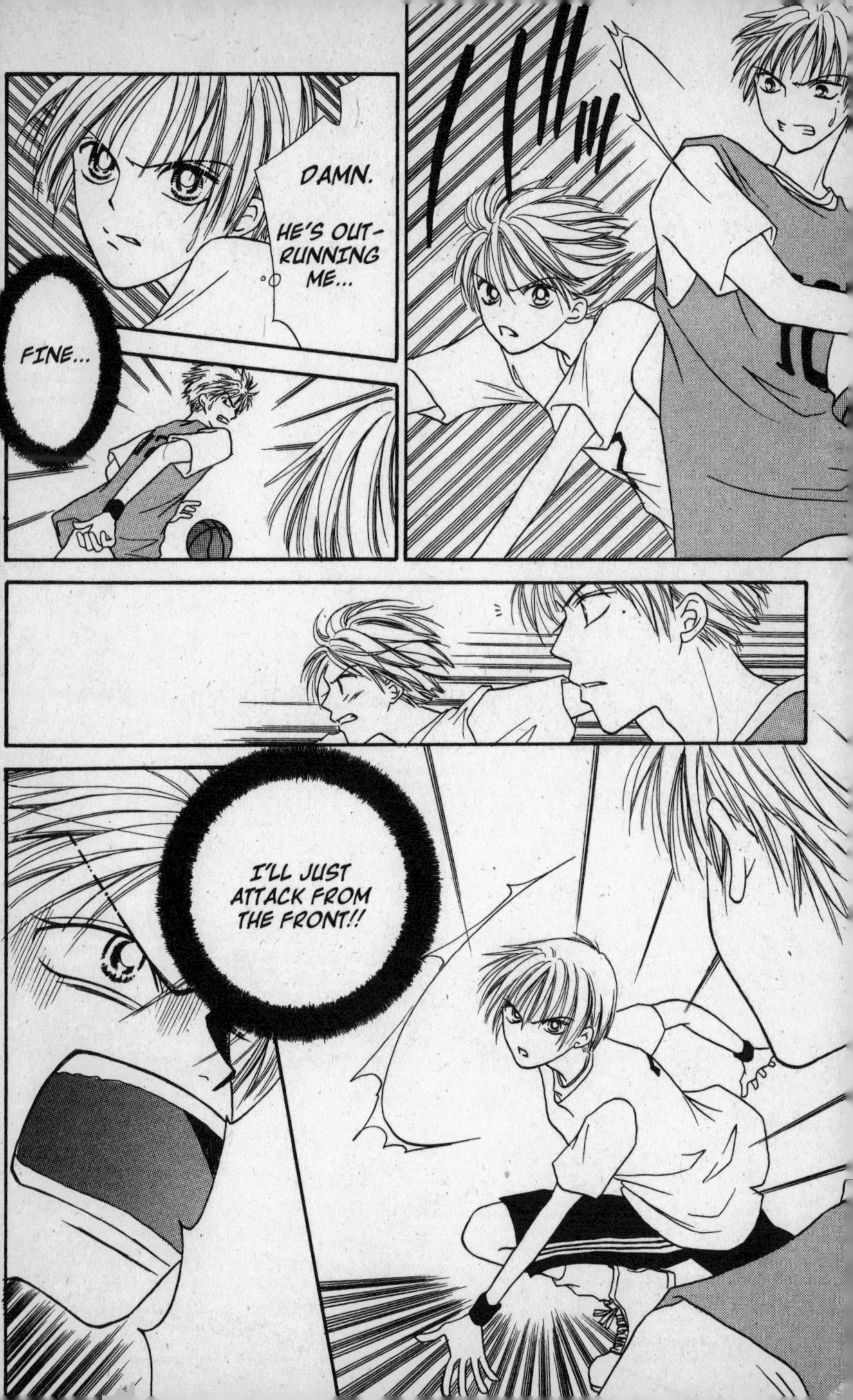
DAMN.
HE'S OUT-RUNNING ME...
FINE...
I'LL JUST ATTACK FROM THE FRONT!!

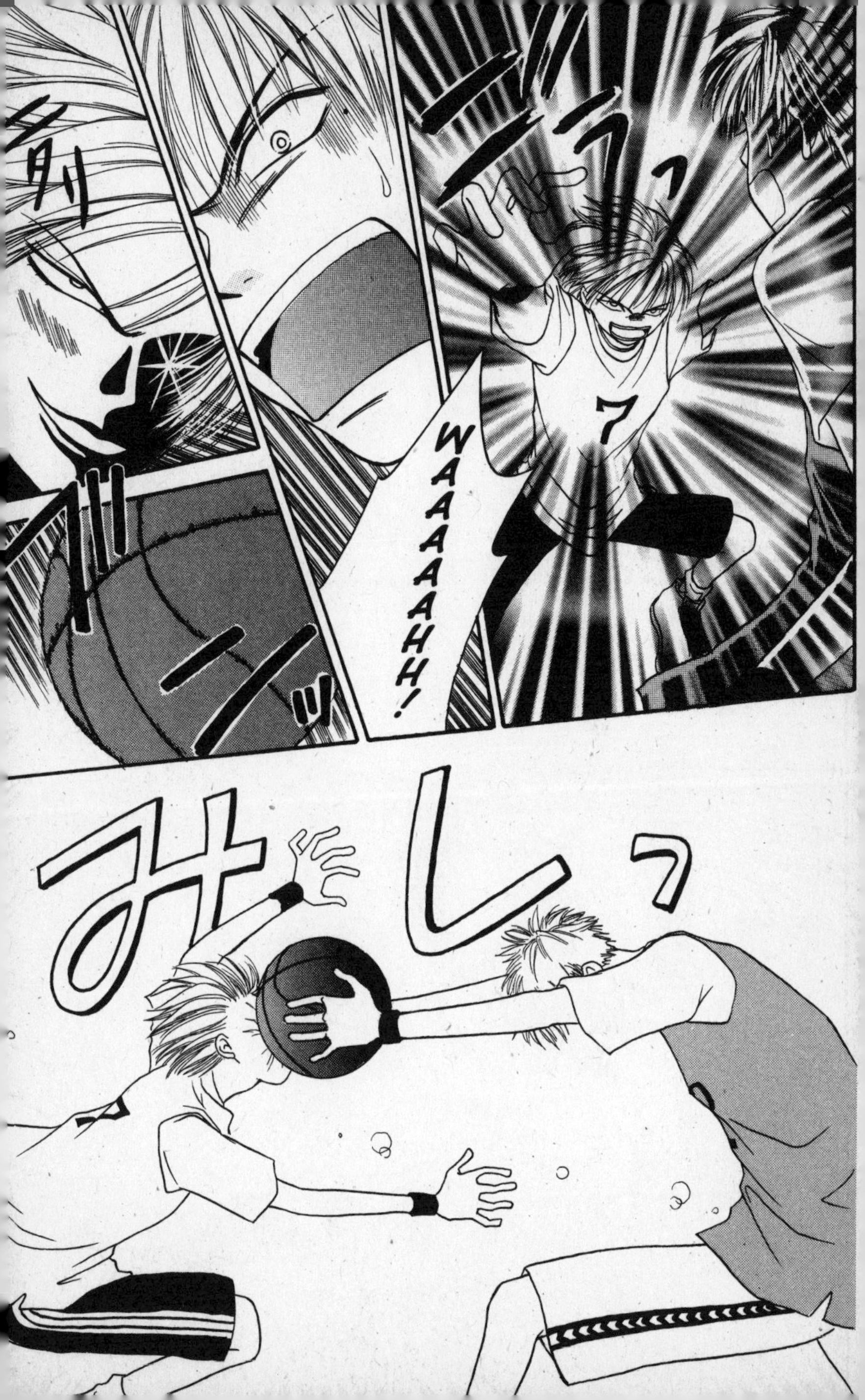
WAAAAAAAHH!
みしっ

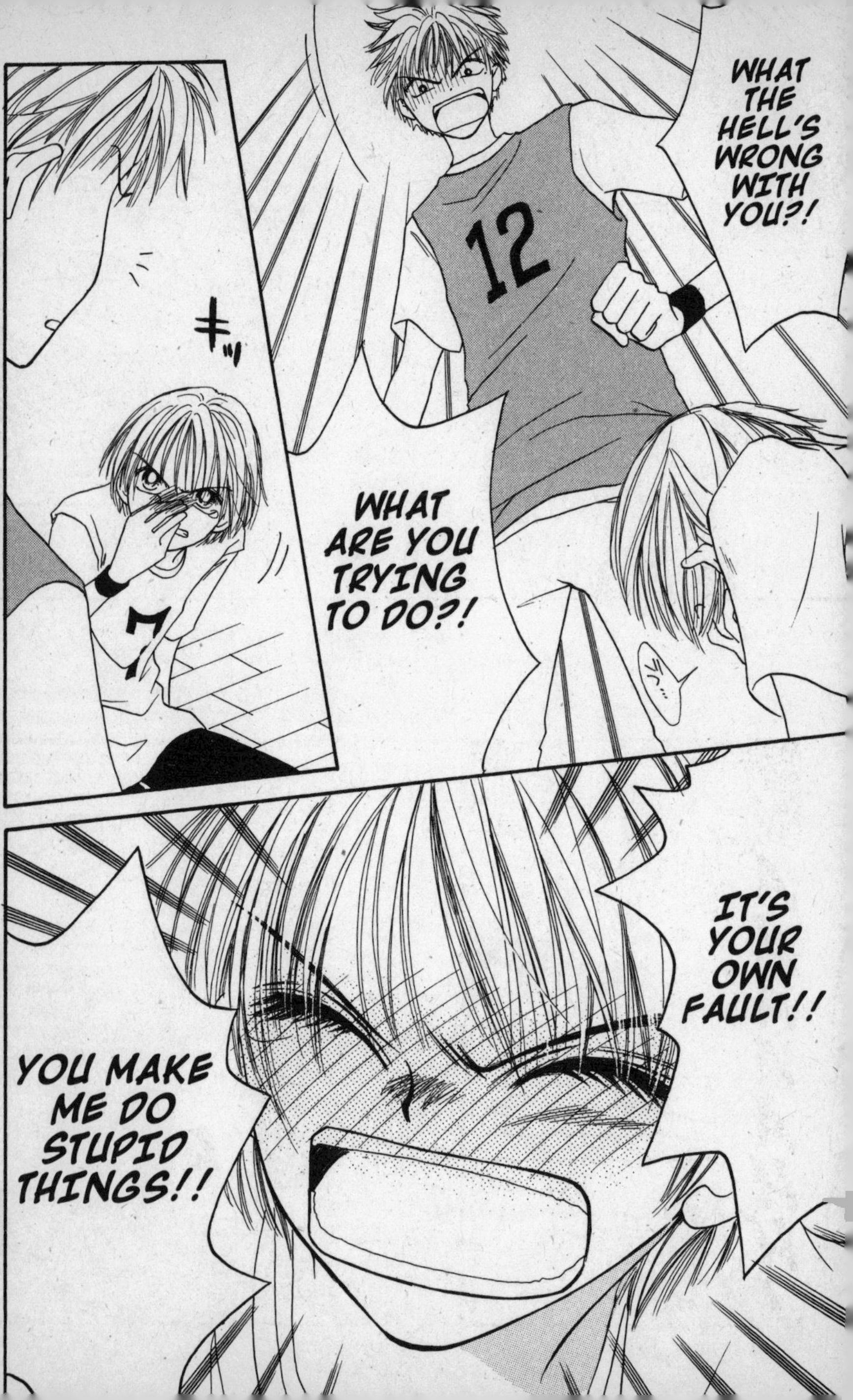
WHAT THE HELL'S WRONG WITH YOU?!
WHAT ARE YOU TRYING TO DO?!
キッ
IT'S YOUR OWN FAULT!!
YOU MAKE ME DO STUPID THINGS!!

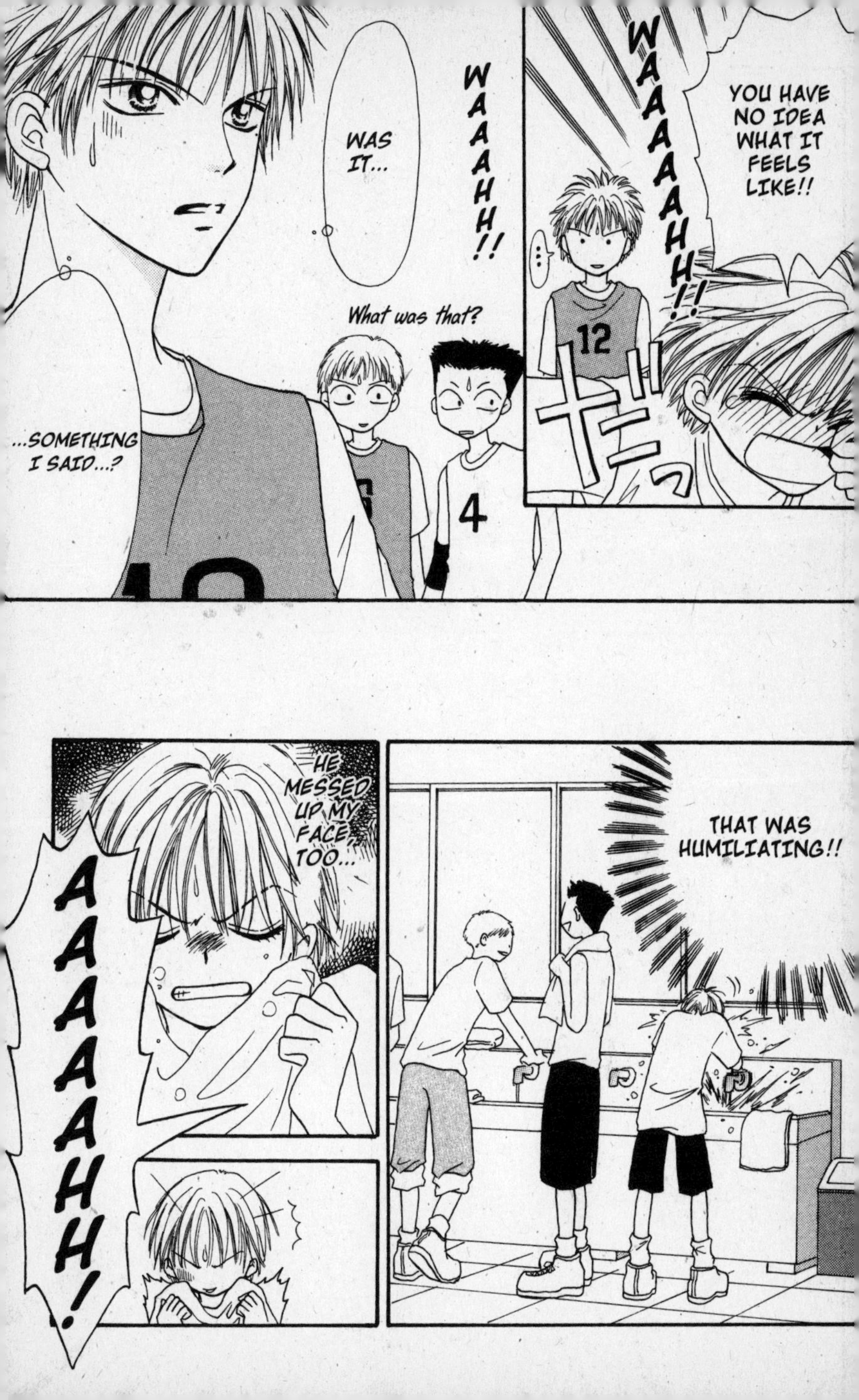
YOU HAVE NO IDEA WHAT IT FEELS LIKE!!
WAAAAAAHH!!
...
ギュっ
WAAAHH!!
WAS IT...
What was that?
...SOMETHING I SAID...?
THAT WAS HUMILIATING!!
HE MESSED UP MY FACE, TOO...
AAAAAAAHH!

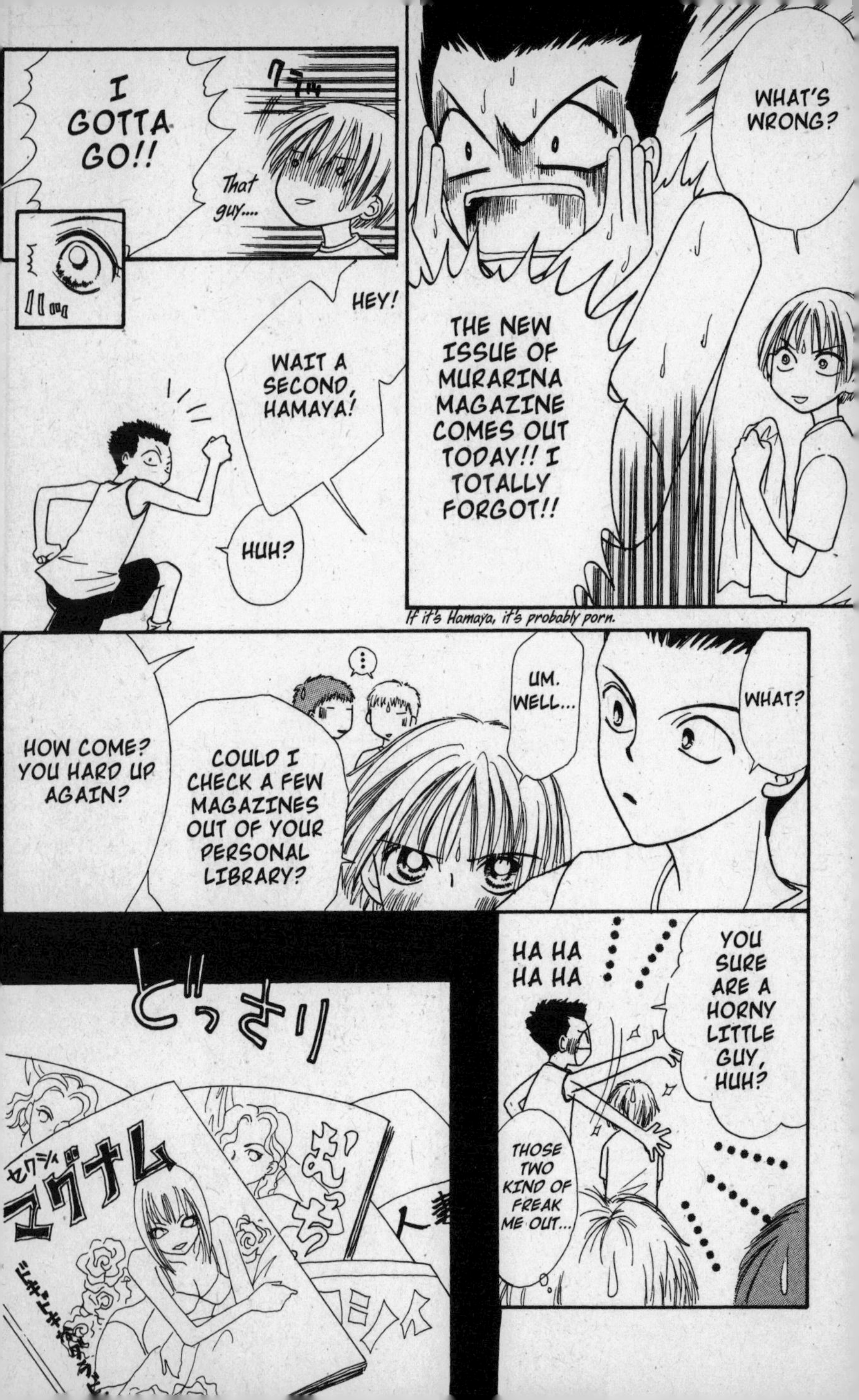
WHAT'S WRONG?
THE NEW ISSUE OF MURARINA MAGAZINE COMES OUT TODAY!! I TOTALLY FORGOT!!
I GOTTA GO!!
That guy....
HEY!
WAIT A SECOND, HAMAYA!
HUH?
If it's Hamaya, it's probably porn.
WHAT?
UM. WELL...
COULD I CHECK A FEW MAGAZINES OUT OF YOUR PERSONAL LIBRARY?
HOW COME? YOU HARD UP AGAIN?
YOU SURE ARE A HORNY LITTLE GUY, HUH?
HA HA HA HA
THOSE TWO KIND OF FREAK ME OUT...

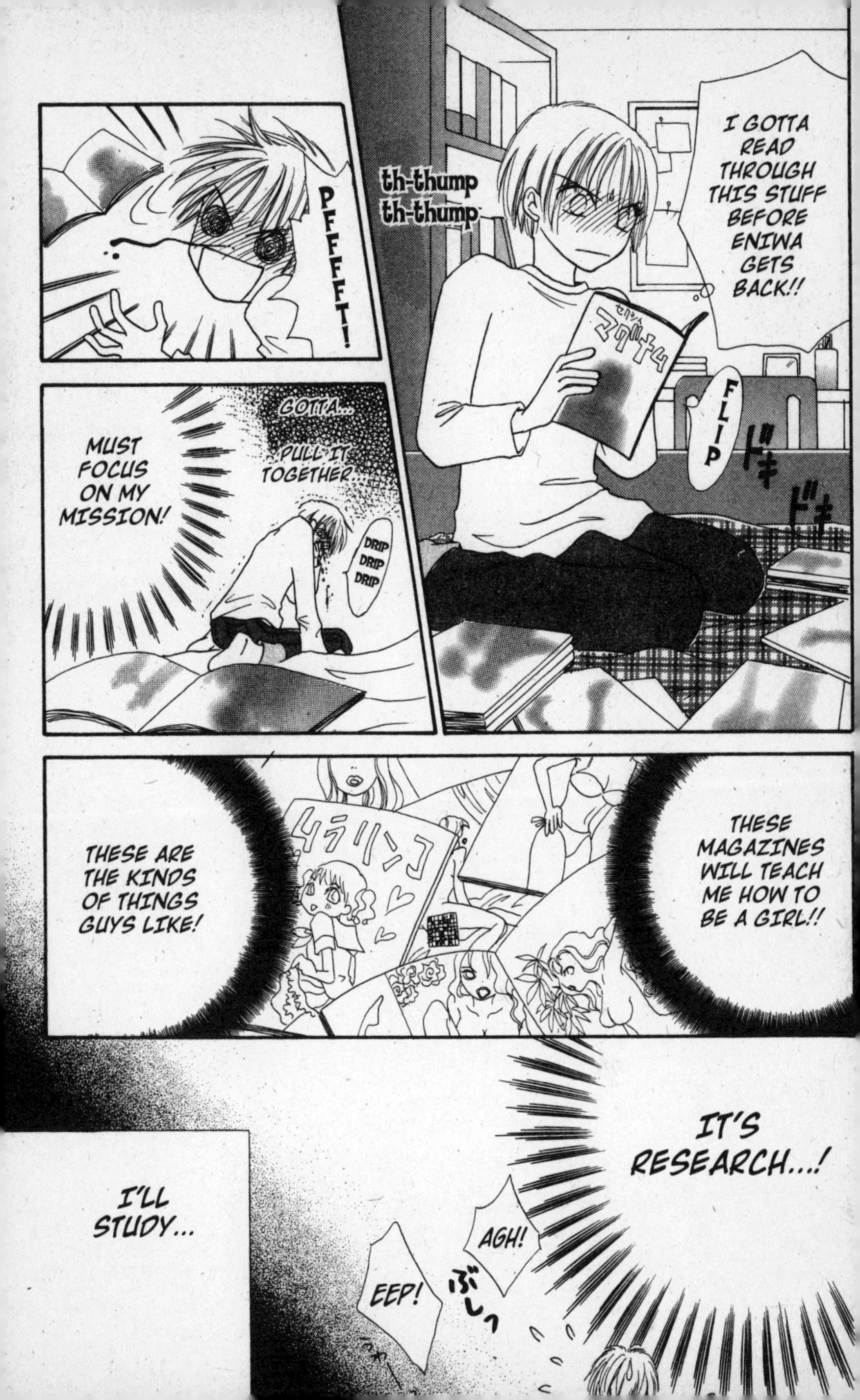
I GOTTA READ THROUGH THIS STUFF BEFORE ENIWA GETS BACK!!
th-thump th-thump
FLIP
ドキドキ
PFFFFT!
GOTTA... PULL IT TOGETHER
MUST FOCUS ON MY MISSION!
DRIP DRIP DRIP
THESE MAGAZINES WILL TEACH ME HOW TO BE A GIRL!!
THESE ARE THE KINDS OF THINGS GUYS LIKE!
IT'S RESEARCH...!
AGH!
ぶしっ
EEP!
I'LL STUDY...

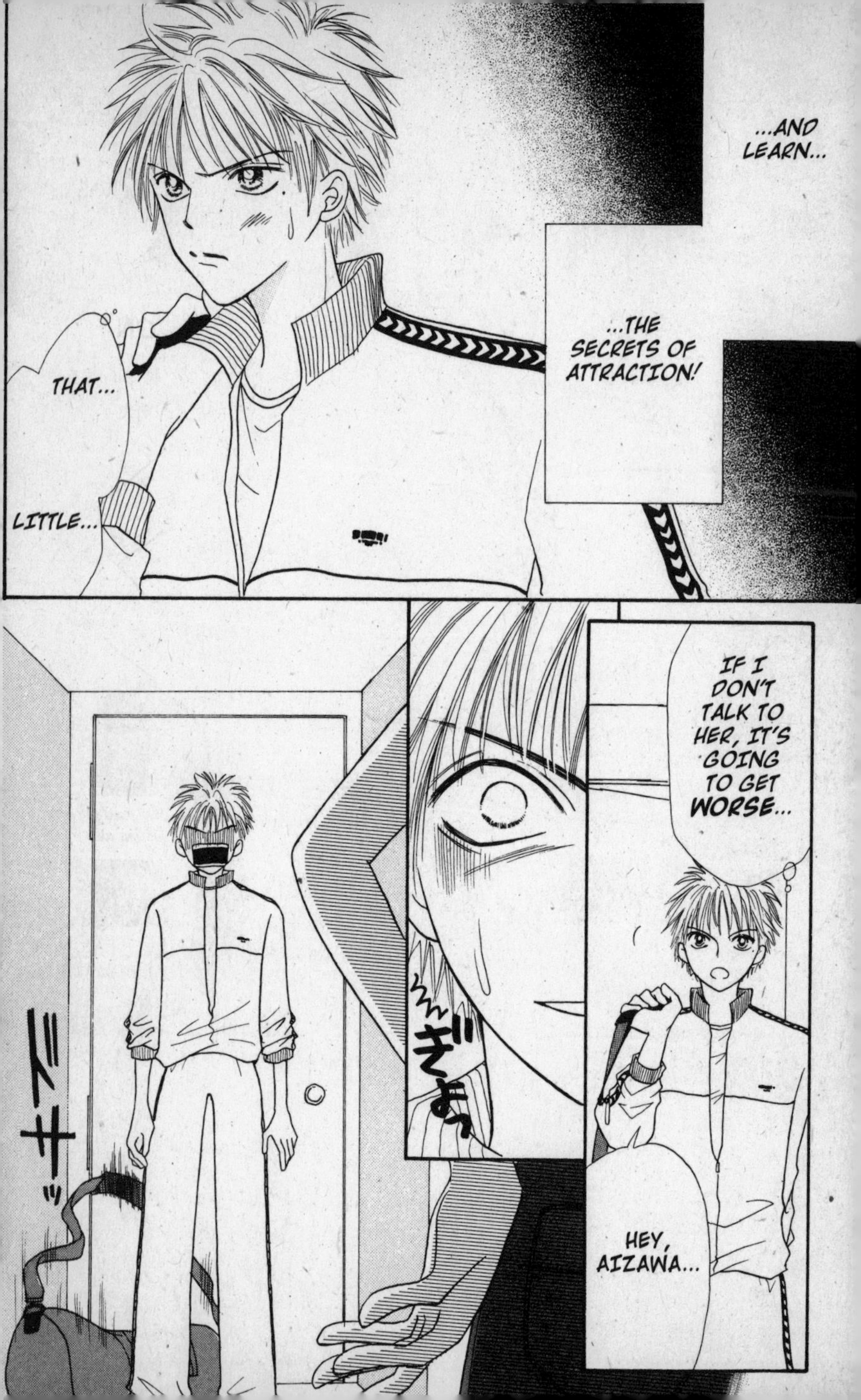
...AND LEARN...
...THE SECRETS OF ATTRACTION!
THAT...
LITTLE...
IF I DON'T TALK TO HER, IT'S GOING TO GET WORSE...
HEY, AIZAWA...
ぎょっ
ドサッ

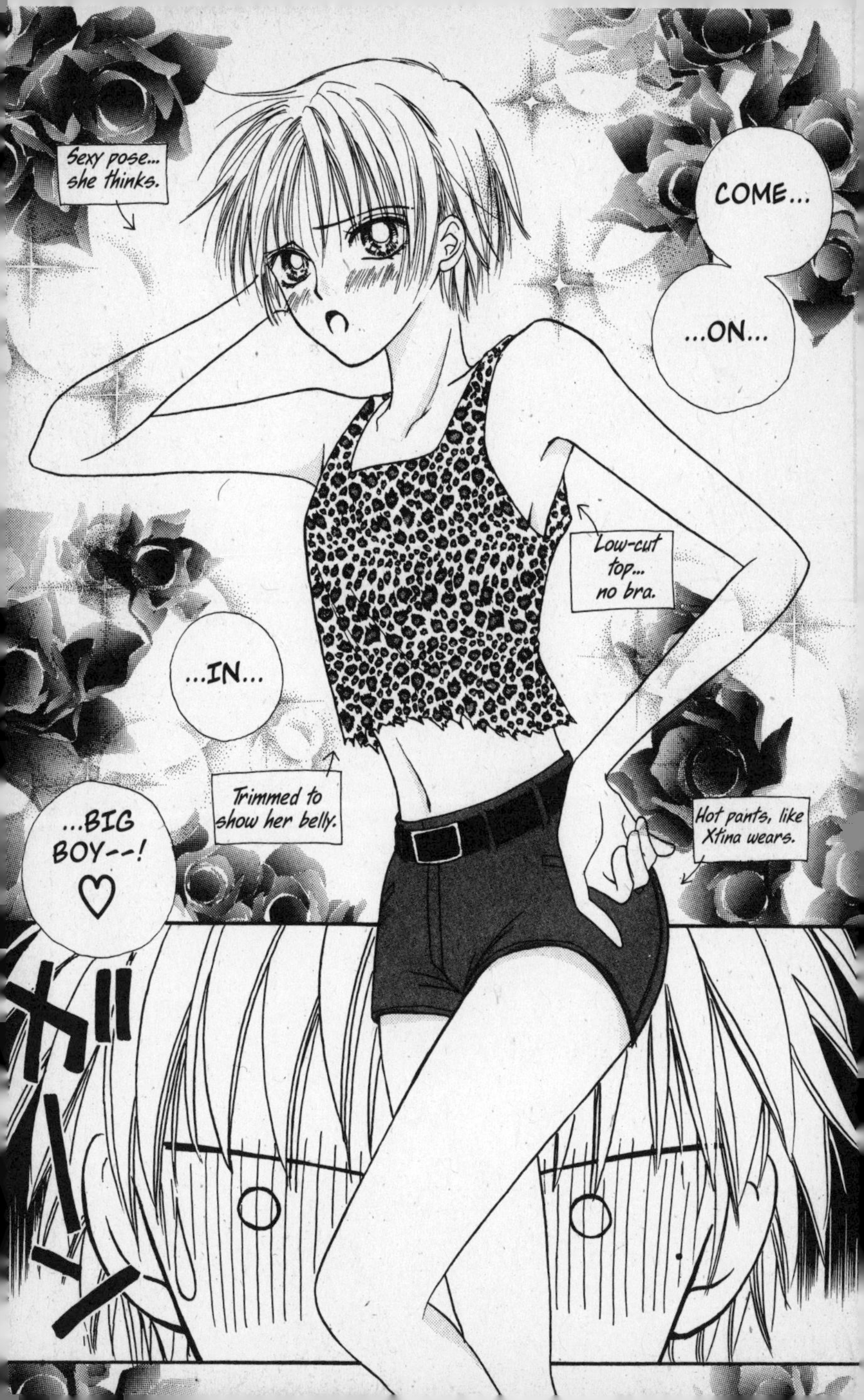

COME...
...ON...
Sexy pose... she thinks.
Low-cut top... no bra.
...IN...
Hot pants, like Xtina wears.
Trimmed to show her belly.
...BIG BOY--! ♥

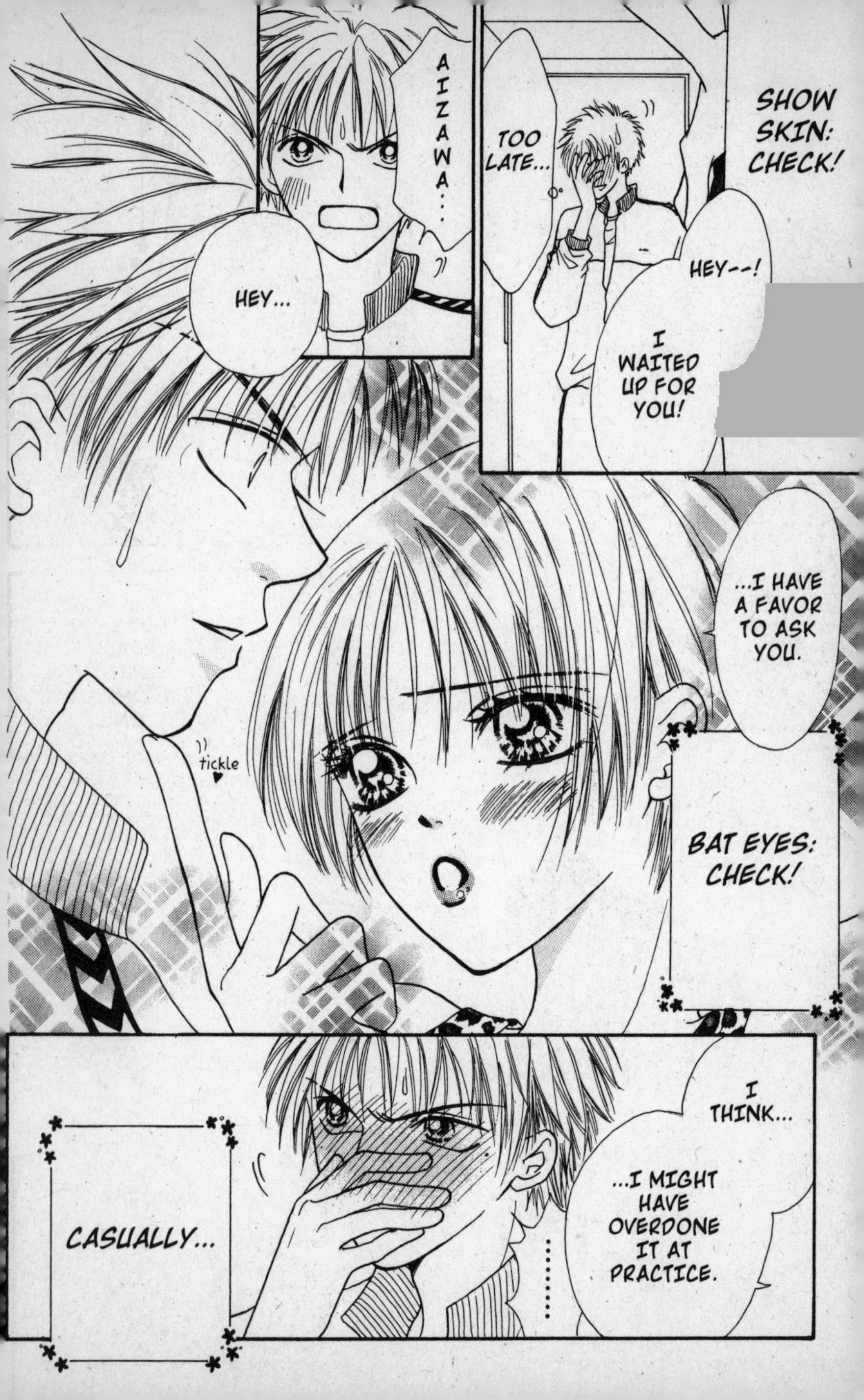
SHOW SKIN: CHECK!
HEY--!
I WAITED UP FOR YOU!
TOO LATE...
AIZAWA...
HEY...
...I HAVE A FAVOR TO ASK YOU.
BAT EYES: CHECK!
tickle
I THINK...
...I MIGHT HAVE OVERDONE IT AT PRACTICE.
......
CASUALLY...

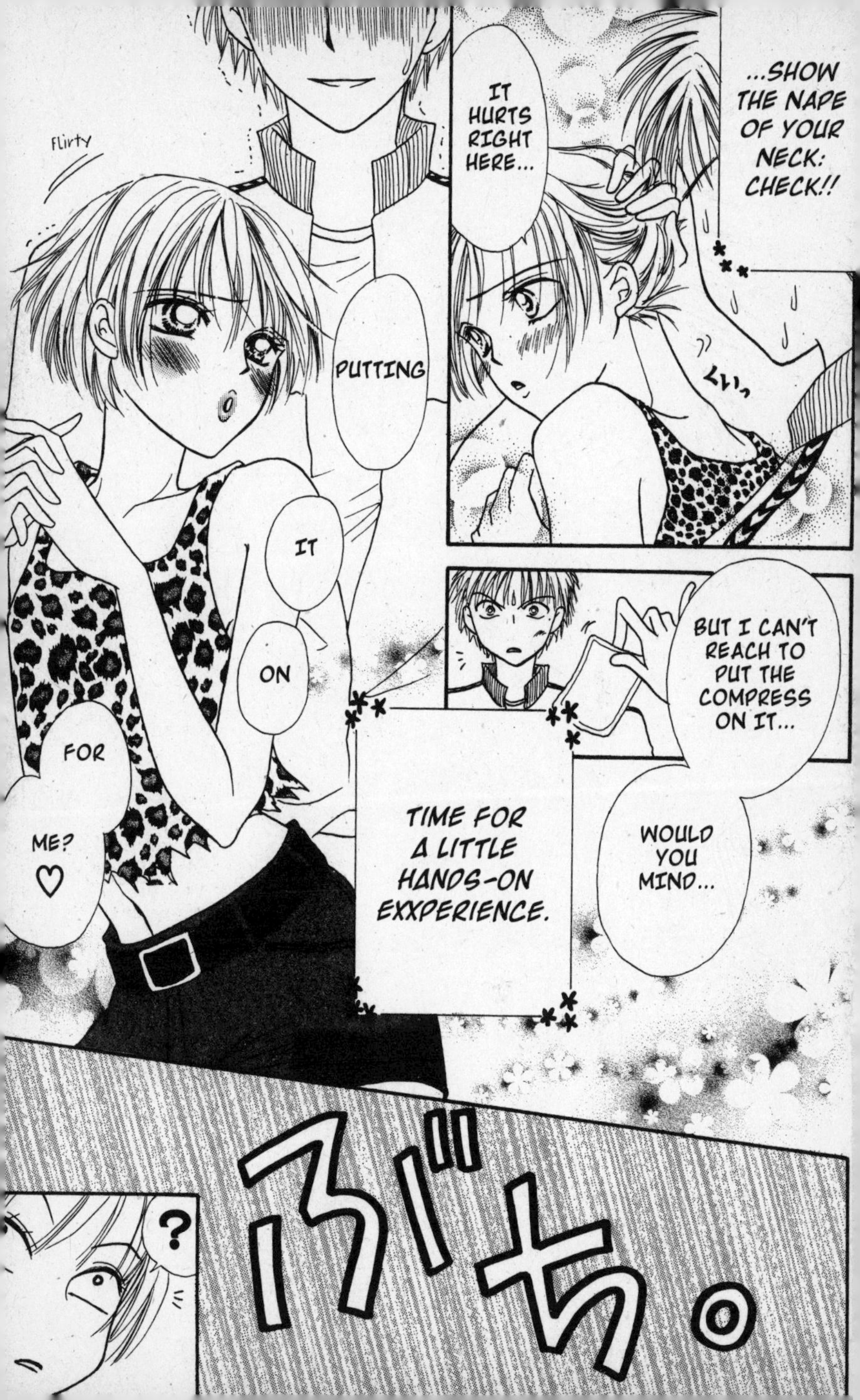
...SHOW THE NAPE OF YOUR NECK: CHECK!!
IT HURTS RIGHT HERE...
BUT I CAN'T REACH TO PUT THE COMPRESS ON IT...
WOULD YOU MIND...
TIME FOR A LITTLE HANDS-ON EXXPERIENCE.
PUTTING
IT
ON
FOR
ME? ♡
Flirty
ぶち。
?

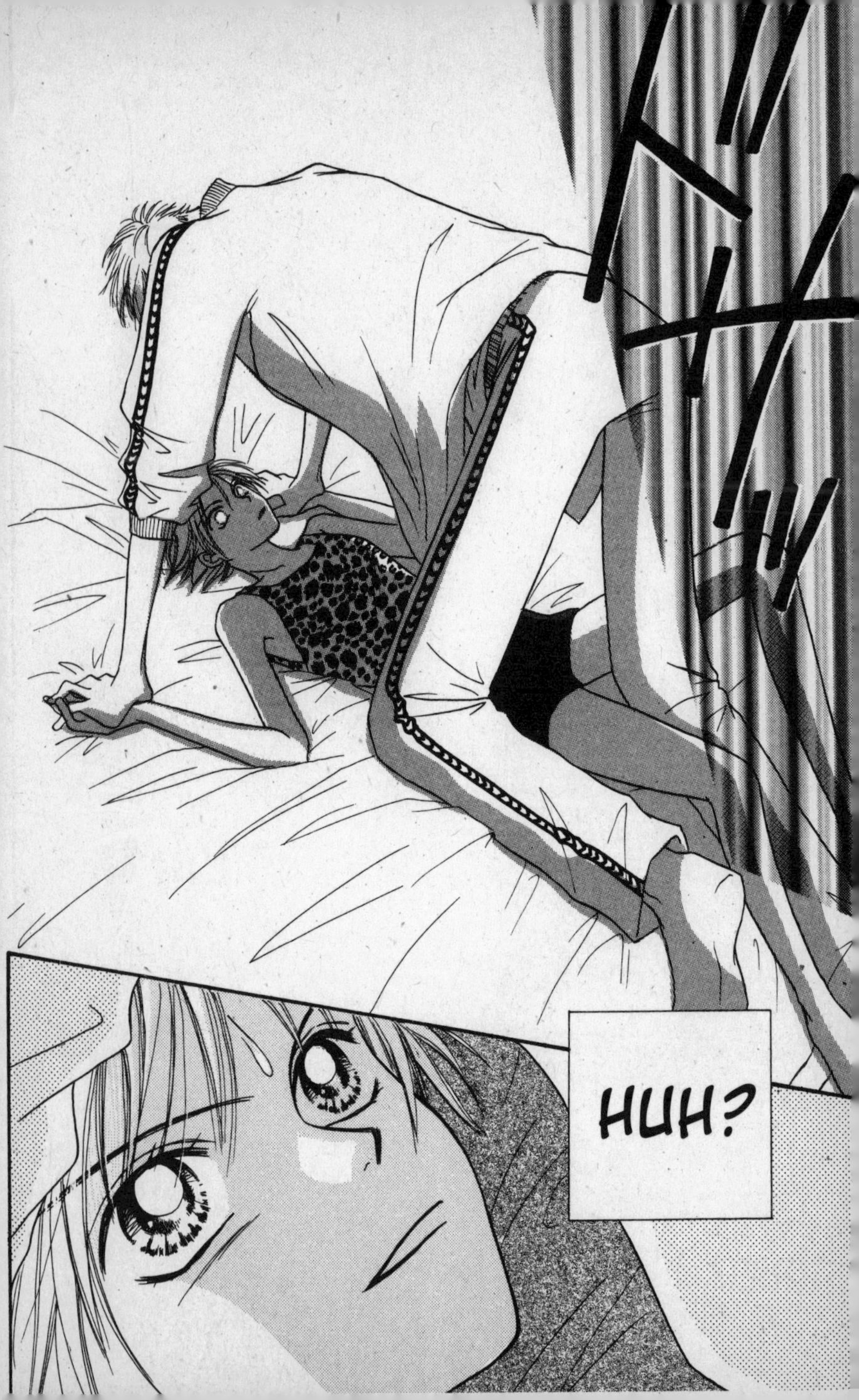
HUH?

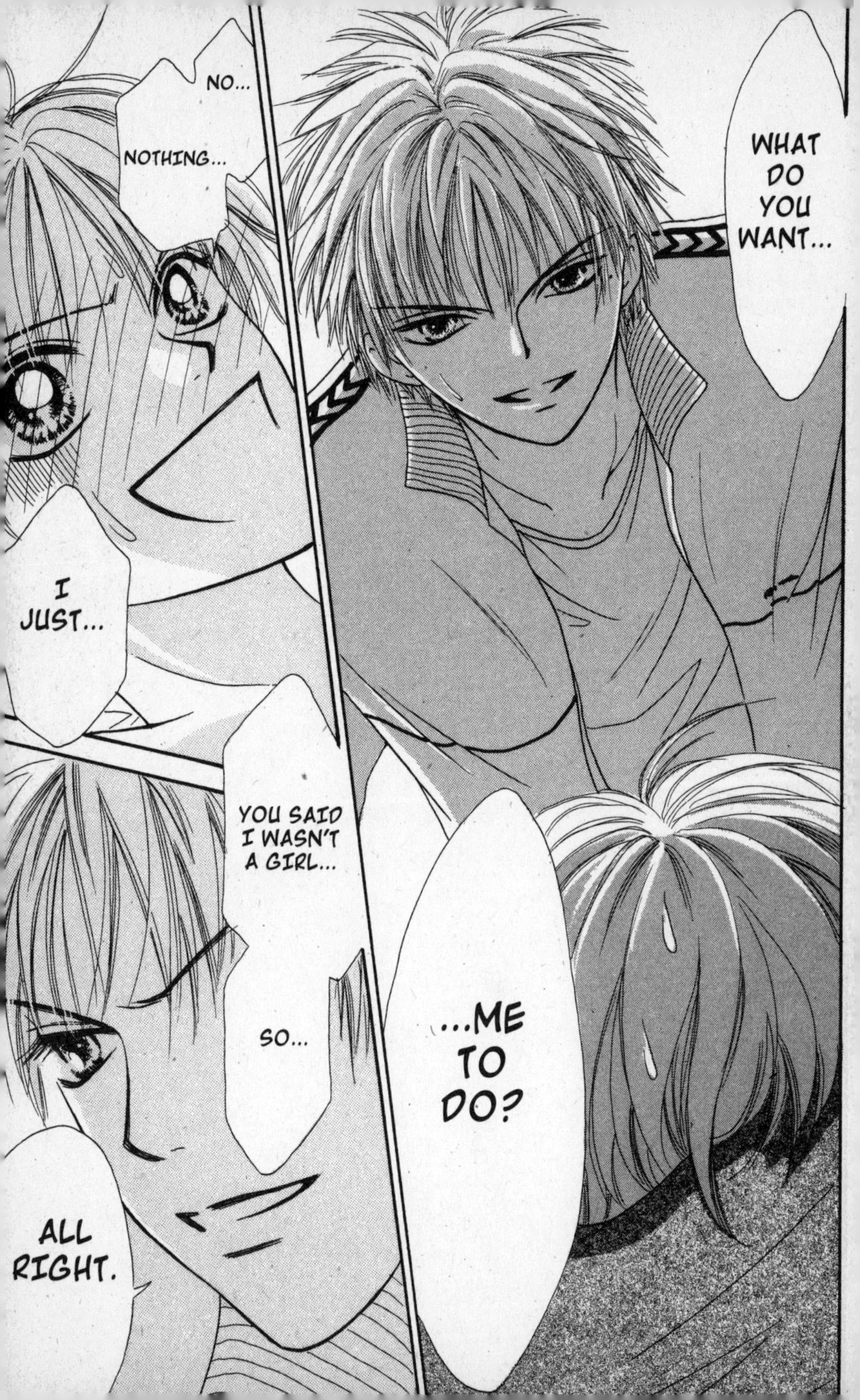
WHAT DO YOU WANT...
...ME TO DO?
NO...
NOTHING...
I JUST...
YOU SAID I WASN'T A GIRL...
SO...
ALL RIGHT.

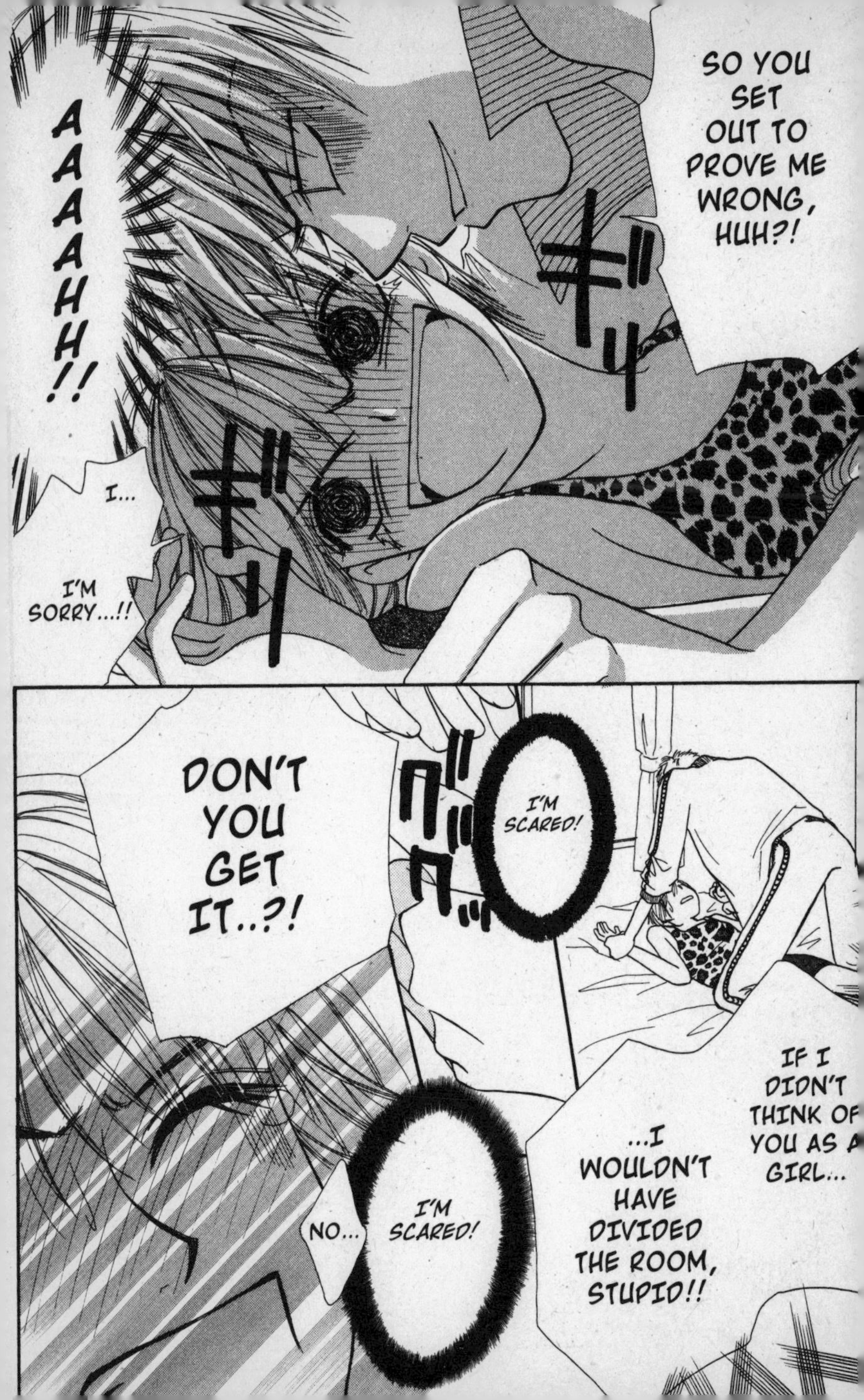
SO YOU SET OUT TO PROVE ME WRONG, HUH?!
AAAAAHH!!
I...
I'M SORRY...!!
DON'T YOU GET IT..?!
IF I DIDN'T THINK OF YOU AS A GIRL...
...I WOULDN'T HAVE DIVIDED THE ROOM, STUPID!!
I'M SCARED!
I'M SCARED!
NO...

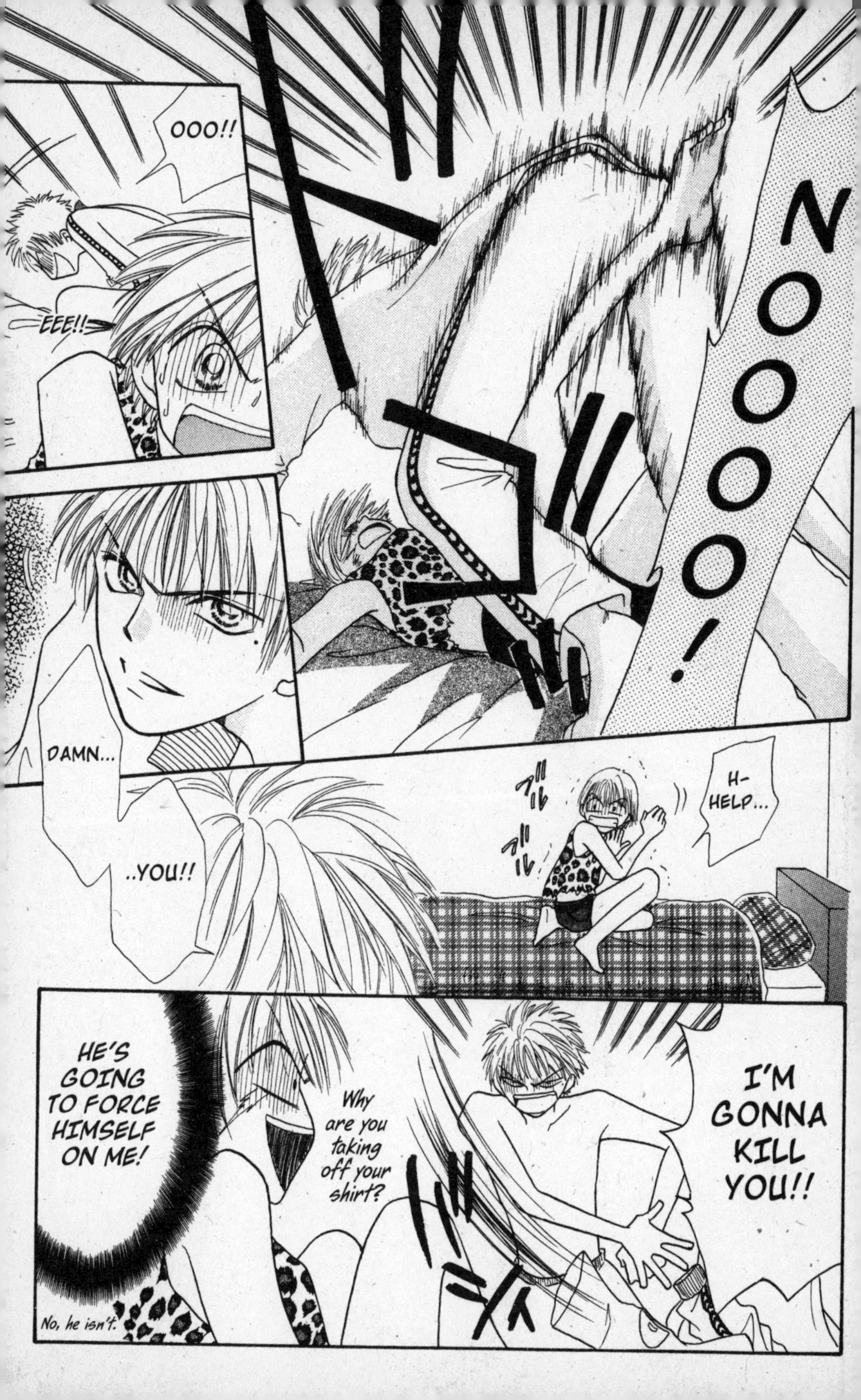
NOOOOO!
OOO!!
EEE!!
DAMN...
H-HELP...
ブル
ブル
..YOU!!
I'M GONNA KILL YOU!!
Why are you taking off your shirt?
HE'S GOING TO FORCE HIMSELF ON ME!
No, he isn't.

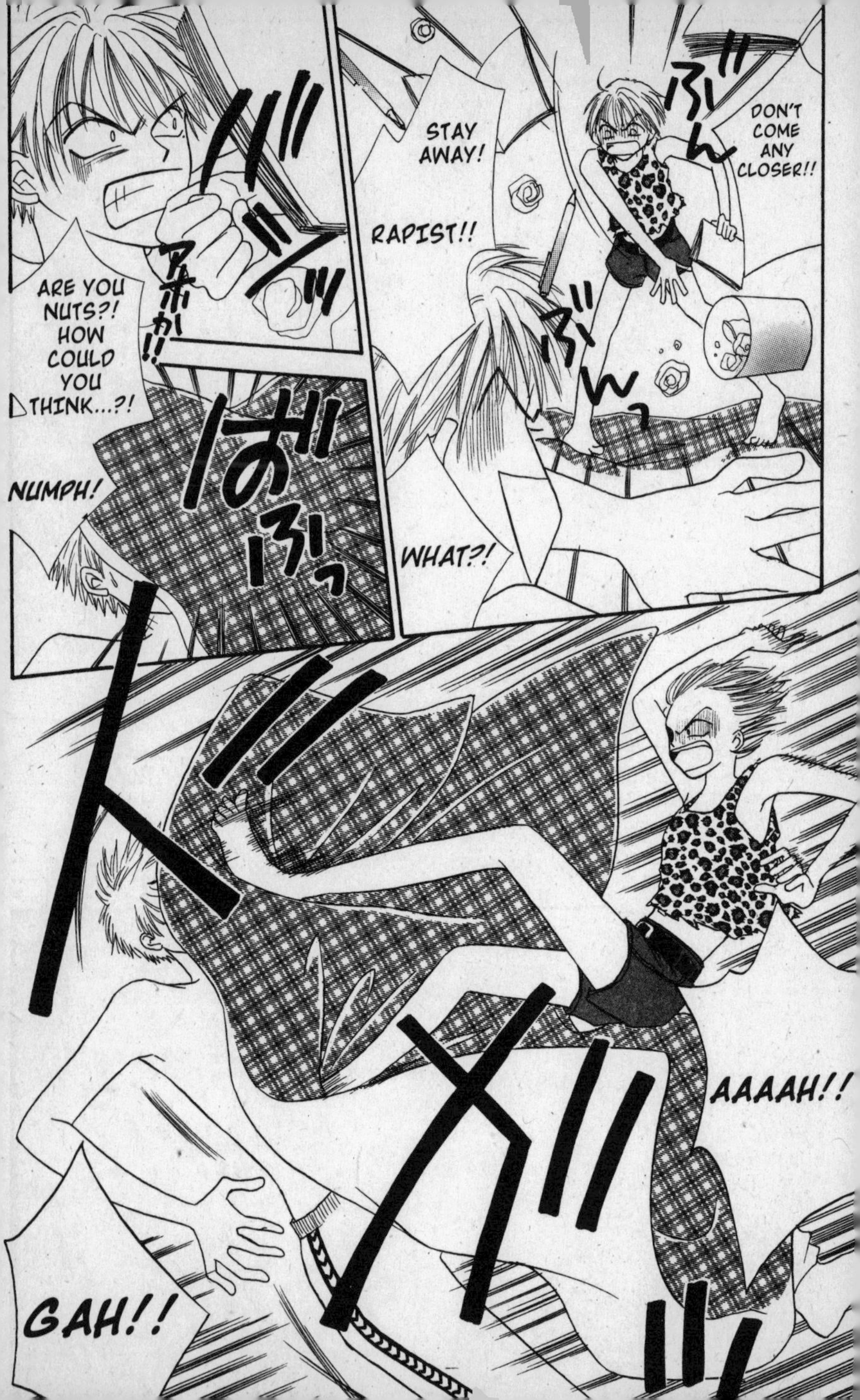
DON'T COME ANY CLOSER!!
STAY AWAY!
RAPIST!!
WHAT?!
ARE YOU NUTS?! HOW COULD YOU THINK...?!
アホか!!
NUMPH!
AAAAH!!
GAH!!

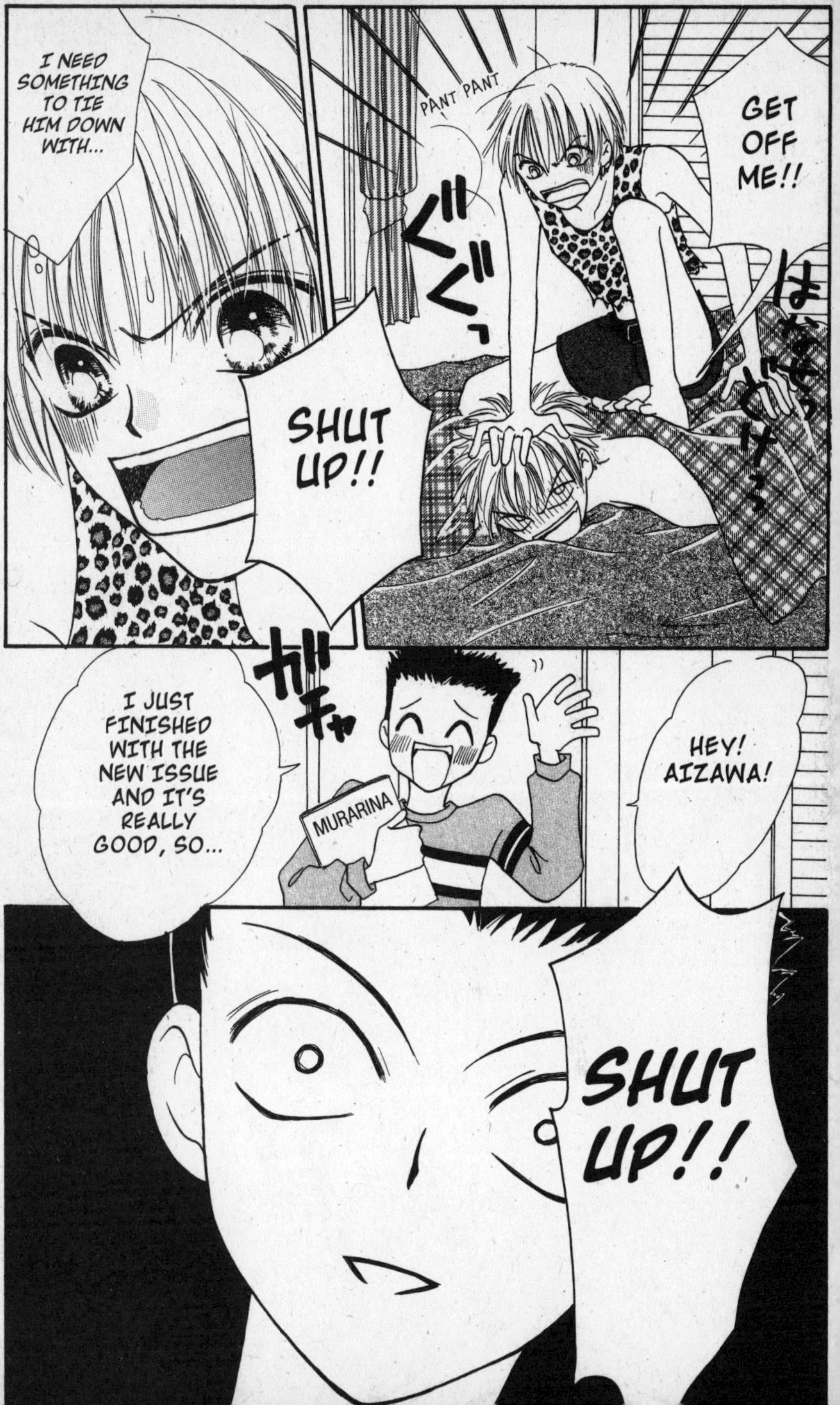
PANT PANT
GET OFF ME!!
I NEED SOMETHING TO TIE HIM DOWN WITH...
SHUT UP!!
HEY! AIZAWA!
I JUST FINISHED WITH THE NEW ISSUE AND IT'S REALLY GOOD, SO...
MURARINA
SHUT UP!!

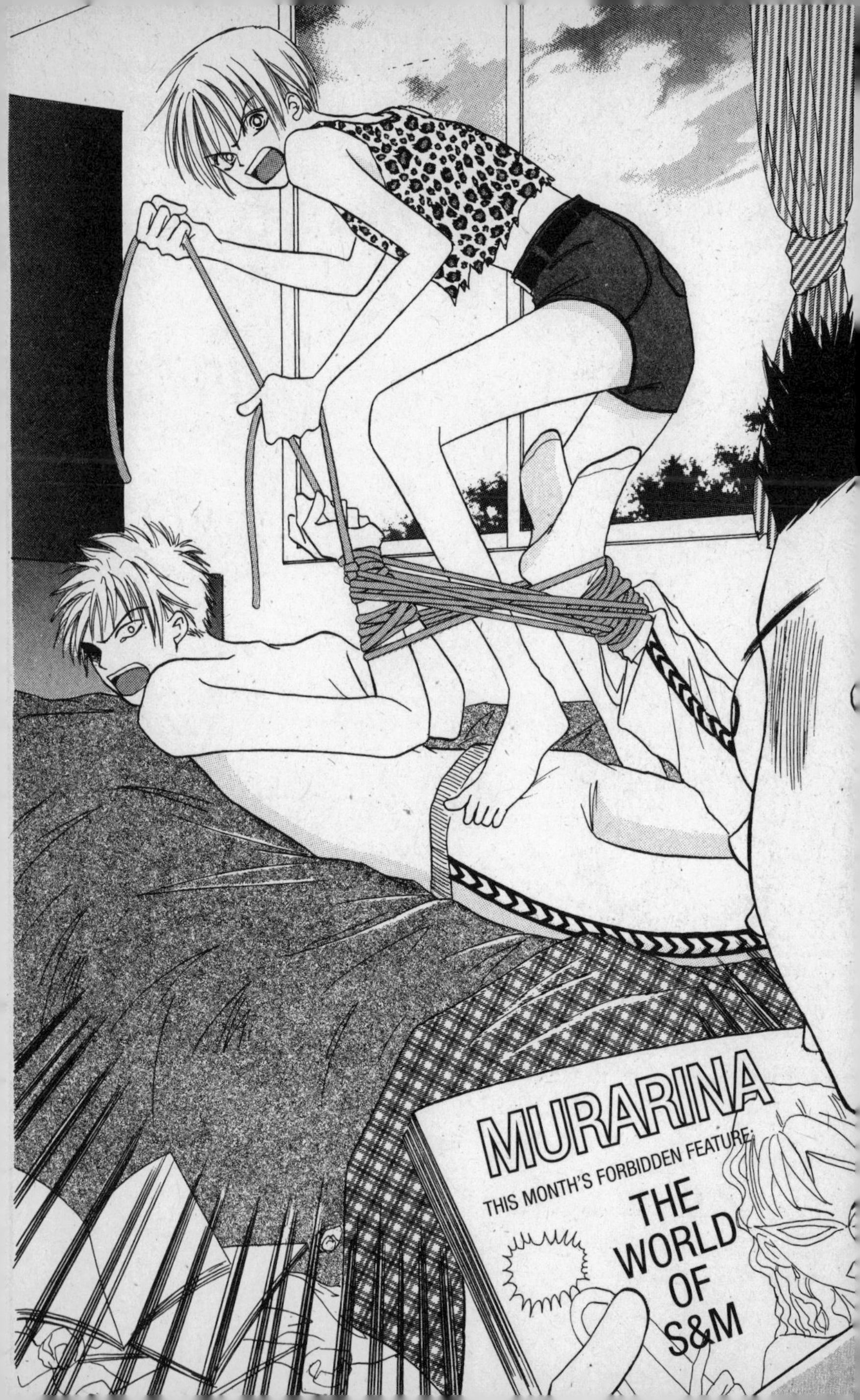
MURARINA
THIS MONTH'S FORBIDDEN FEATURE:
THE WORLD OF S&M

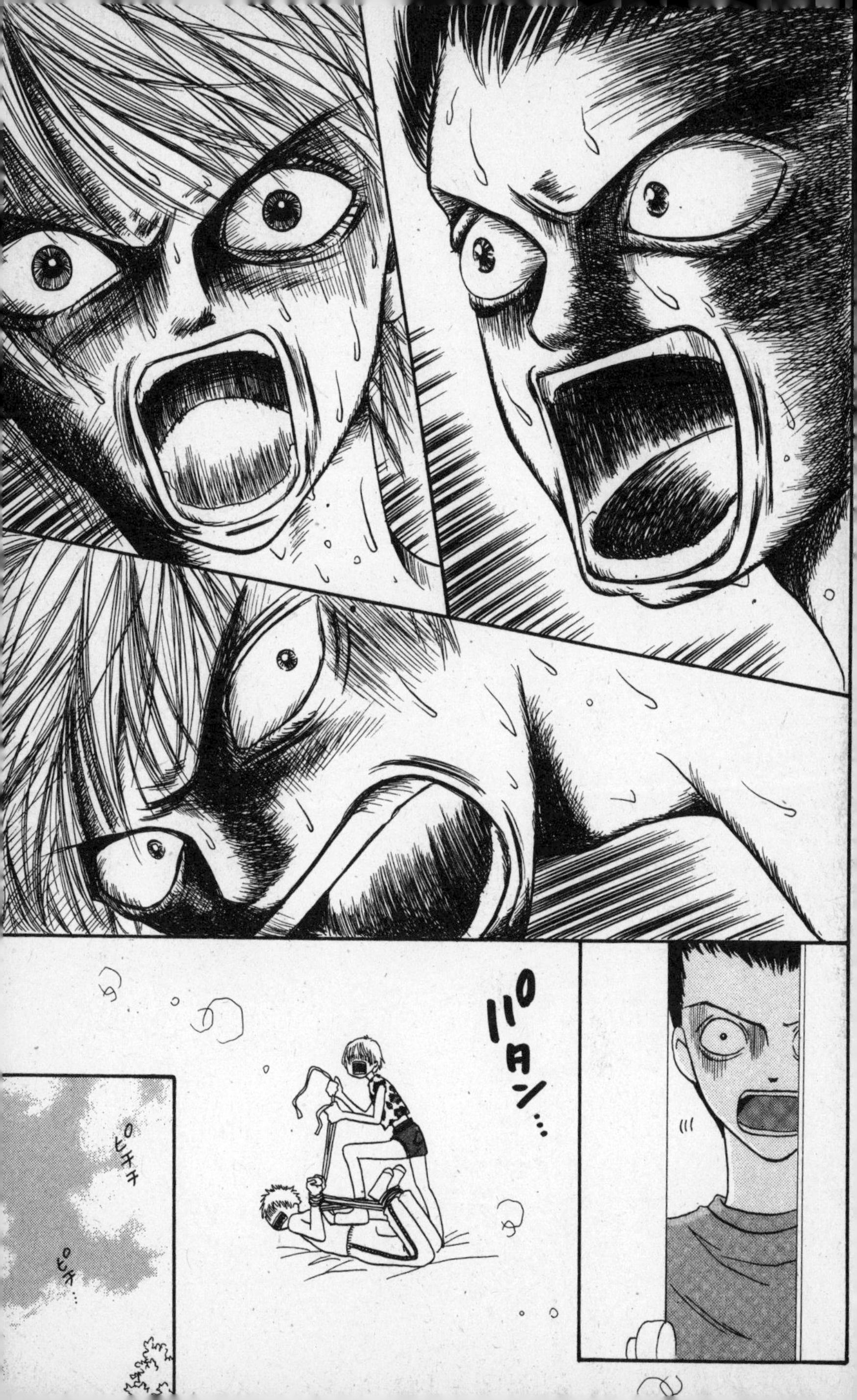
パタン…
ピチチ
ピチ…

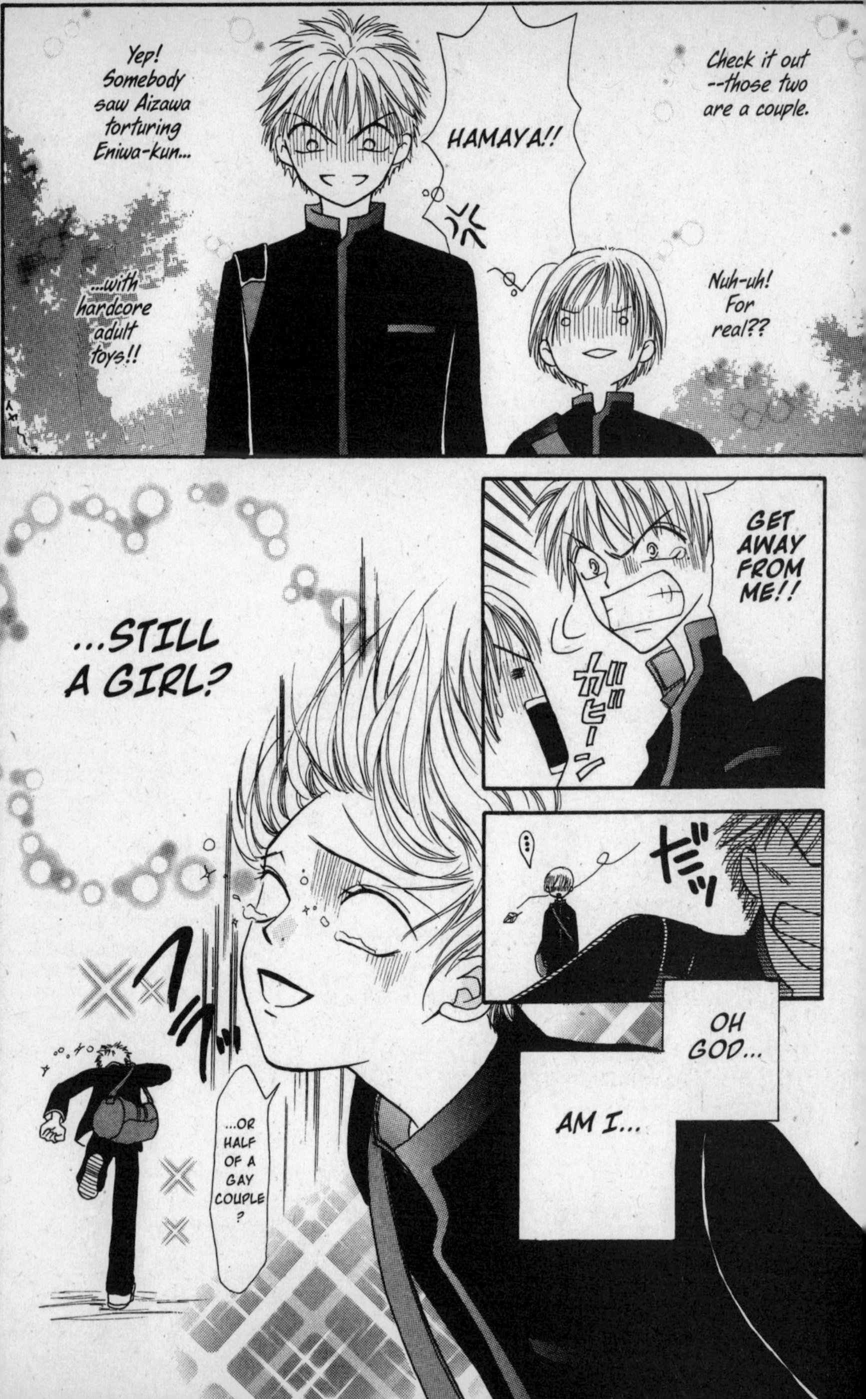

Check it out --those two are a couple.
HAMAYA!!
Nuh-uh! For real??
Yep! Somebody saw Aizawa torturing Eniwa-kun...
...with hardcore adult toys!!
GET AWAY FROM ME!!
ガビーン
ダッ
OH GOD...
AM I...
...STILL A GIRL?
...OR HALF OF A GAY COUPLE?

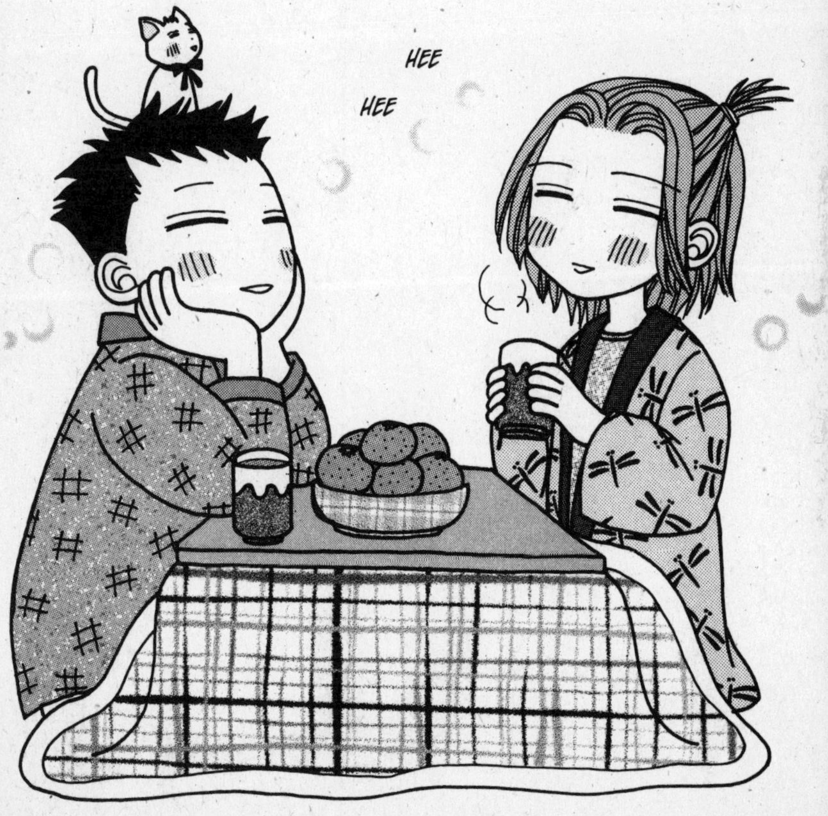
HEE
HEE

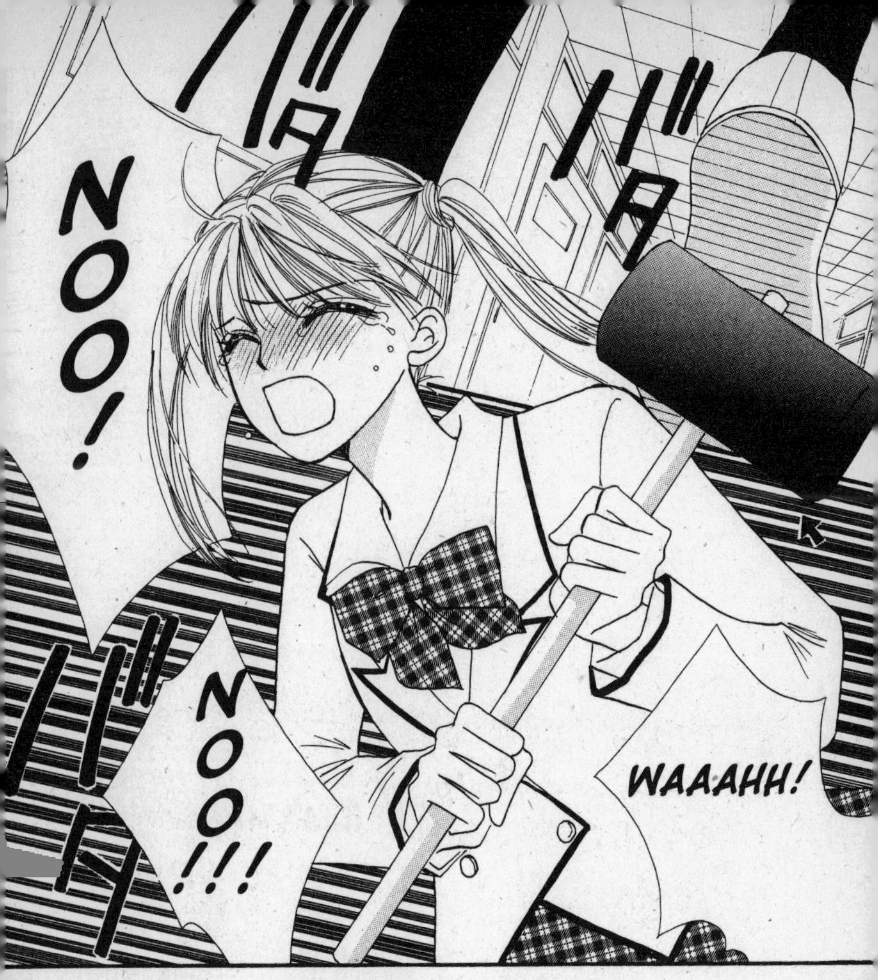
バタ
バタ
NOOO!
WAAAHH!
NOOO!!!
バタ

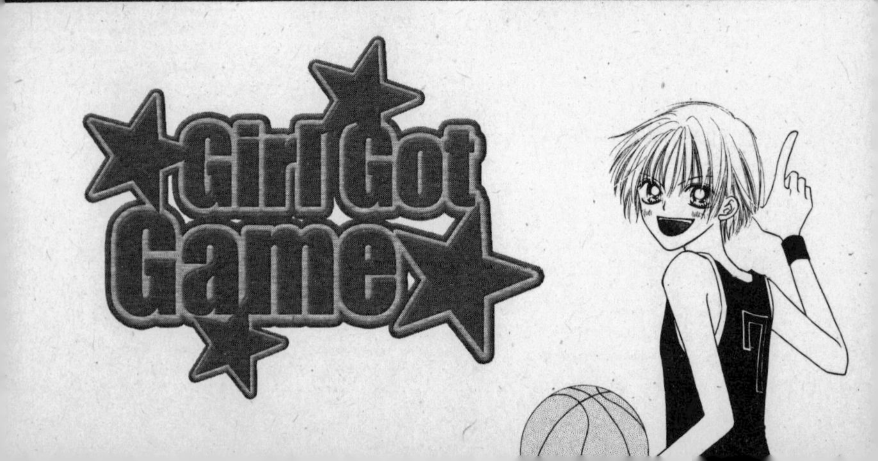
Girl Got Game

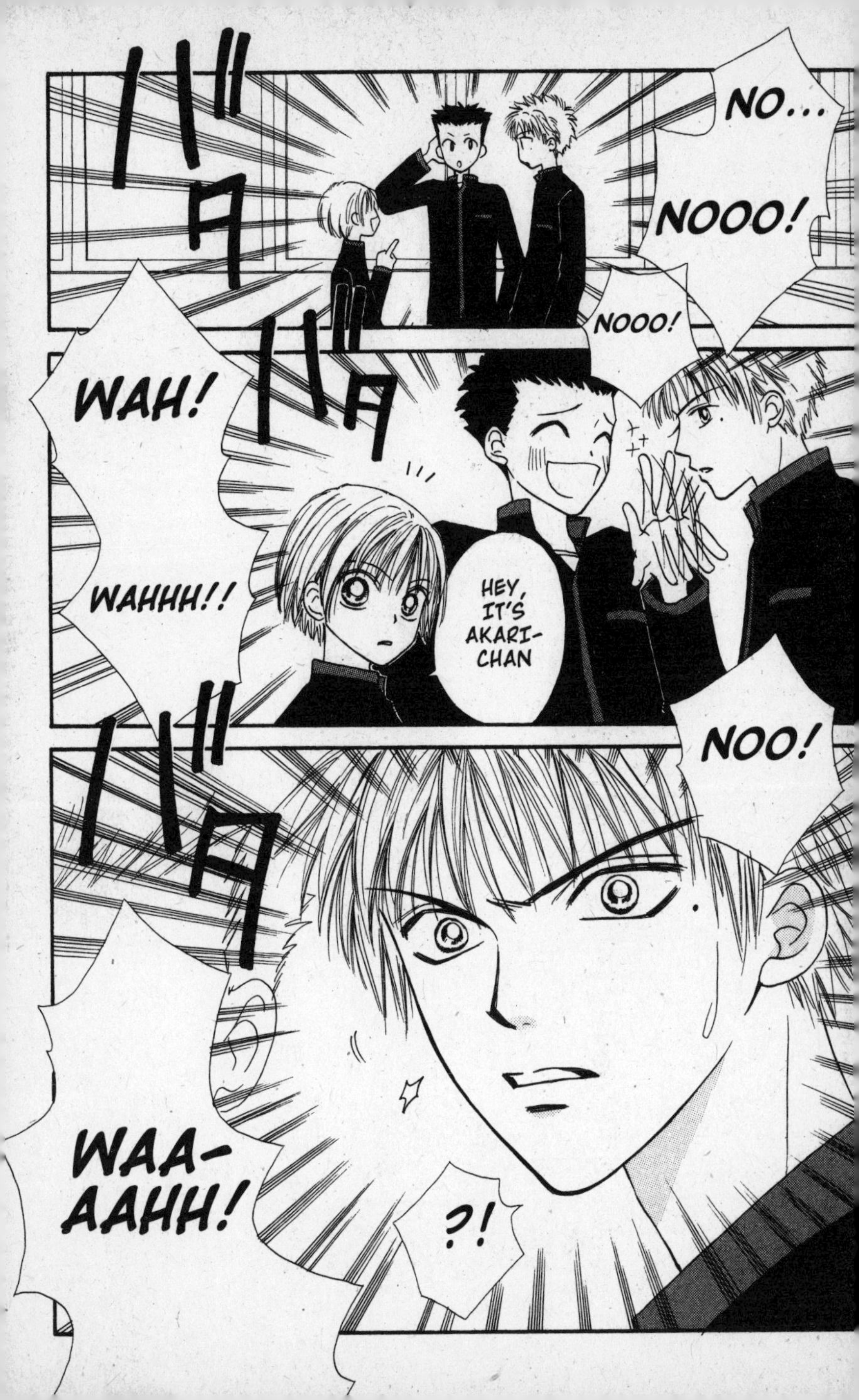
NO... NOOO!
NOOO!
バタ
WAH!
HEY, IT'S AKARI-CHAN
バタ
WAHHH!!
NOO!
?!
バタ
WAA-AAHH!

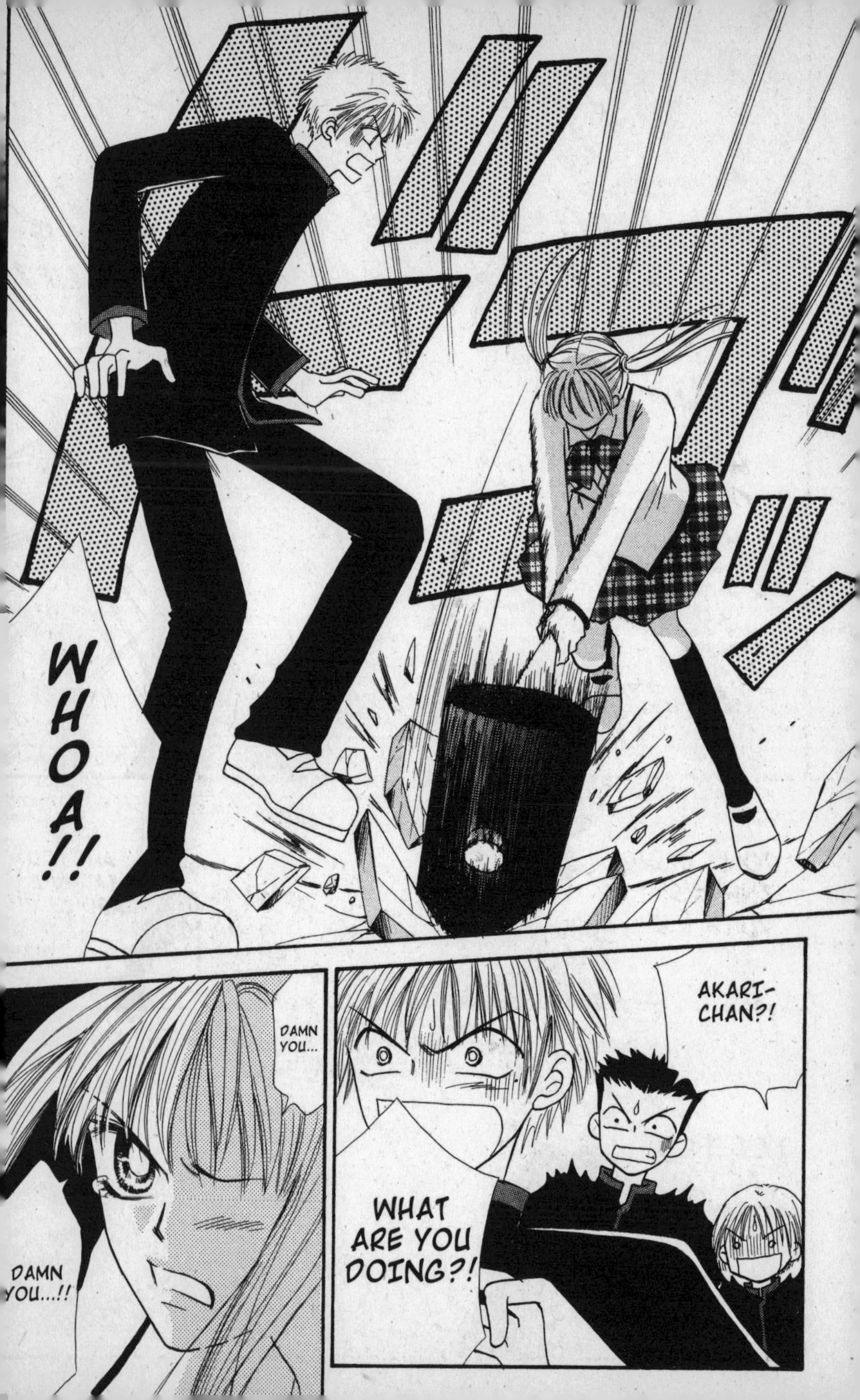
WHOA!!
AKARI-CHAN?!
WHAT ARE YOU DOING?!
DAMN YOU...
DAMN YOU...!!

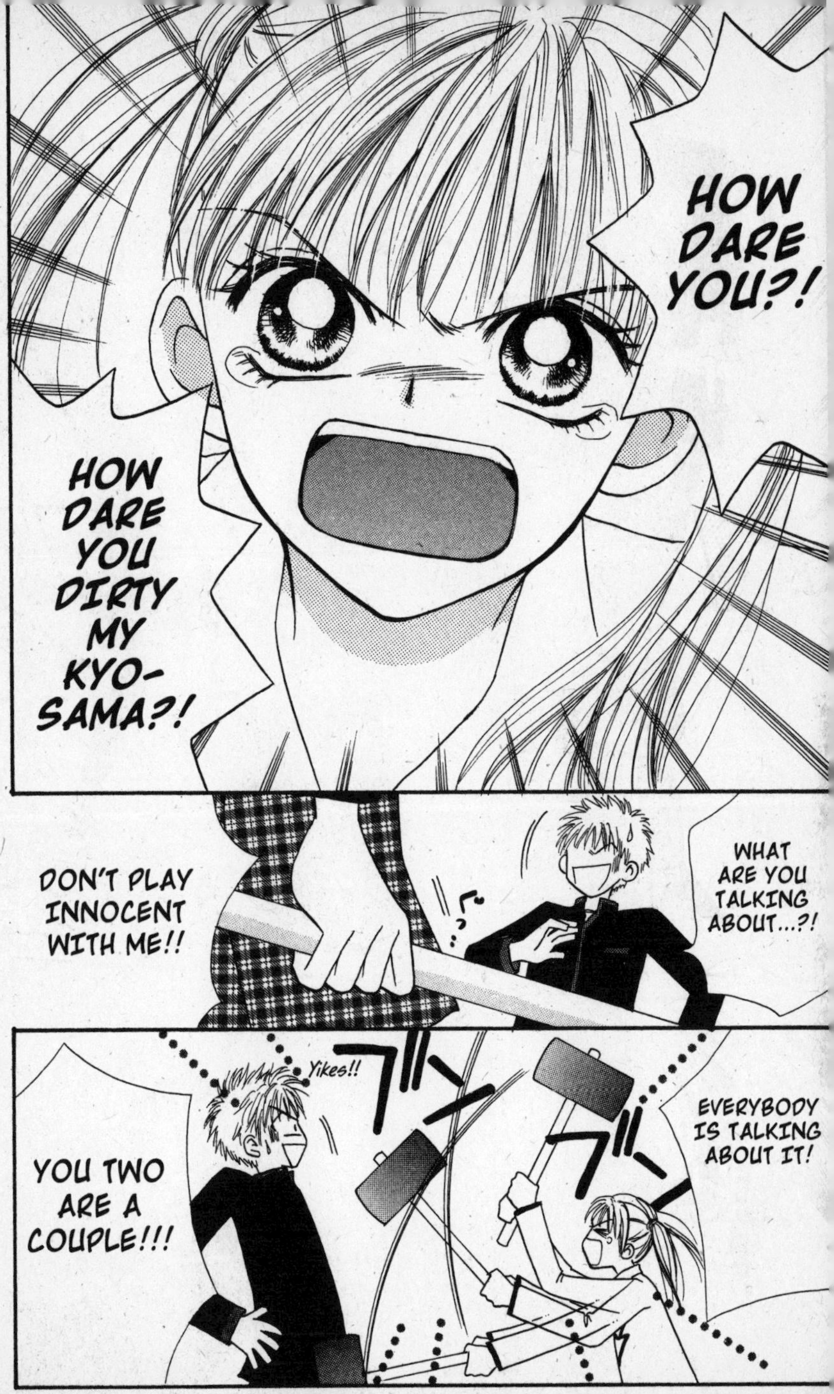
HOW DARE YOU?!
HOW DARE YOU DIRTY MY KYO-SAMA?!
WHAT ARE YOU TALKING ABOUT...?!
DON'T PLAY INNOCENT WITH ME!!
EVERYBODY IS TALKING ABOUT IT!
Yikes!!
YOU TWO ARE A COUPLE!!!

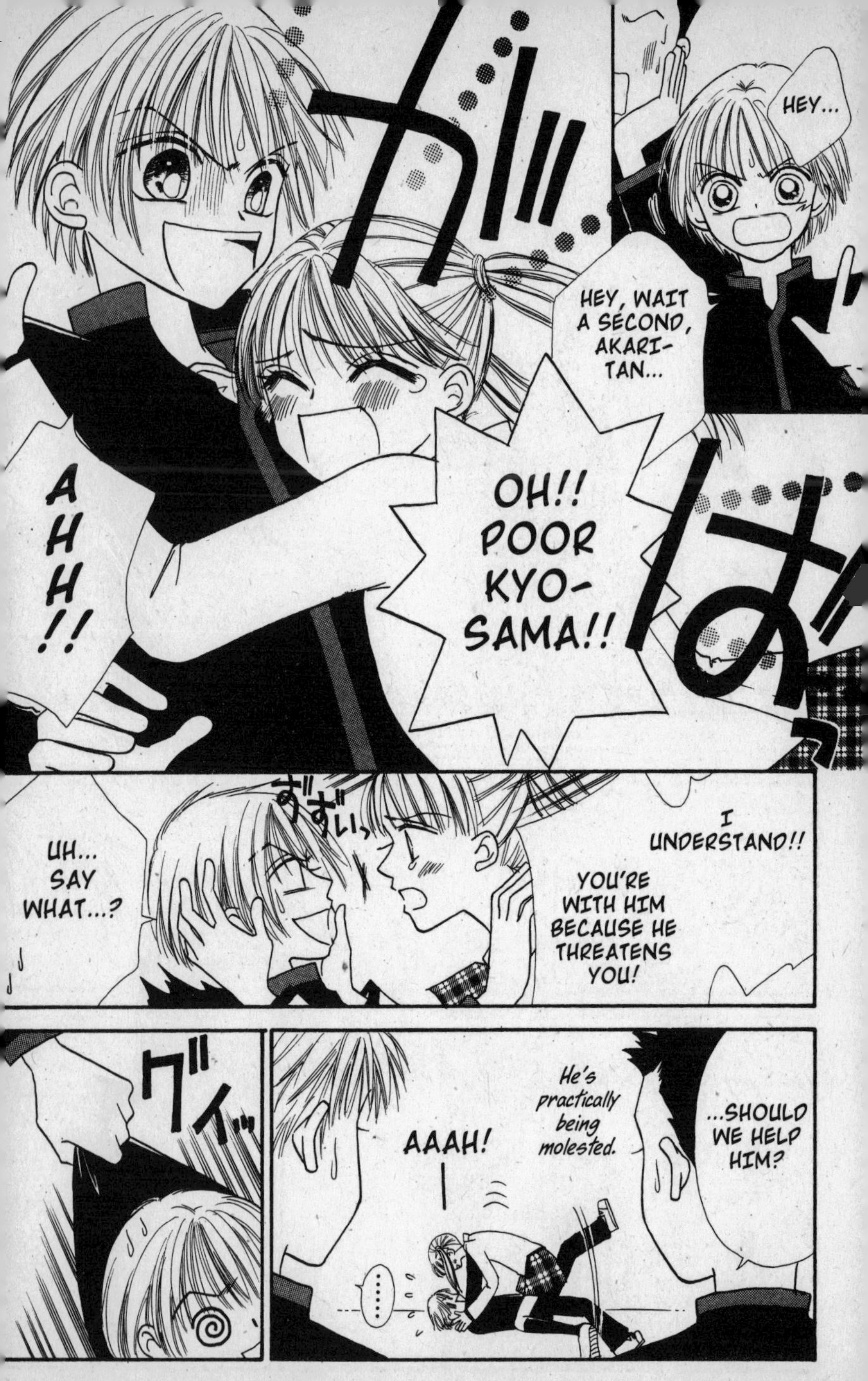
HEY...
HEY, WAIT A SECOND, AKARI-TAN...
OH!! POOR KYO-SAMA!!
AHHH!!
I UNDERSTAND!!
YOU'RE WITH HIM BECAUSE HE THREATENS YOU!
UH... SAY WHAT...?
...SHOULD WE HELP HIM?
He's practically being molested.
AAAH!
......

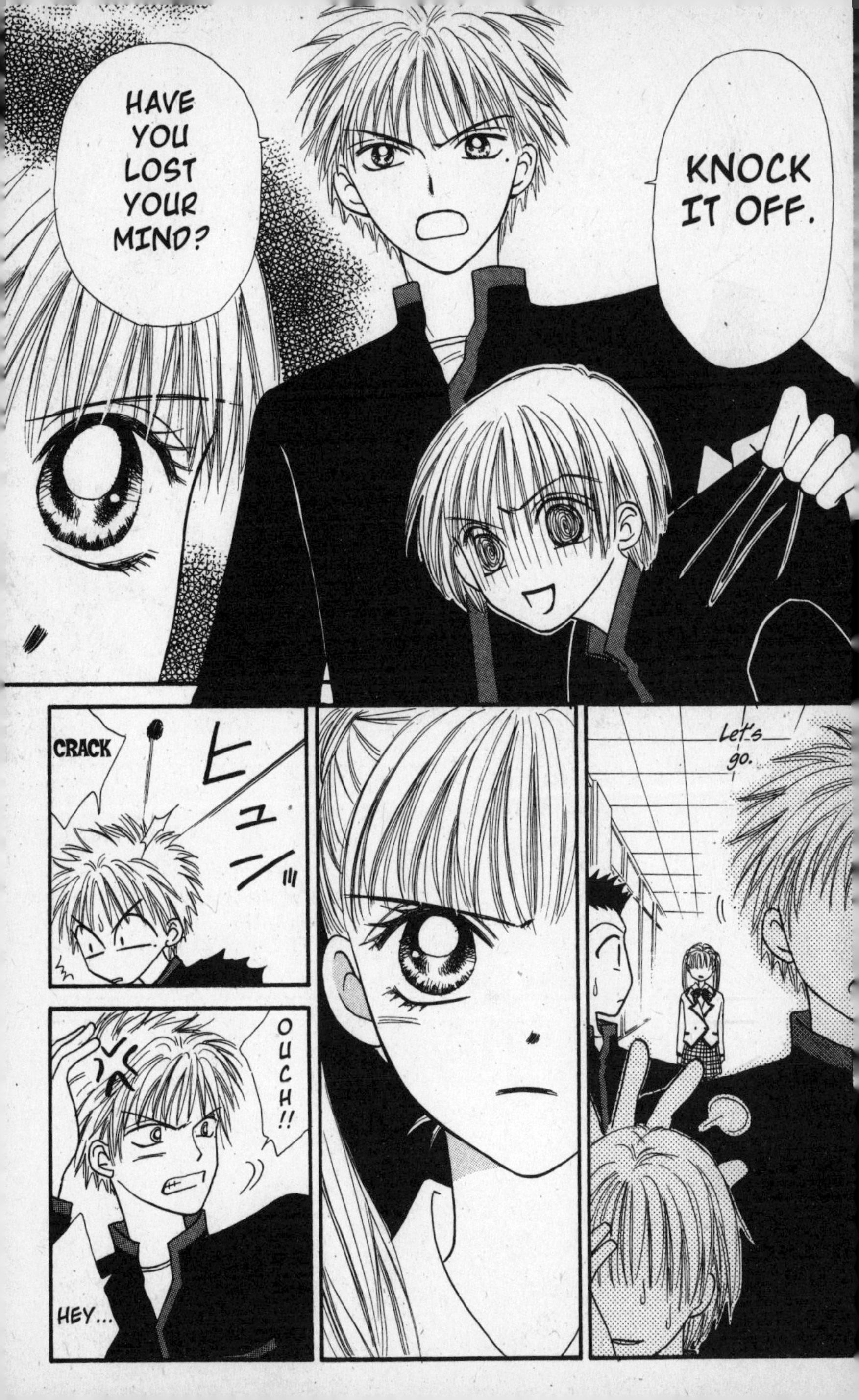
KNOCK IT OFF.
HAVE YOU LOST YOUR MIND?
Let's go.
CRACK
ヒュン
OUCH!!
HEY...

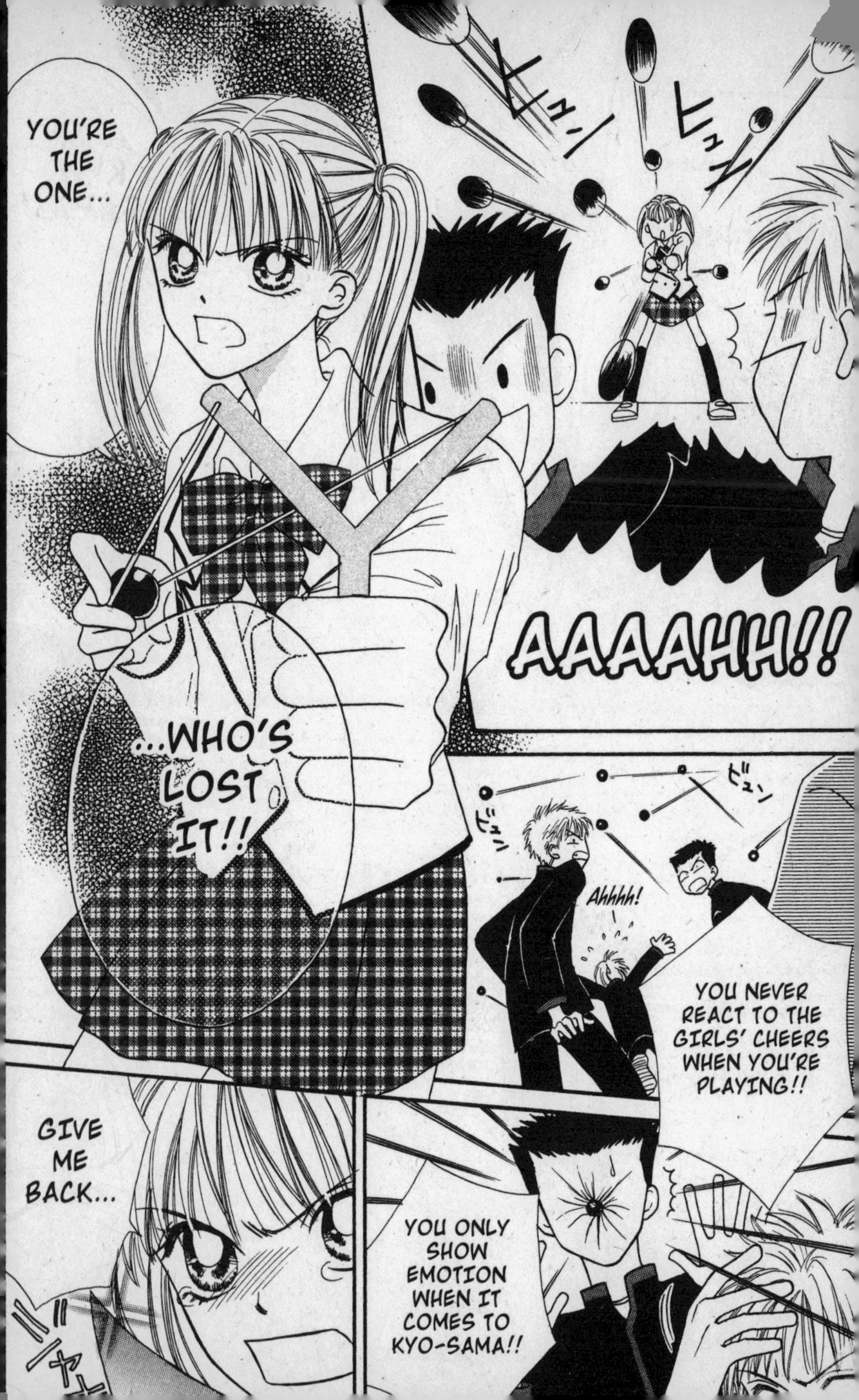
AAAAHH!!
Ahhhh!
YOU NEVER REACT TO THE GIRLS' CHEERS WHEN YOU'RE PLAYING!!
YOU'RE THE ONE...
...WHO'S LOST IT!!
YOU ONLY SHOW EMOTION WHEN IT COMES TO KYO-SAMA!!
GIVE ME BACK...

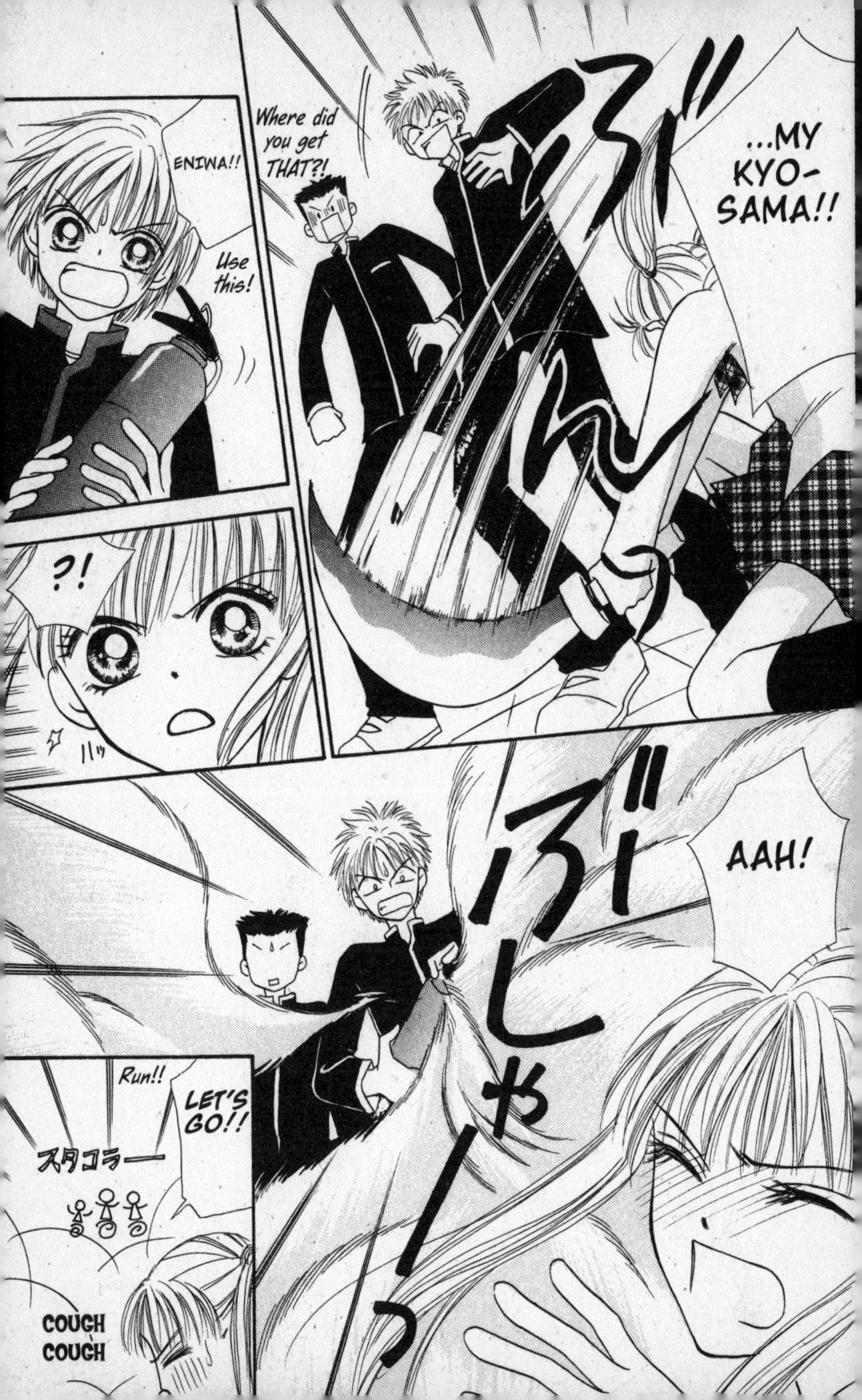
ぶんっ
...MY KYO-SAMA!!
Where did you get THAT?!
ENIWA!!
Use this!
?!
ハッ
AAH!
ぶしゃーっ
Run!!
LET'S GO!!
スタコラー
COUGH COUGH

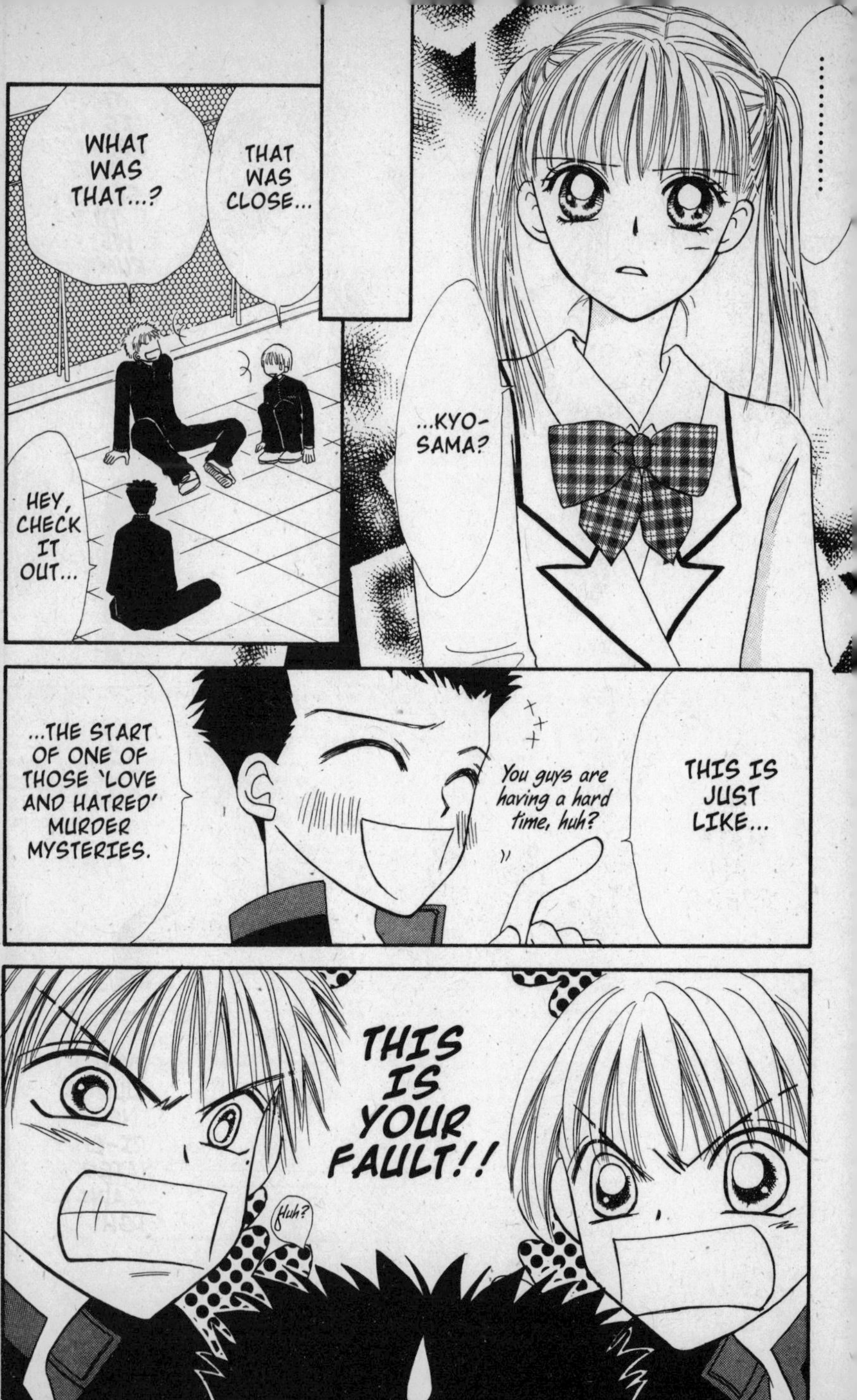

......
...KYO-SAMA?
THAT WAS CLOSE...
WHAT WAS THAT...?
HEY, CHECK IT OUT...
THIS IS JUST LIKE...
You guys are having a hard time, huh?
...THE START OF ONE OF THOSE 'LOVE AND HATRED' MURDER MYSTERIES.
THIS IS YOUR FAULT!!
Huh?

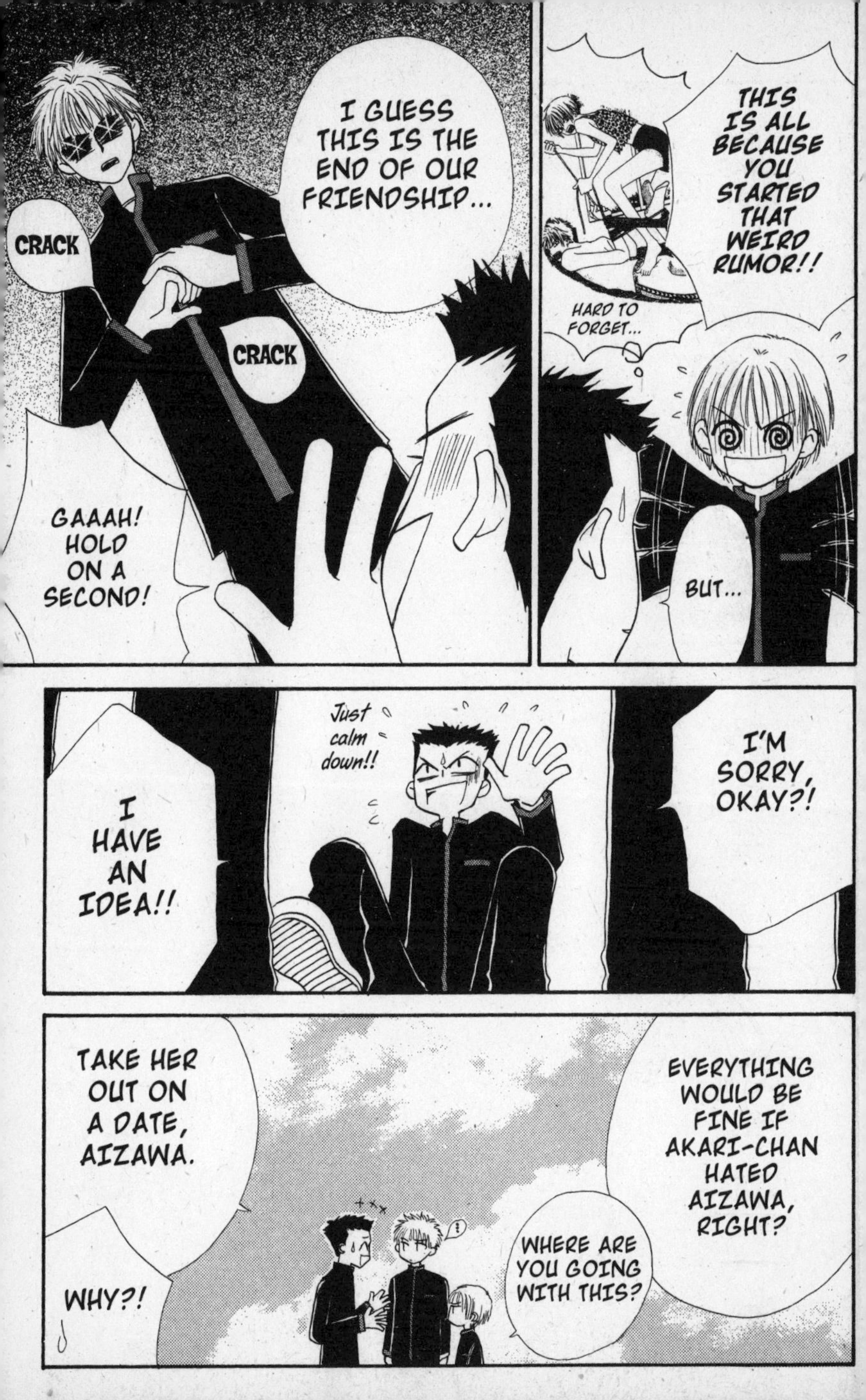
THIS IS ALL BECAUSE YOU STARTED THAT WEIRD RUMOR!!
HARD TO FORGET...
BUT...
I GUESS THIS IS THE END OF OUR FRIENDSHIP...
CRACK
CRACK
GAAAH! HOLD ON A SECOND!
I'M SORRY, OKAY?!
Just calm down!!
I HAVE AN IDEA!!
EVERYTHING WOULD BE FINE IF AKARI-CHAN HATED AIZAWA, RIGHT?
WHERE ARE YOU GOING WITH THIS?
TAKE HER OUT ON A DATE, AIZAWA.
WHY?!

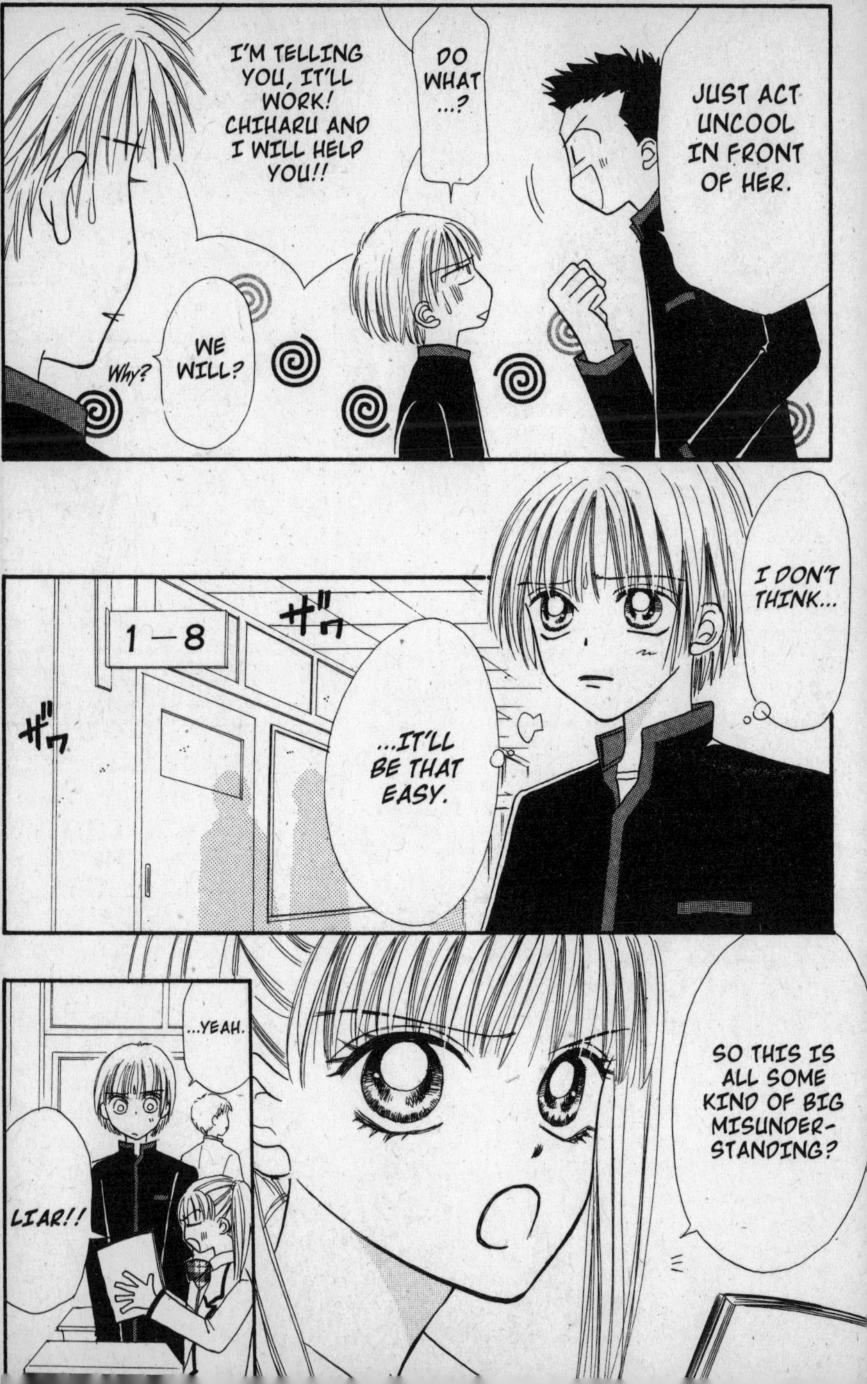
JUST ACT UNCOOL IN FRONT OF HER.
DO WHAT ...?
I'M TELLING YOU, IT'LL WORK! CHIHARU AND I WILL HELP YOU!!
WE WILL?
Why?
I DON'T THINK...
...IT'LL BE THAT EASY.
ザワ
1-8
ザワ
SO THIS IS ALL SOME KIND OF BIG MISUNDER-STANDING?
...YEAH.
LIAR!!

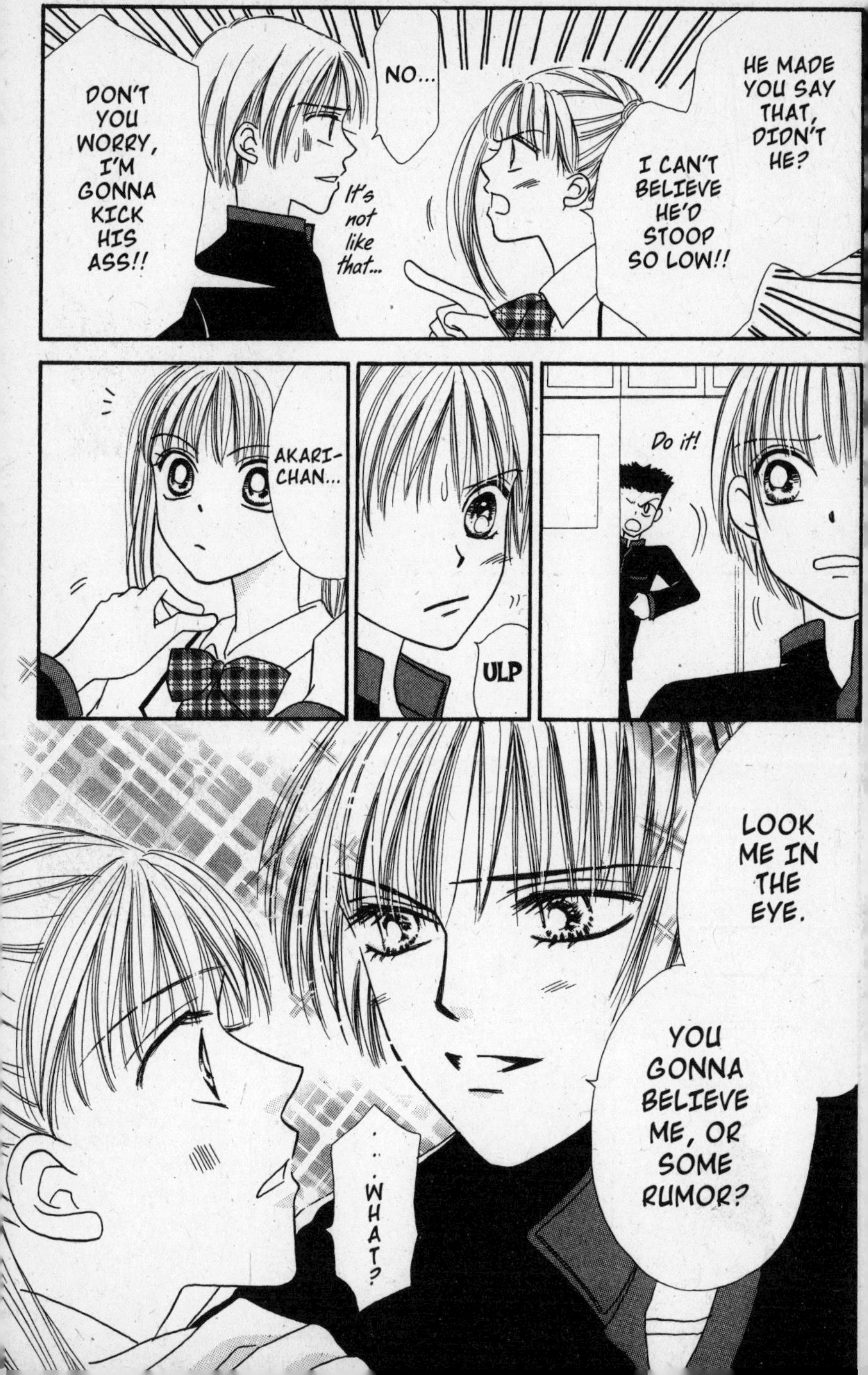
HE MADE YOU SAY THAT, DIDN'T HE?
I CAN'T BELIEVE HE'D STOOP SO LOW!!
NO...
It's not like that...
DON'T YOU WORRY, I'M GONNA KICK HIS ASS!!
Do it!
ULP
AKARI-CHAN...
LOOK ME IN THE EYE.
YOU GONNA BELIEVE ME, OR SOME RUMOR?
...WHAT?

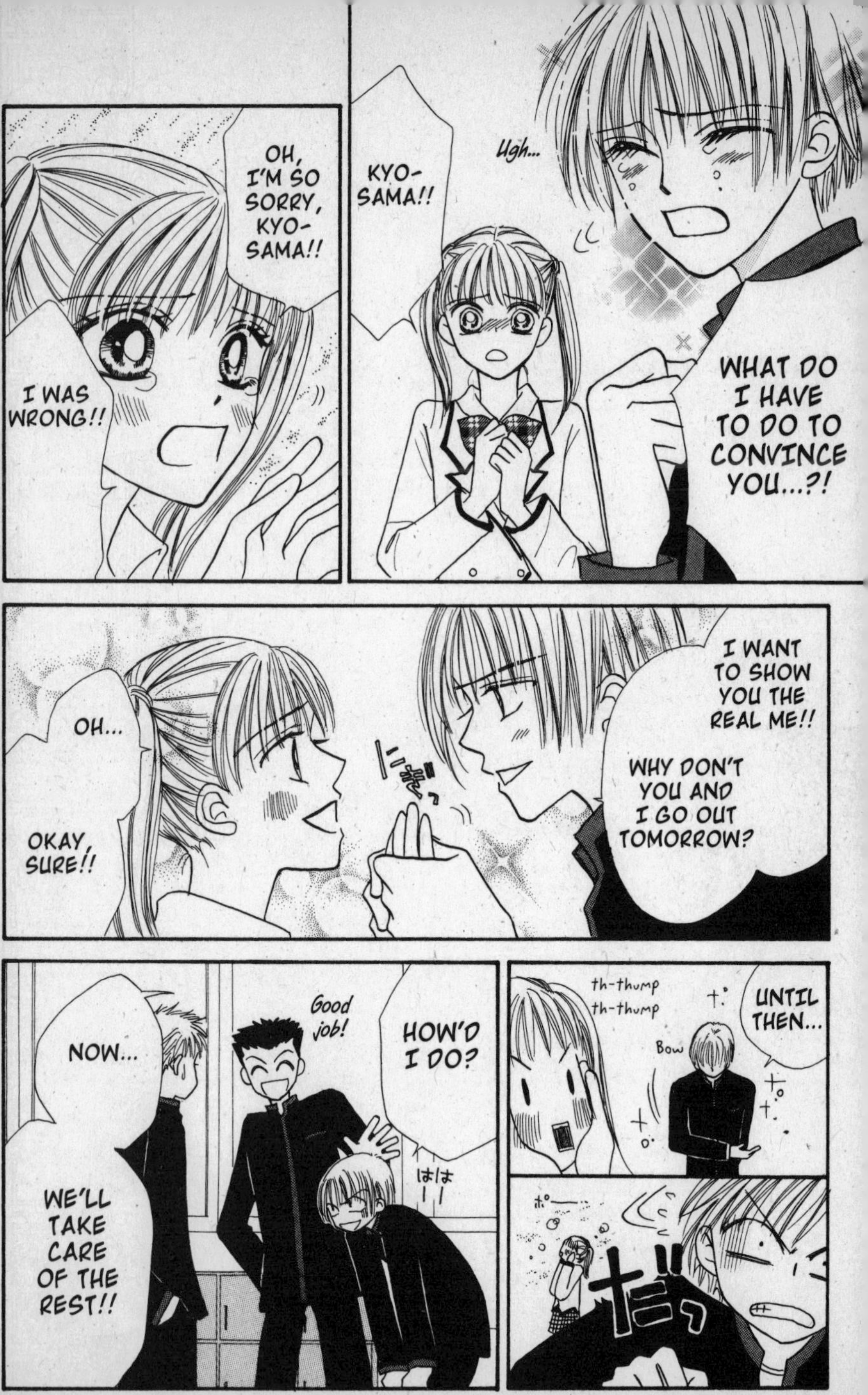
Ugh...
KYO-SAMA!!
WHAT DO I HAVE TO DO TO CONVINCE YOU...?!
OH, I'M SO SORRY, KYO-SAMA!!
I WAS WRONG!!
I WANT TO SHOW YOU THE REAL ME!!
WHY DON'T YOU AND I GO OUT TOMORROW?
OH...
OKAY, SURE!!
UNTIL THEN...
th-thump
th-thump
Bow
HOW'D I DO?
Good job!
NOW...
WE'LL TAKE CARE OF THE REST!!

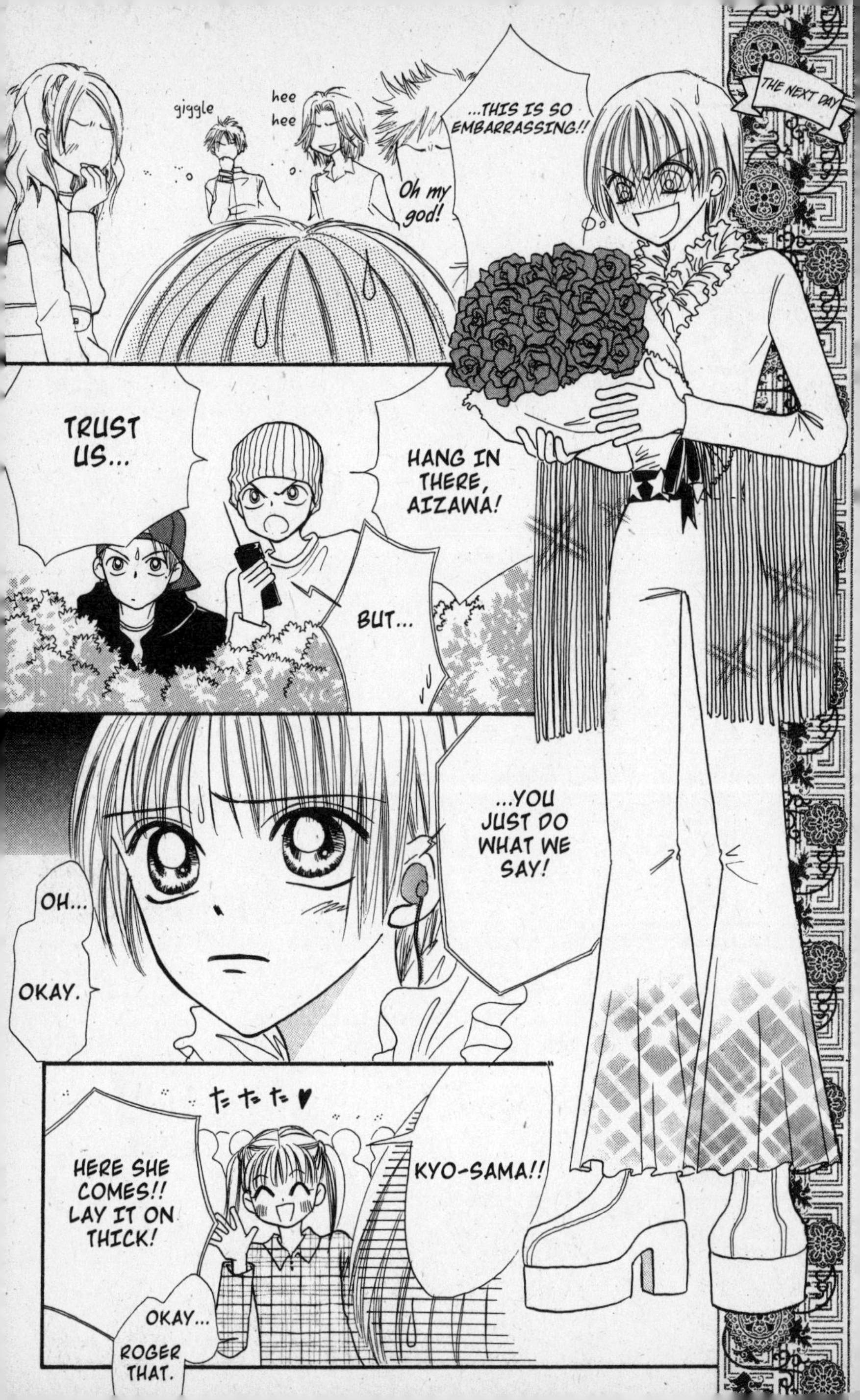
THE NEXT DAY
...THIS IS SO EMBARRASSING!!
Oh my god!
hee hee
giggle
HANG IN THERE, AIZAWA!
TRUST US...
BUT...
...YOU JUST DO WHAT WE SAY!
OH...
OKAY.
KYO-SAMA!!
たたた♥
HERE SHE COMES!! LAY IT ON THICK!
OKAY...
ROGER THAT.

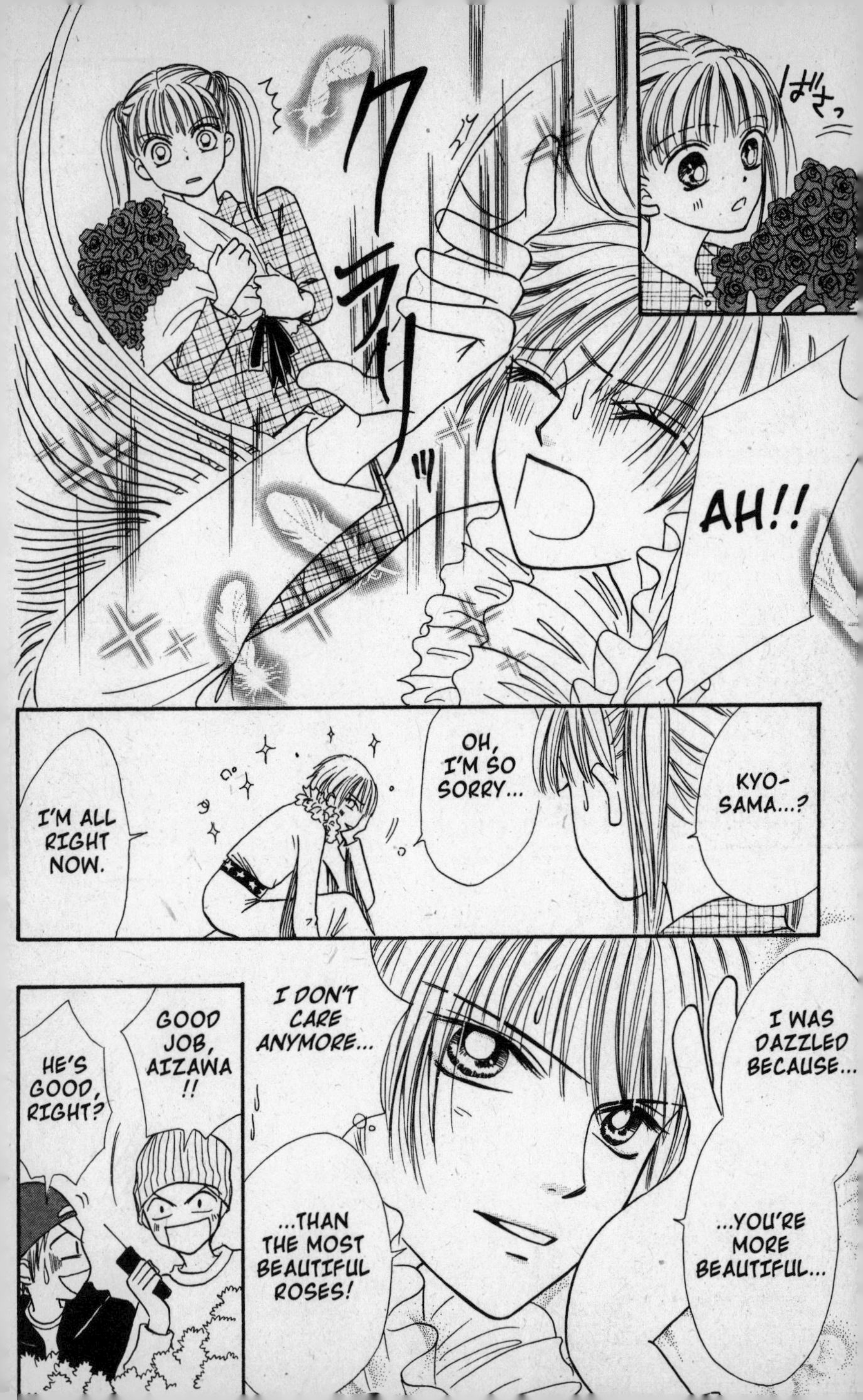
ばさっ
AH!!
クラリ
KYO-SAMA...?
OH, I'M SO SORRY...
I'M ALL RIGHT NOW.
I WAS DAZZLED BECAUSE...
...YOU'RE MORE BEAUTIFUL...
...THAN THE MOST BEAUTIFUL ROSES!
I DON'T CARE ANYMORE...
GOOD JOB, AIZAWA!!
HE'S GOOD, RIGHT?

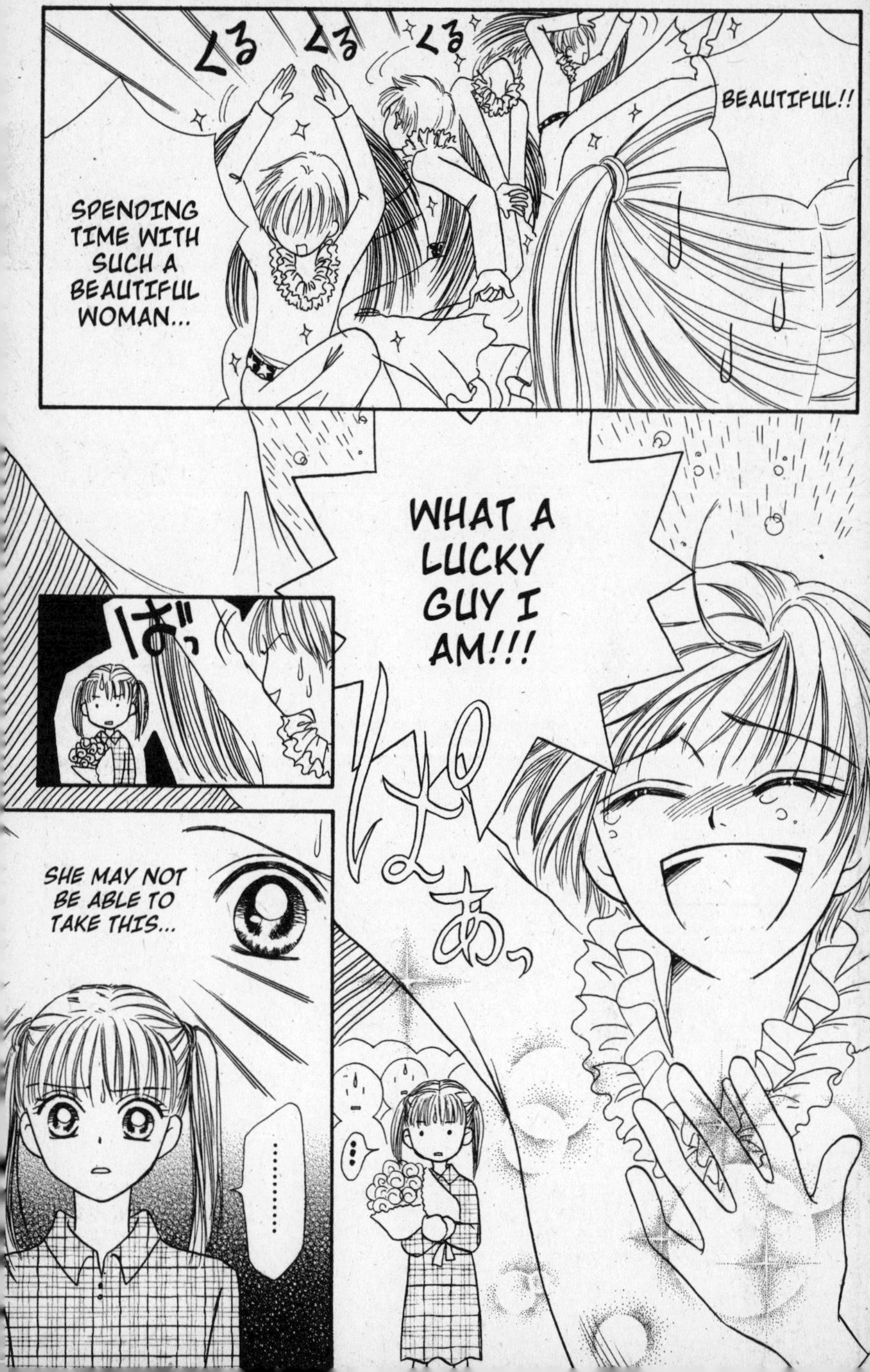
くる くる くる
BEAUTIFUL!!
SPENDING TIME WITH SUCH A BEAUTIFUL WOMAN...
WHAT A LUCKY GUY I AM!!!
はあっ
...
ばっ
SHE MAY NOT BE ABLE TO TAKE THIS...
......

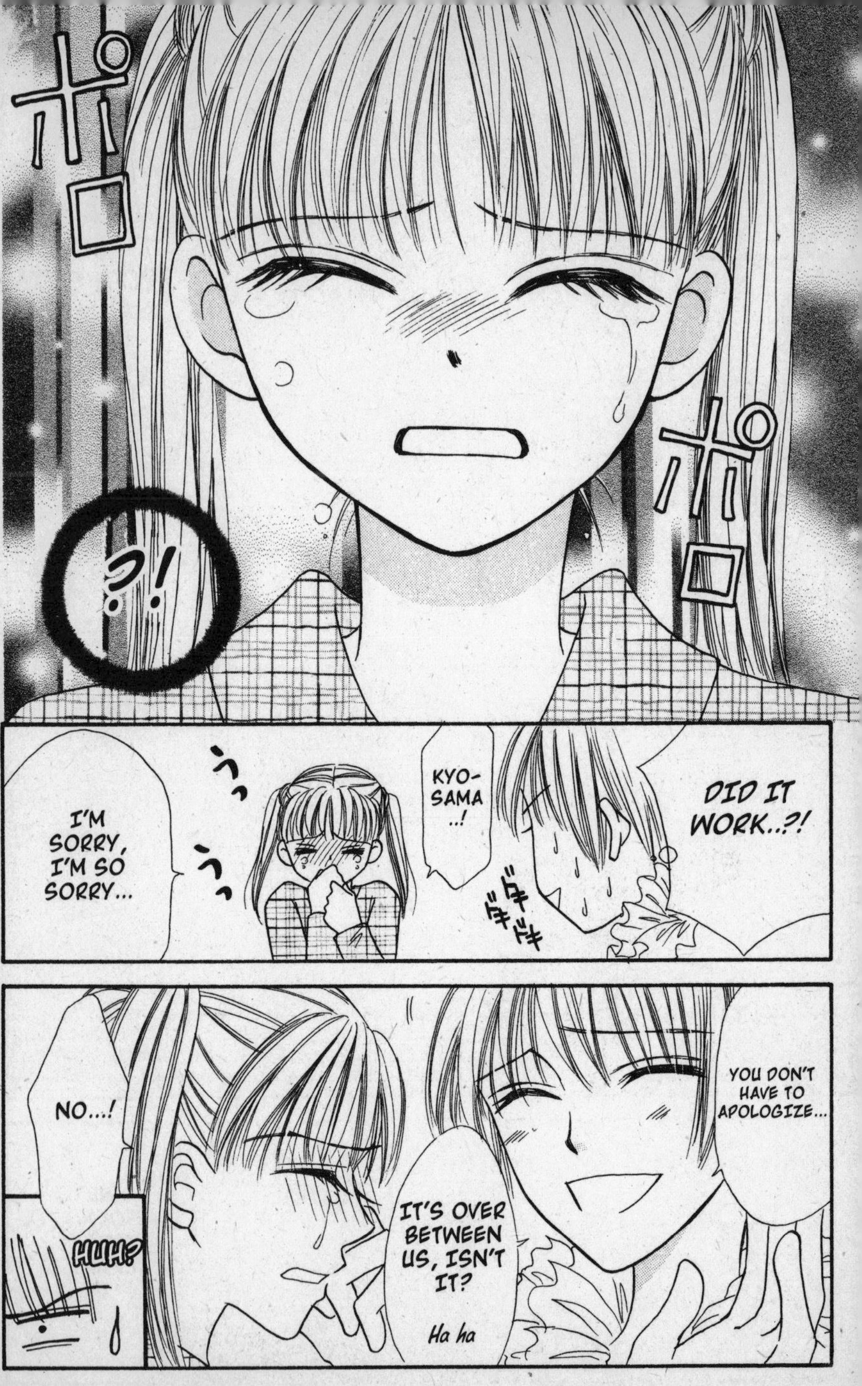
ポロ
?!
ポロ
DID IT WORK..?!
ドキドキ
KYO-SAMA..!
うっ
うっ
I'M SORRY, I'M SO SORRY...
YOU DON'T HAVE TO APOLOGIZE...
IT'S OVER BETWEEN US, ISN'T IT?
Ha ha
NO...!
HUH?

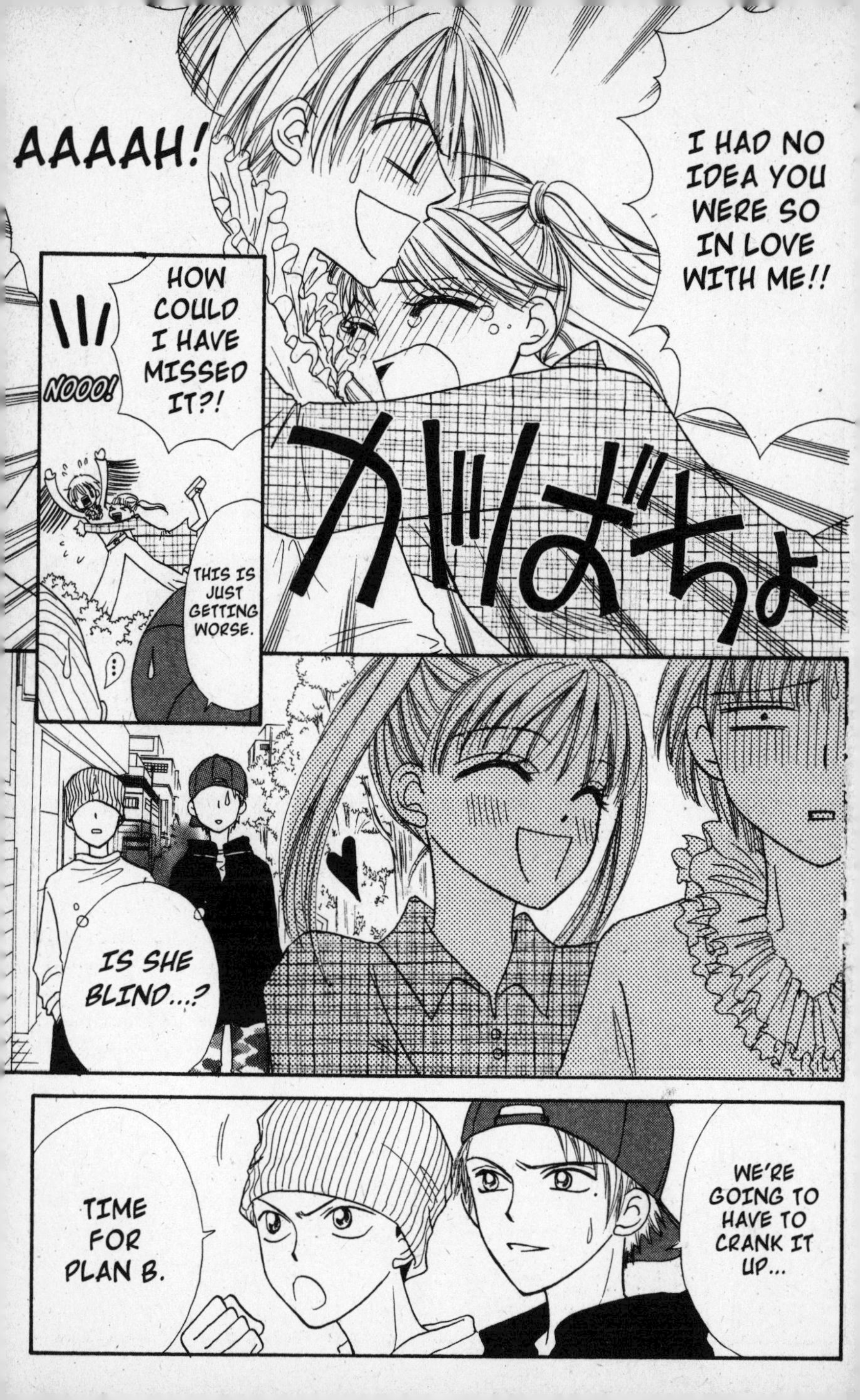
I HAD NO IDEA YOU WERE SO IN LOVE WITH ME!!
AAAAH!
HOW COULD I HAVE MISSED IT?!
NOOO!
THIS IS JUST GETTING WORSE.
...
IS SHE BLIND...?
WE'RE GOING TO HAVE TO CRANK IT UP...
TIME FOR PLAN B.

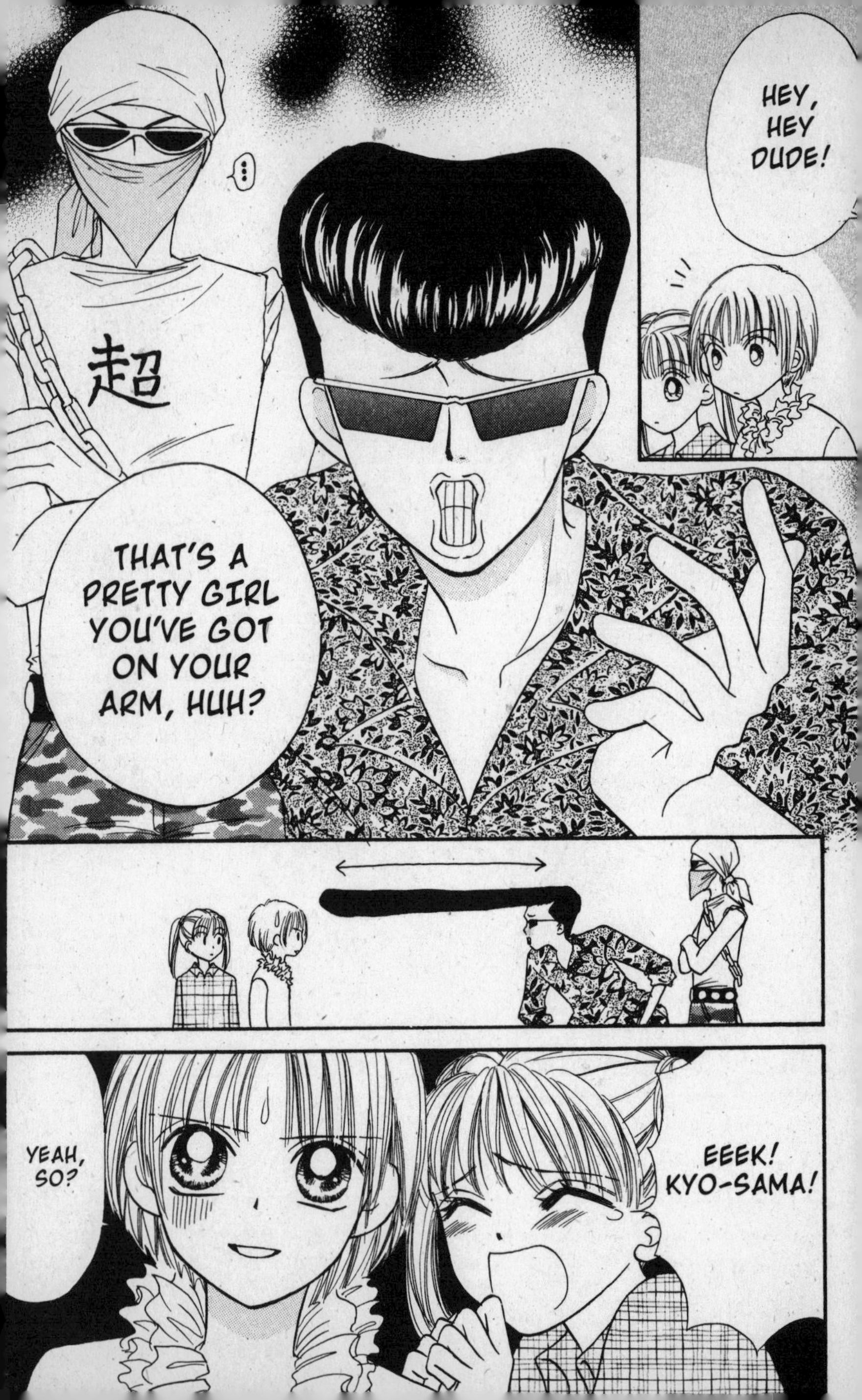
HEY, HEY DUDE!
...
THAT'S A PRETTY GIRL YOU'VE GOT ON YOUR ARM, HUH?
EEEK! KYO-SAMA!
YEAH, SO?

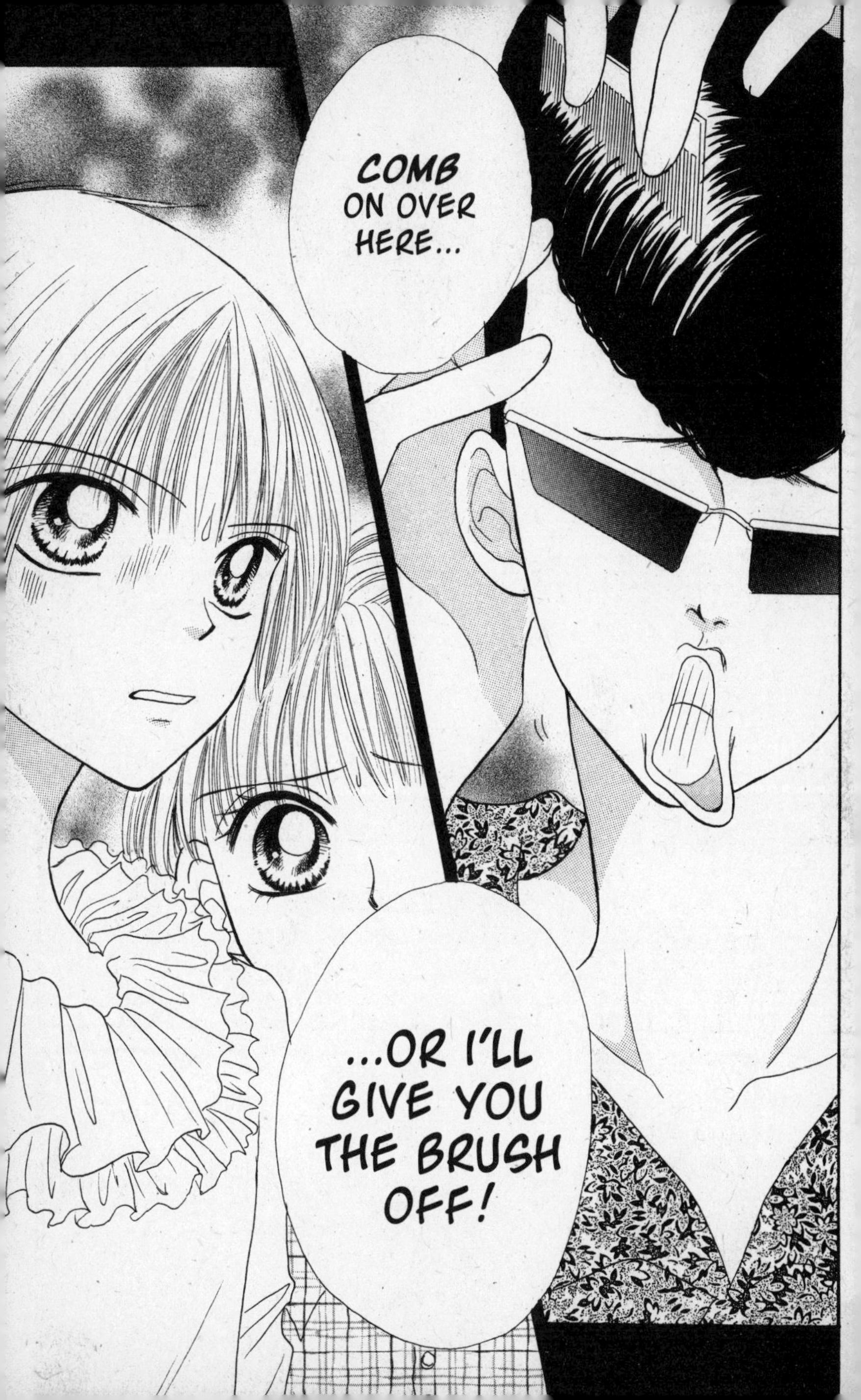
COMB ON OVER HERE...
...OR I'LL GIVE YOU THE BRUSH OFF!

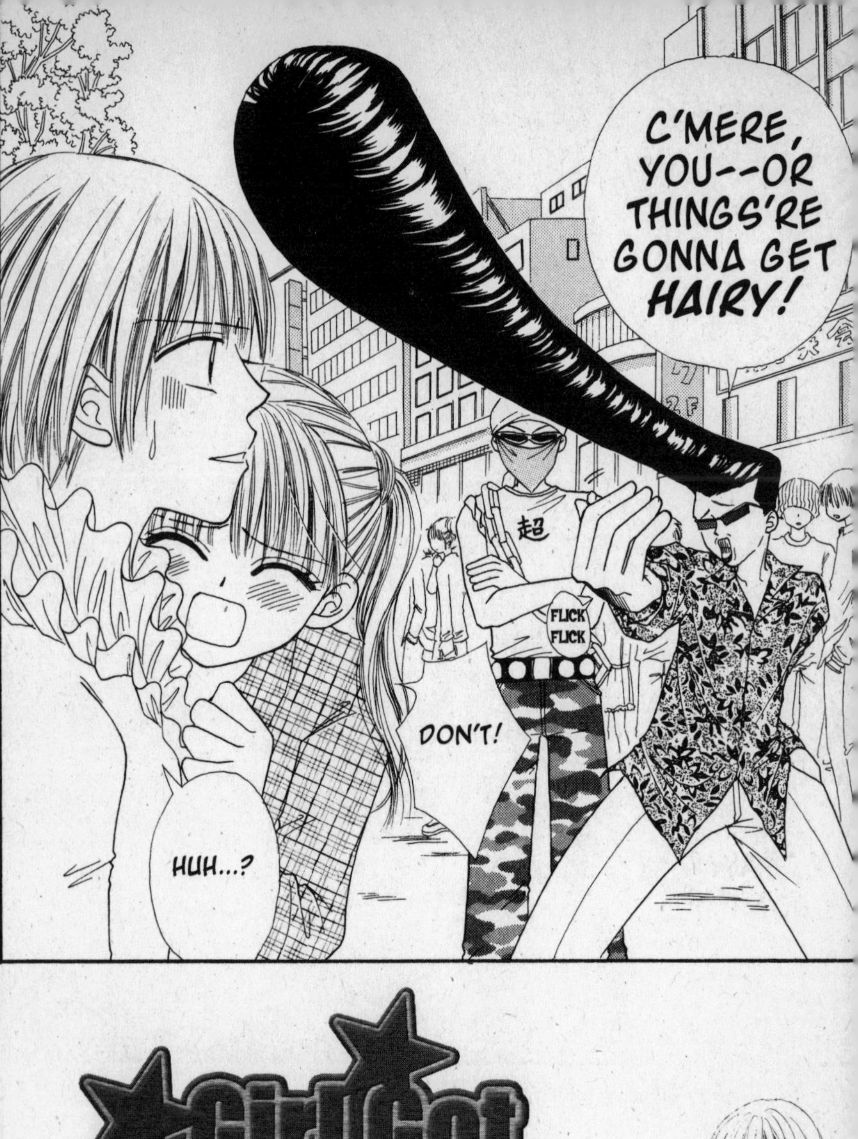
C'MERE, YOU--OR THINGS'RE GONNA GET HAIRY!
FLICK FLICK
超
DON'T!
HUH...?

# ★Girl Got Game★

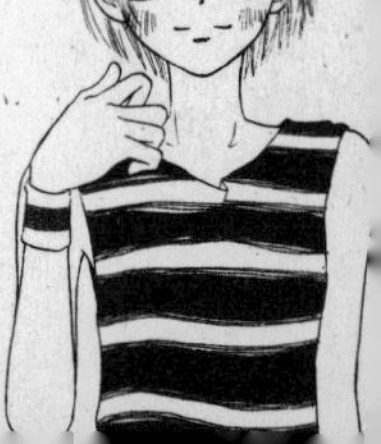

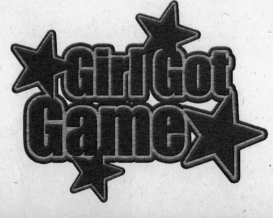

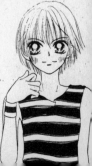

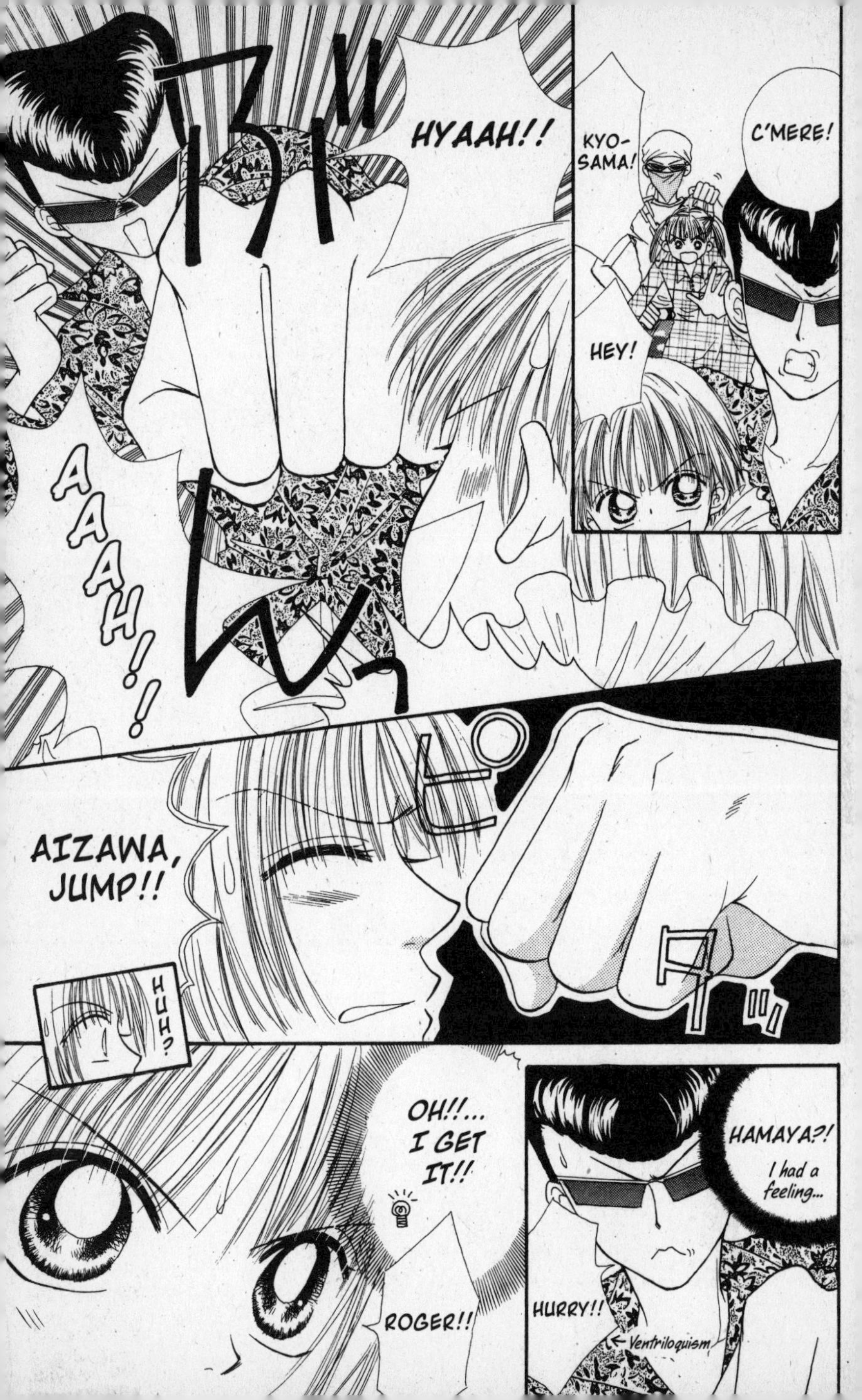
C'MERE!
KYO-SAMA!
HEY!
HYAAH!!
AAAAH!!
AIZAWA, JUMP!!
HUH?
HAMAYA?!
I had a feeling...
HURRY!!
← Ventriloquism
OH!!... I GET IT!!
ROGER!!

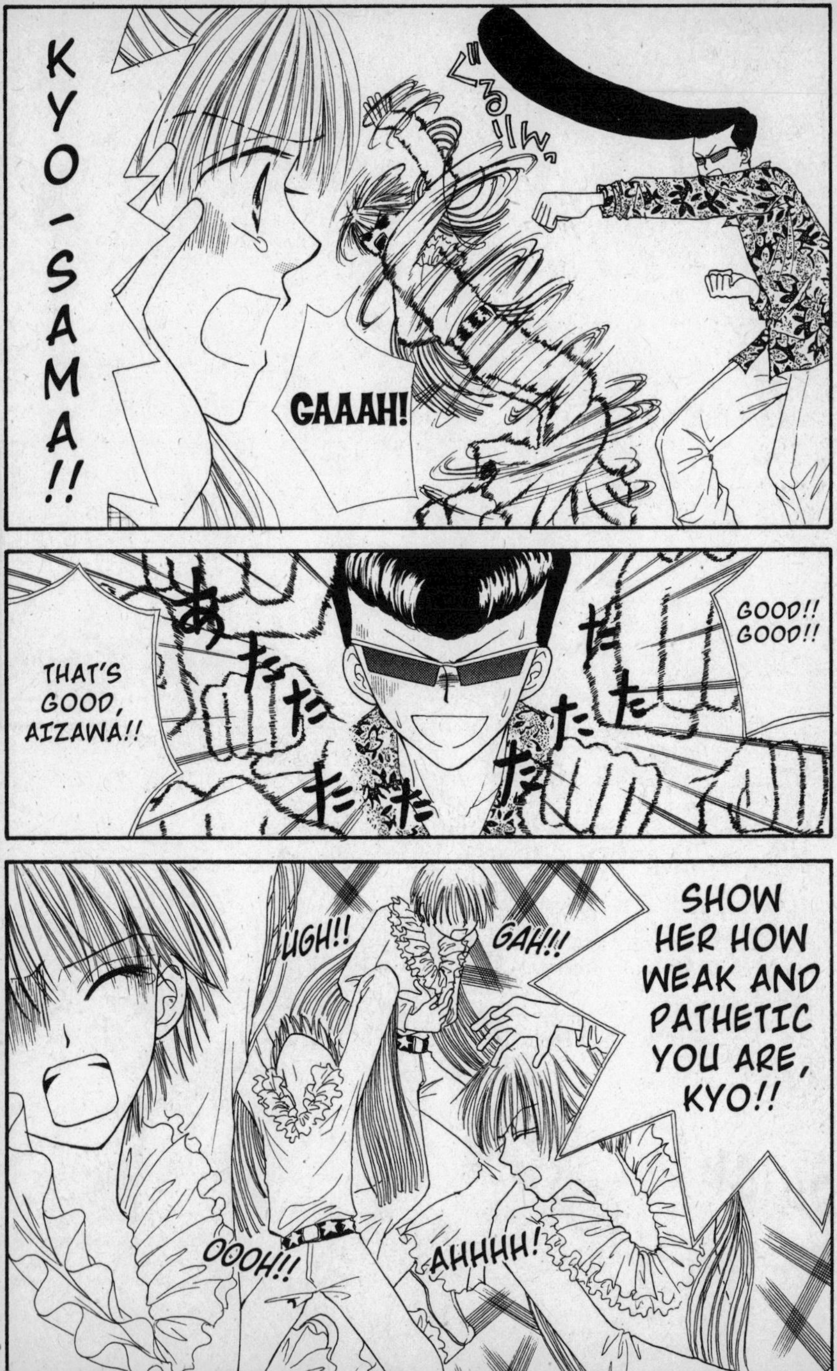
GAAAH!
KYO-SAMA!!
GOOD!! GOOD!!
THAT'S GOOD, AIZAWA!!
SHOW HER HOW WEAK AND PATHETIC YOU ARE, KYO!!
GAH!!
UGH!!
AHHHH!
OOOH!!

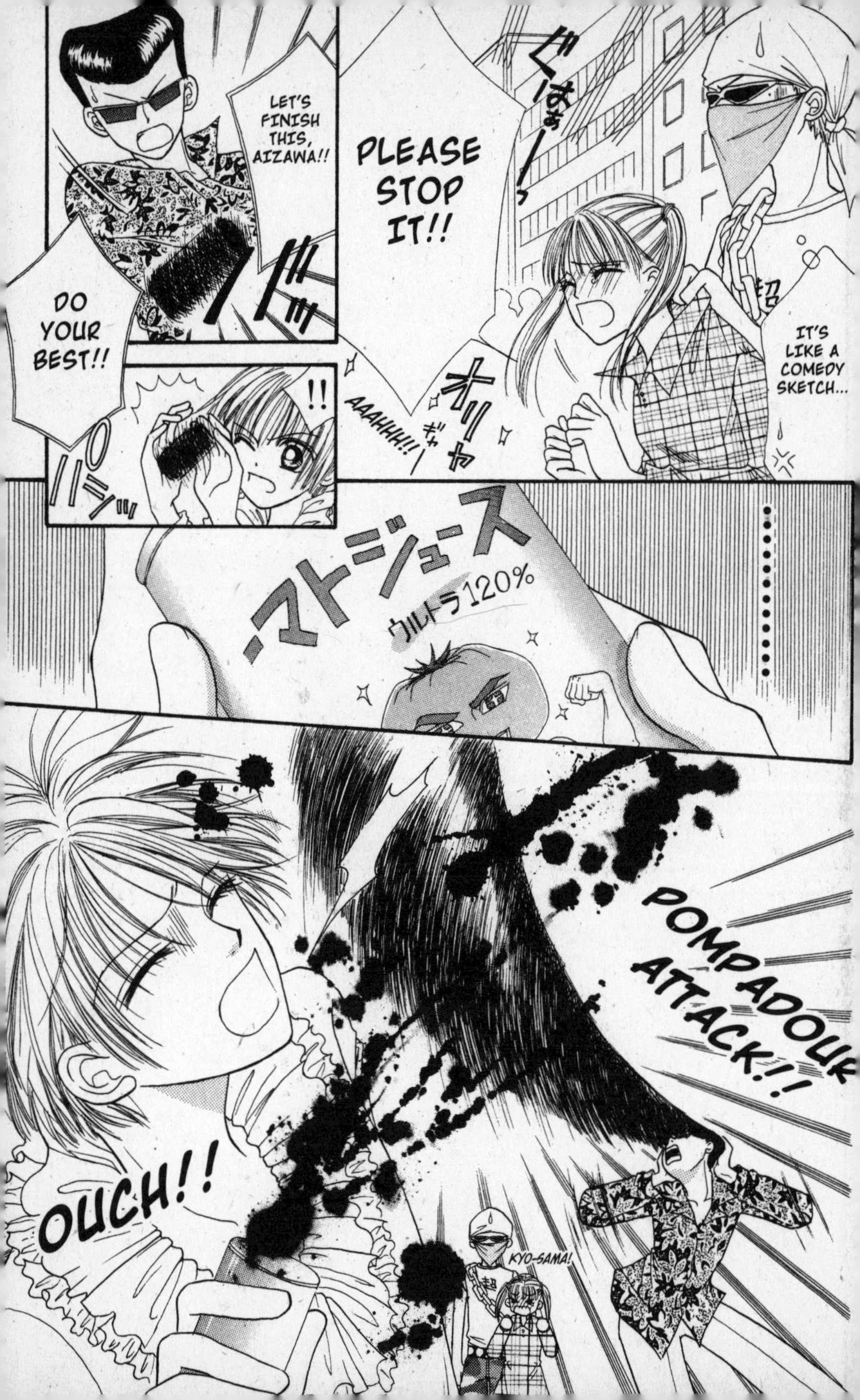
ぐはぁー!
PLEASE STOP IT!!
オリャ
ギャ
AAAHHH!!!
IT'S LIKE A COMEDY SKETCH...
LET'S FINISH THIS, AIZAWA!!
DO YOUR BEST!!
!!
........
マトジュース
ウルトラ120%
POMPADOUR ATTACK!!
KYO-SAMA!
OUCH!!

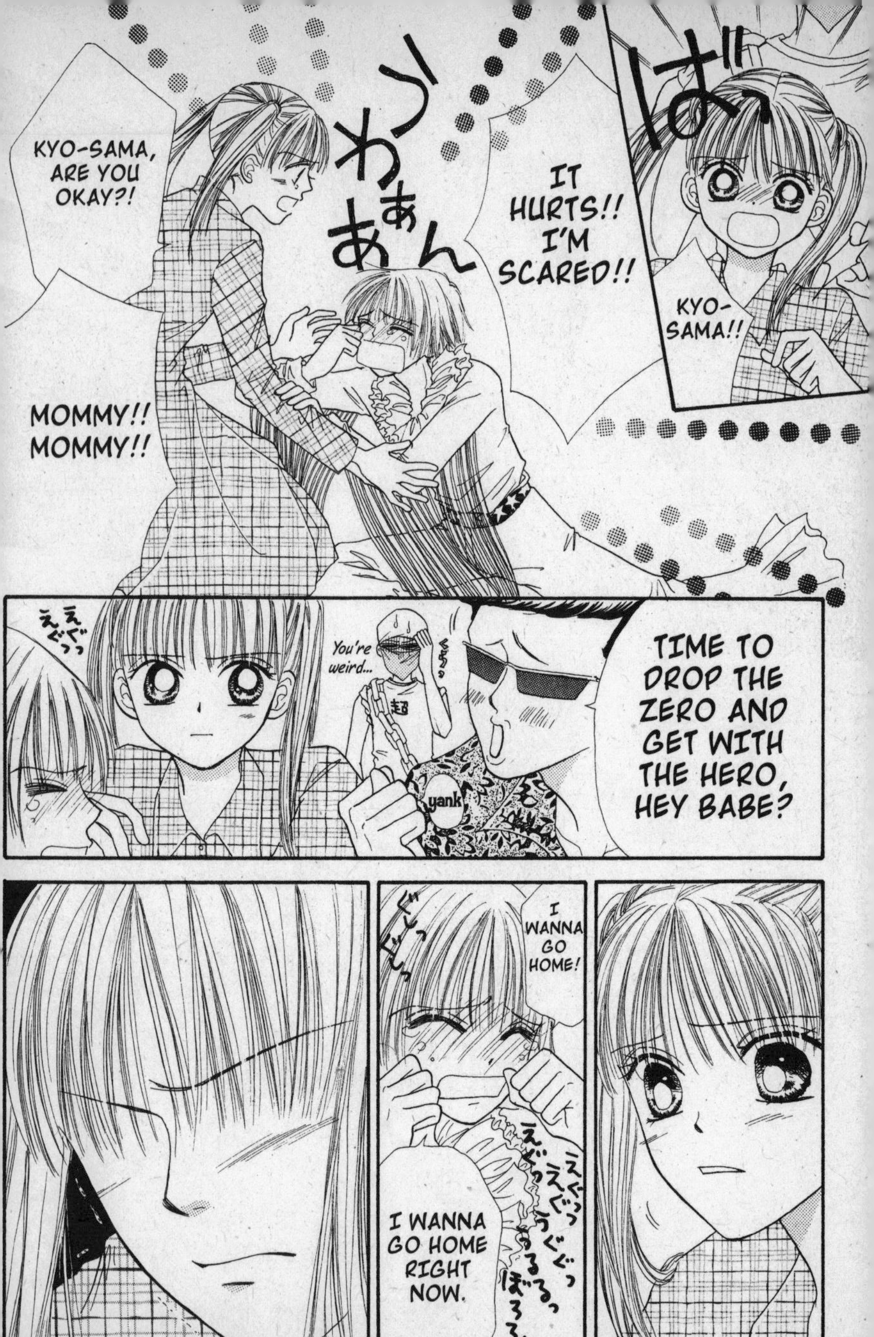
ばっ
KYO-SAMA!!
うわぁあん
IT HURTS!! I'M SCARED!!
KYO-SAMA, ARE YOU OKAY?!
MOMMY!! MOMMY!!
TIME TO DROP THE ZERO AND GET WITH THE HERO, HEY BABE?
You're weird...
超
yank
えぐっ えぐっ
I WANNA GO HOME!
I WANNA GO HOME RIGHT NOW.

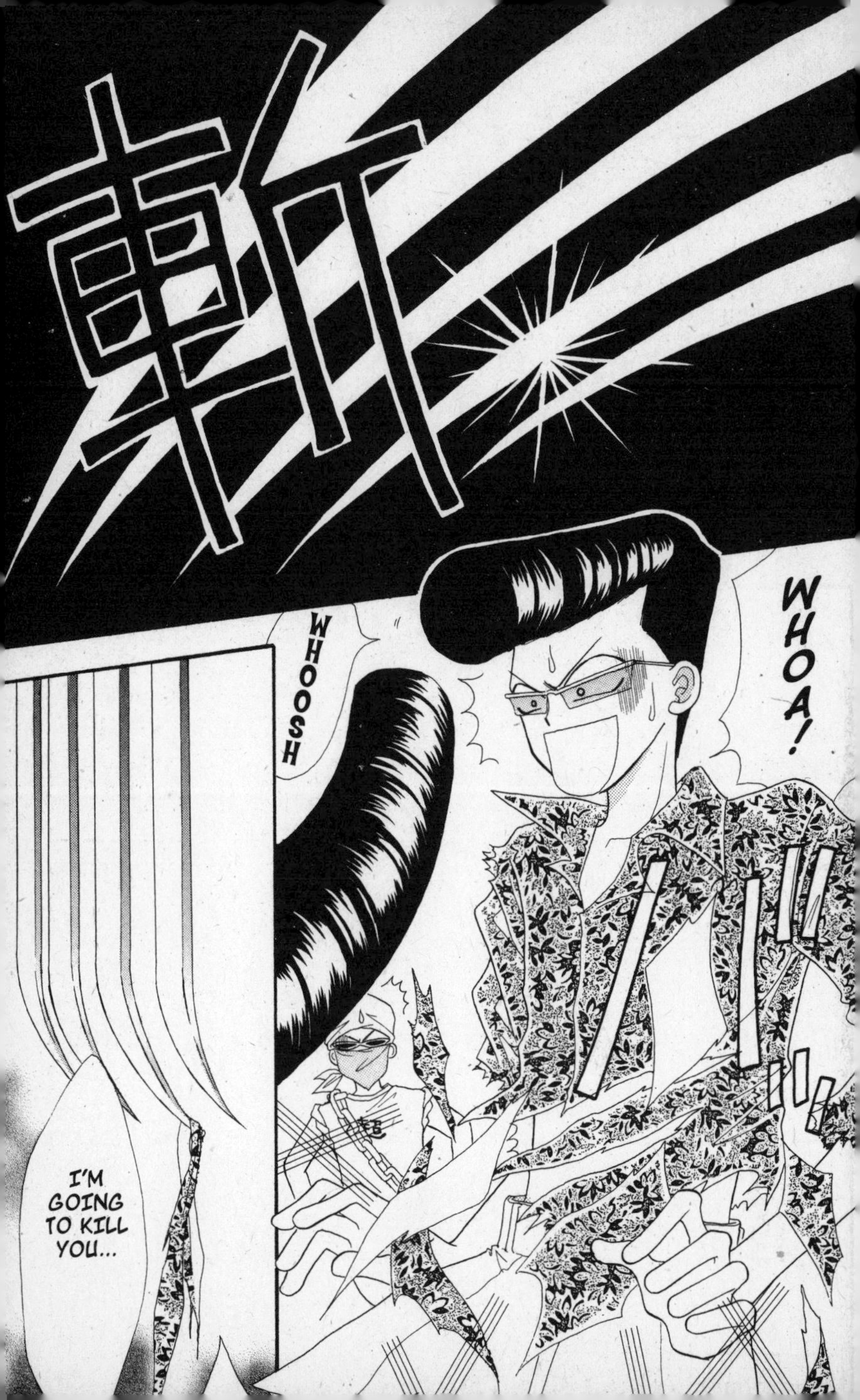
斬
WHOA!
WHOOSH
I'M GOING TO KILL YOU...

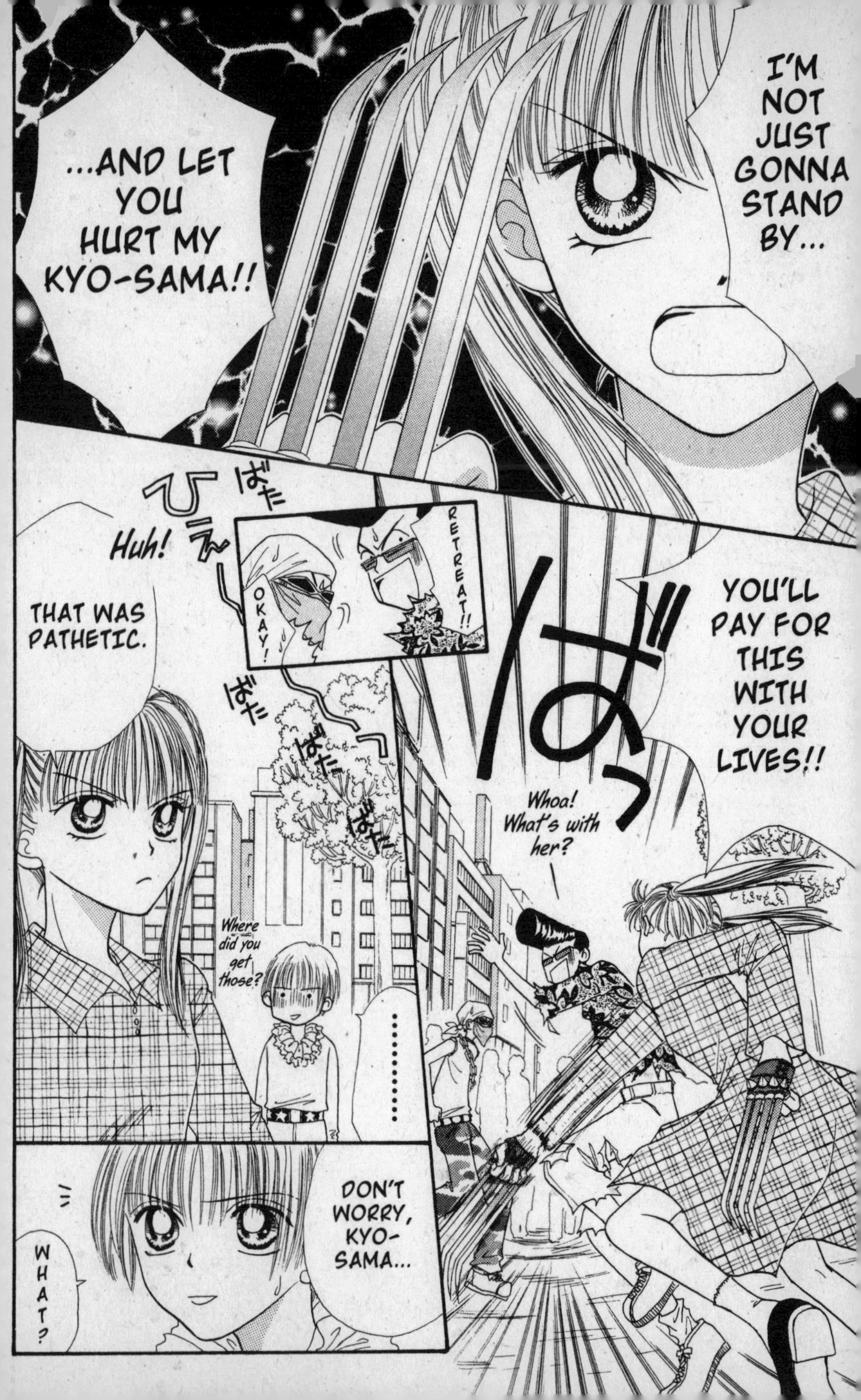

I'M NOT JUST GONNA STAND BY...
...AND LET YOU HURT MY KYO-SAMA!!
YOU'LL PAY FOR THIS WITH YOUR LIVES!!
ばっ
Whoa! What's with her?
ばた
ひぇ～
RETREAT!!
OKAY!
Huh!
THAT WAS PATHETIC.
ばた
ばた
ばた
Where did you get those?
......
DON'T WORRY, KYO-SAMA...
WHAT?

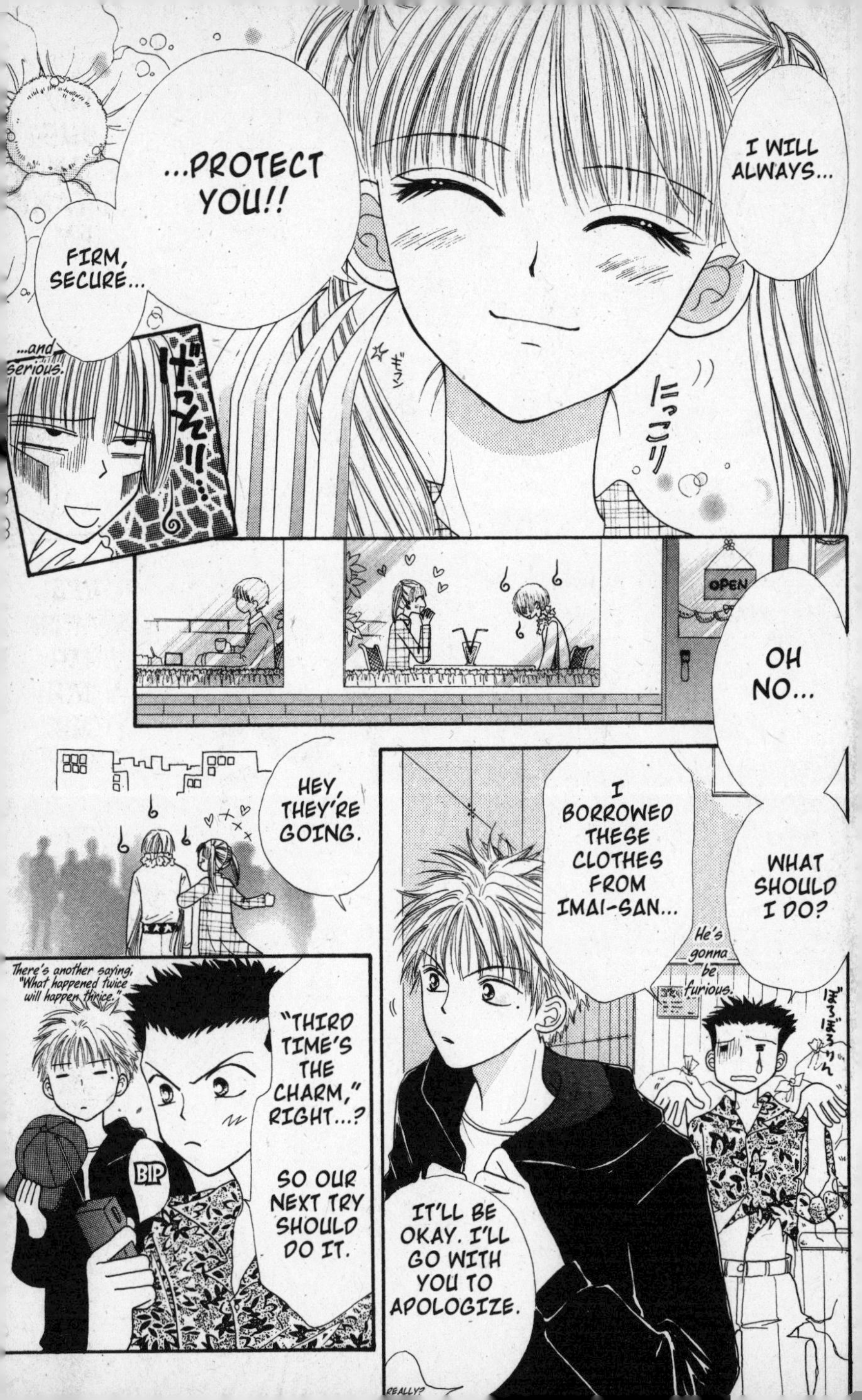
I WILL ALWAYS...
...PROTECT YOU!!
にっこり
FIRM, SECURE...
...and serious.
げっそり…
OH NO...
WHAT SHOULD I DO?
I BORROWED THESE CLOTHES FROM IMAI-SAN...
He's gonna be furious.
ぼろぼろりん
IT'LL BE OKAY. I'LL GO WITH YOU TO APOLOGIZE.
REALLY?
HEY, THEY'RE GOING.
There's another saying, "What happened twice will happen thrice."
"THIRD TIME'S THE CHARM," RIGHT...?
SO OUR NEXT TRY SHOULD DO IT.
BIP

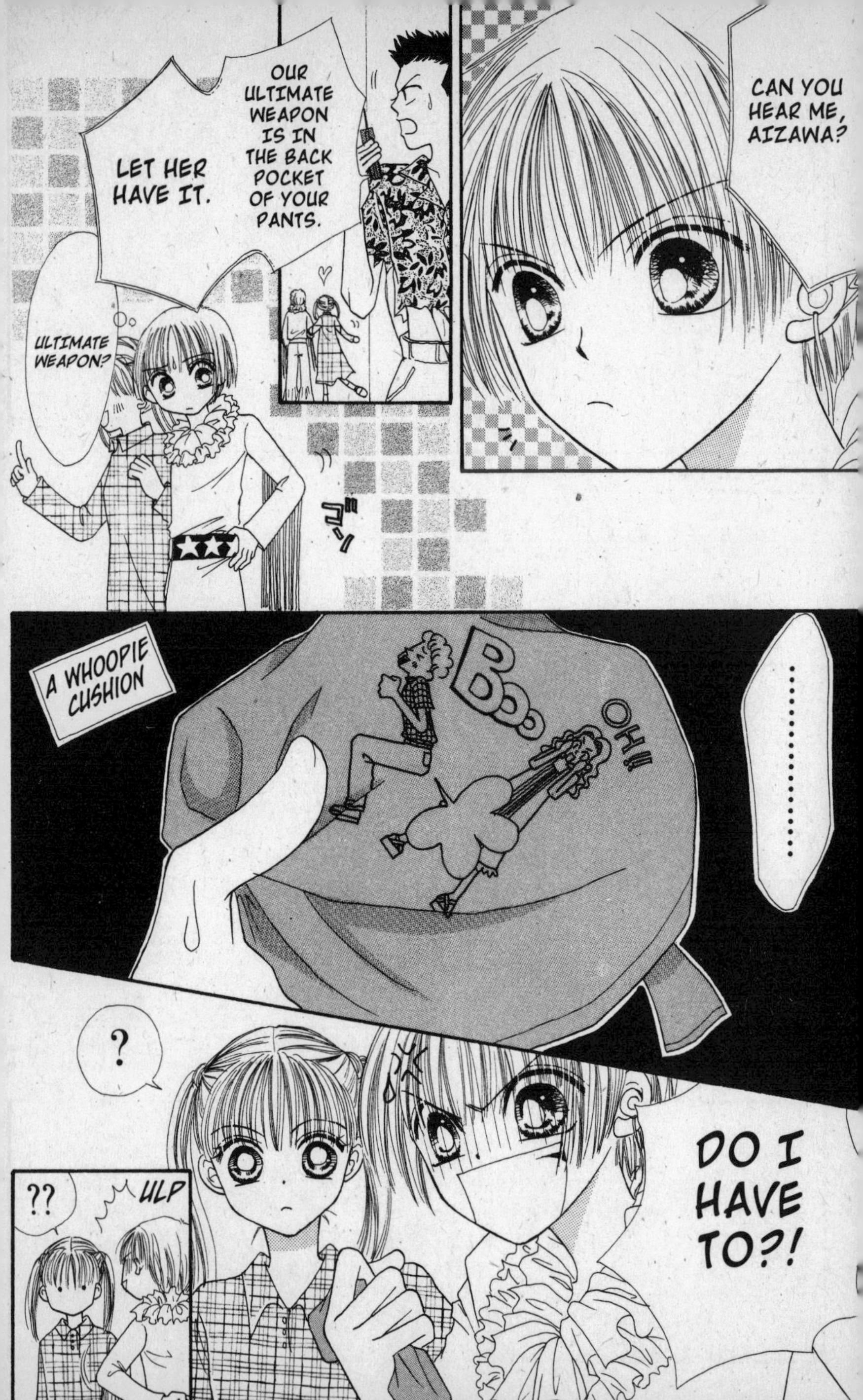
CAN YOU HEAR ME, AIZAWA?
OUR ULTIMATE WEAPON IS IN THE BACK POCKET OF YOUR PANTS.
LET HER HAVE IT.
ULTIMATE WEAPON?
......
BOOO
OH!!
A WHOOPIE CUSHION
DO I HAVE TO?!
?
ULP
??

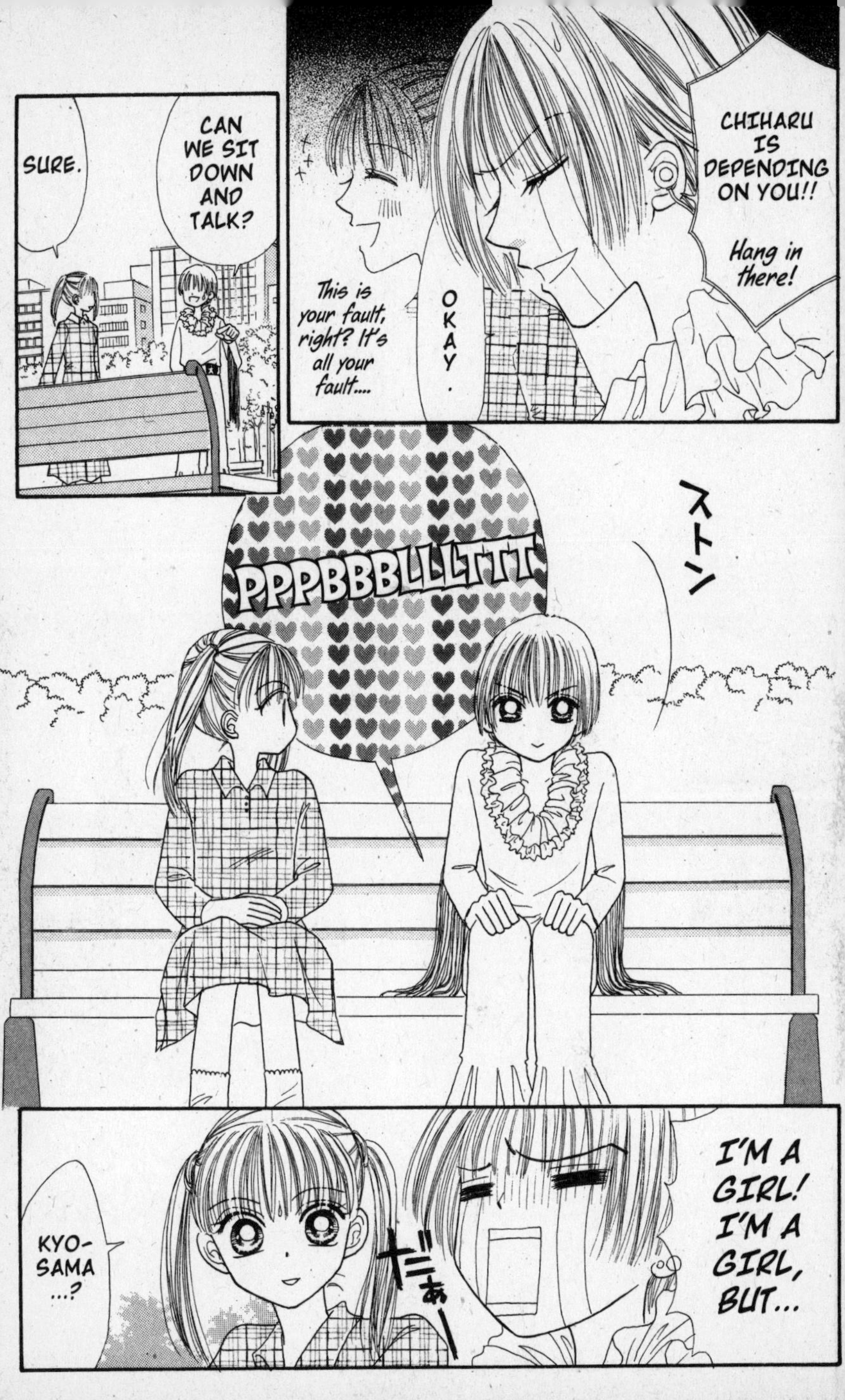

CHIHARU IS DEPENDING ON YOU!!
Hang in there!
OKAY.
This is your fault, right? It's all your fault....
CAN WE SIT DOWN AND TALK?
SURE.
ストン
PPPBBBLLLTTT
I'M A GIRL! I'M A GIRL, BUT...
だあー
KYO-SAMA ...?

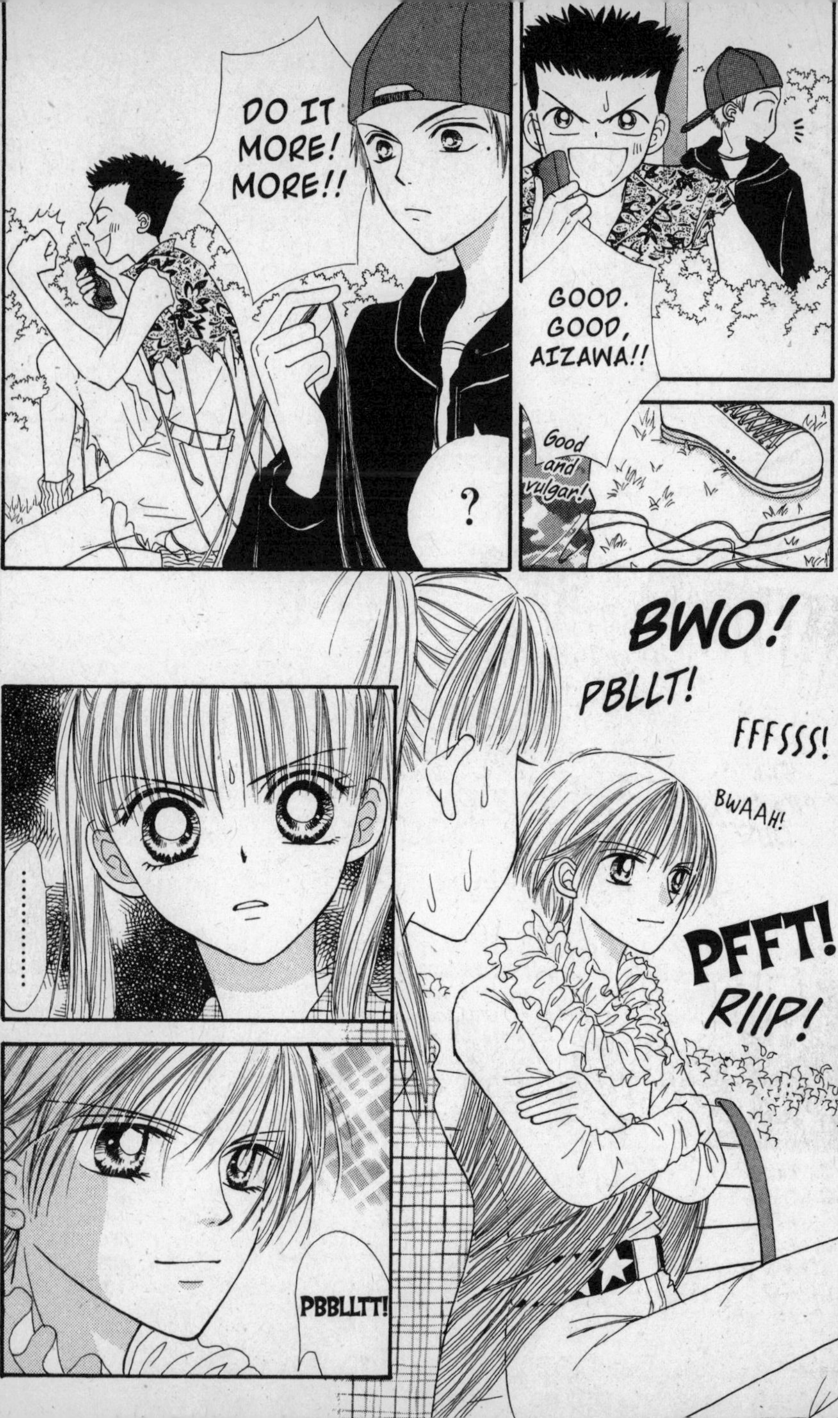
GOOD. GOOD, AIZAWA!!
Good and vulgar!
DO IT MORE! MORE!!
?
BWO!
PBLLT!
FFFSSS!
BWAAH!
PFFT!
RIIP!
……
PBBLLTT!

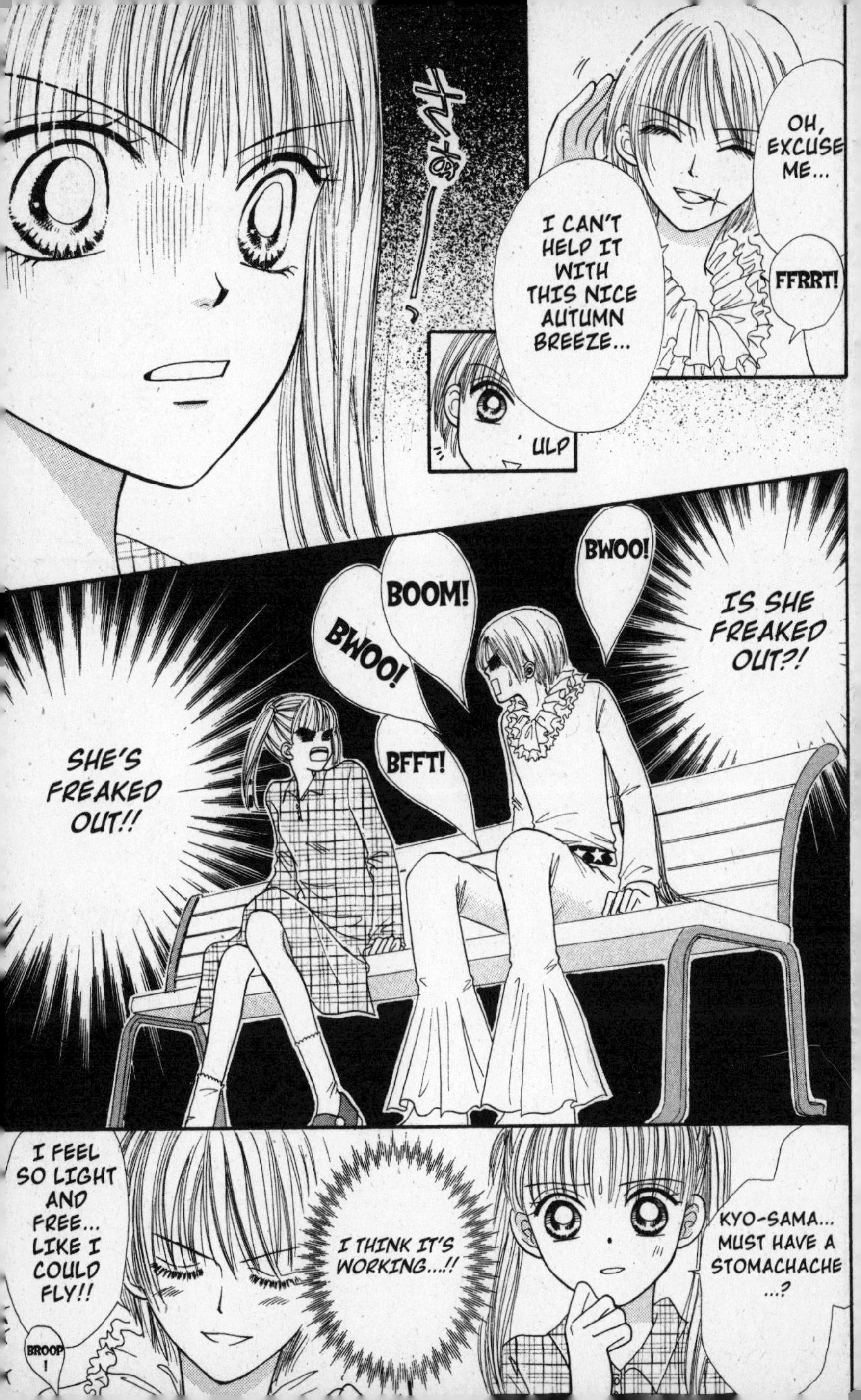
OH, EXCUSE ME...
FFRRT!
I CAN'T HELP IT WITH THIS NICE AUTUMN BREEZE...
ULP
IS SHE FREAKED OUT?!
BWOO!
BOOM!
BWOO!
BFFT!
SHE'S FREAKED OUT!!
KYO-SAMA... MUST HAVE A STOMACHACHE ...?
I THINK IT'S WORKING...!!
I FEEL SO LIGHT AND FREE... LIKE I COULD FLY!!
BROOP!

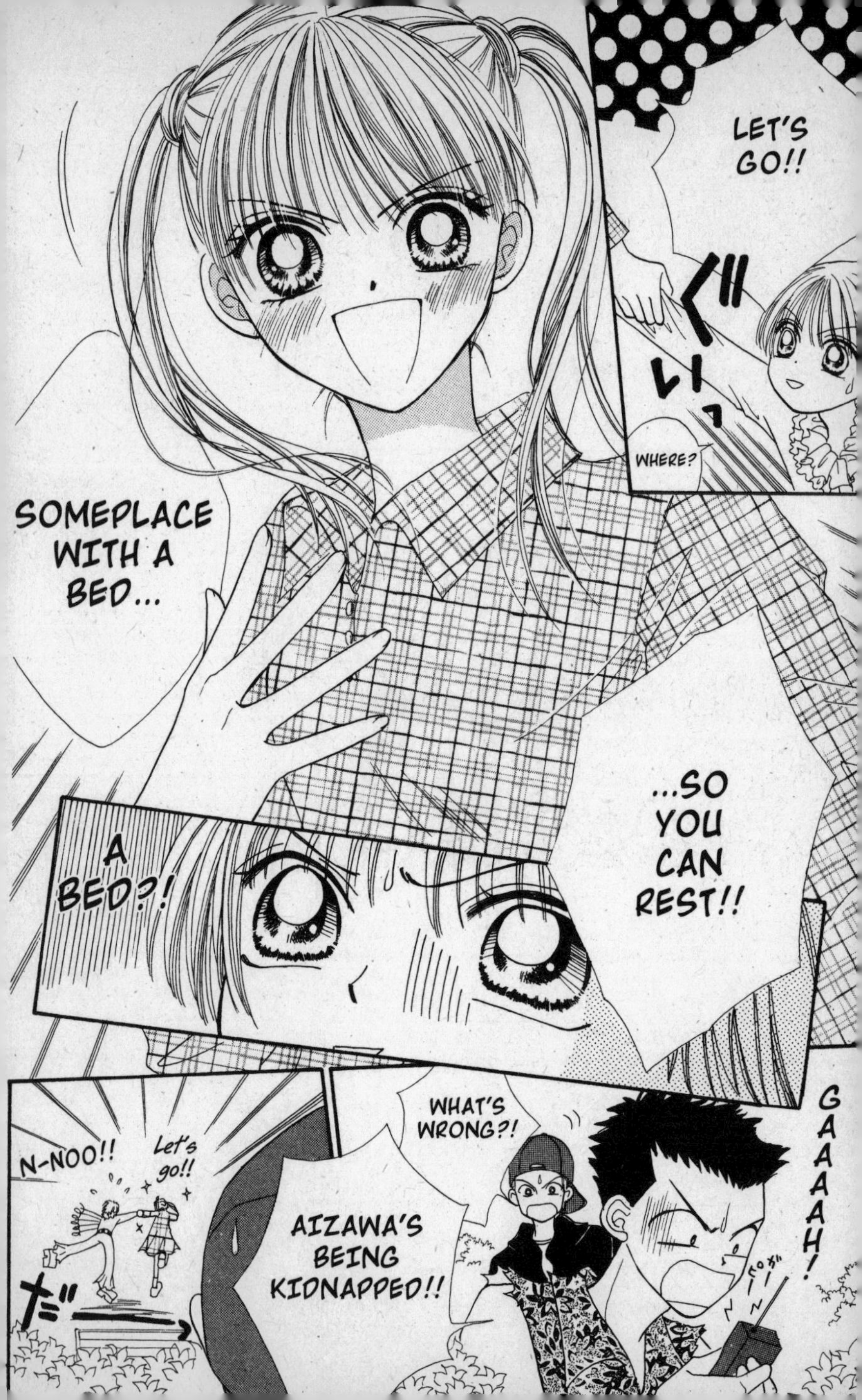
LET'S GO!!
WHERE?
SOMEPLACE WITH A BED...
...SO YOU CAN REST!!
A BED?!
GAAAAH!
WHAT'S WRONG?!
AIZAWA'S BEING KIDNAPPED!!
Let's go!!
N-NOO!!

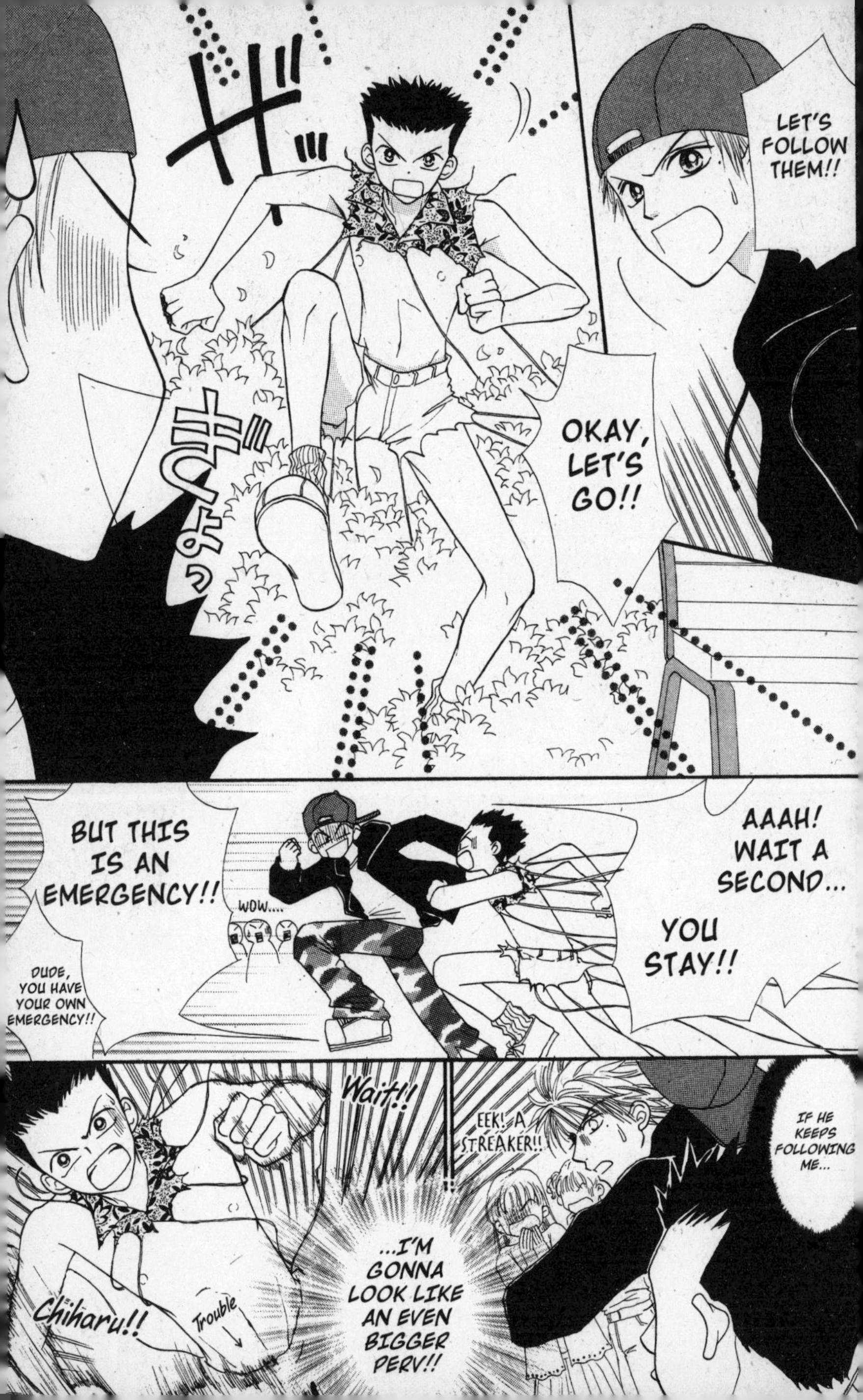
LET'S FOLLOW THEM!!
ザッ
OKAY, LET'S GO!!
ぎょっ
AAAH! WAIT A SECOND...
YOU STAY!!
BUT THIS IS AN EMERGENCY!!
WOW....
DUDE, YOU HAVE YOUR OWN EMERGENCY!!
IF HE KEEPS FOLLOWING ME...
EEK! A STREAKER!!
...I'M GONNA LOOK LIKE AN EVEN BIGGER PERV!!
Wait!!
Chiharu!!
Trouble

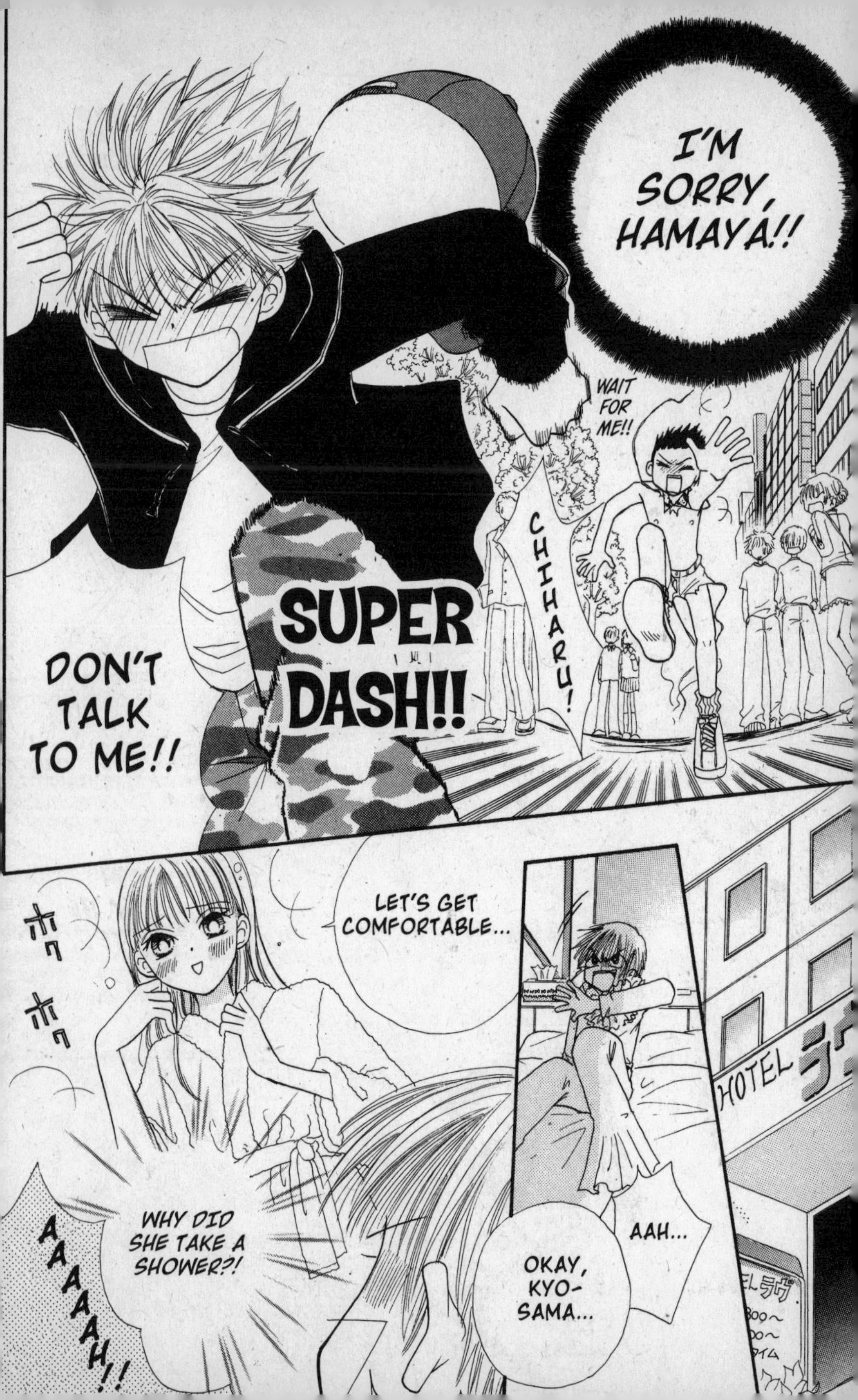
I'M SORRY, HAMAYA!!
WAIT FOR ME!!
CHIHARU!
SUPER DASH!!
DON'T TALK TO ME!!
HOTEL
AAH...
OKAY, KYO-SAMA...
LET'S GET COMFORTABLE...
WHY DID SHE TAKE A SHOWER?!
AAAAAAH!!

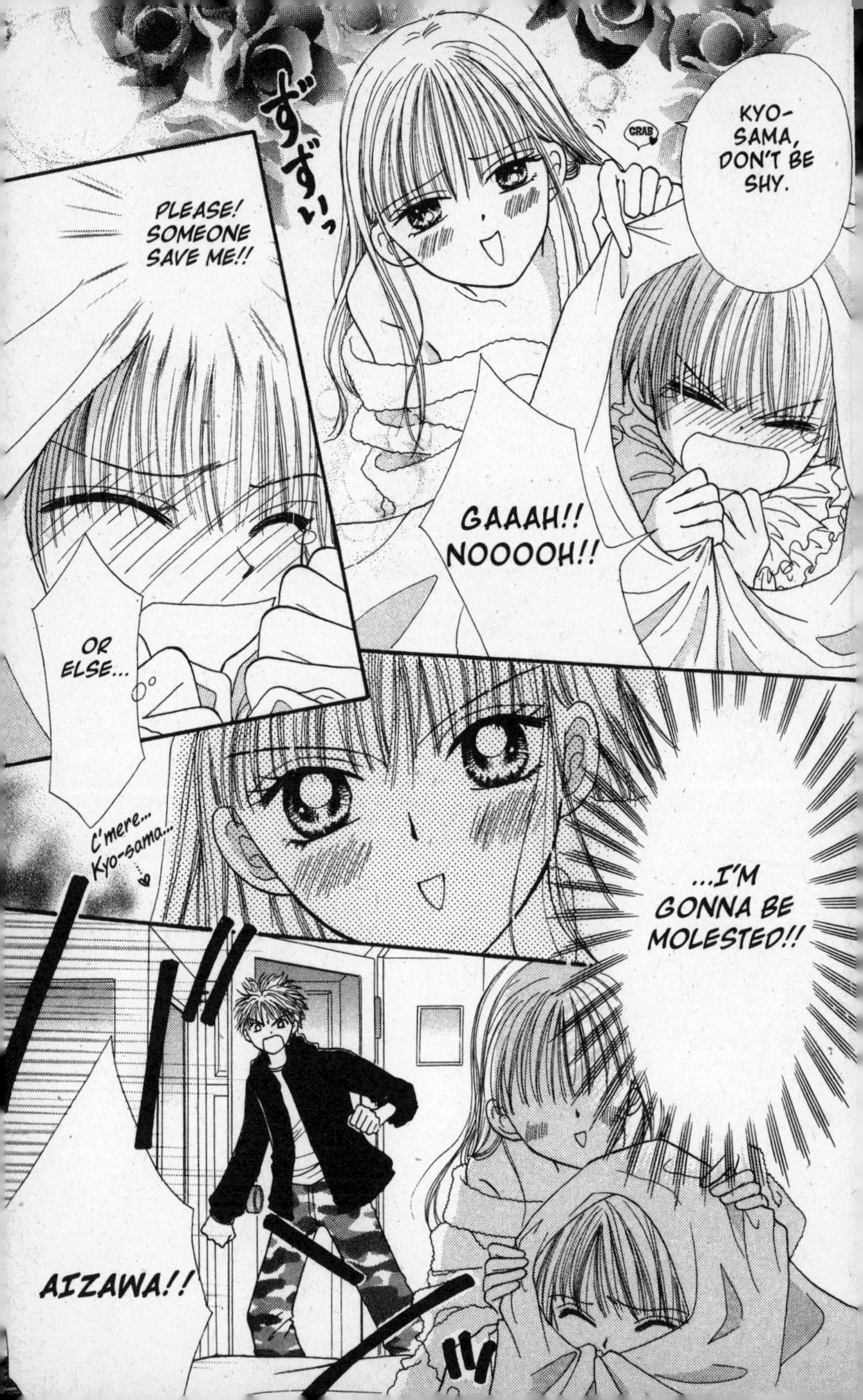

KYO-SAMA, DON'T BE SHY.
GRAB
ずずいっ
GAAAH!! NOOOOH!!
PLEASE! SOMEONE SAVE ME!!
OR ELSE...
...I'M GONNA BE MOLESTED!!
C'mere... Kyo-sama...
AIZAWA!!

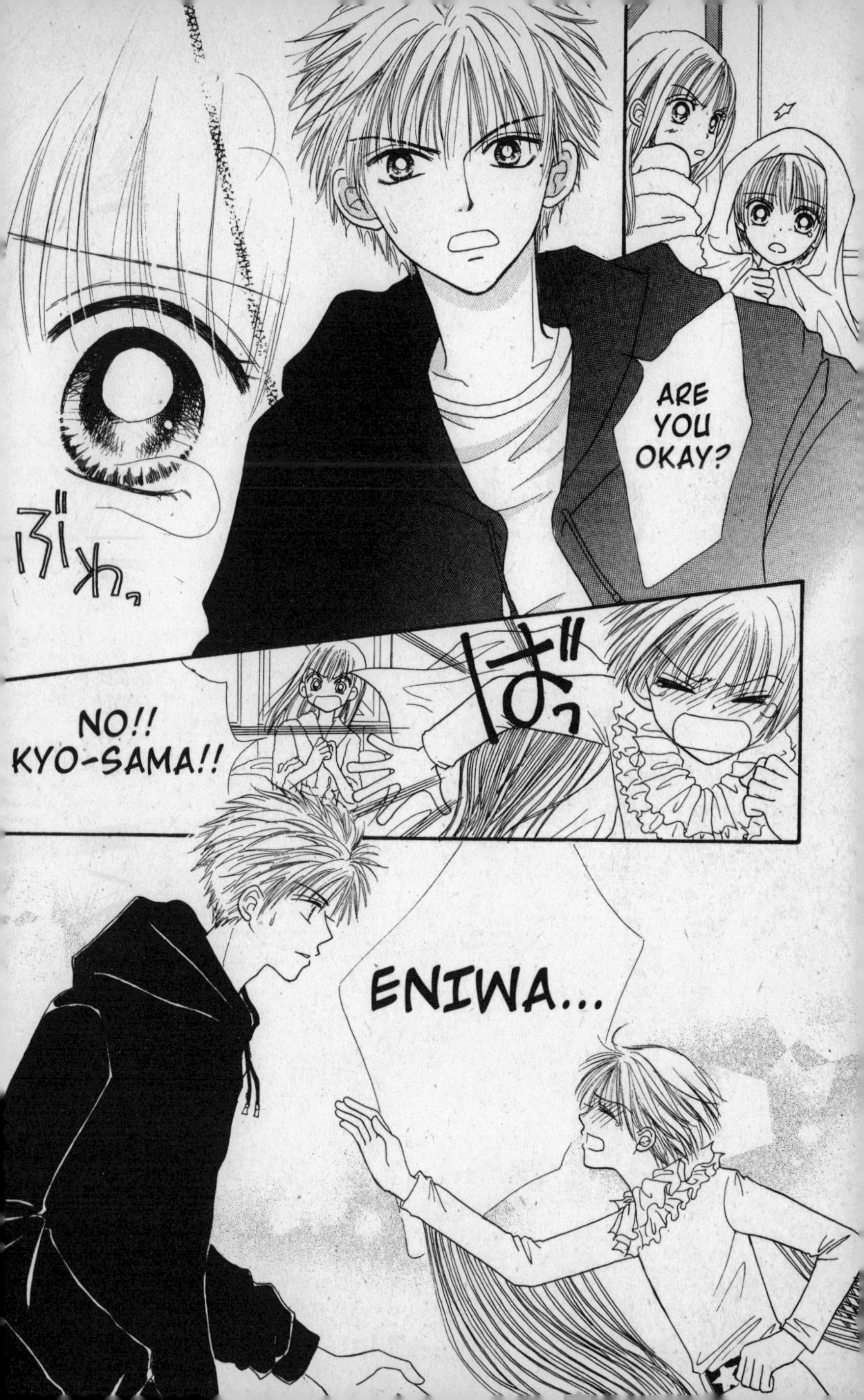
ARE YOU OKAY?
ぶわっ
ばっ
NO!! KYO-SAMA!!
ENIWA...

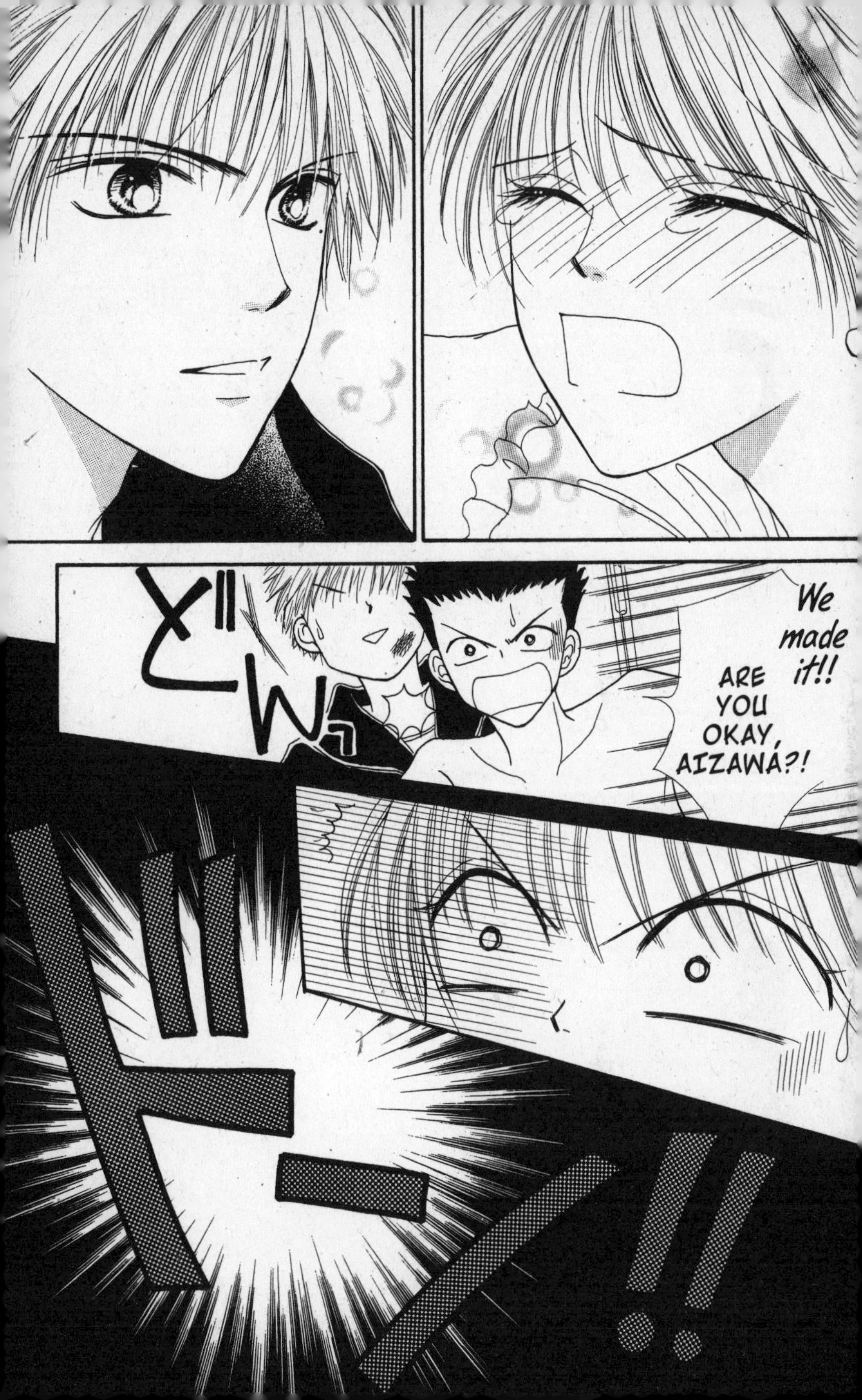
We made it!!
ARE YOU OKAY, AIZAWA?!

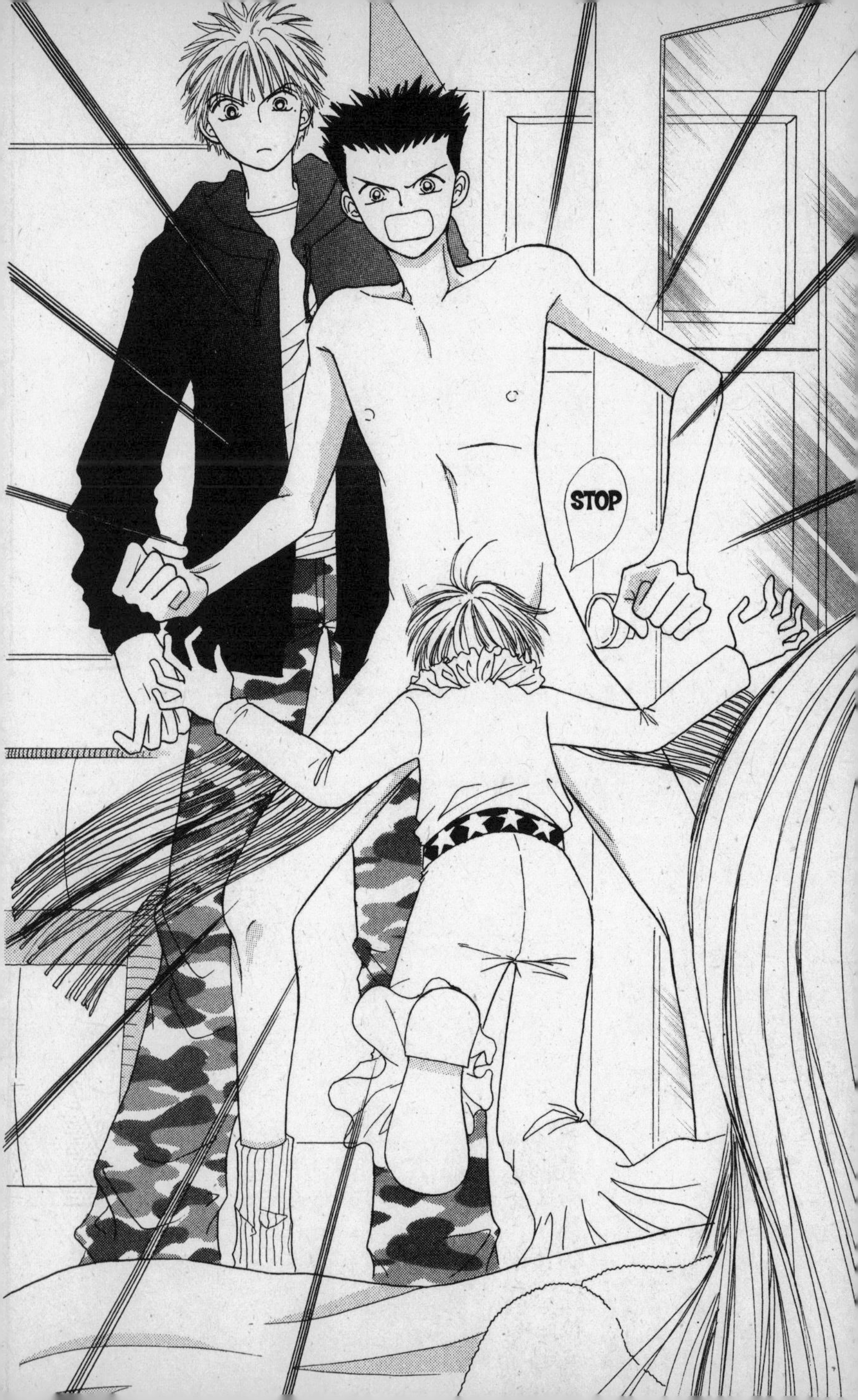
STOP

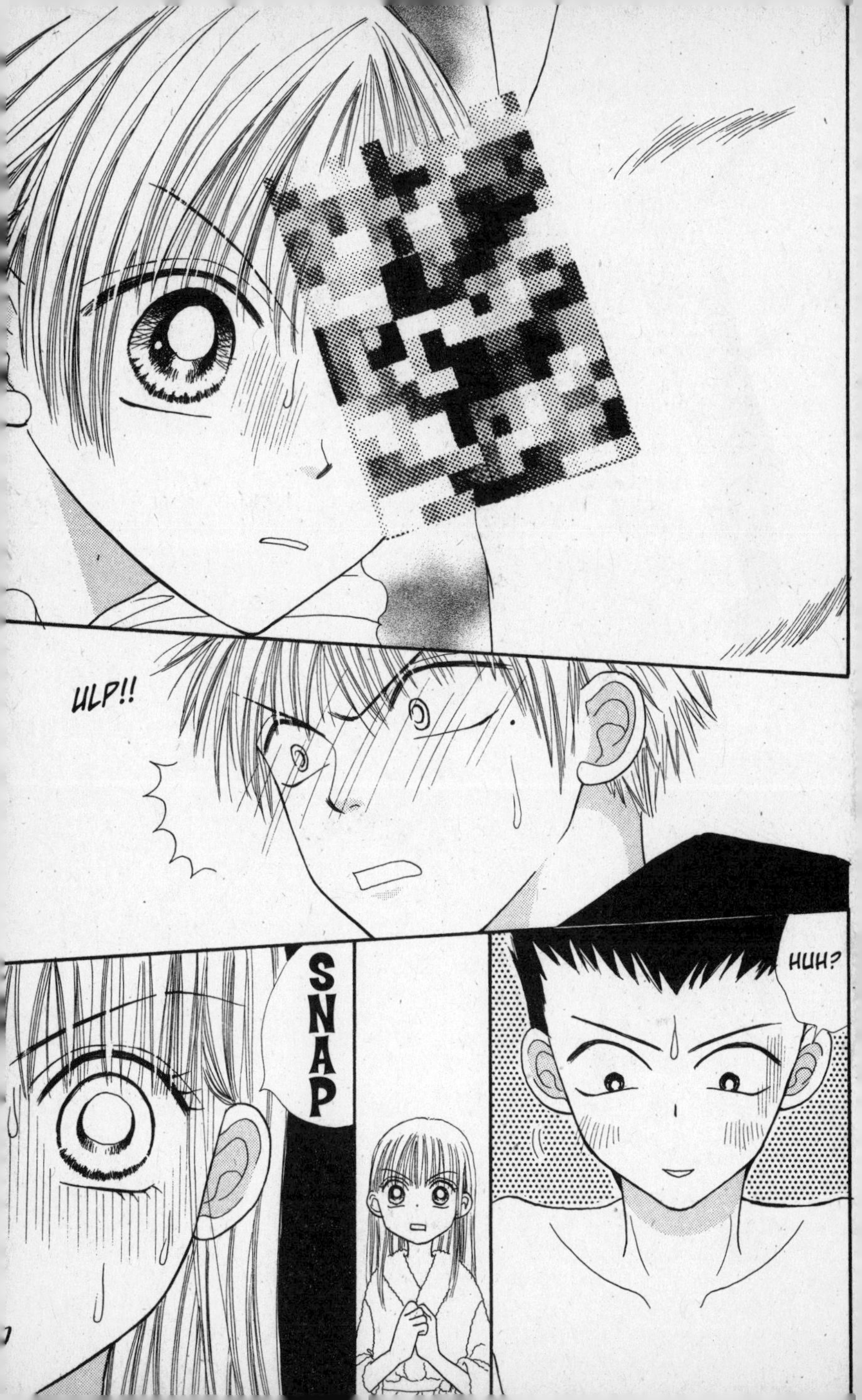
ULP!!
HUH?
SNAP

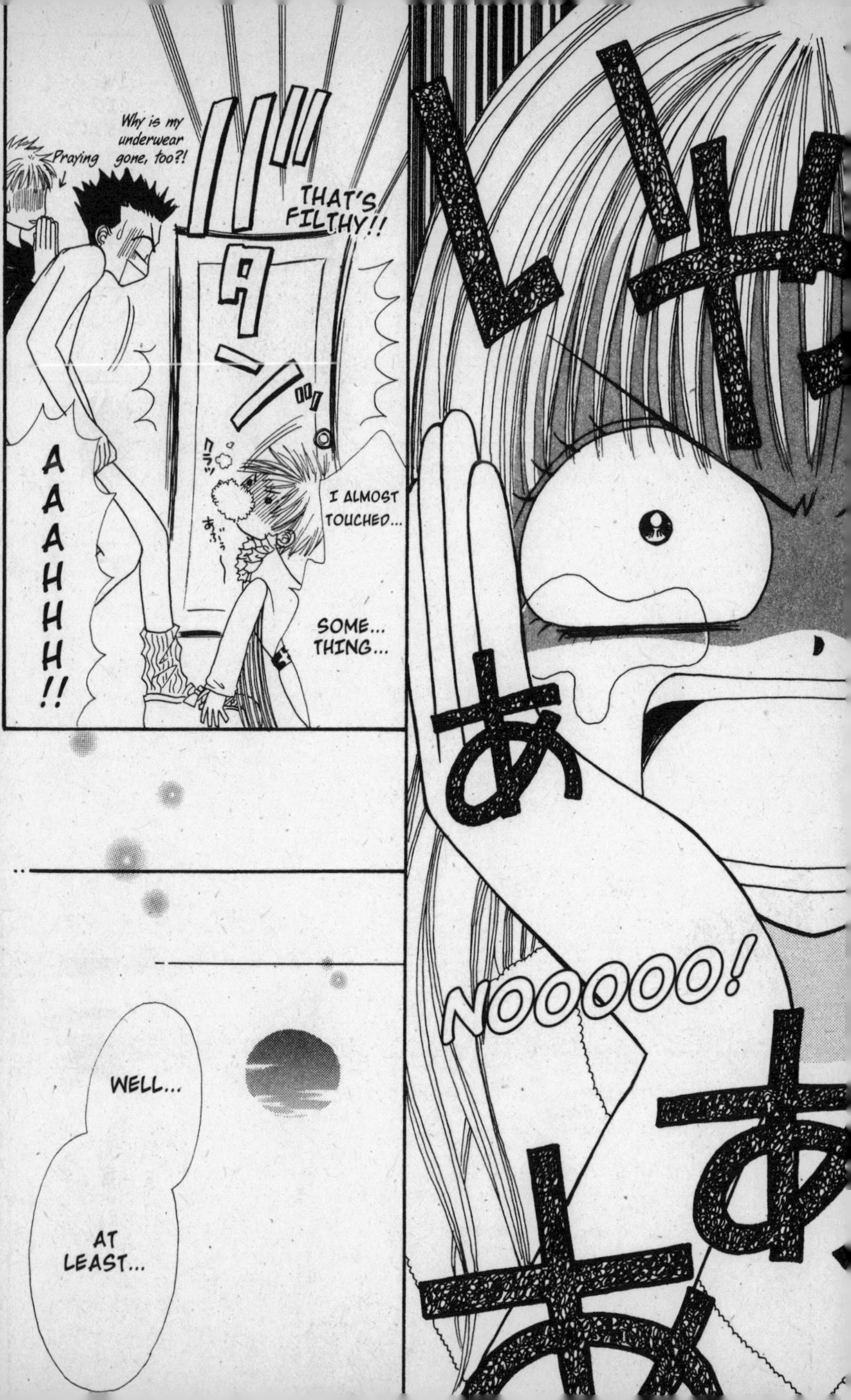
NOOOOO!
THAT'S FILTHY!!
Why is my underwear gone, too?!
Praying
I ALMOST TOUCHED...
SOME... THING...
AAAAHHHH!!
WELL...
AT LEAST...

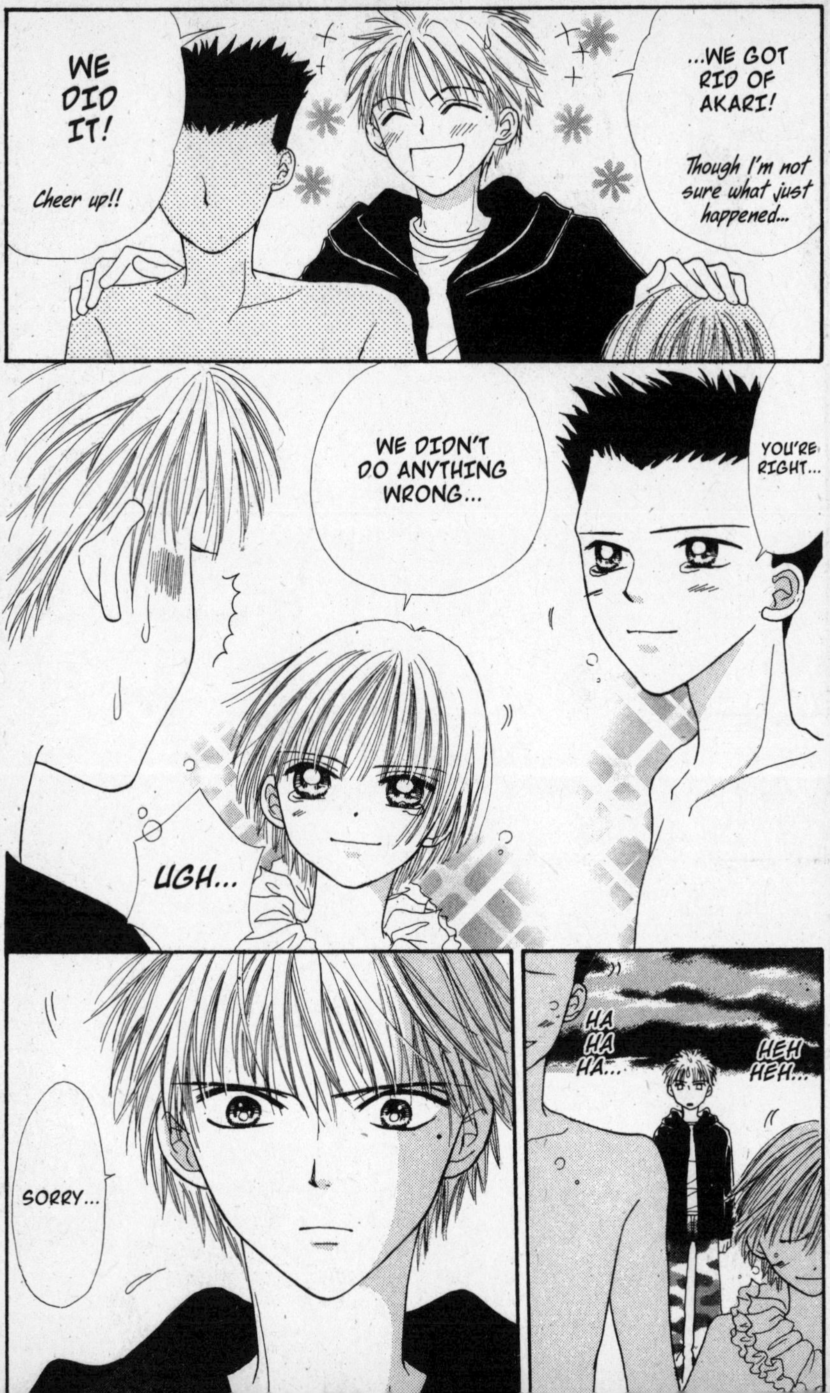
...WE GOT RID OF AKARI!
Though I'm not sure what just happened...
WE DID IT!
Cheer up!!
YOU'RE RIGHT...
WE DIDN'T DO ANYTHING WRONG...
UGH...
HEH HEH...
HA HA HA...
SORRY...

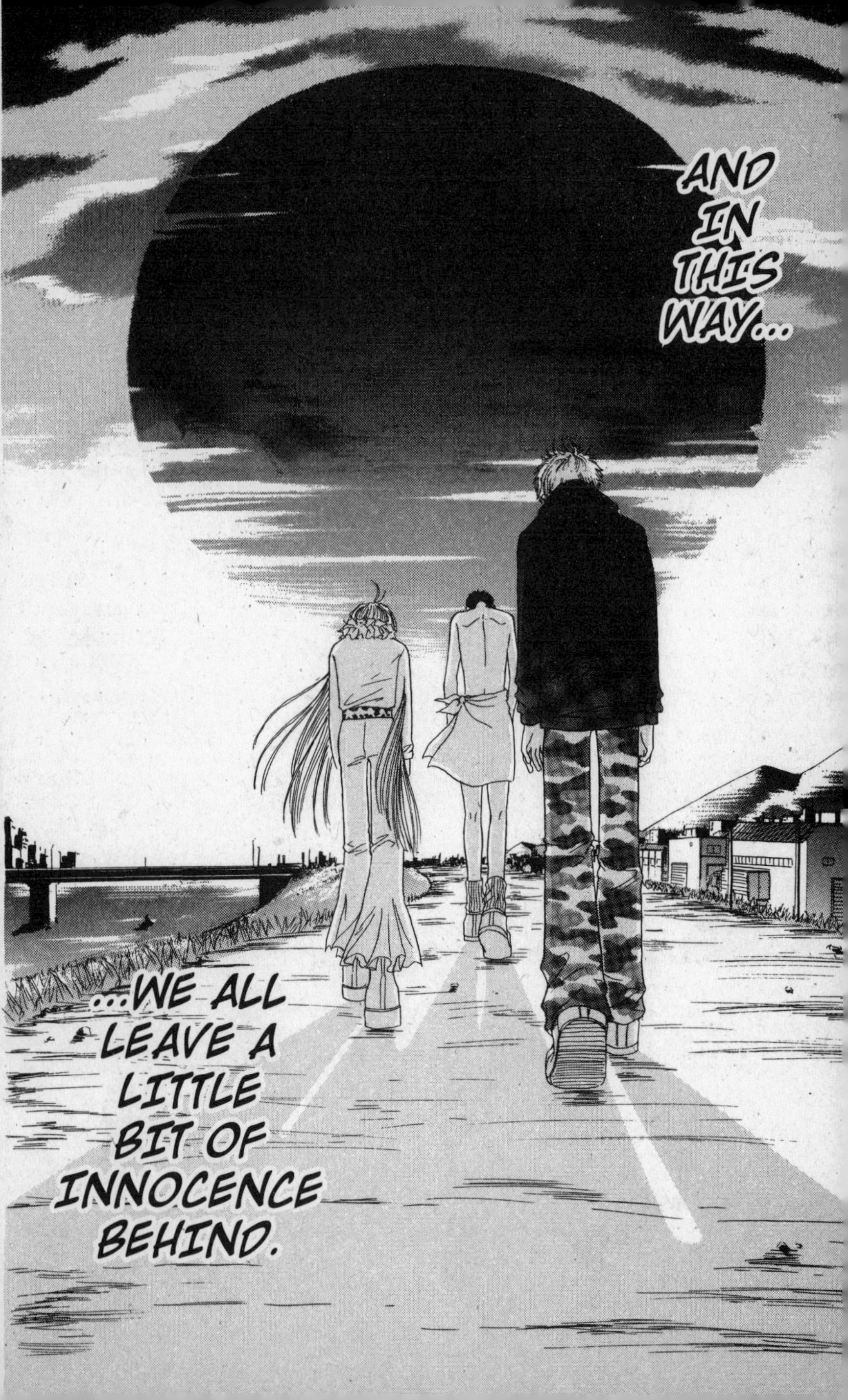
AND IN THIS WAY...
...WE ALL LEAVE A LITTLE BIT OF INNOCENCE BEHIND.

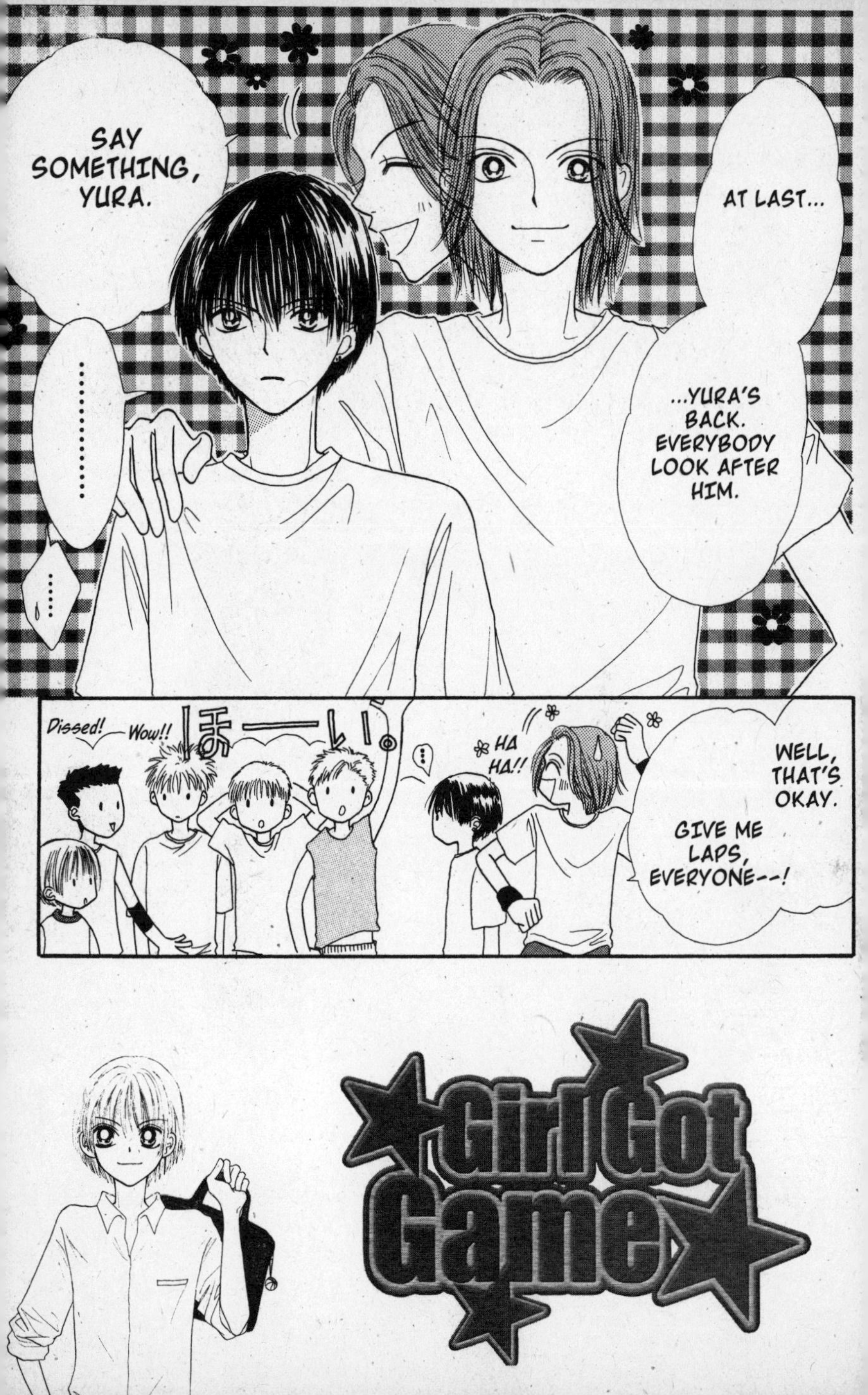
AT LAST...
...YURA'S BACK. EVERYBODY LOOK AFTER HIM.
SAY SOMETHING, YURA.
..............
......
WELL, THAT'S OKAY.
GIVE ME LAPS, EVERYONE--!
HA HA!!
!
ほーーい。
Wow!!
Dissed!
Girl Got Game

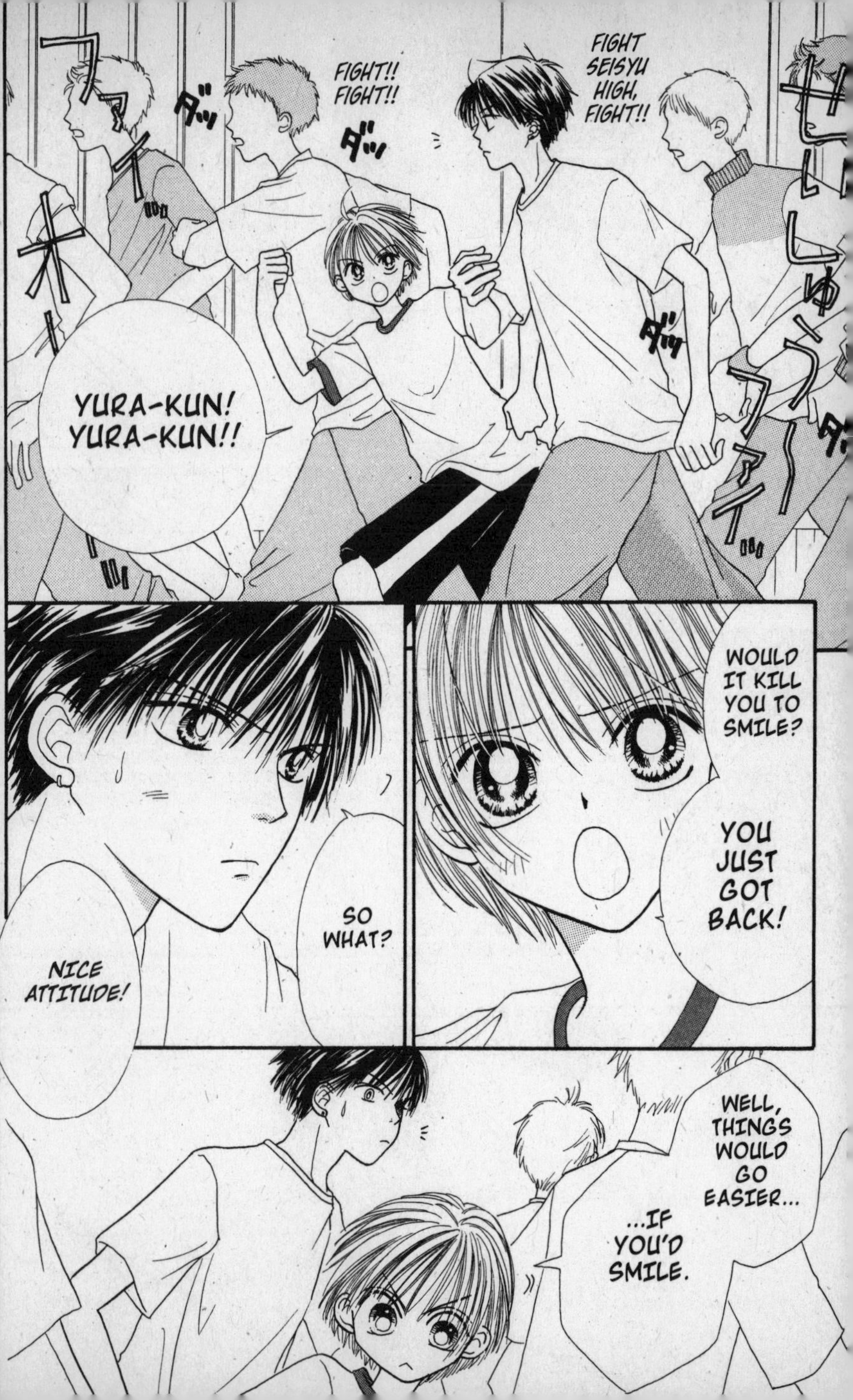
FIGHT SEISYU HIGH, FIGHT!!
FIGHT!! FIGHT!!
ダッ
ダッ
YURA-KUN! YURA-KUN!!
WOULD IT KILL YOU TO SMILE?
YOU JUST GOT BACK!
SO WHAT?
NICE ATTITUDE!
WELL, THINGS WOULD GO EASIER...
...IF YOU'D SMILE.

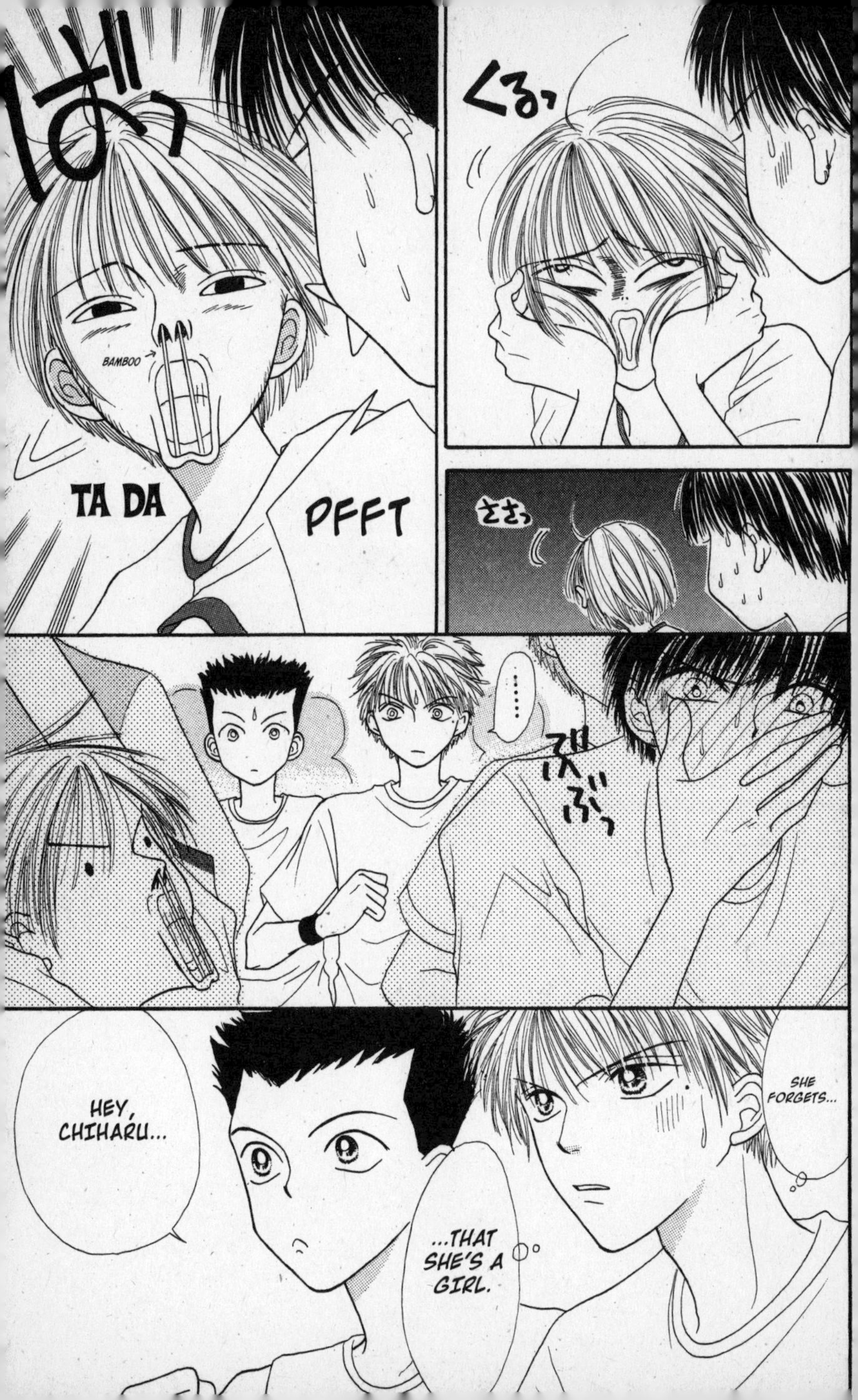
くるっ
ささっ
ばっ
BAMBOO
TA DA
PFFT
......
ぶぶっ
SHE FORGETS...
...THAT SHE'S A GIRL.
HEY, CHIHARU...

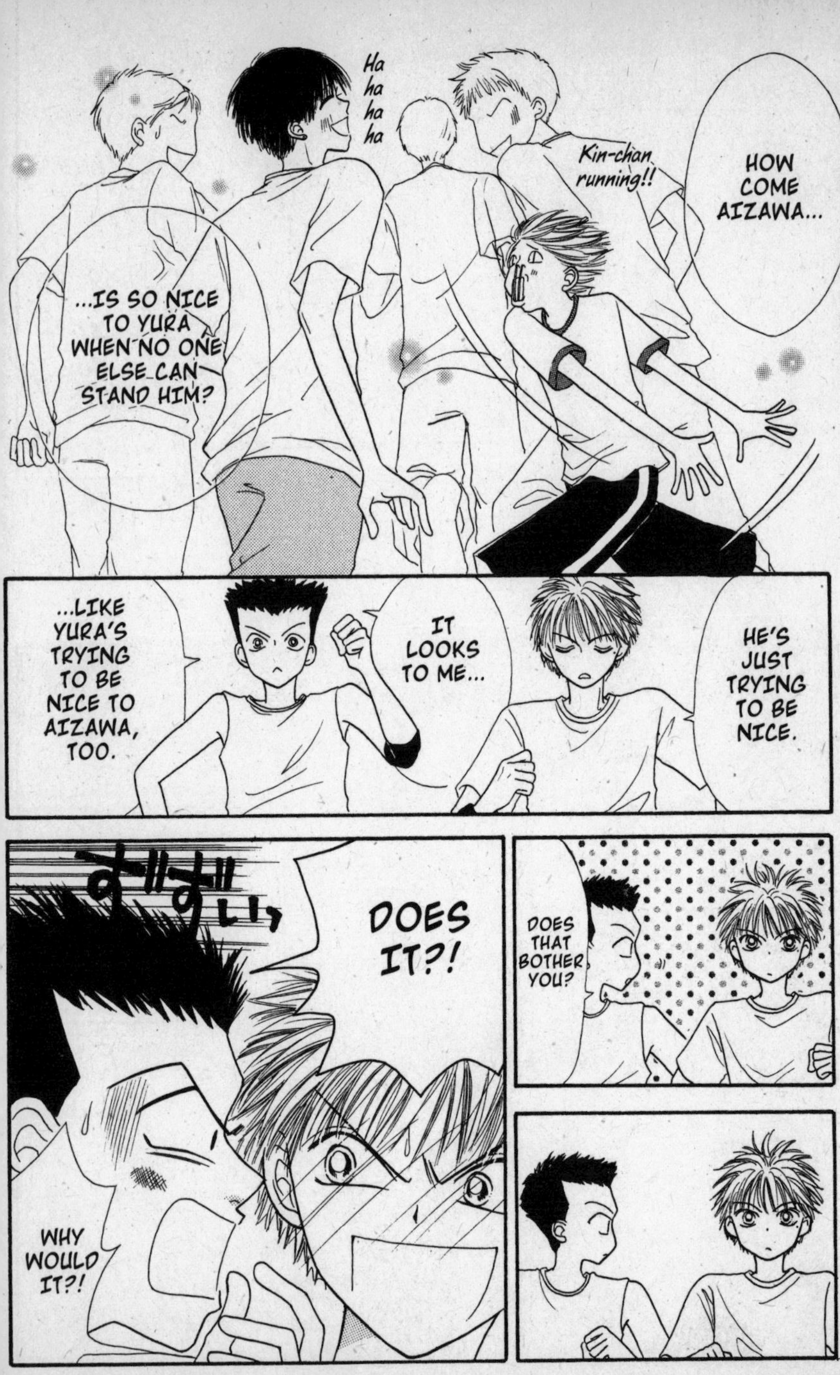
HOW COME AIZAWA...
Kin-chan running!!
Ha ha ha ha
...IS SO NICE TO YURA WHEN NO ONE ELSE CAN STAND HIM?
HE'S JUST TRYING TO BE NICE.
IT LOOKS TO ME...
...LIKE YURA'S TRYING TO BE NICE TO AIZAWA, TOO.
DOES THAT BOTHER YOU?
DOES IT?!
WHY WOULD IT?!

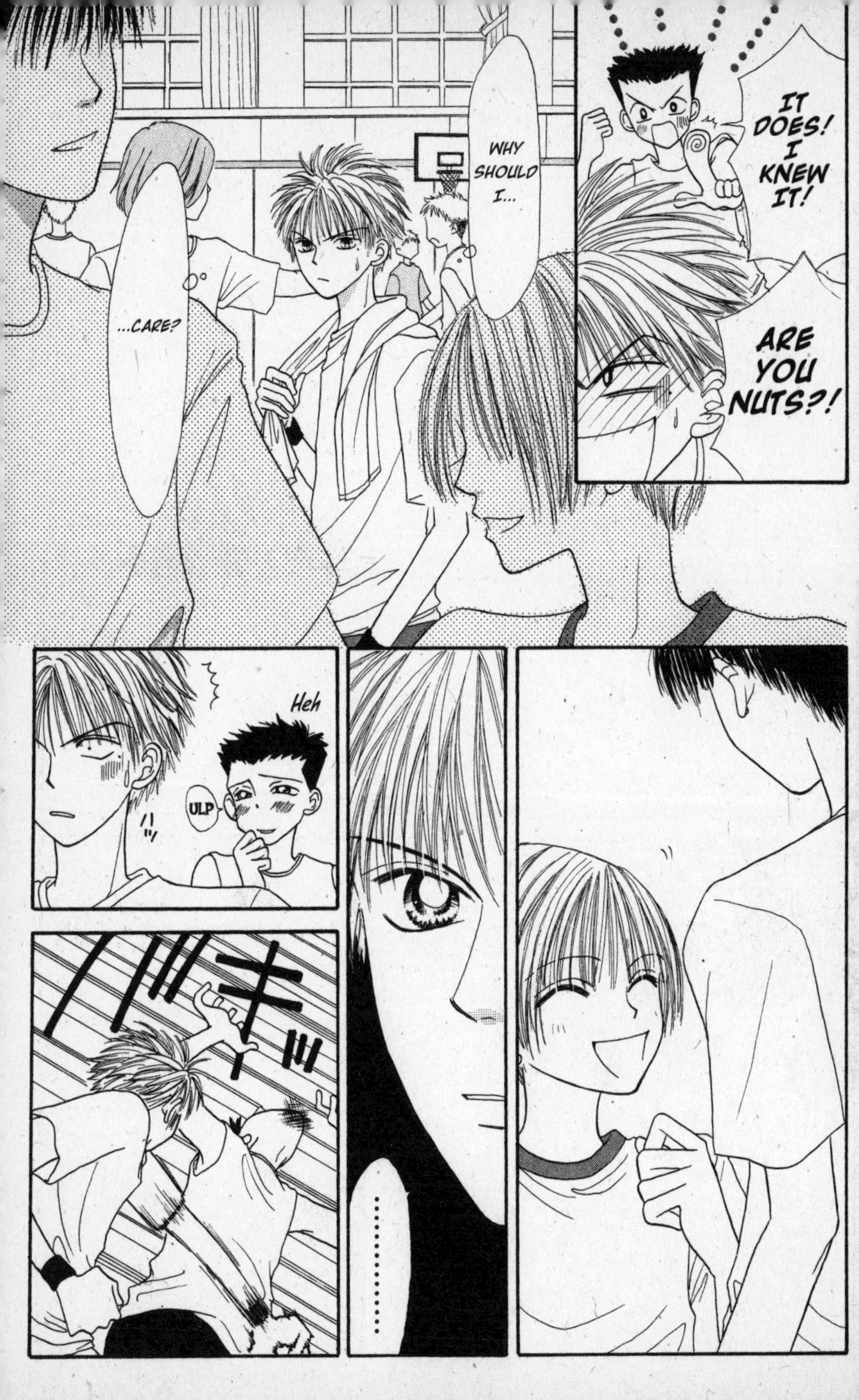
IT DOES! I KNEW IT!
ARE YOU NUTS?!
WHY SHOULD I...
...CARE?
Heh
ULP

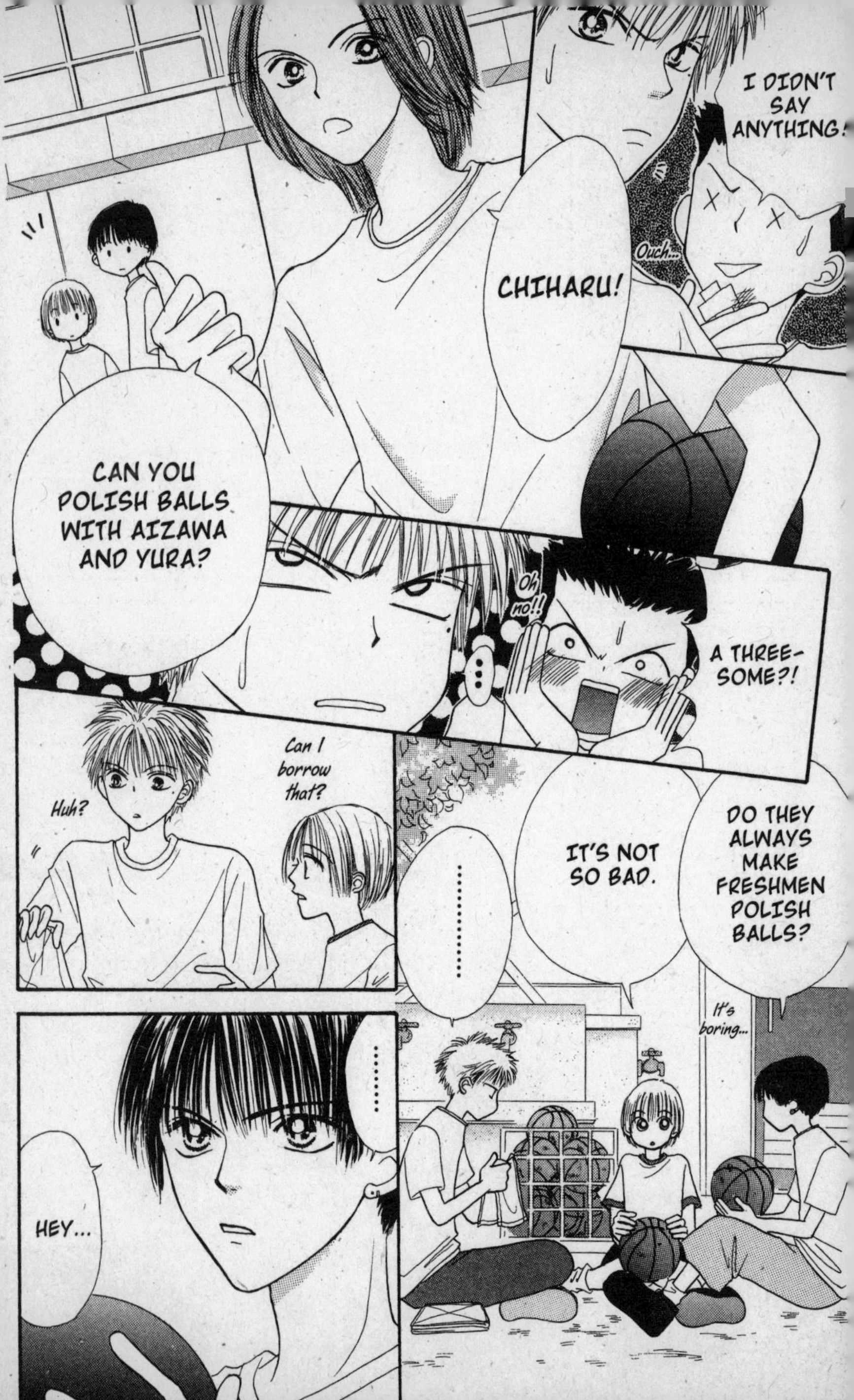
I DIDN'T SAY ANYTHING!
Ouch...
CHIHARU!
CAN YOU POLISH BALLS WITH AIZAWA AND YURA?
A THREE-SOME?!
Oh no!!
...
DO THEY ALWAYS MAKE FRESHMEN POLISH BALLS?
It's boring...
IT'S NOT SO BAD.
.........
Can I borrow that?
Huh?
......
HEY...

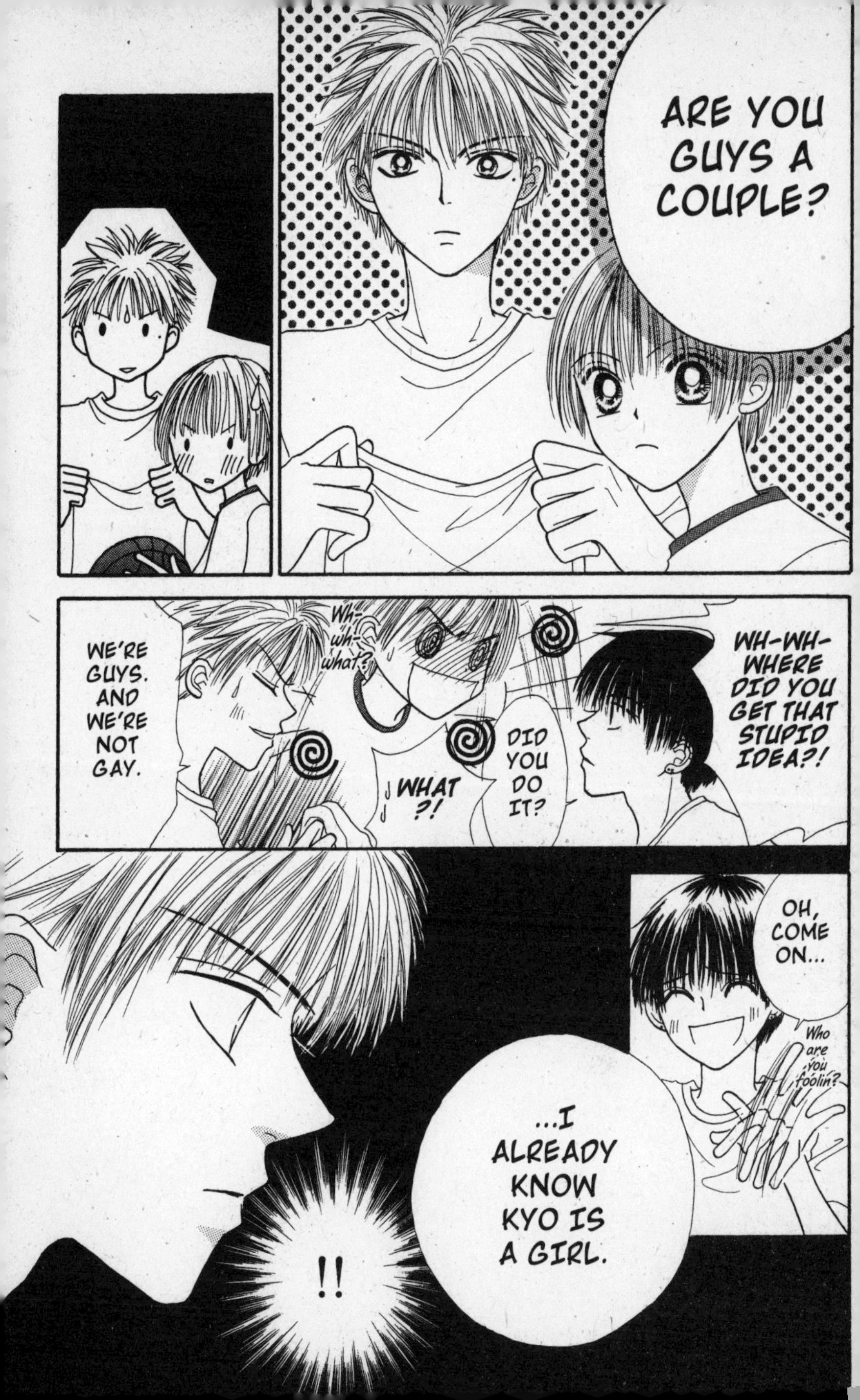
ARE YOU GUYS A COUPLE?
WH-WH-WHERE DID YOU GET THAT STUPID IDEA?!
Wh-wh-what?
DID YOU DO IT?
WHAT?!
WE'RE GUYS. AND WE'RE NOT GAY.
OH, COME ON...
Who are you foolin'?
...I ALREADY KNOW KYO IS A GIRL.
!!

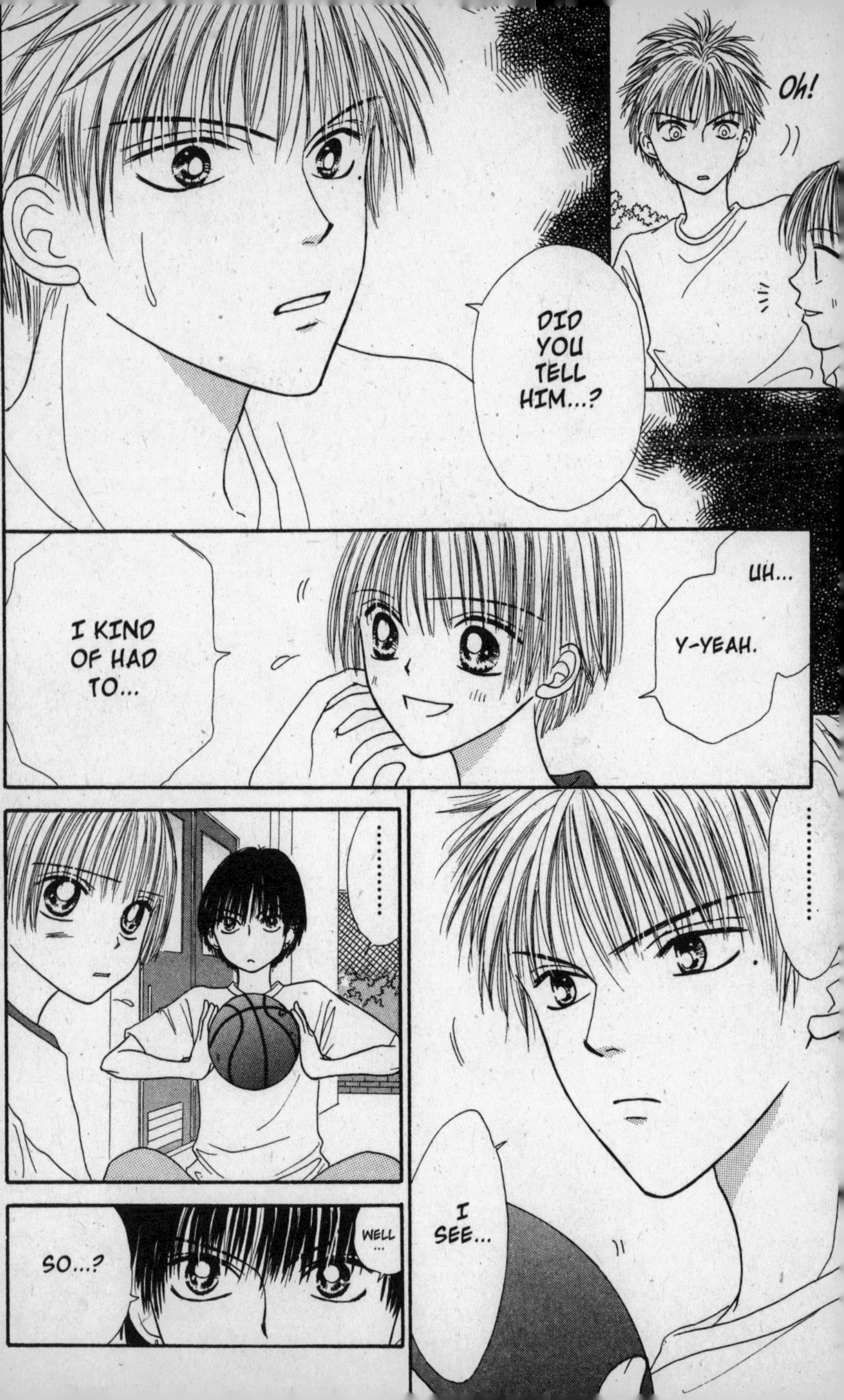
Oh!
DID YOU TELL HIM...?
UH... Y-YEAH.
I KIND OF HAD TO...
......
I SEE...
......
WELL...
SO...?

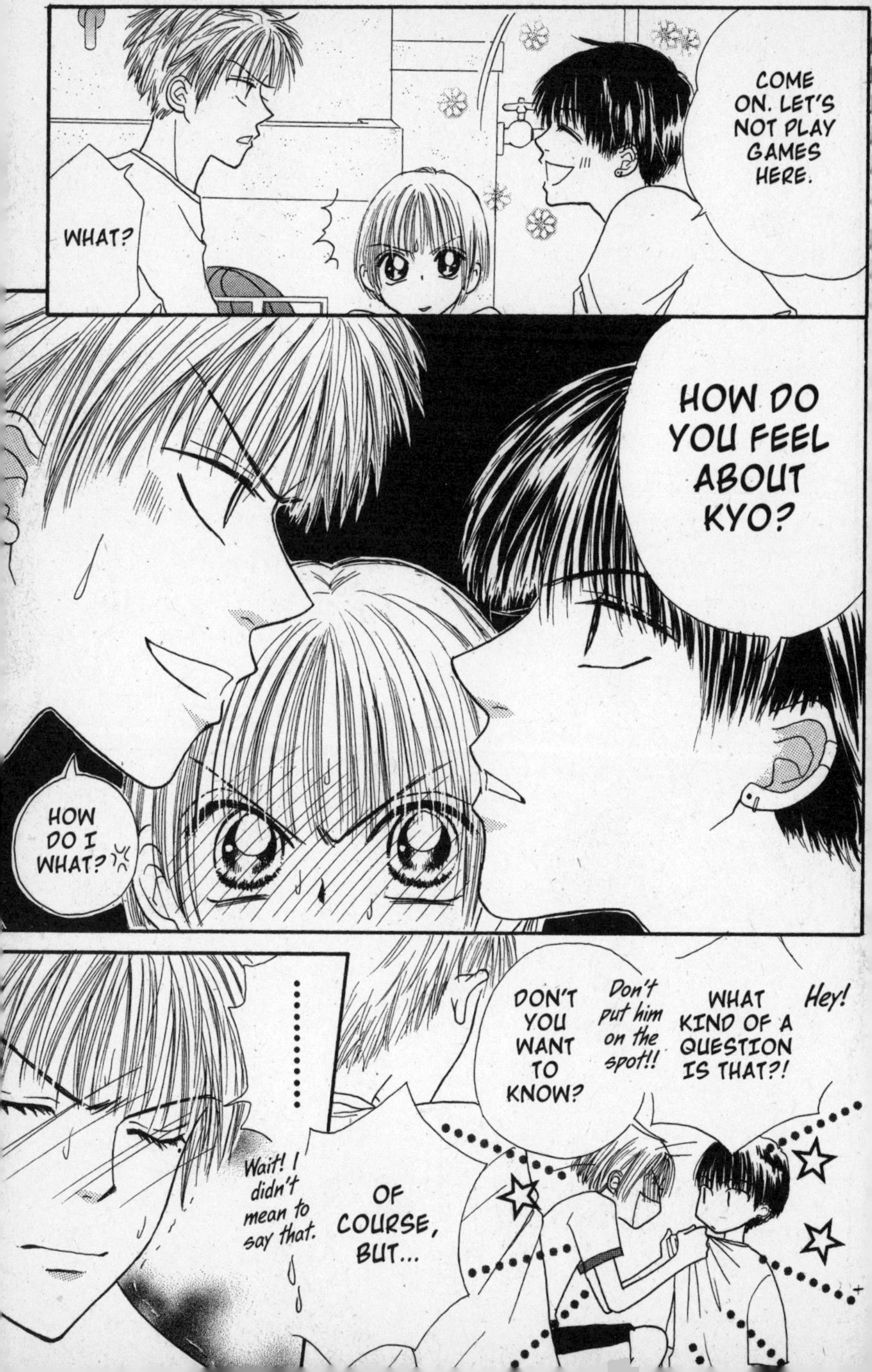
COME ON. LET'S NOT PLAY GAMES HERE.
WHAT?
HOW DO YOU FEEL ABOUT KYO?
HOW DO I WHAT?
Hey!
WHAT KIND OF A QUESTION IS THAT?!
Don't put him on the spot!!
DON'T YOU WANT TO KNOW?
OF COURSE, BUT...
Wait! I didn't mean to say that.
......

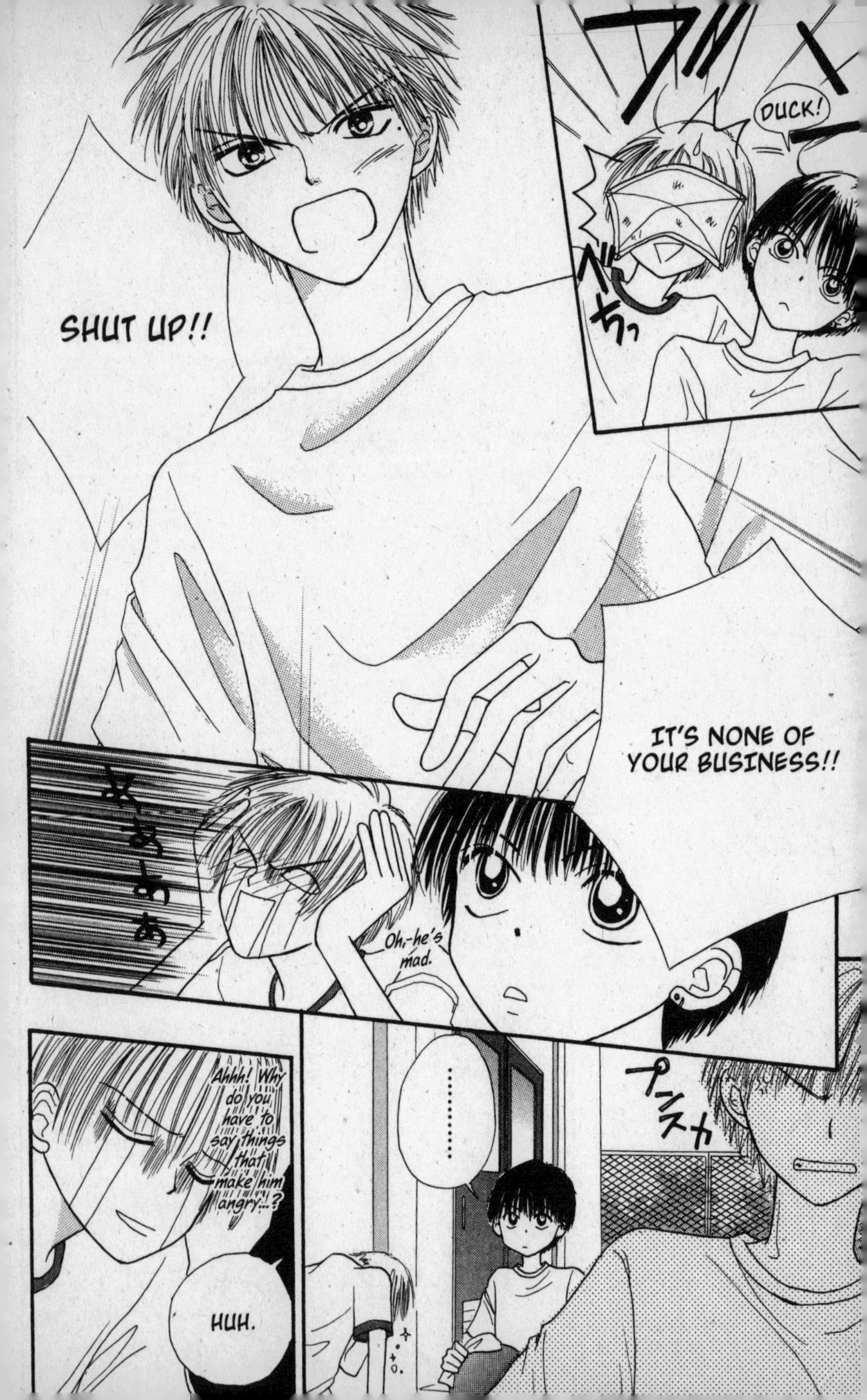
DUCK!
SHUT UP!!
IT'S NONE OF YOUR BUSINESS!!
Oh,-he's mad.
......
Ahhh! Why do you have to say things that make him angry...?
HUH.

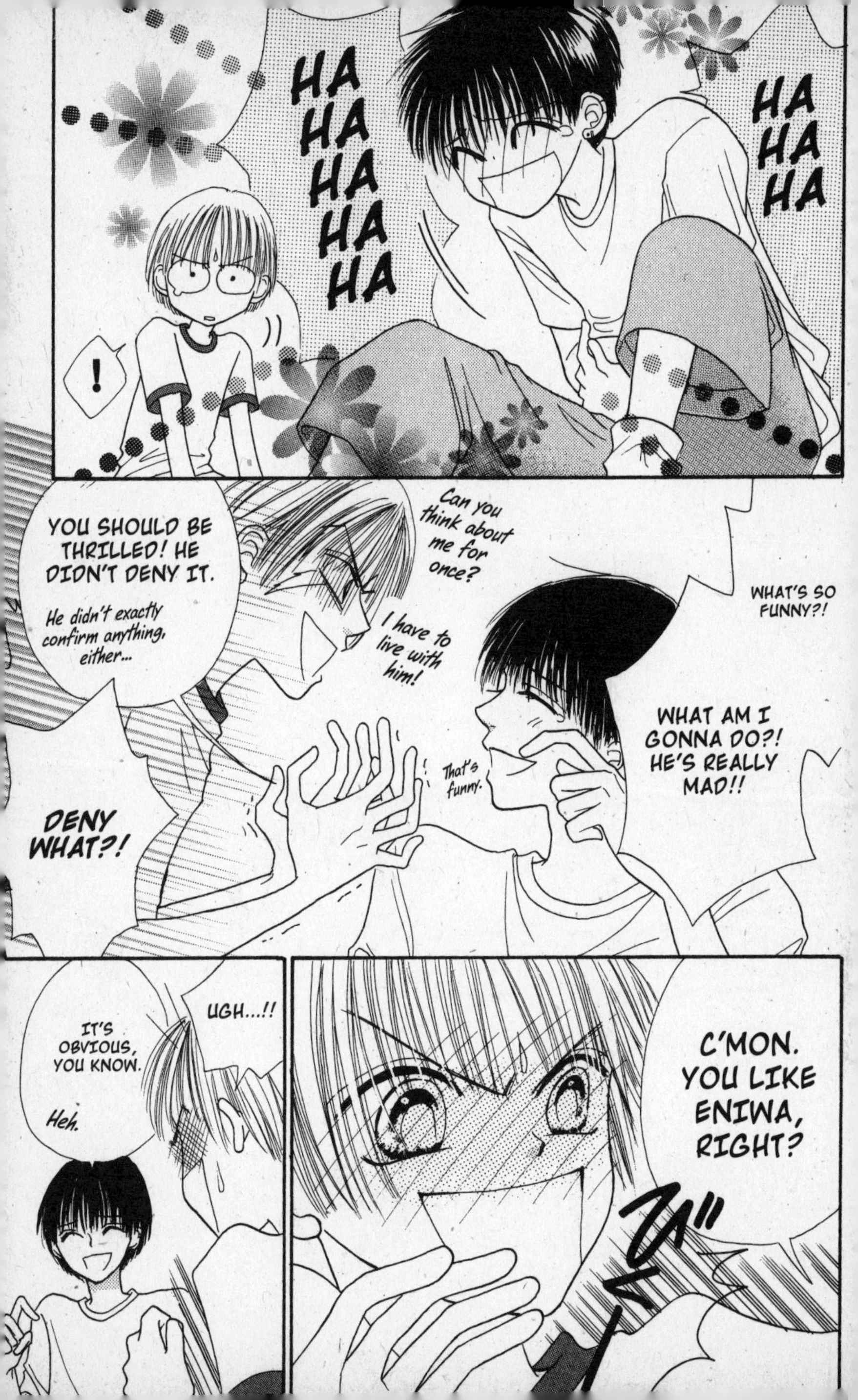
HA HA HA
HA HA HA HA HA
!
WHAT'S SO FUNNY?!
WHAT AM I GONNA DO?! HE'S REALLY MAD!!
Can you think about me for once?
I have to live with him!
That's funny.
YOU SHOULD BE THRILLED! HE DIDN'T DENY IT.
He didn't exactly confirm anything, either...
DENY WHAT?!
C'MON. YOU LIKE ENIWA, RIGHT?
UGH...!!
IT'S OBVIOUS, YOU KNOW.
Heh.

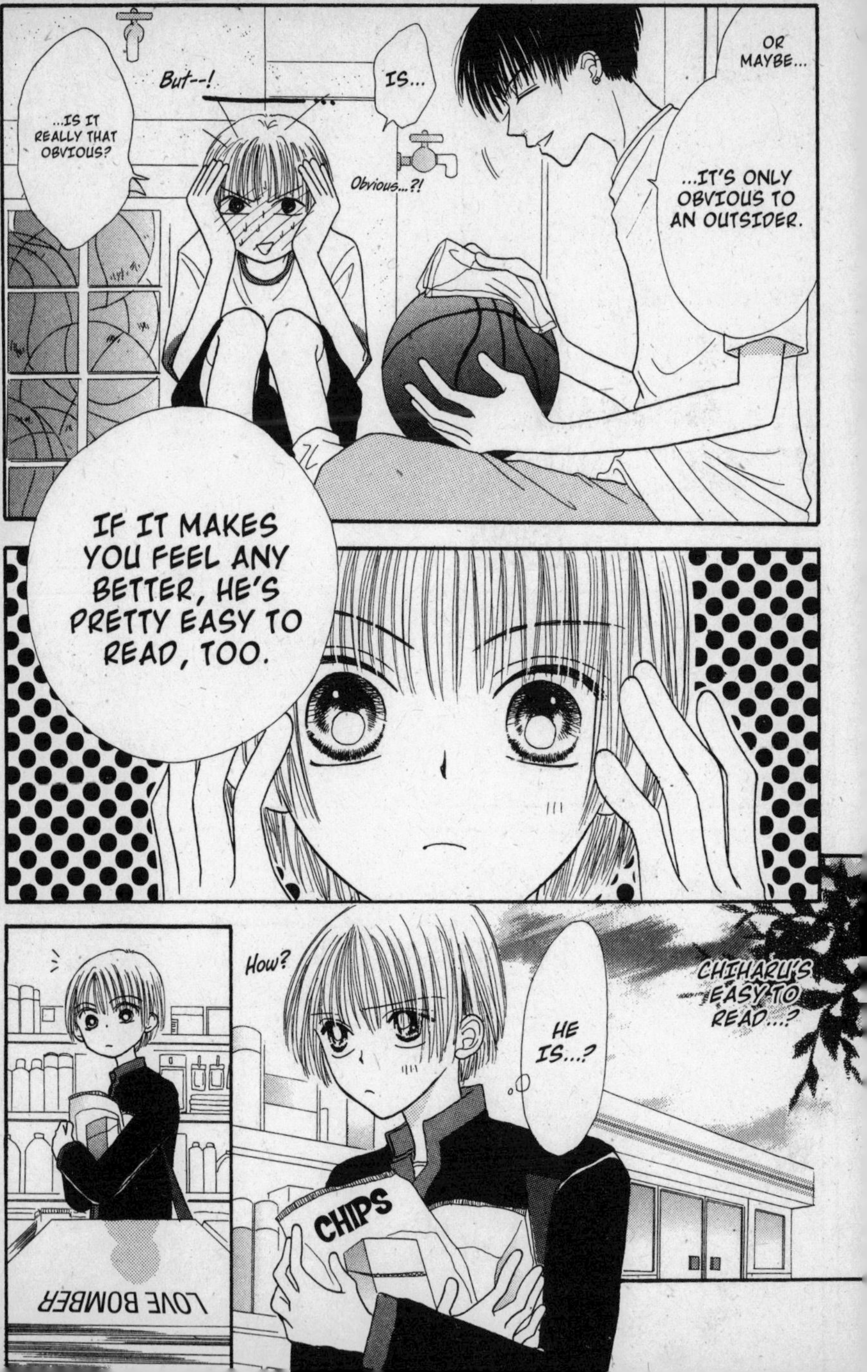
OR MAYBE...
...IT'S ONLY OBVIOUS TO AN OUTSIDER.
IS...
Obvious...?!
But--!
...IS IT REALLY THAT OBVIOUS?
IF IT MAKES YOU FEEL ANY BETTER, HE'S PRETTY EASY TO READ, TOO.
CHIHARU'S EASY TO READ...?
HE IS...?
How?
CHIPS
LOVE BOMBER

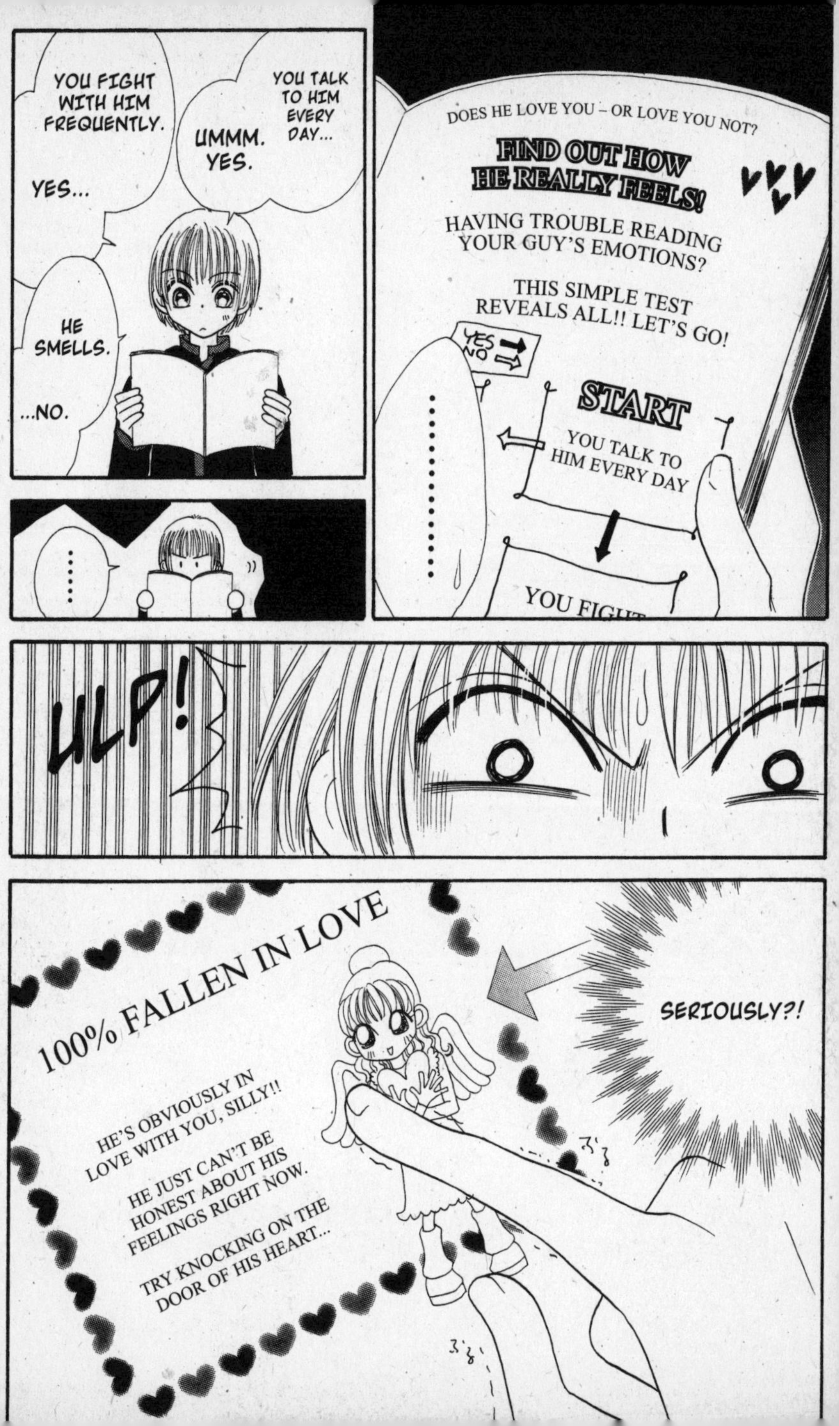
DOES HE LOVE YOU – OR LOVE YOU NOT?
FIND OUT HOW HE REALLY FEELS!
HAVING TROUBLE READING YOUR GUY'S EMOTIONS?
THIS SIMPLE TEST REVEALS ALL!! LET'S GO!
YES
NO
START
YOU TALK TO HIM EVERY DAY
YOU FIGHT
......
YOU TALK TO HIM EVERY DAY...
UMMM. YES.
YOU FIGHT WITH HIM FREQUENTLY.
YES...
HE SMELLS.
...NO.
......
ULP!
SERIOUSLY?!
100% FALLEN IN LOVE
HE'S OBVIOUSLY IN LOVE WITH YOU, SILLY!!
HE JUST CAN'T BE HONEST ABOUT HIS FEELINGS RIGHT NOW.
TRY KNOCKING ON THE DOOR OF HIS HEART...

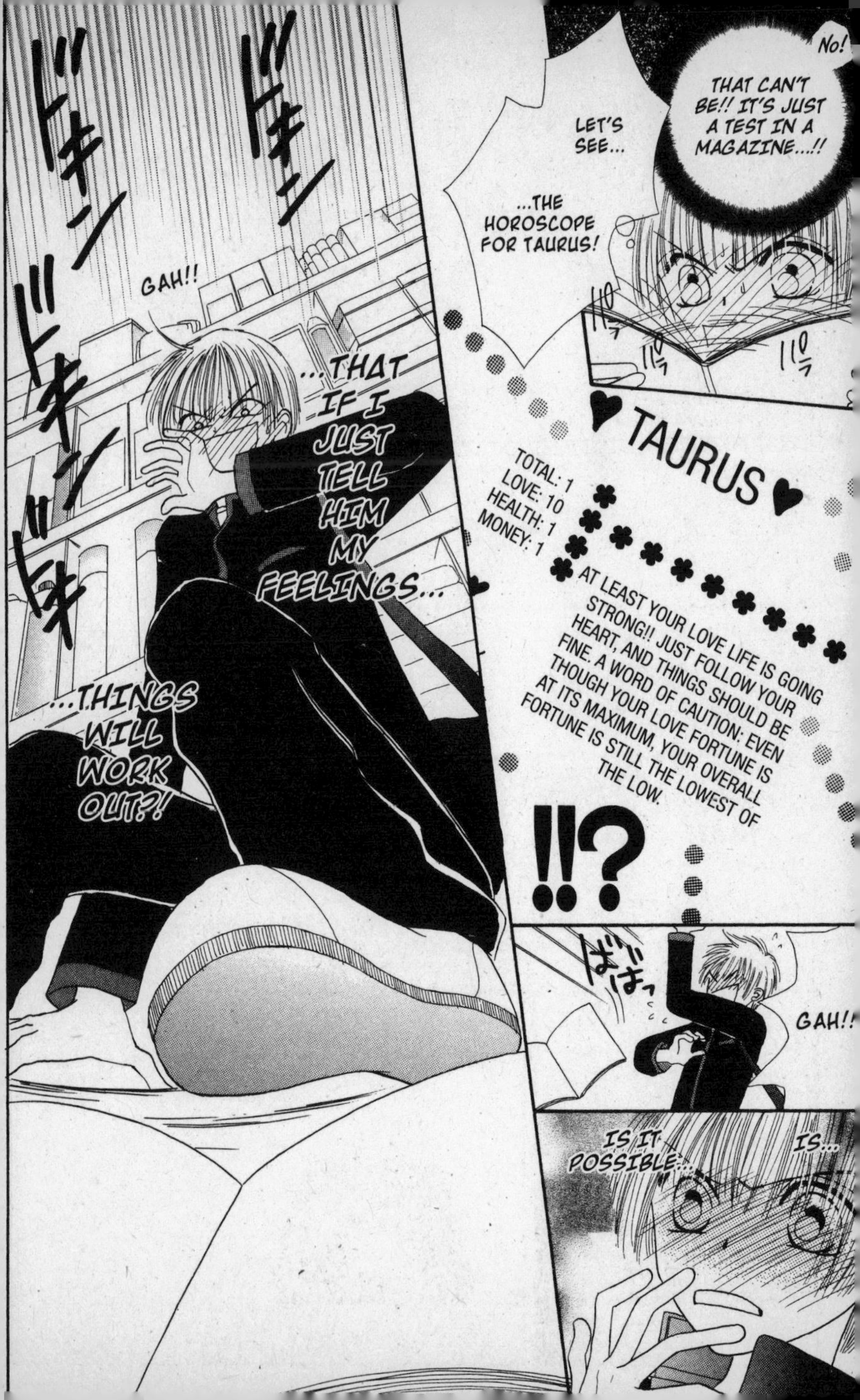
No!
THAT CAN'T BE!! IT'S JUST A TEST IN A MAGAZINE...!!
LET'S SEE...
...THE HOROSCOPE FOR TAURUS!
TAURUS
TOTAL: 1
LOVE: 10
HEALTH: 1
MONEY: 1
AT LEAST YOUR LOVE LIFE IS GOING STRONG!! JUST FOLLOW YOUR HEART, AND THINGS SHOULD BE FINE. A WORD OF CAUTION: EVEN THOUGH YOUR LOVE FORTUNE IS AT ITS MAXIMUM, YOUR OVERALL FORTUNE IS STILL THE LOWEST OF THE LOW.
!!?
GAH!!
IS...
IS IT POSSIBLE...
...THAT IF I JUST TELL HIM MY FEELINGS...
...THINGS WILL WORK OUT?!
GAH!!

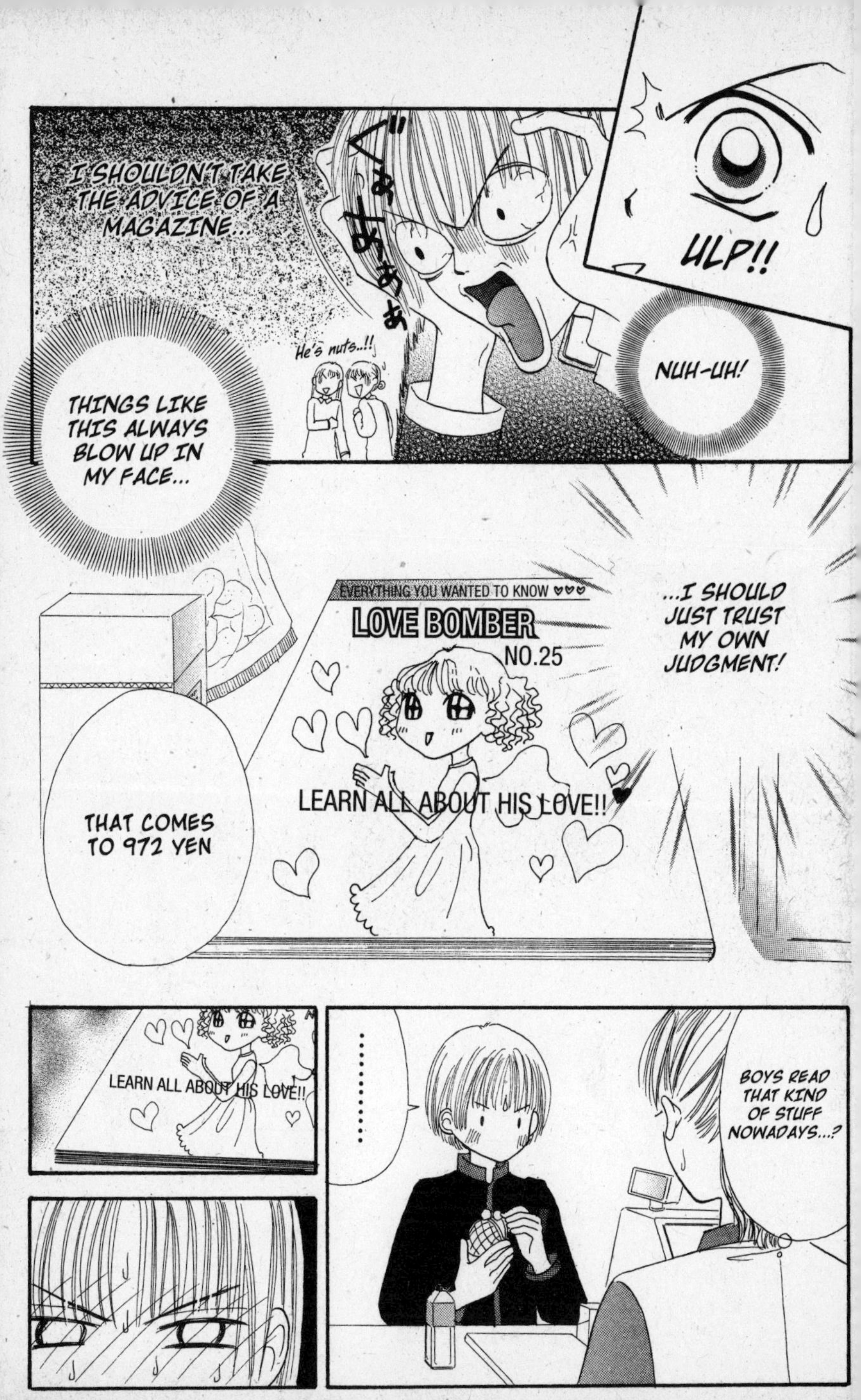
ULP!!
NUH-UH!
I SHOULDN'T TAKE THE ADVICE OF A MAGAZINE...
He's nuts..!!
THINGS LIKE THIS ALWAYS BLOW UP IN MY FACE...
...I SHOULD JUST TRUST MY OWN JUDGMENT!
EVERYTHING YOU WANTED TO KNOW
LOVE BOMBER
NO.25
LEARN ALL ABOUT HIS LOVE!!
THAT COMES TO 972 YEN
BOYS READ THAT KIND OF STUFF NOWADAYS...?
......
LEARN ALL ABOUT HIS LOVE!!

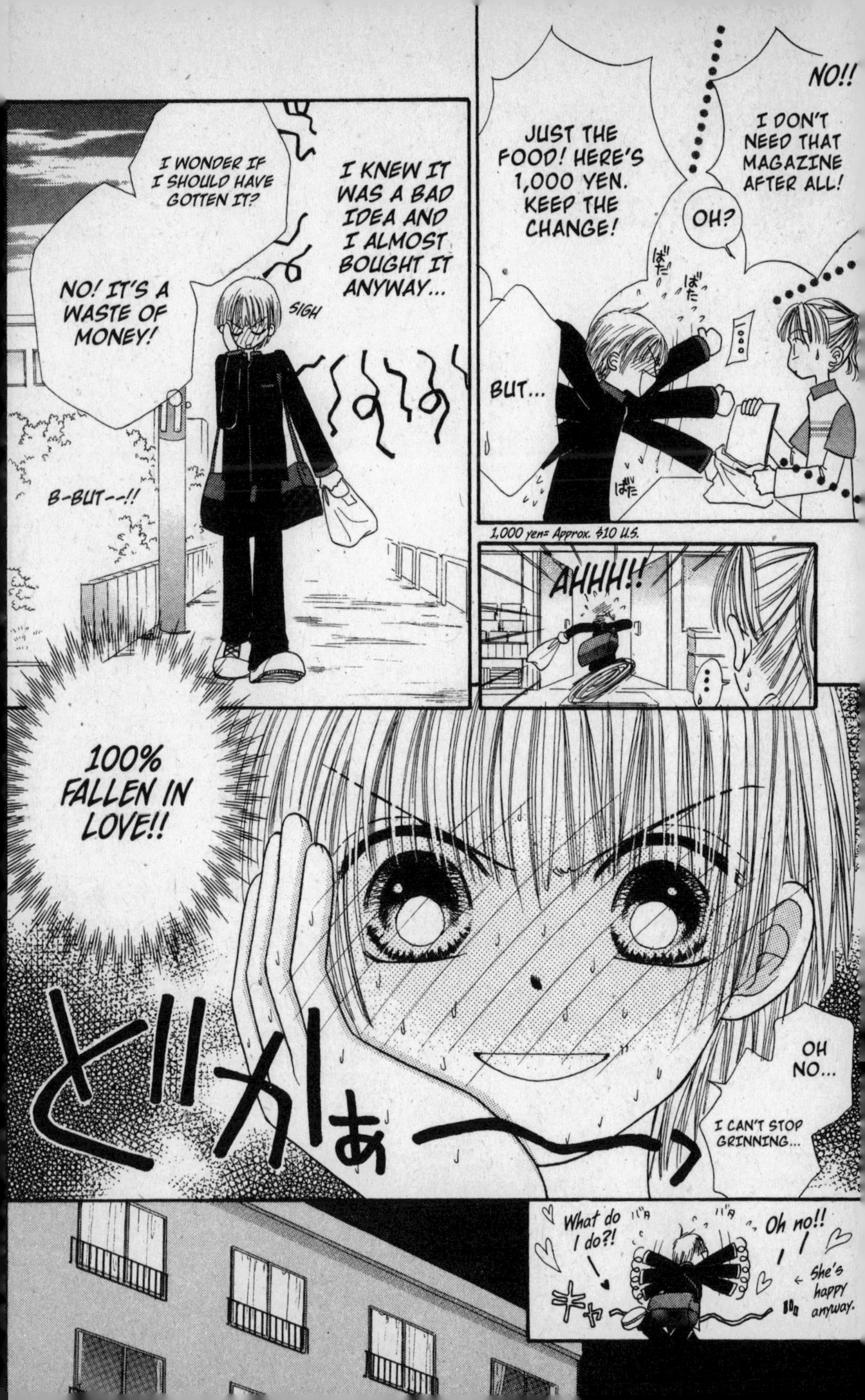
NO!!
I DON'T NEED THAT MAGAZINE AFTER ALL!
JUST THE FOOD! HERE'S 1,000 YEN. KEEP THE CHANGE!
OH?
ばた
ばた
BUT...
...
ばた
1,000 yen= Approx. $10 U.S.
AHHH!!
...
I KNEW IT WAS A BAD IDEA AND I ALMOST BOUGHT IT ANYWAY...
I WONDER IF I SHOULD HAVE GOTTEN IT?
SIGH
NO! IT'S A WASTE OF MONEY!
B-BUT--!!
OH NO...
I CAN'T STOP GRINNING...
100% FALLEN IN LOVE!!
とりかぁ〜っ
Oh no!!
She's happy anyway.
バタ
バタ
What do I do?!
キャ〜

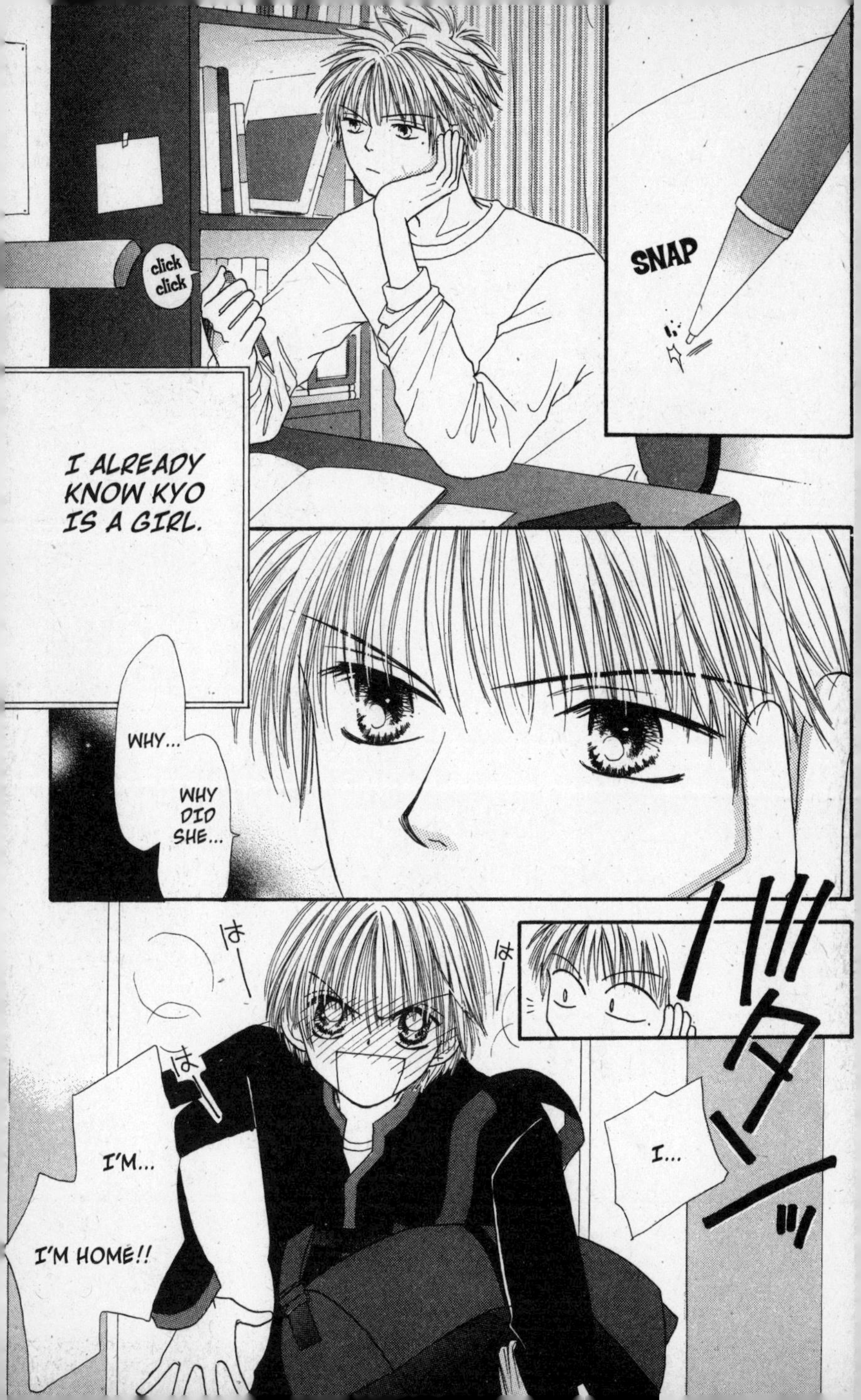
SNAP
click click
I ALREADY KNOW KYO IS A GIRL.
WHY...
WHY DID SHE...
バターンッ
はー
I...
はー
はー
I'M...
I'M HOME!!

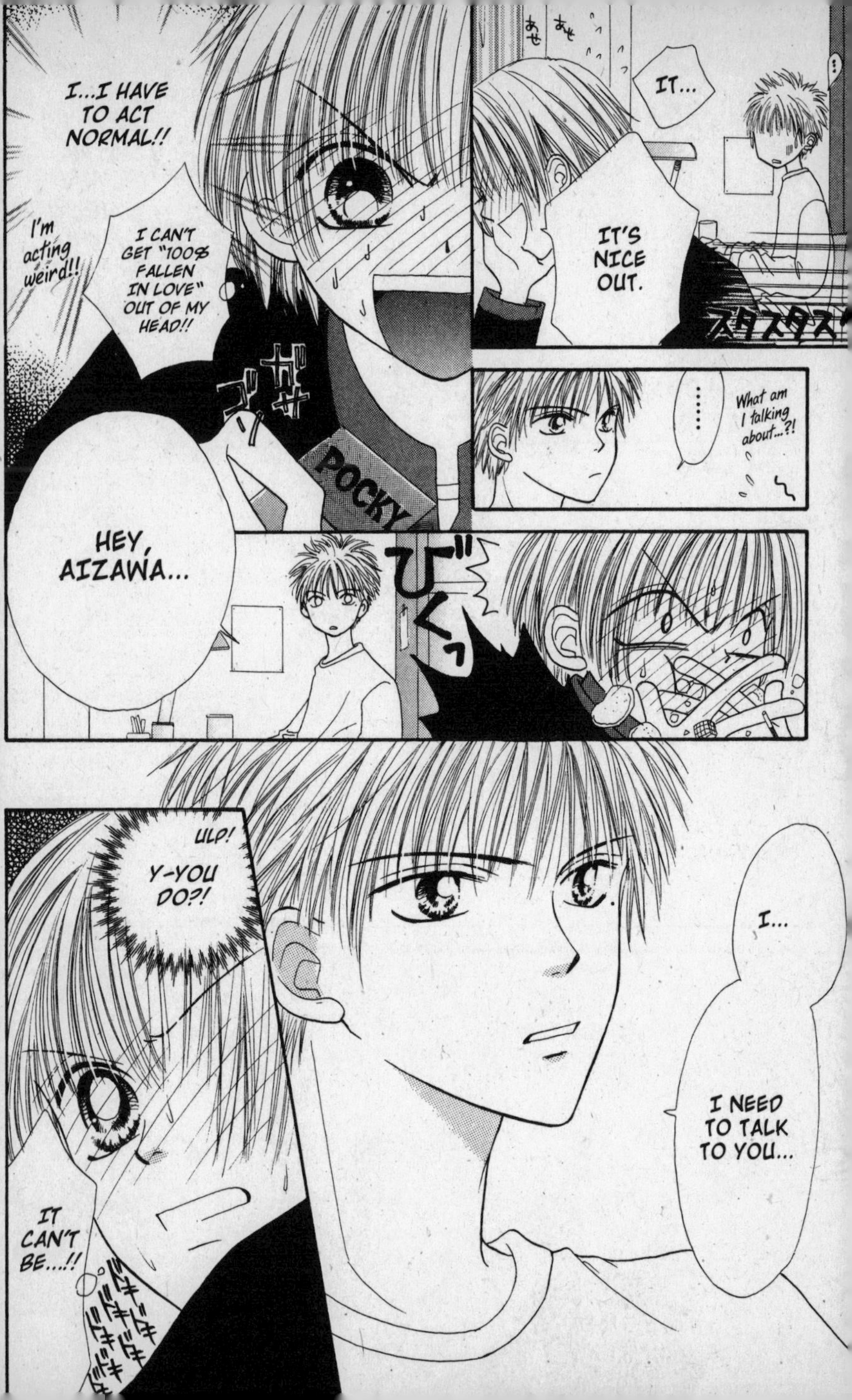
IT...
IT'S NICE OUT.
......
What am I talking about...?!
I...I HAVE TO ACT NORMAL!!
I'm acting weird!!
I CAN'T GET "100% FALLEN IN LOVE" OUT OF MY HEAD!!
POCKY
びくっ
HEY, AIZAWA...
I...
I NEED TO TALK TO YOU...
ULP!
Y-YOU DO?!
IT CAN'T BE...!!

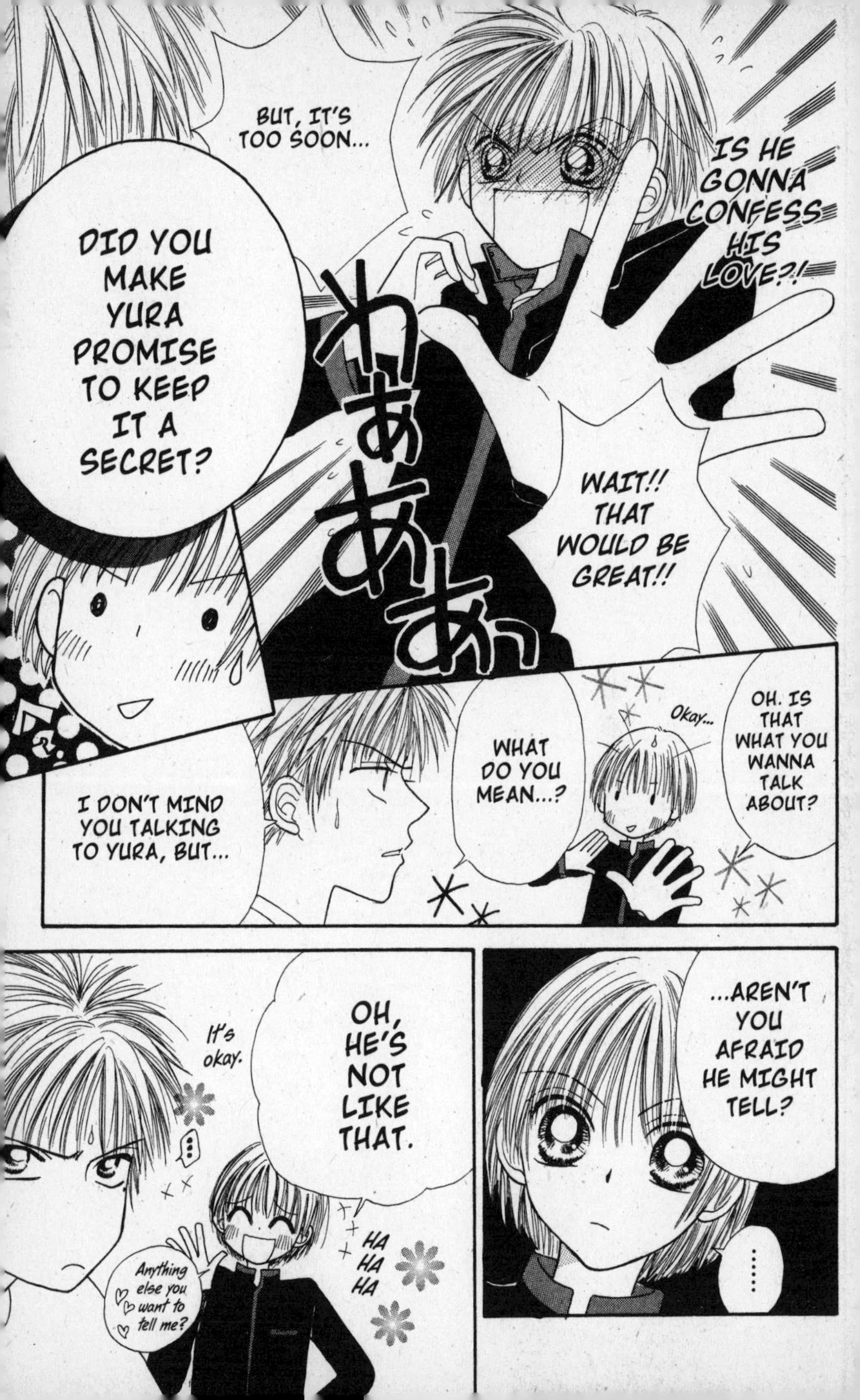
IS HE GONNA CONFESS HIS LOVE?!
BUT, IT'S TOO SOON...
WAIT!! THAT WOULD BE GREAT!!
わあああっ
DID YOU MAKE YURA PROMISE TO KEEP IT A SECRET?
OH. IS THAT WHAT YOU WANNA TALK ABOUT?
Okay...
WHAT DO YOU MEAN...?
I DON'T MIND YOU TALKING TO YURA, BUT...
...AREN'T YOU AFRAID HE MIGHT TELL?
......
OH, HE'S NOT LIKE THAT.
HA HA HA
It's okay.
...
Anything else you want to tell me?

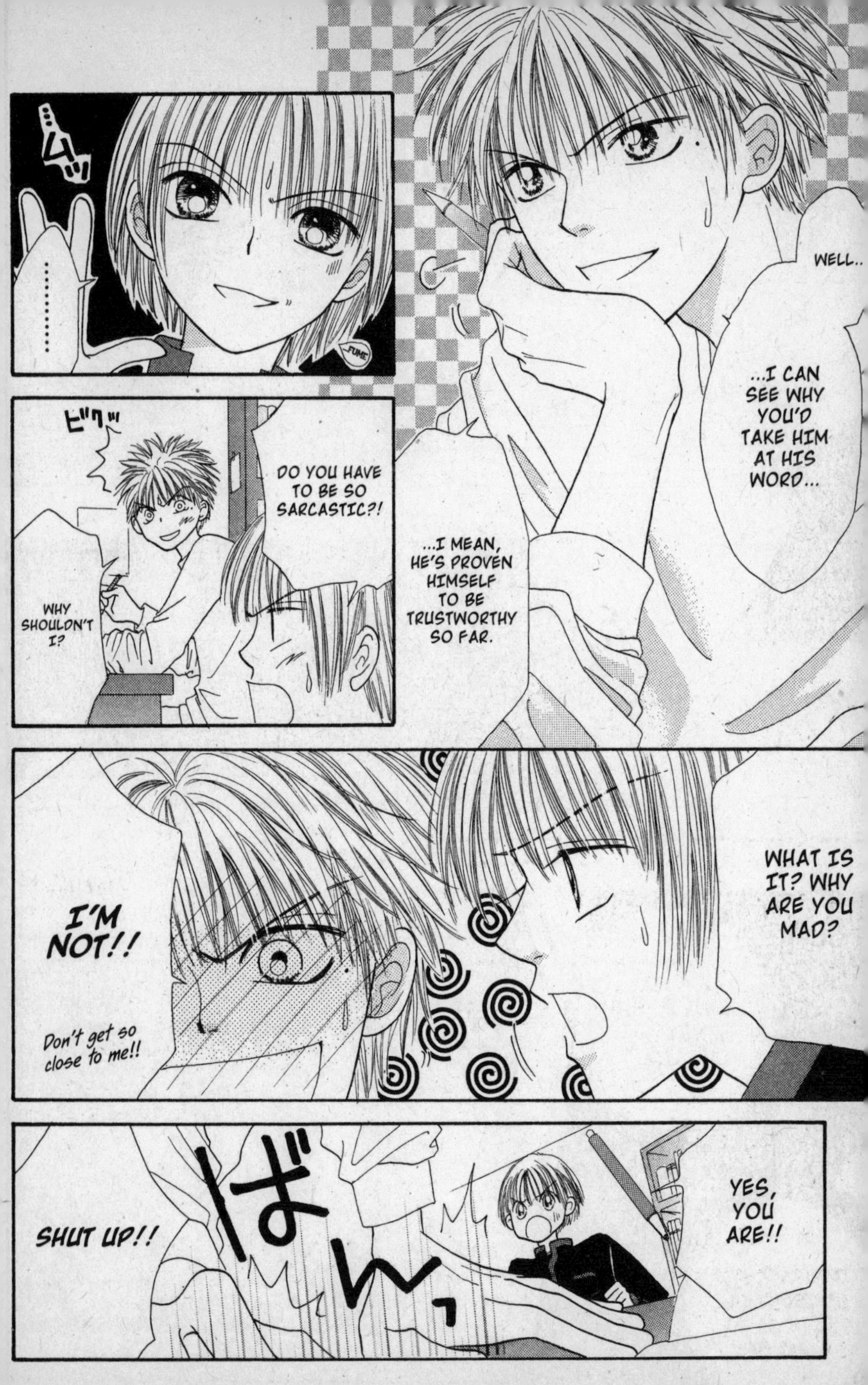
WELL..
...I CAN SEE WHY YOU'D TAKE HIM AT HIS WORD...
...I MEAN, HE'S PROVEN HIMSELF TO BE TRUSTWORTHY SO FAR.
ムッ
......
FUME
DO YOU HAVE TO BE SO SARCASTIC?!
ビクッ
WHY SHOULDN'T I?
WHAT IS IT? WHY ARE YOU MAD?
I'M NOT!!
Don't get so close to me!!
YES, YOU ARE!!
ばんっ
SHUT UP!!

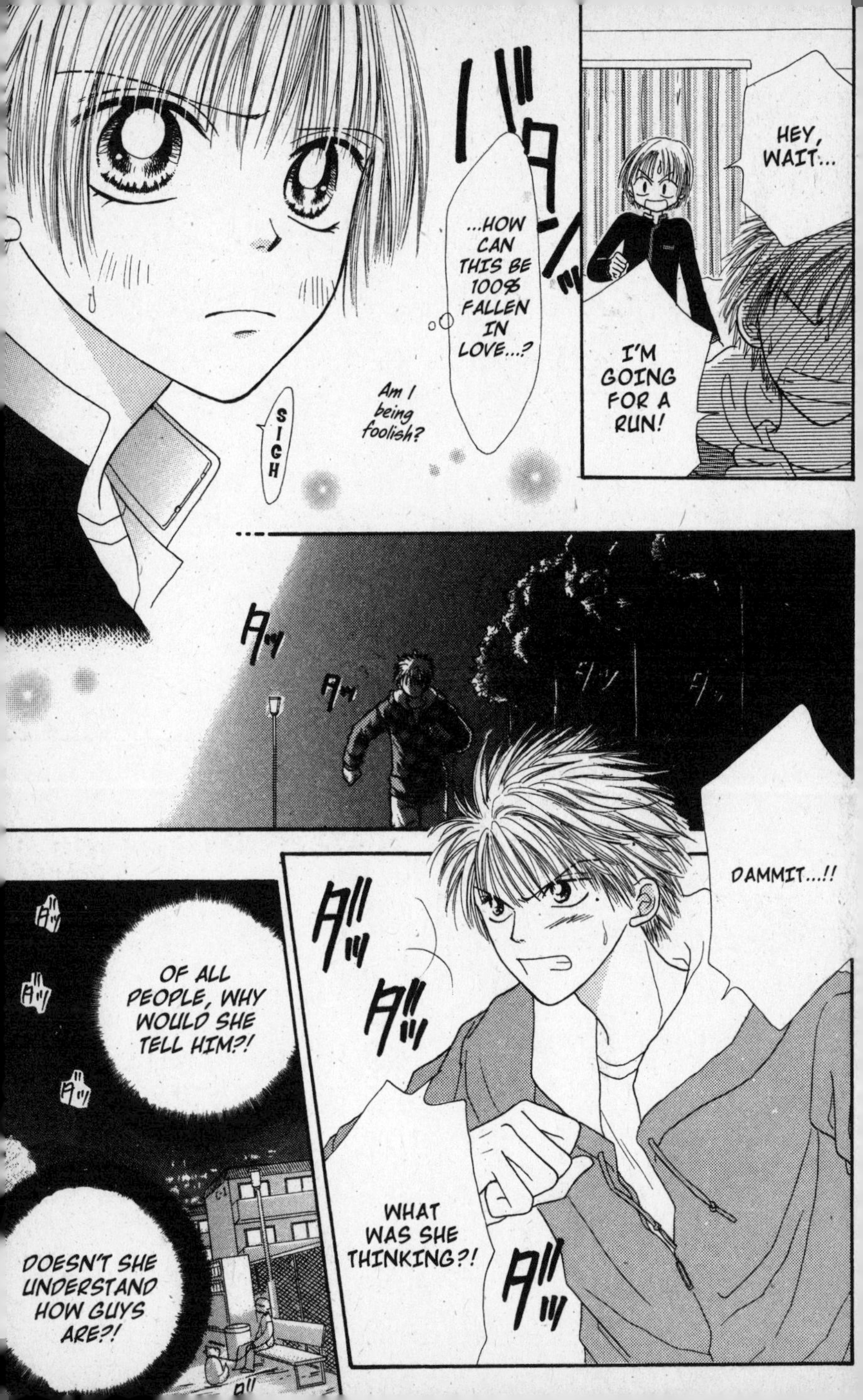
HEY, WAIT...
I'M GOING FOR A RUN!
バタン
...HOW CAN THIS BE 100% FALLEN IN LOVE...?
Am I being foolish?
SIGH
DAMMIT...!!
WHAT WAS SHE THINKING?!
OF ALL PEOPLE, WHY WOULD SHE TELL HIM?!
DOESN'T SHE UNDERSTAND HOW GUYS ARE?!

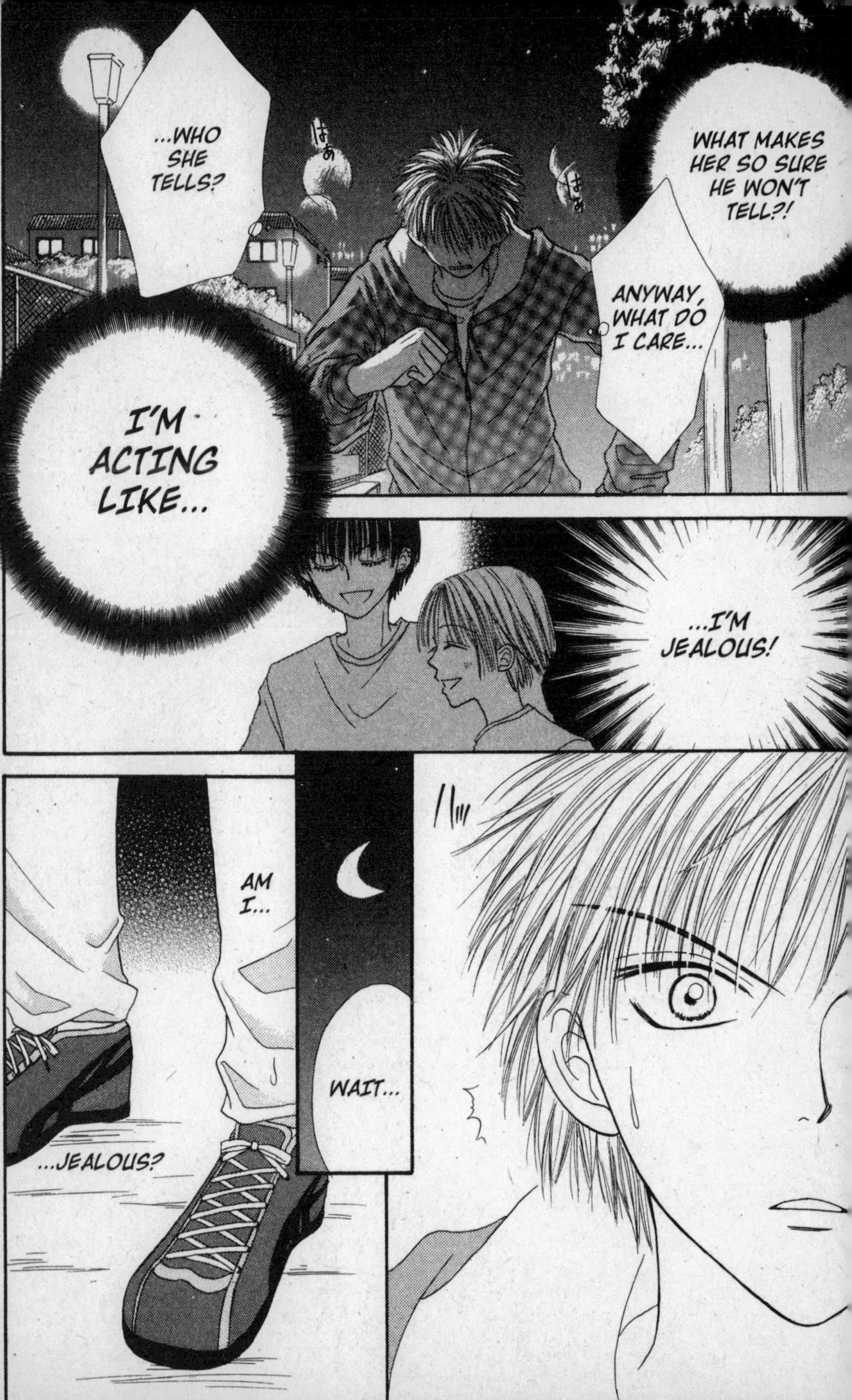
WHAT MAKES HER SO SURE HE WON'T TELL?!
ANYWAY, WHAT DO I CARE...
...WHO SHE TELLS?
I'M ACTING LIKE...
...I'M JEALOUS!
WAIT...
AM I...
...JEALOUS?

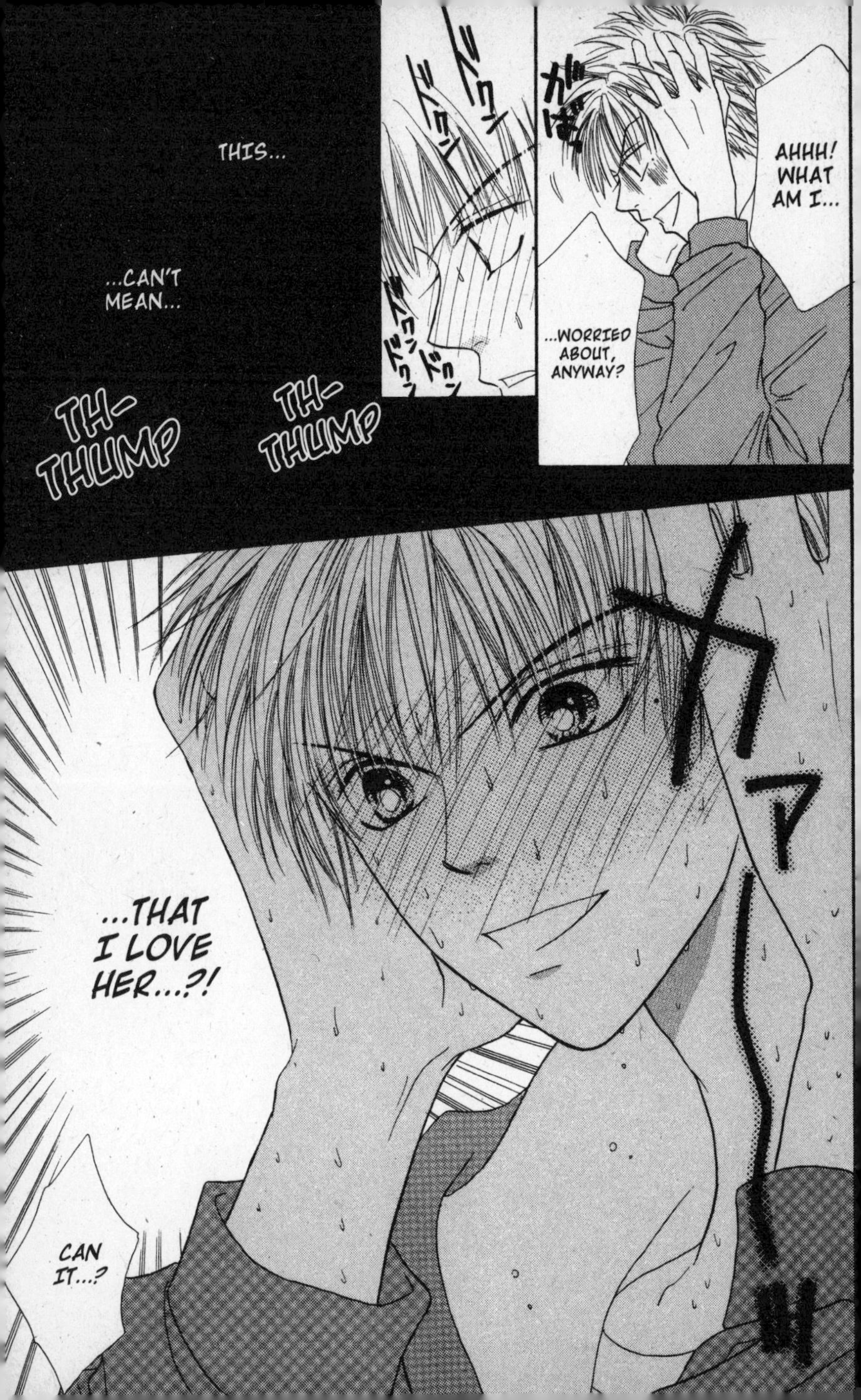
AHHH! WHAT AM I...
...WORRIED ABOUT, ANYWAY?
THIS...
...CAN'T MEAN...
TH-THUMP
TH-THUMP
...THAT I LOVE HER...?!
CAN IT...?

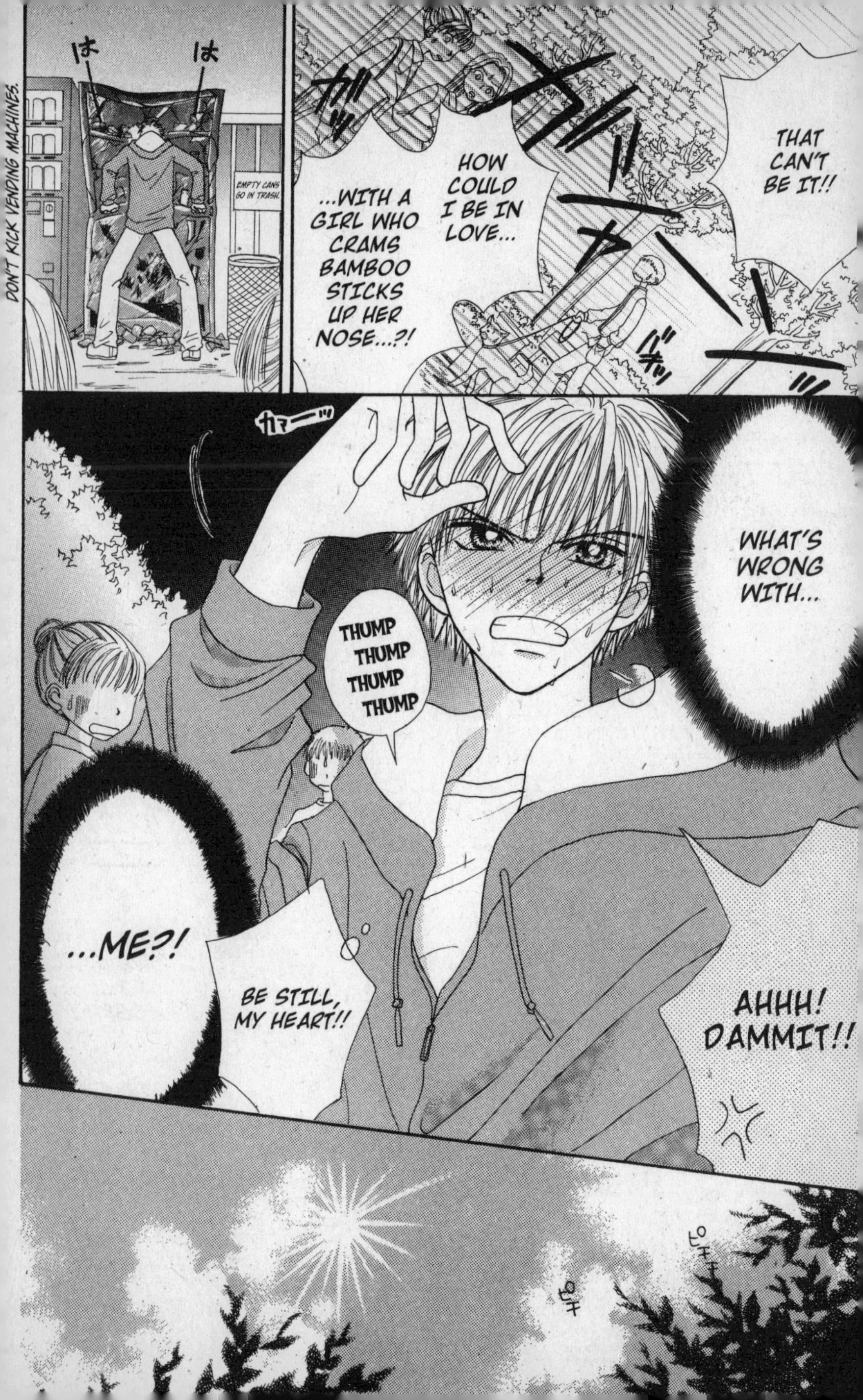
THAT CAN'T BE IT!!
HOW COULD I BE IN LOVE...
...WITH A GIRL WHO CRAMS BAMBOO STICKS UP HER NOSE...?!
は
は
EMPTY CANS GO IN TRASH.
DON'T KICK VENDING MACHINES.
カァーッ
WHAT'S WRONG WITH...
THUMP THUMP THUMP THUMP
...ME?!
AHHH! DAMMIT!!
BE STILL, MY HEART!!
ピチチ
ピチ

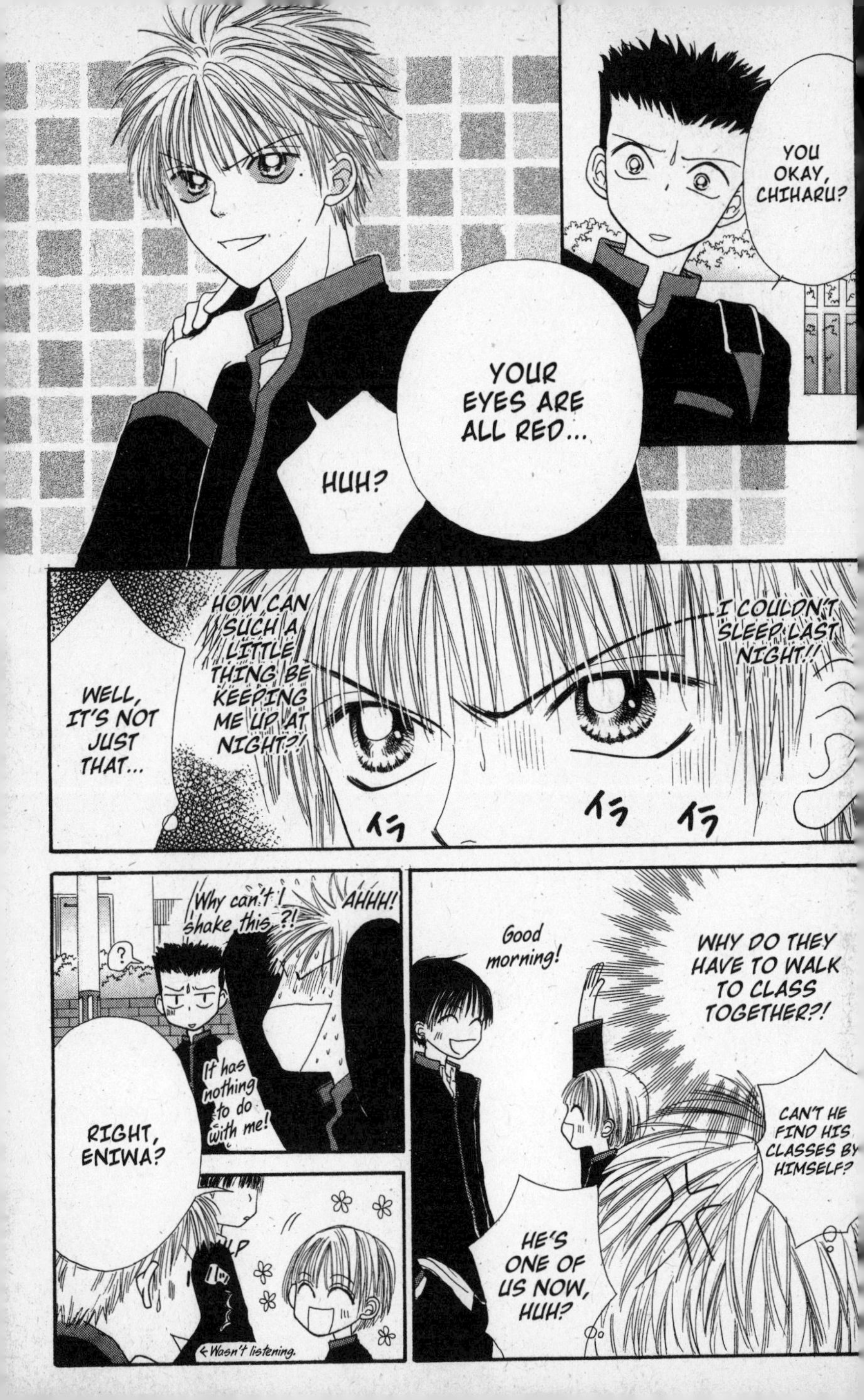
YOU OKAY, CHIHARU?
YOUR EYES ARE ALL RED...
HUH?
I COULDN'T SLEEP LAST NIGHT!!
HOW CAN SUCH A LITTLE THING BE KEEPING ME UP AT NIGHT?!
WELL, IT'S NOT JUST THAT...
イラ
イラ
イラ
Good morning!
WHY DO THEY HAVE TO WALK TO CLASS TOGETHER?!
CAN'T HE FIND HIS CLASSES BY HIMSELF?
HE'S ONE OF US NOW, HUH?
AHHH!
Why can't I shake this?!
?
It has nothing to do with me!
RIGHT, ENIWA?
← Wasn't listening.

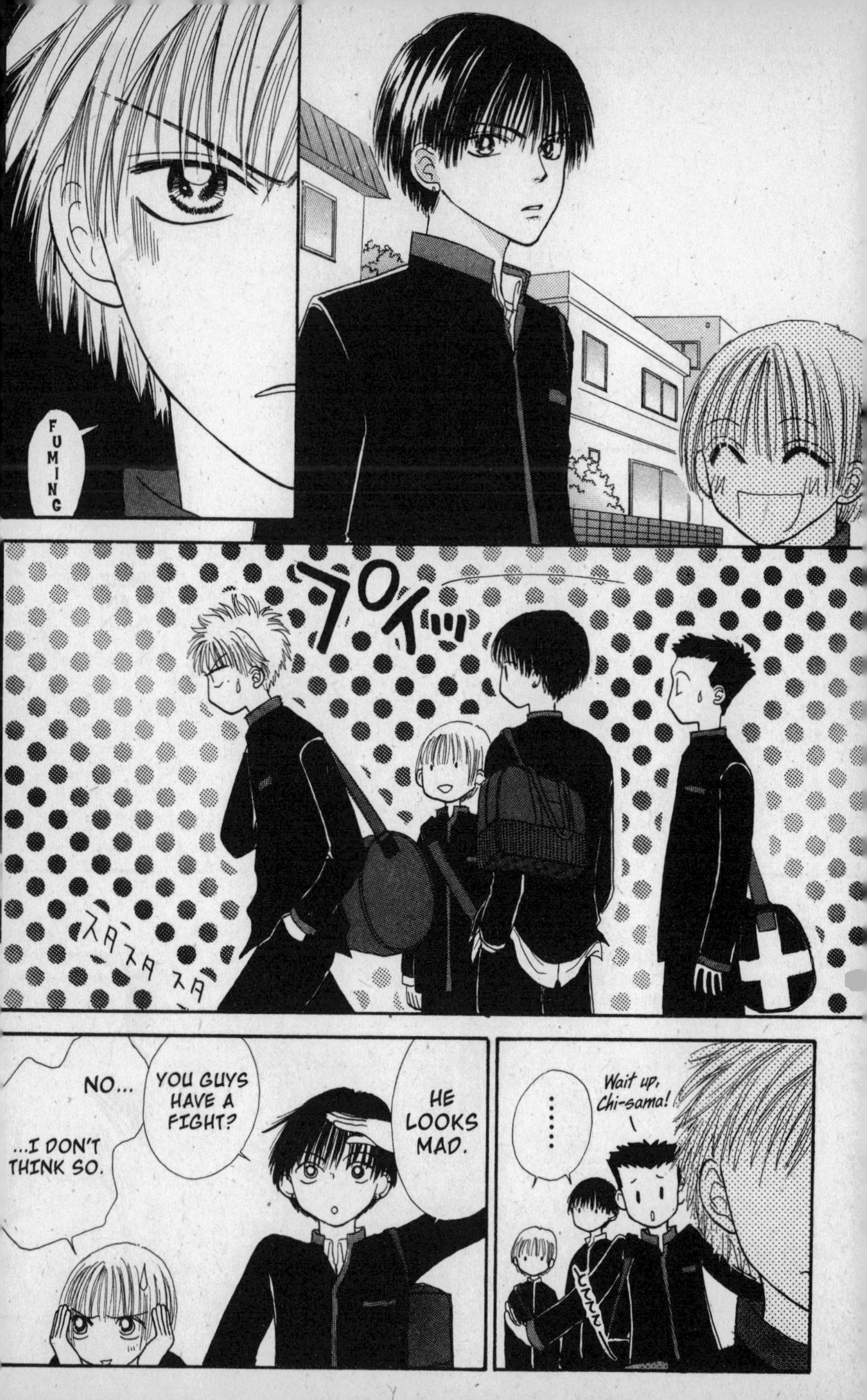
FUMING
プイッ
スタスタ スタ
Wait up, Chi-sama!
......
HE LOOKS MAD.
YOU GUYS HAVE A FIGHT?
NO...
...I DON'T THINK SO.

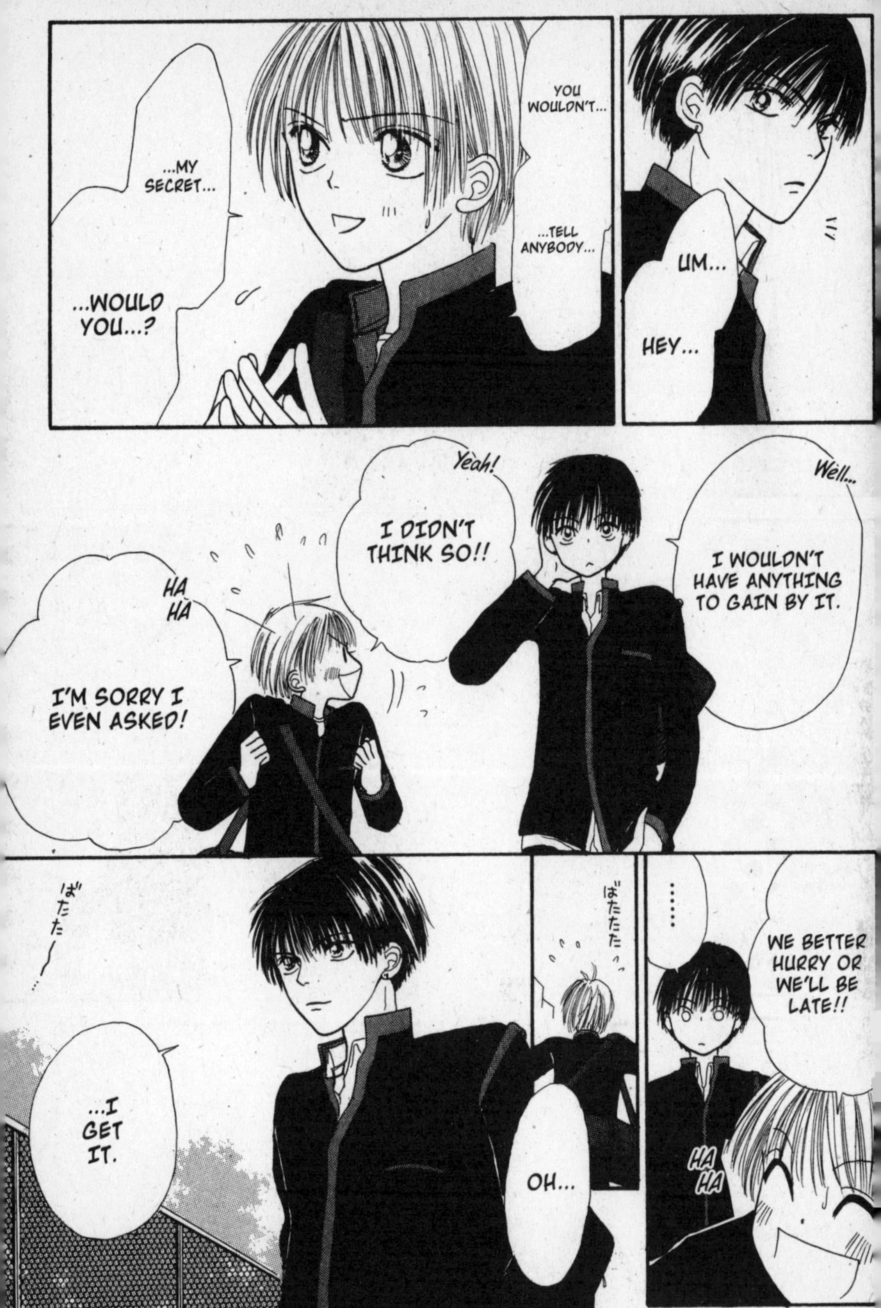
UM...
HEY...
YOU WOULDN'T...
...TELL ANYBODY...
...MY SECRET...
...WOULD YOU...?
Well...
I WOULDN'T HAVE ANYTHING TO GAIN BY IT.
Yeah!
I DIDN'T THINK SO!!
HA HA
I'M SORRY I EVEN ASKED!
WE BETTER HURRY OR WE'LL BE LATE!!
......
HA HA
ばたたた
OH...
ばたた—…
...I GET IT.

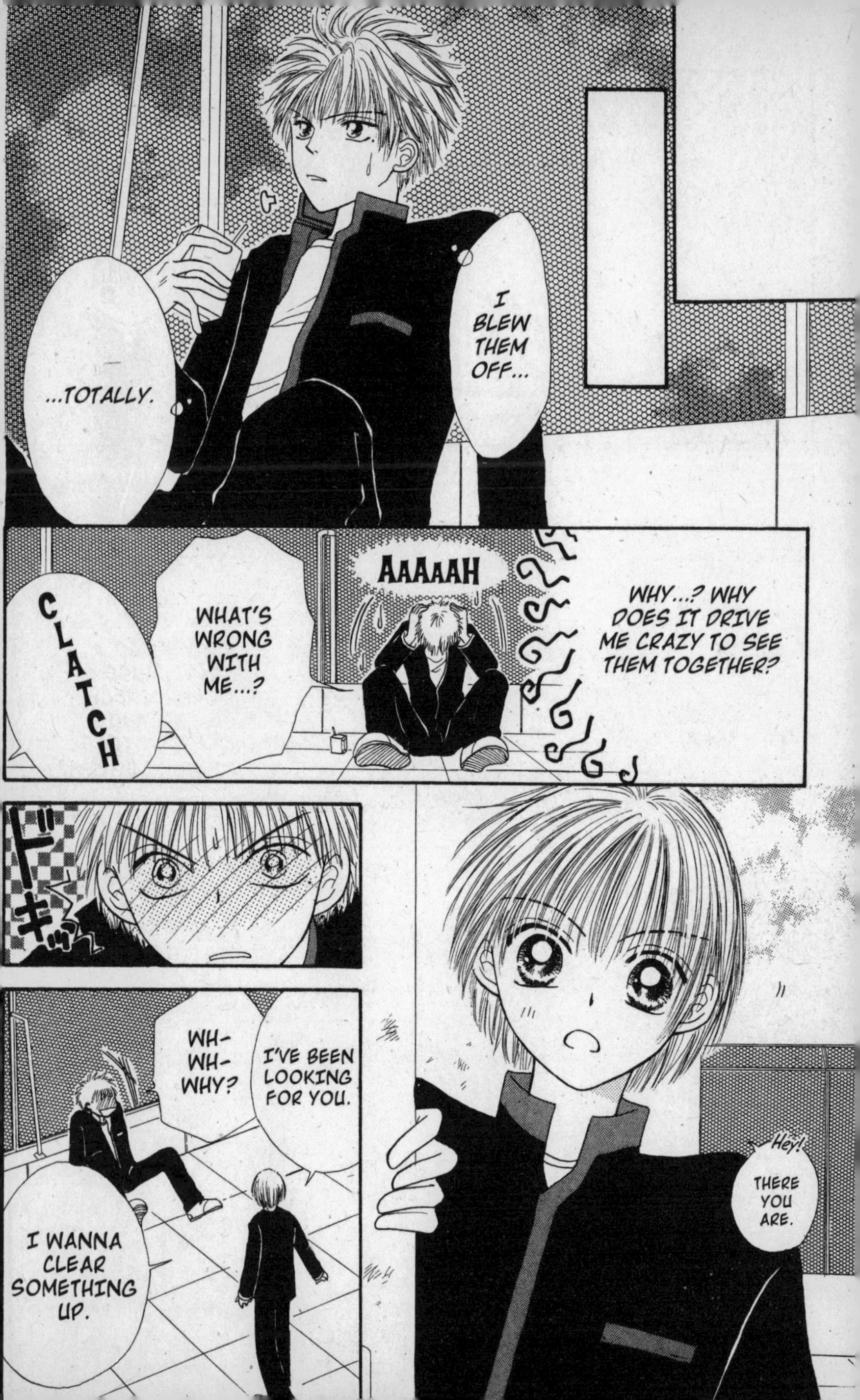
I BLEW THEM OFF...
...TOTALLY.
WHY...? WHY DOES IT DRIVE ME CRAZY TO SEE THEM TOGETHER?
AAAAAH
WHAT'S WRONG WITH ME...?
CLATCH
Hey!
THERE YOU ARE.
ドキッ
I'VE BEEN LOOKING FOR YOU.
WH-WH-WHY?
I WANNA CLEAR SOMETHING UP.

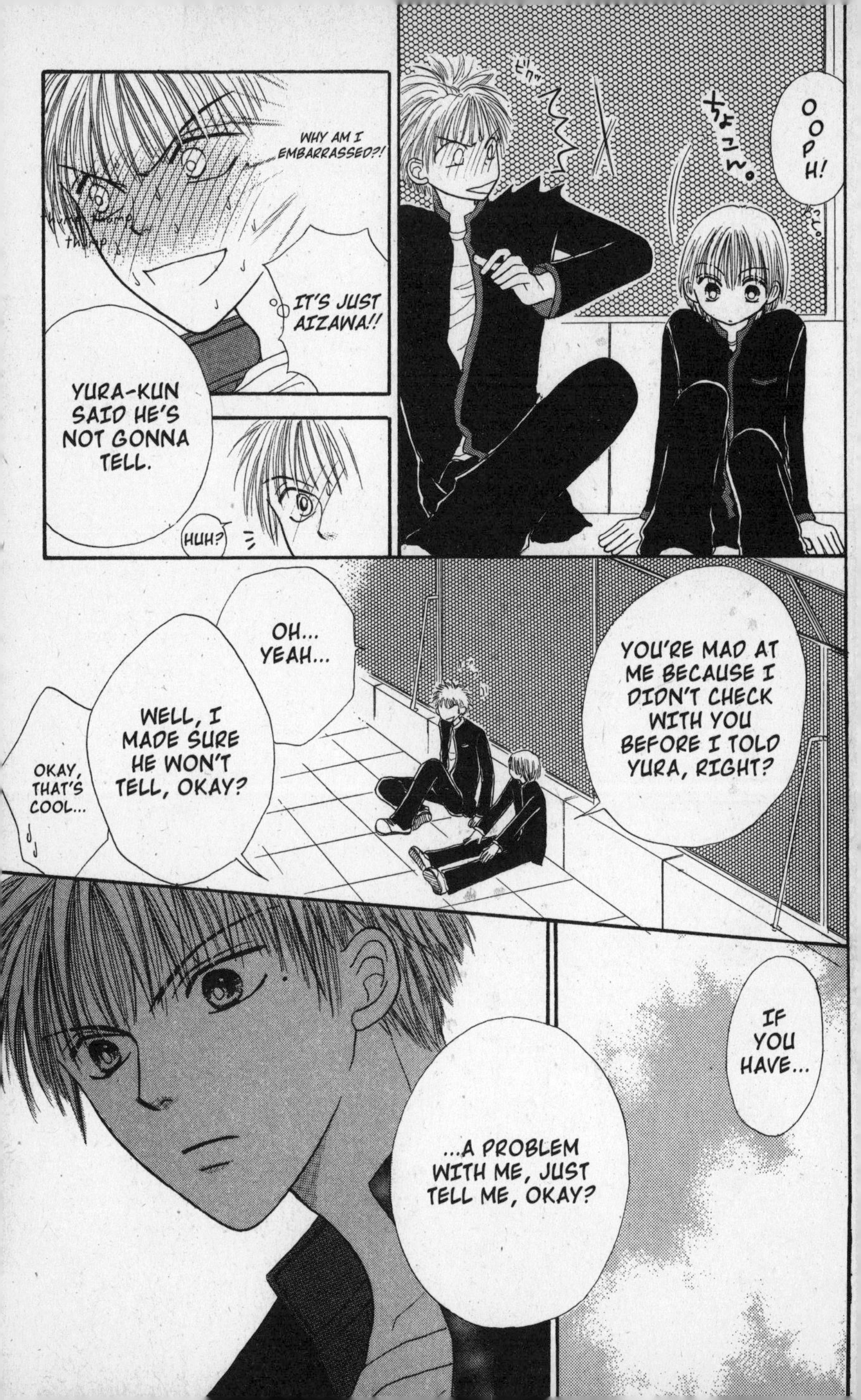
OOPH!
ちょこん。
WHY AM I EMBARRASSED?!
IT'S JUST AIZAWA!!
YURA-KUN SAID HE'S NOT GONNA TELL.
HUH?
YOU'RE MAD AT ME BECAUSE I DIDN'T CHECK WITH YOU BEFORE I TOLD YURA, RIGHT?
OH... YEAH...
WELL, I MADE SURE HE WON'T TELL, OKAY?
OKAY, THAT'S COOL...
IF YOU HAVE...
...A PROBLEM WITH ME, JUST TELL ME, OKAY?

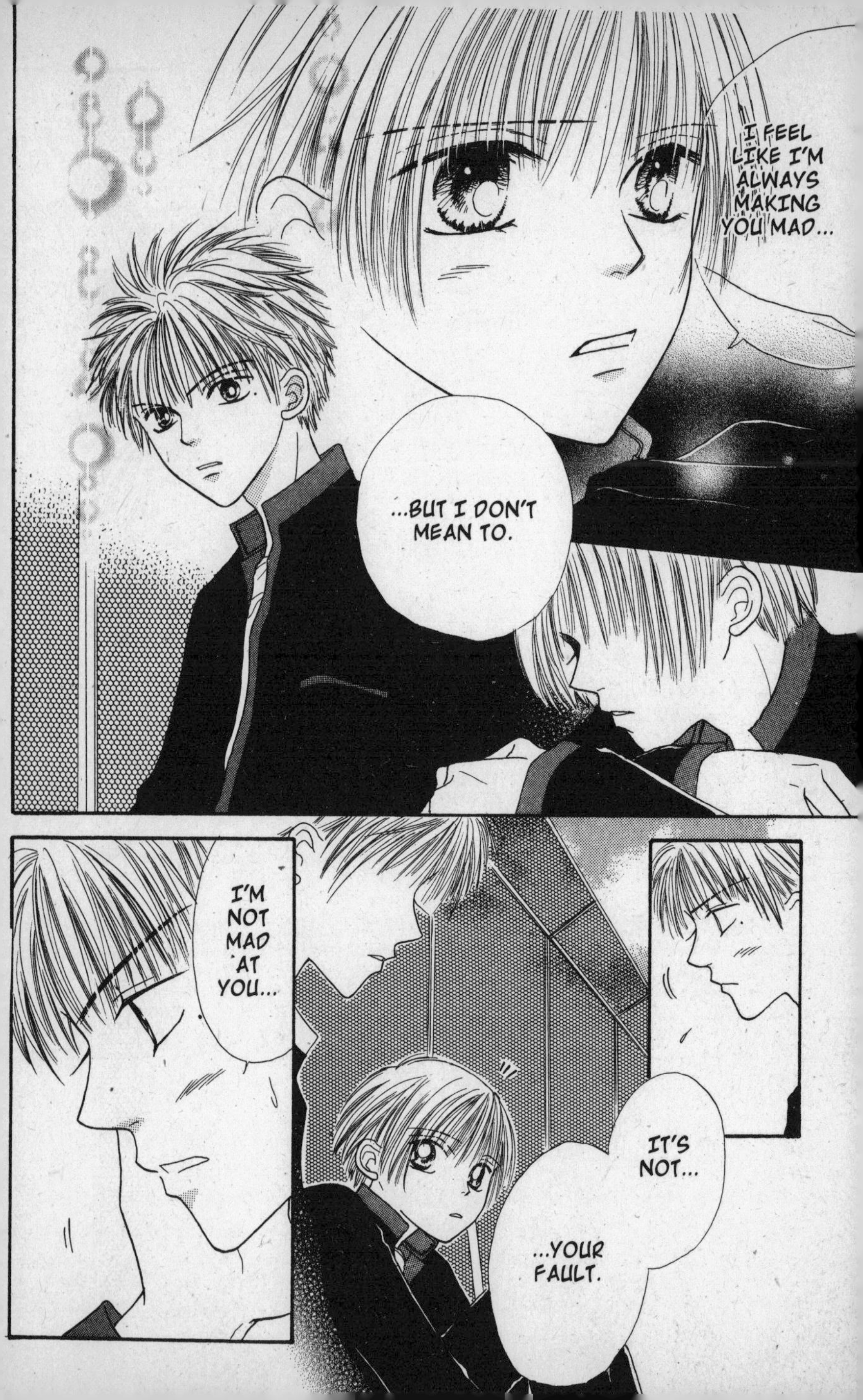
I FEEL LIKE I'M ALWAYS MAKING YOU MAD...
...BUT I DON'T MEAN TO.
I'M NOT MAD AT YOU...
IT'S NOT...
...YOUR FAULT.

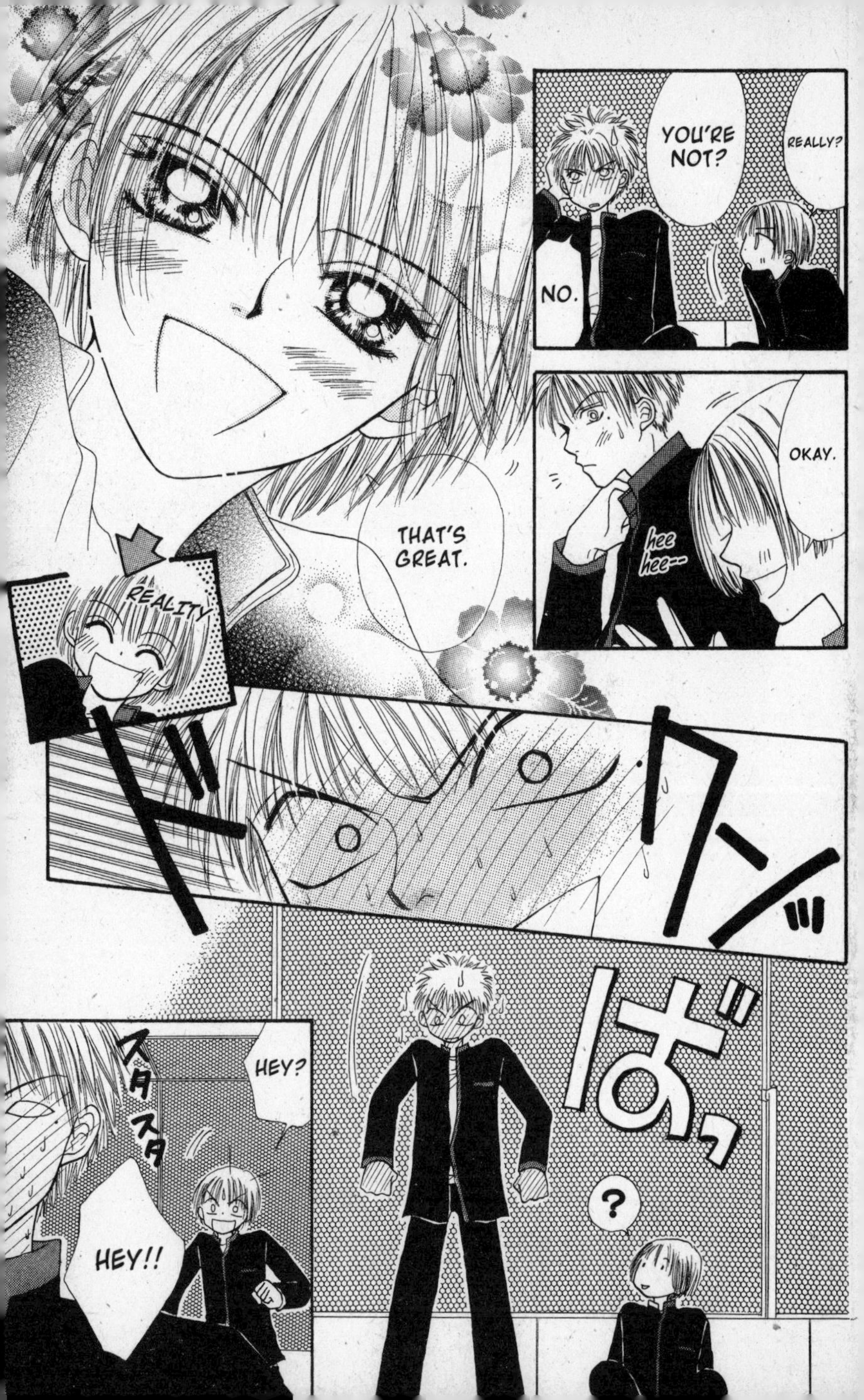
REALLY?
YOU'RE NOT?
NO.
OKAY.
hee hee--
THAT'S GREAT.
REALITY
ばっ
?
HEY?
スタスタ
HEY!!

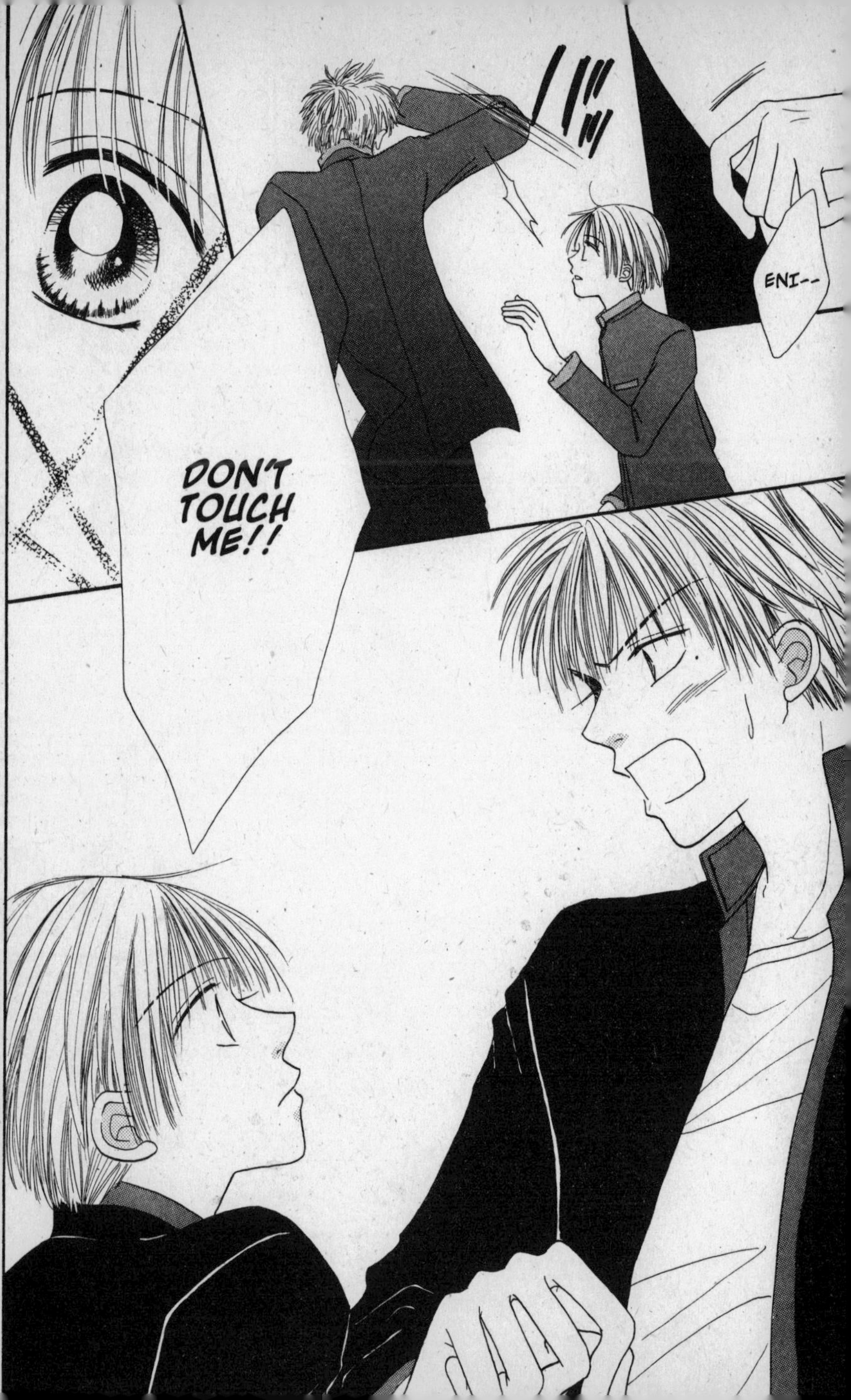
ENI--
DON'T TOUCH ME!!

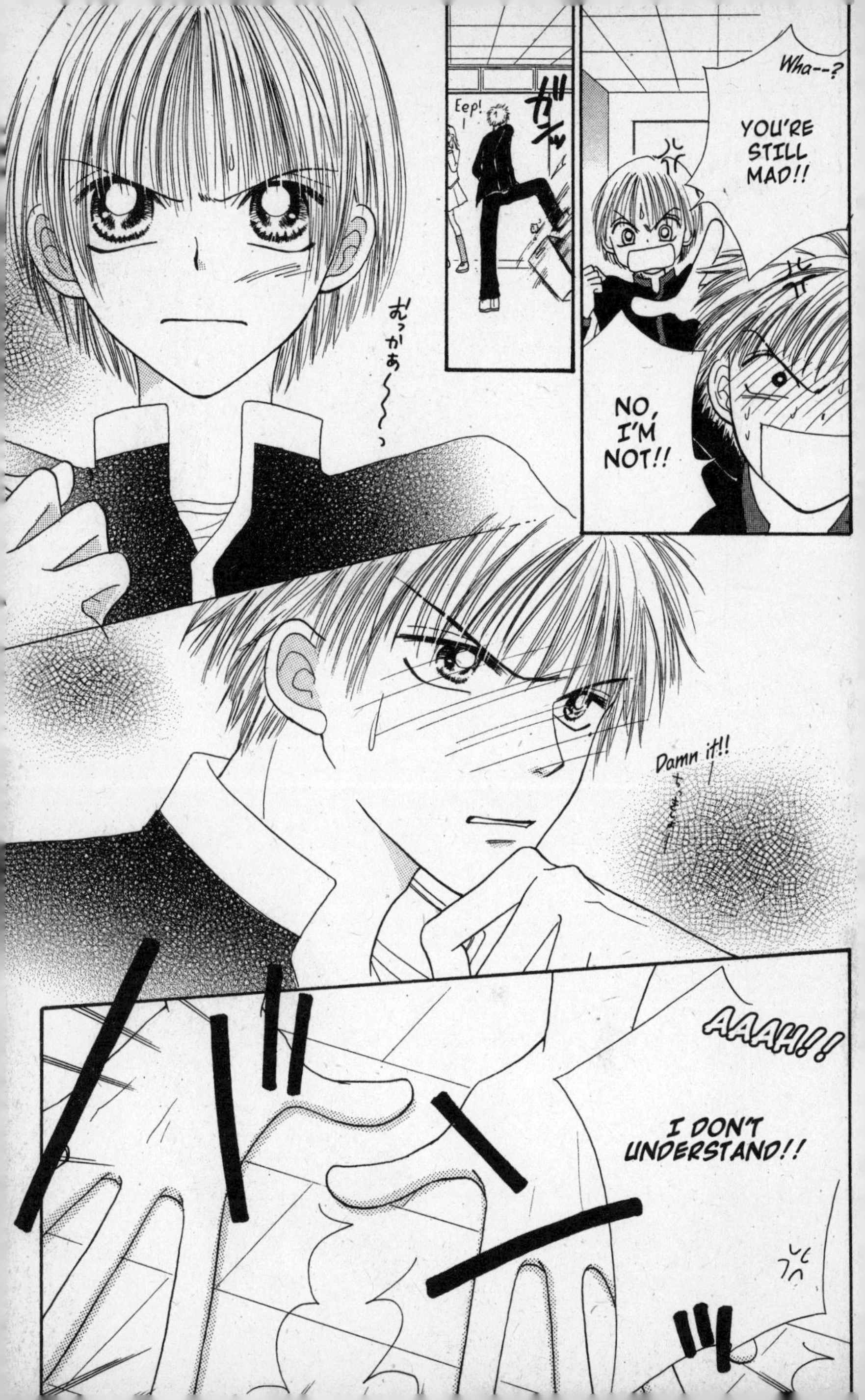
Wha--?
YOU'RE STILL MAD!!
NO, I'M NOT!!
Eep!
おっかあ〜〜っ
Damn it!!
AAAH!!
I DON'T UNDERSTAND!!

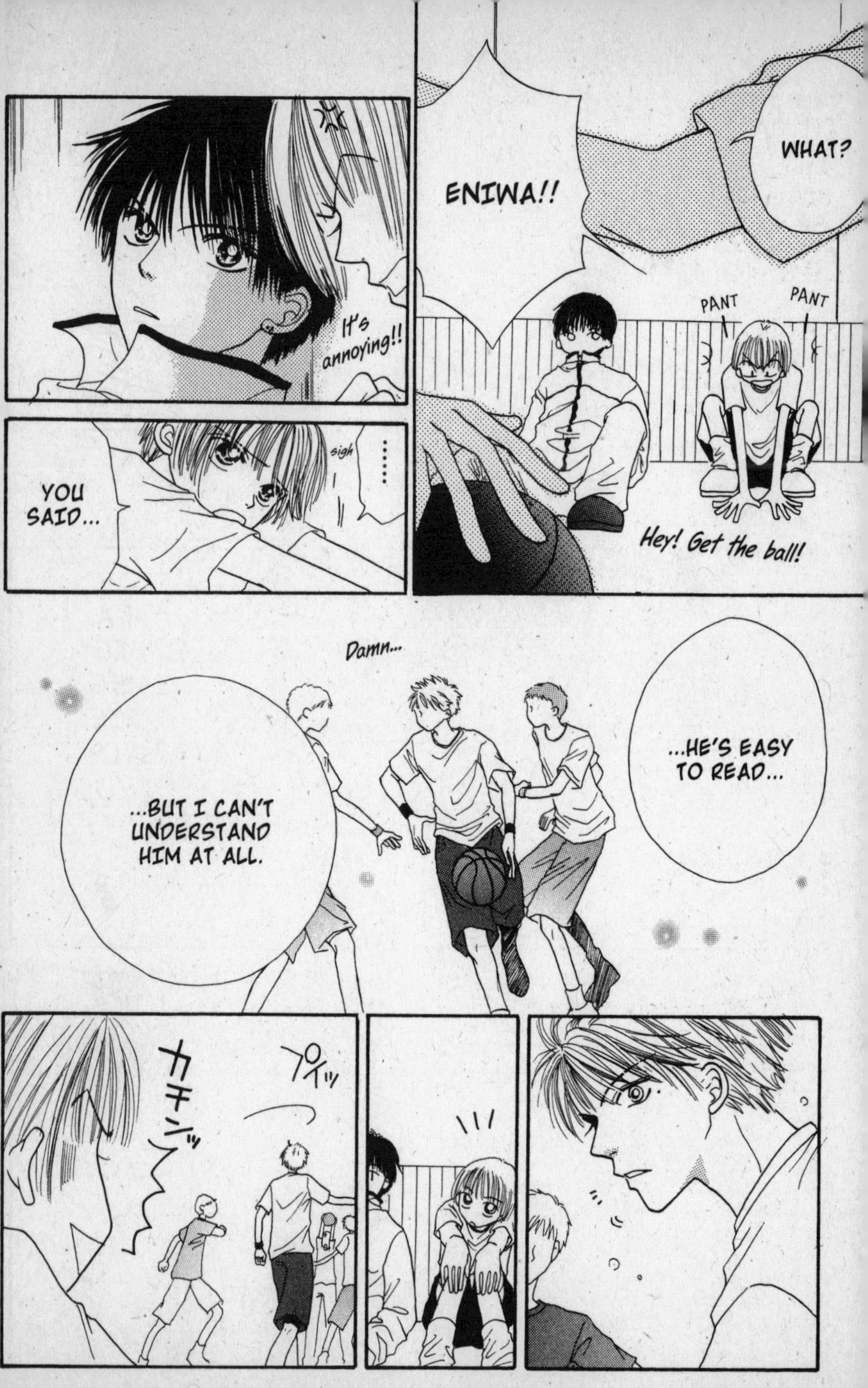
WHAT?
ENIWA!!
PANT
PANT
Hey! Get the ball!
It's annoying!!
sigh
……
YOU SAID...
Damn...
...HE'S EASY TO READ...
...BUT I CAN'T UNDERSTAND HIM AT ALL.
プイッ
カチンッ

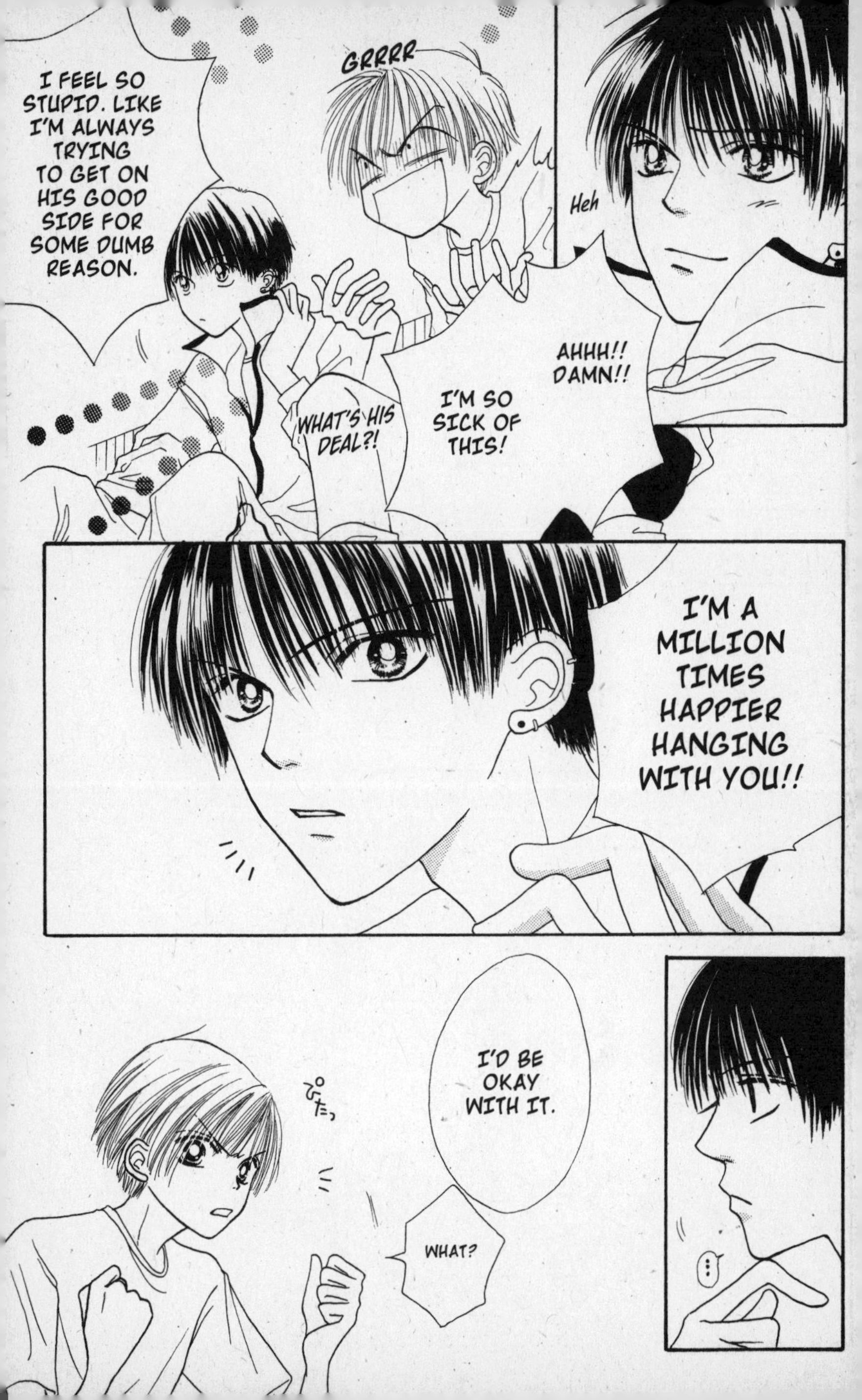
Heh
AHHH!! DAMN!!
I'M SO SICK OF THIS!
WHAT'S HIS DEAL?!
GRRRR
I FEEL SO STUPID. LIKE I'M ALWAYS TRYING TO GET ON HIS GOOD SIDE FOR SOME DUMB REASON.
I'M A MILLION TIMES HAPPIER HANGING WITH YOU!!
...
I'D BE OKAY WITH IT.
ぴたっ
WHAT?

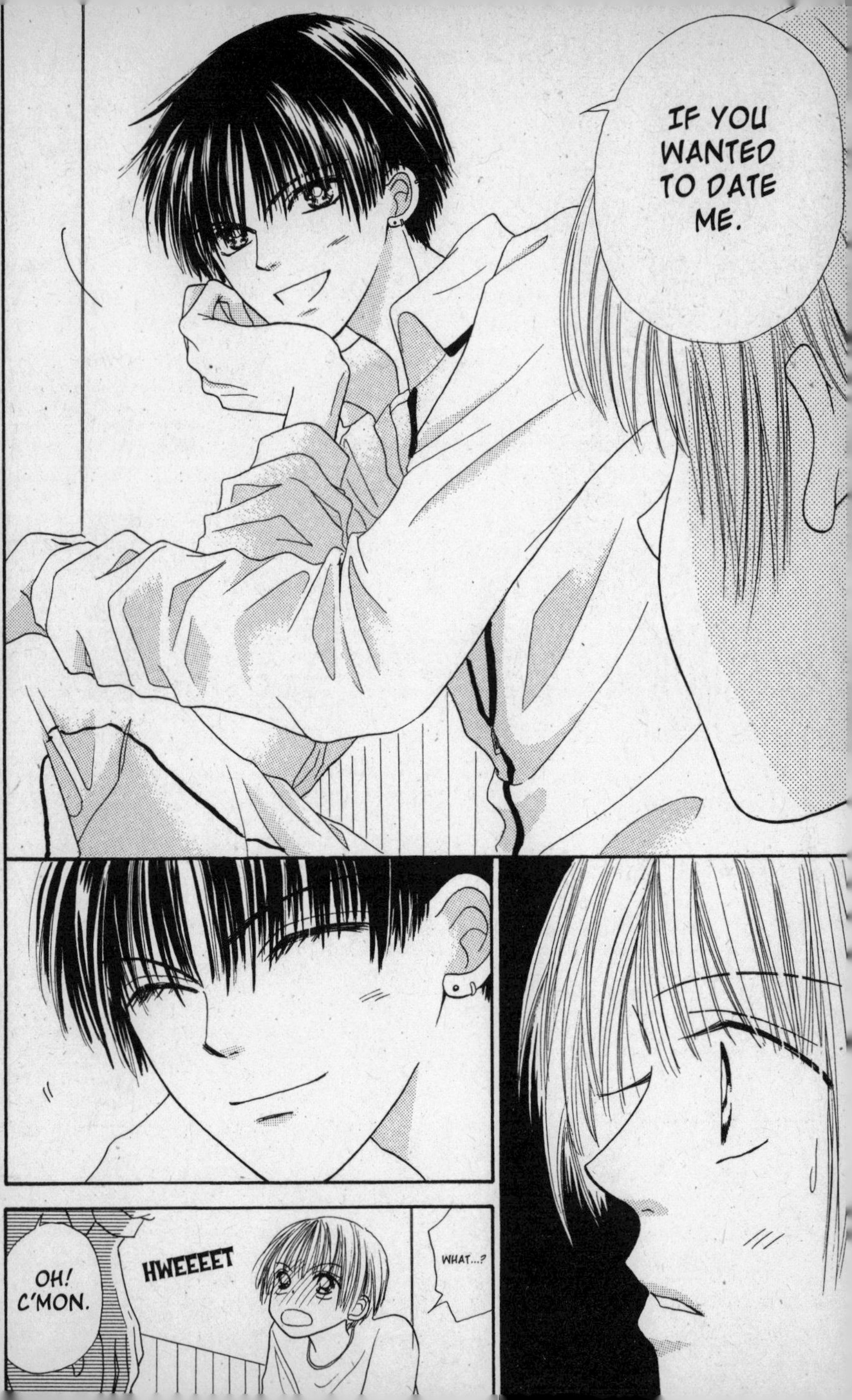
IF YOU WANTED TO DATE ME.
WHAT...?
HWEEEET
OH! C'MON.

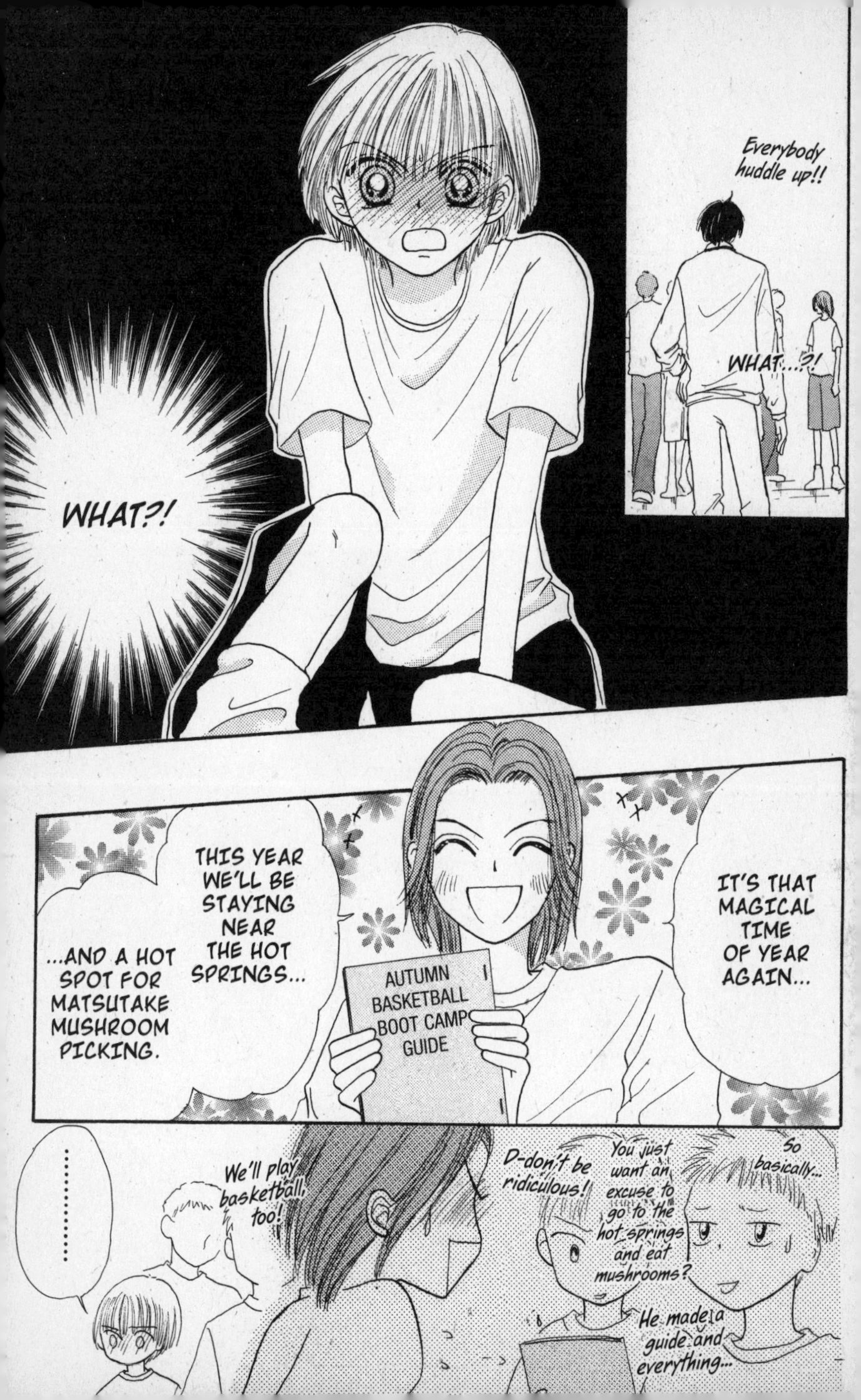
Everybody huddle up!!
WHAT...?!
WHAT?!
IT'S THAT MAGICAL TIME OF YEAR AGAIN...
AUTUMN BASKETBALL BOOT CAMP GUIDE
THIS YEAR WE'LL BE STAYING NEAR THE HOT SPRINGS...
...AND A HOT SPOT FOR MATSUTAKE MUSHROOM PICKING.
So basically...
You just want an excuse to go to the hot springs and eat mushrooms?
He made a guide and everything...
D-don't be ridiculous!
We'll play basketball, too!
.........

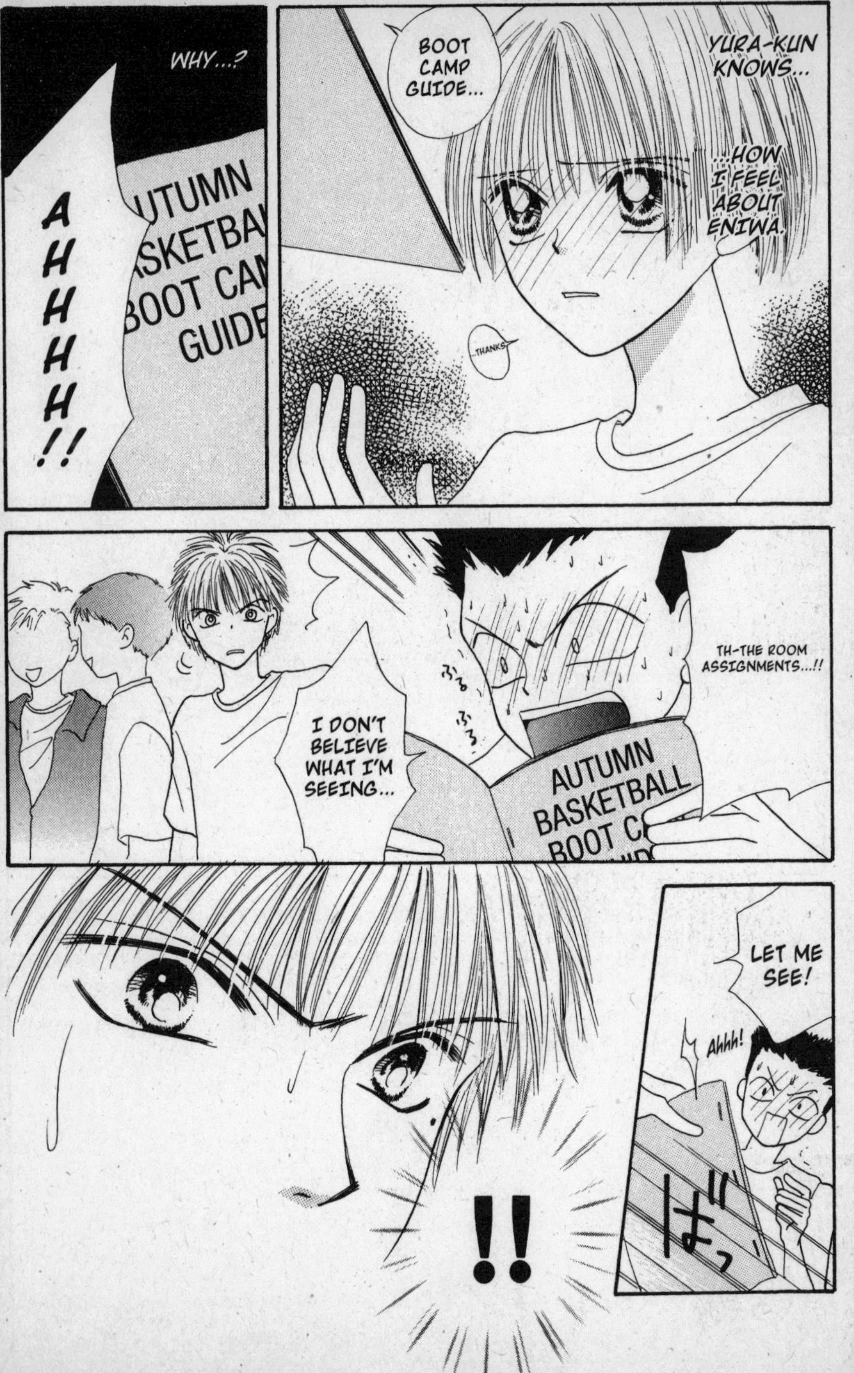
YURA-KUN KNOWS...
...HOW I FEEL ABOUT ENIWA.
BOOT CAMP GUIDE...
...THANKS
WHY...?
AHHHHH!!
TH-THE ROOM ASSIGNMENTS...!!
ぶる ぶる
AUTUMN BASKETBALL
I DON'T BELIEVE WHAT I'M SEEING...
LET ME SEE!
Ahhh!
ばっ
!!

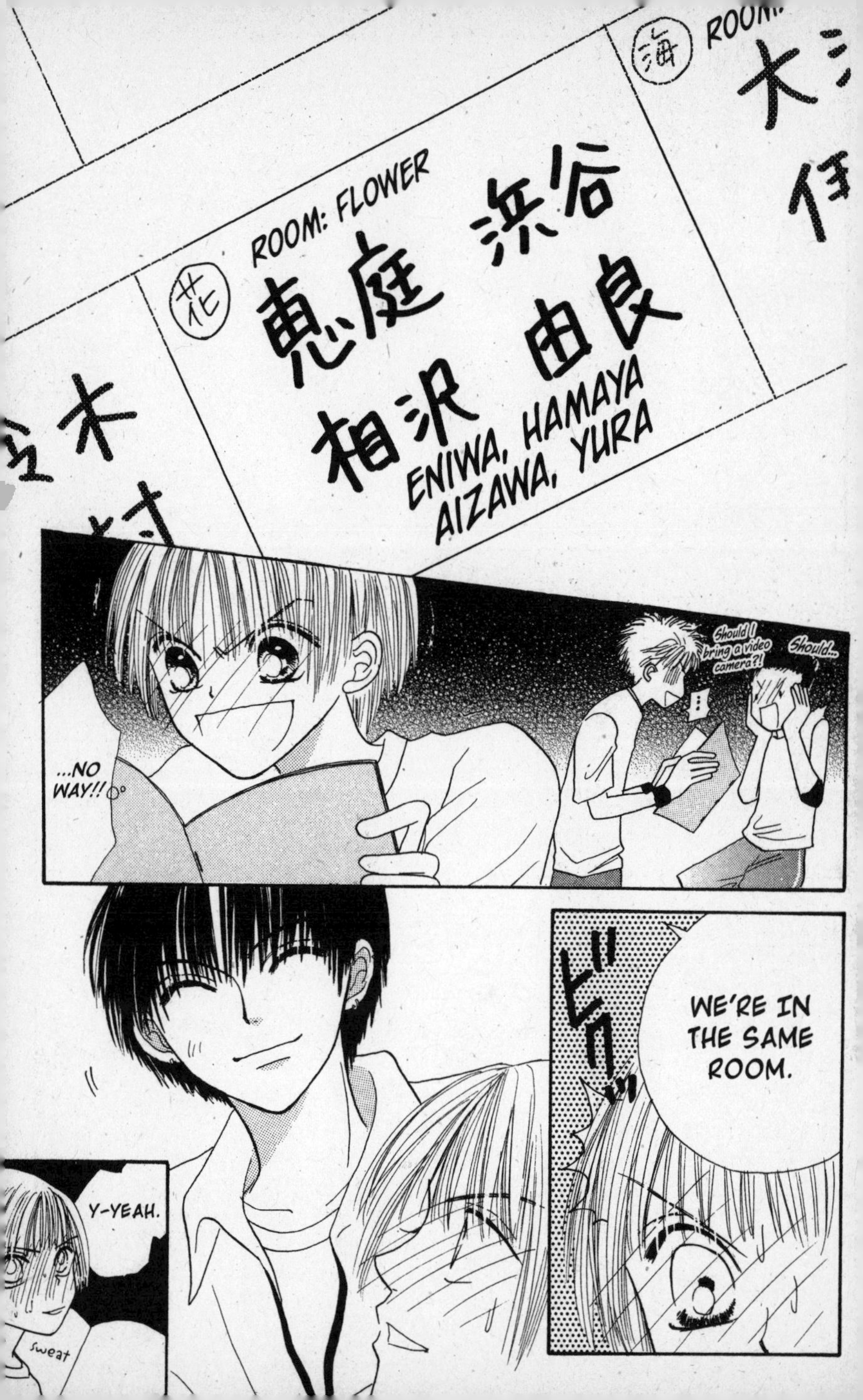
ROOM: FLOWER
恵庭 浜谷
相沢 由良
ENIWA, HAMAYA
AIZAWA, YURA
Should...
Should I bring a video camera?!
...NO WAY!!
WE'RE IN THE SAME ROOM.
Y-YEAH.
sweat

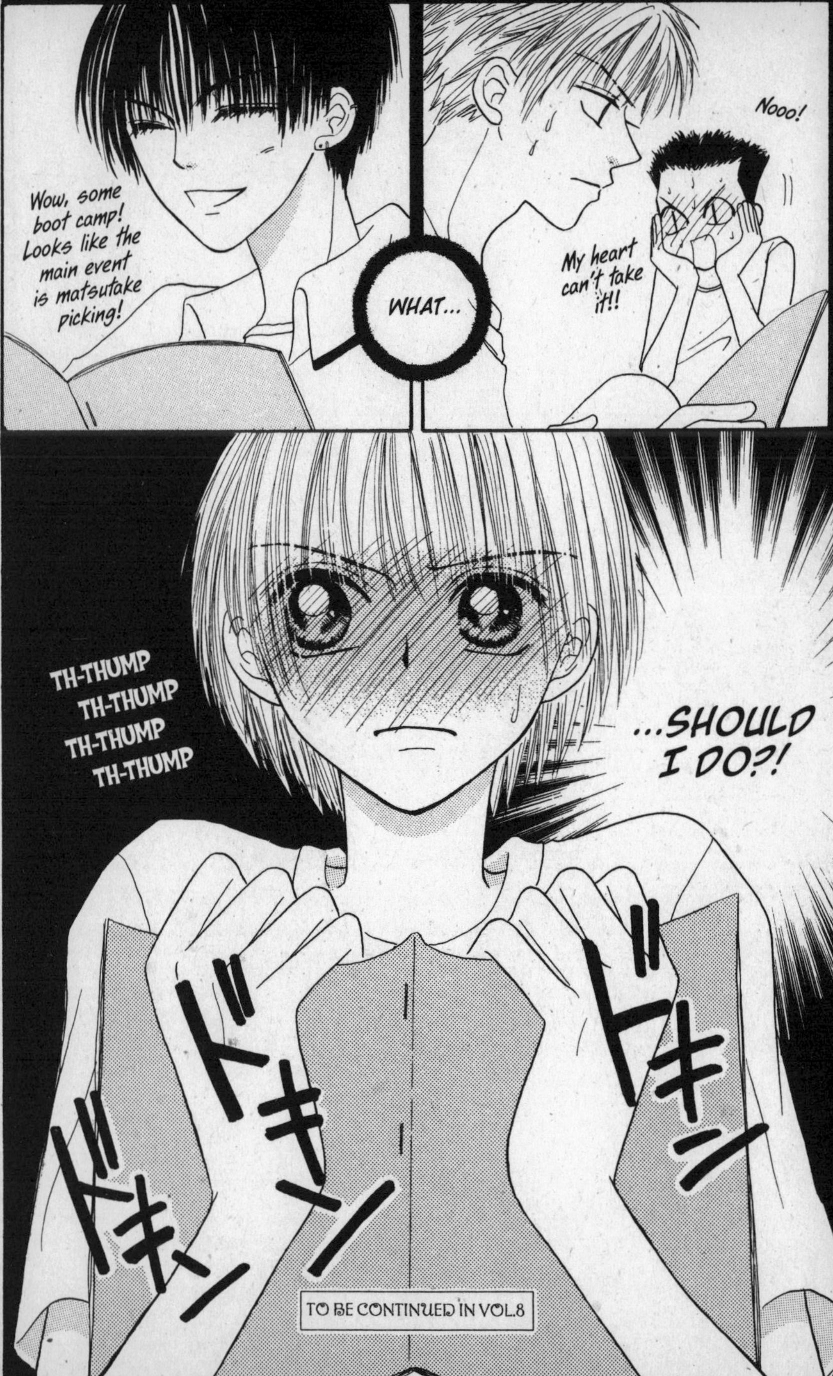
Nooo!
My heart can't take it!!
Wow, some boot camp! Looks like the main event is matsutake picking!
WHAT...
...SHOULD I DO?!
ドキン
ドキン
TH-THUMP TH-THUMP TH-THUMP TH-THUMP
ドキン
ドキン
TO BE CONTINUED IN VOL.8

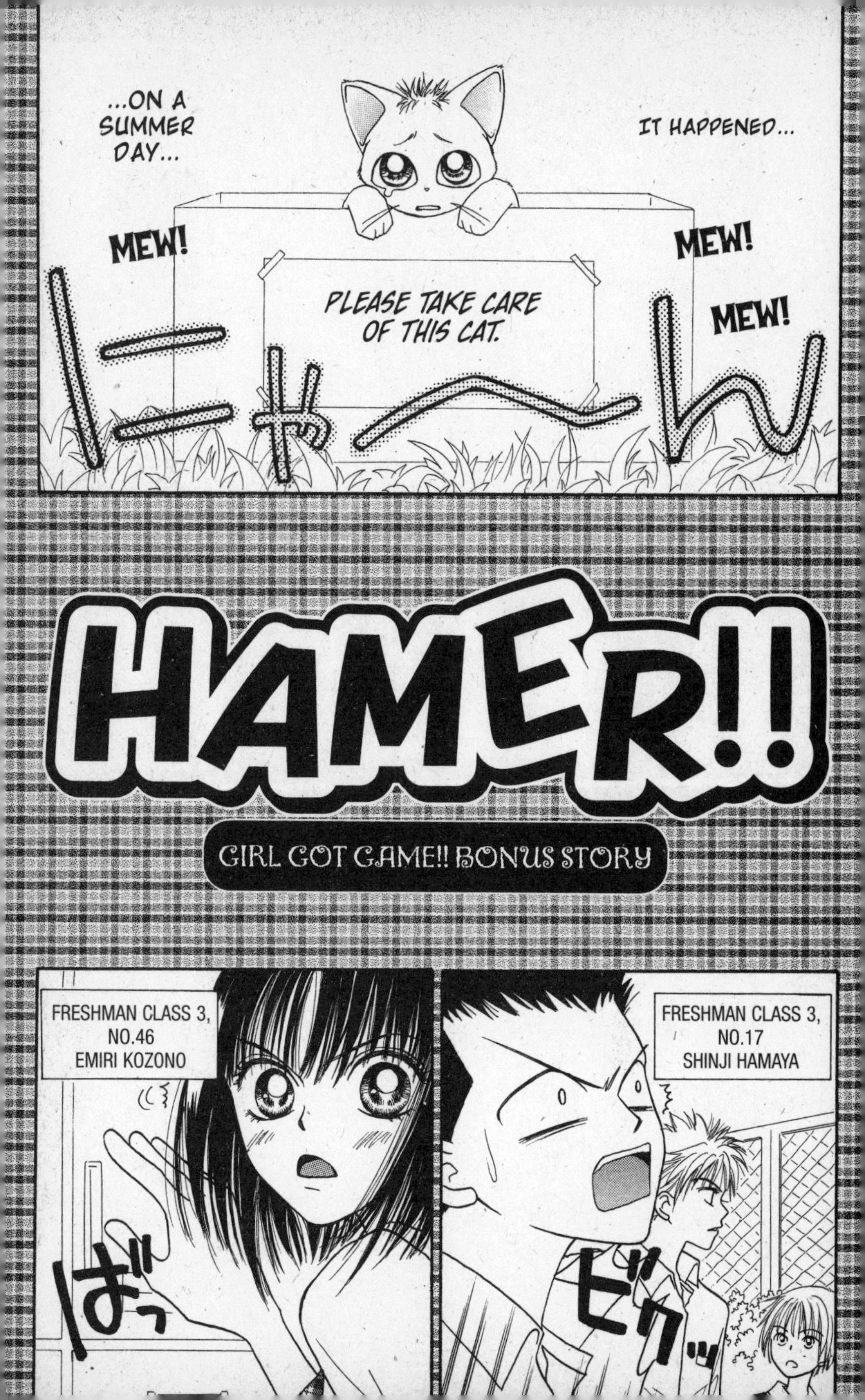

IT HAPPENED...
MEW!
MEW!
PLEASE TAKE CARE OF THIS CAT.
MEW!
にゃーん
...ON A SUMMER DAY...
HAMER!!
GIRL GOT GAME!! BONUS STORY
FRESHMAN CLASS 3, NO.17 SHINJI HAMAYA
ビクッ
FRESHMAN CLASS 3, NO.46 EMIRI KOZONO
ばっ

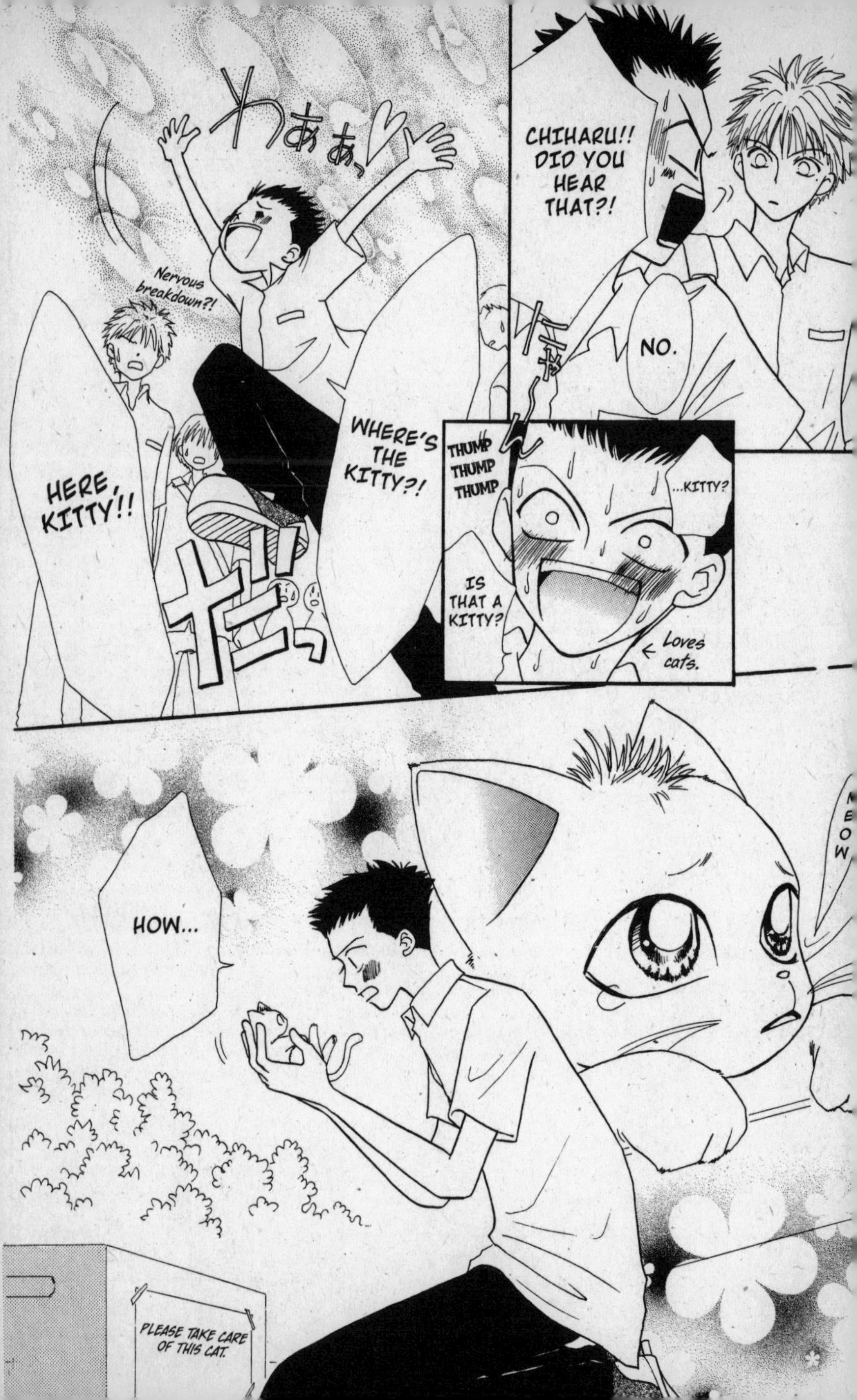
CHIHARU!! DID YOU HEAR THAT?!
NO.
THUMP THUMP THUMP
...KITTY?
IS THAT A KITTY?
Loves cats.
WHERE'S THE KITTY?!
Nervous breakdown?!
HERE, KITTY!!
MEOW
HOW...
PLEASE TAKE CARE OF THIS CAT.

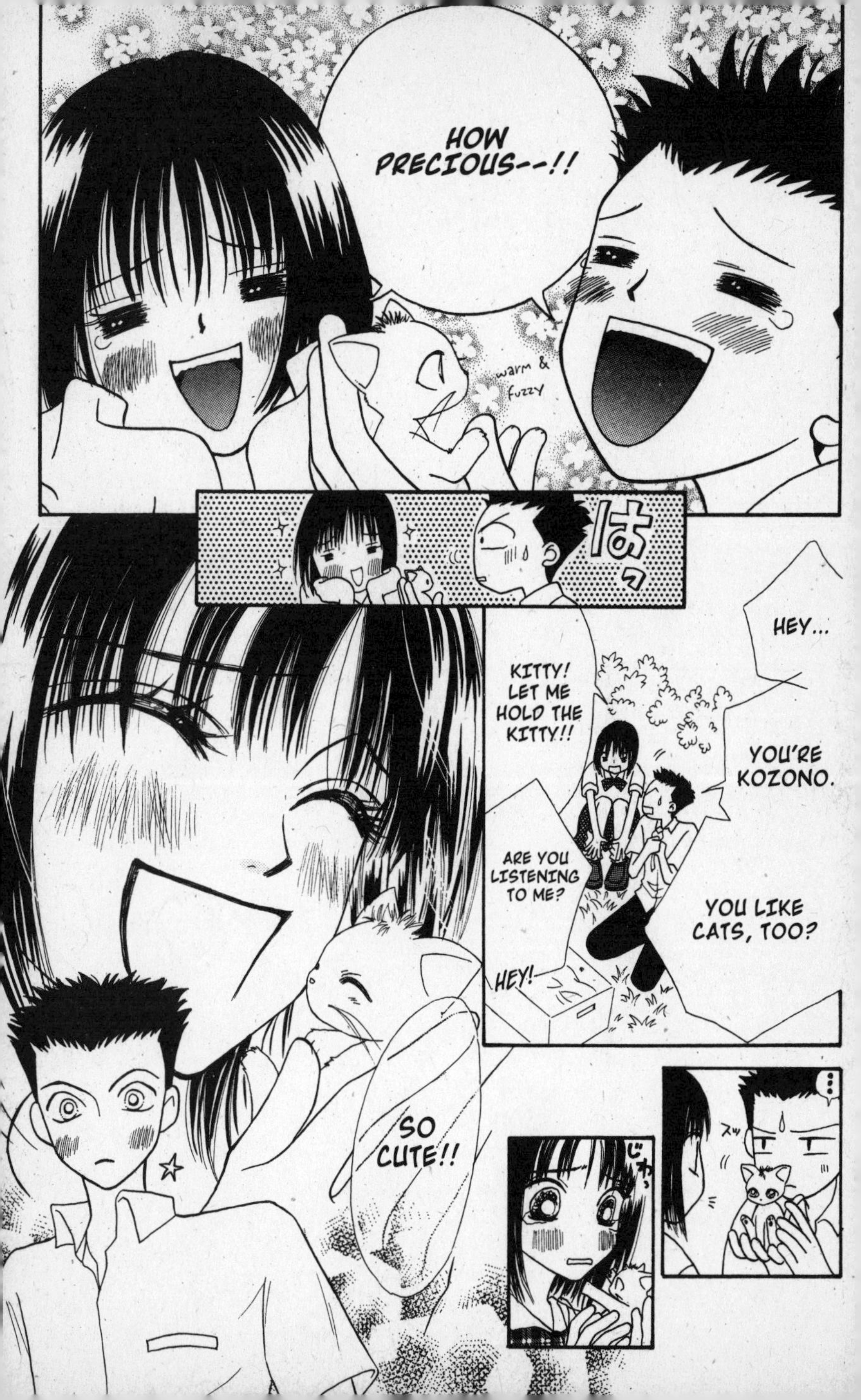
HOW PRECIOUS--!!
warm & fuzzy
はっ
HEY...
YOU'RE KOZONO.
KITTY! LET ME HOLD THE KITTY!!
YOU LIKE CATS, TOO?
ARE YOU LISTENING TO ME?
HEY!
...
スッ
じわっ
SO CUTE!!

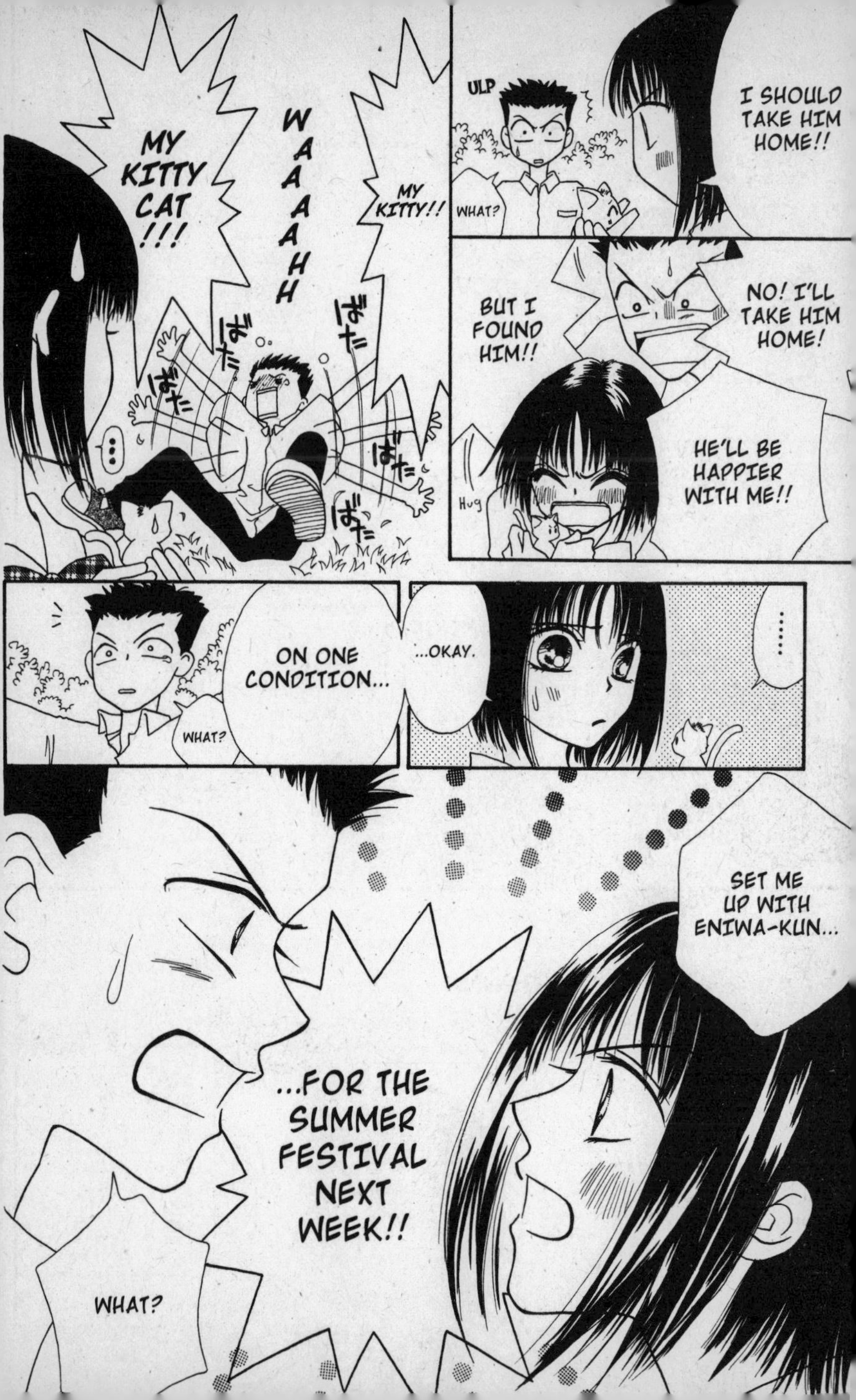
ULP
I SHOULD TAKE HIM HOME!!
WHAT?
NO! I'LL TAKE HIM HOME!
BUT I FOUND HIM!!
HE'LL BE HAPPIER WITH ME!!
Hug
MY KITTY!!
WAAAAHH
MY KITTY CAT!!!
ばた
ばた
ばた
ばた
ばた
ばた
...
......
...OKAY.
ON ONE CONDITION...
WHAT?
SET ME UP WITH ENIWA-KUN...
...FOR THE SUMMER FESTIVAL NEXT WEEK!!
WHAT?

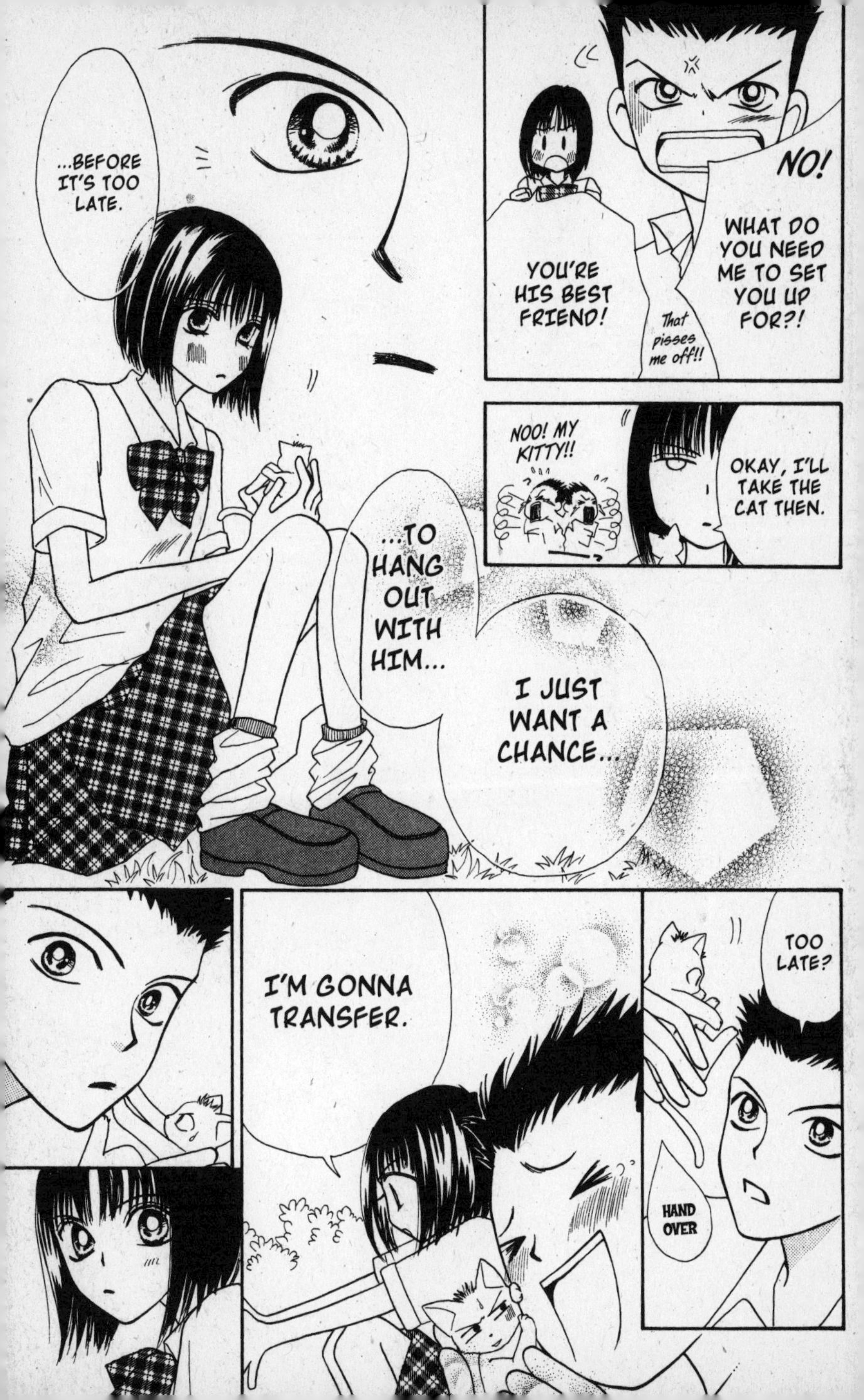
NO!
WHAT DO YOU NEED ME TO SET YOU UP FOR?!
That pisses me off!!
YOU'RE HIS BEST FRIEND!
OKAY, I'LL TAKE THE CAT THEN.
NOO! MY KITTY!!
I JUST WANT A CHANCE...
...TO HANG OUT WITH HIM...
...BEFORE IT'S TOO LATE.
TOO LATE?
HAND OVER
I'M GONNA TRANSFER.

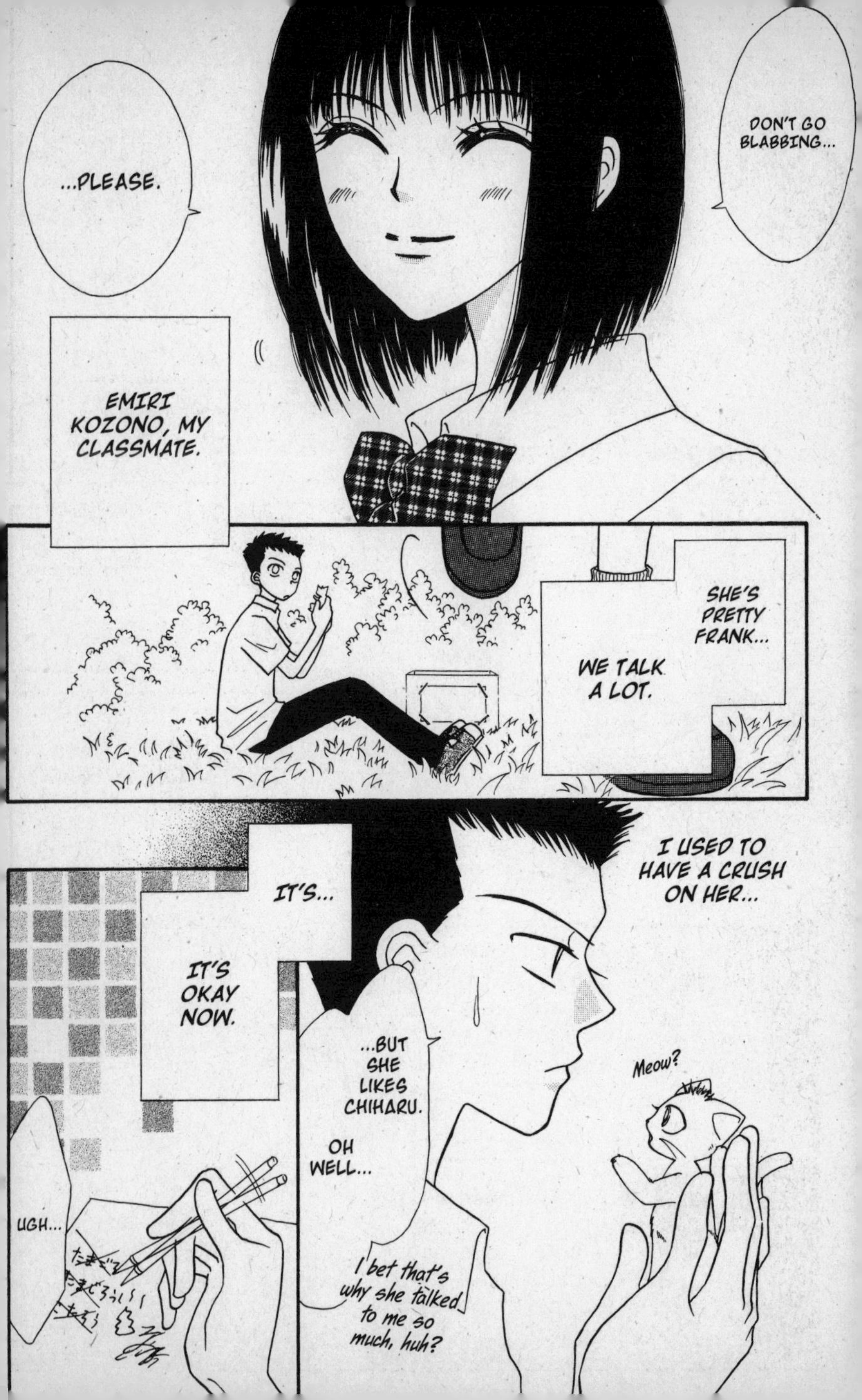
DON'T GO BLABBING...
...PLEASE.
EMIRI KOZONO, MY CLASSMATE.
SHE'S PRETTY FRANK...
WE TALK A LOT.
I USED TO HAVE A CRUSH ON HER...
...BUT SHE LIKES CHIHARU.
OH WELL...
Meow?
I bet that's why she talked to me so much, huh?
IT'S...
IT'S OKAY NOW.
UGH...

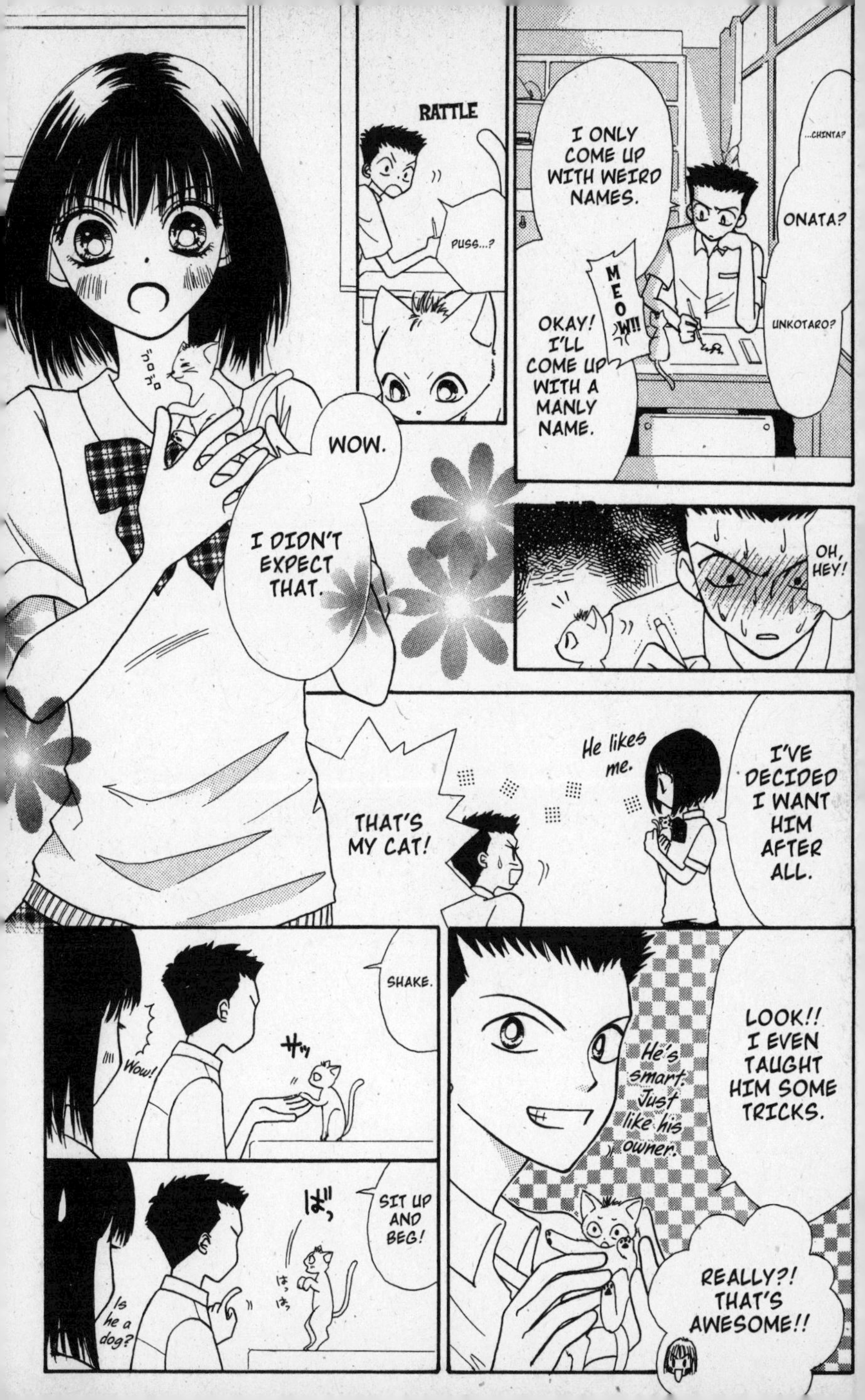
...CHINTA?
ONATA?
UNKOTARO?
I ONLY COME UP WITH WEIRD NAMES.
MEOW!!
OKAY! I'LL COME UP WITH A MANLY NAME.
RATTLE
PUSS...?
OH, HEY!
WOW.
I DIDN'T EXPECT THAT.
I'VE DECIDED I WANT HIM AFTER ALL.
He likes me.
THAT'S MY CAT!
LOOK!! I EVEN TAUGHT HIM SOME TRICKS.
He's smart. Just like his owner.
REALLY?! THAT'S AWESOME!!
SHAKE.
Wow!
SIT UP AND BEG!
Is he a dog?

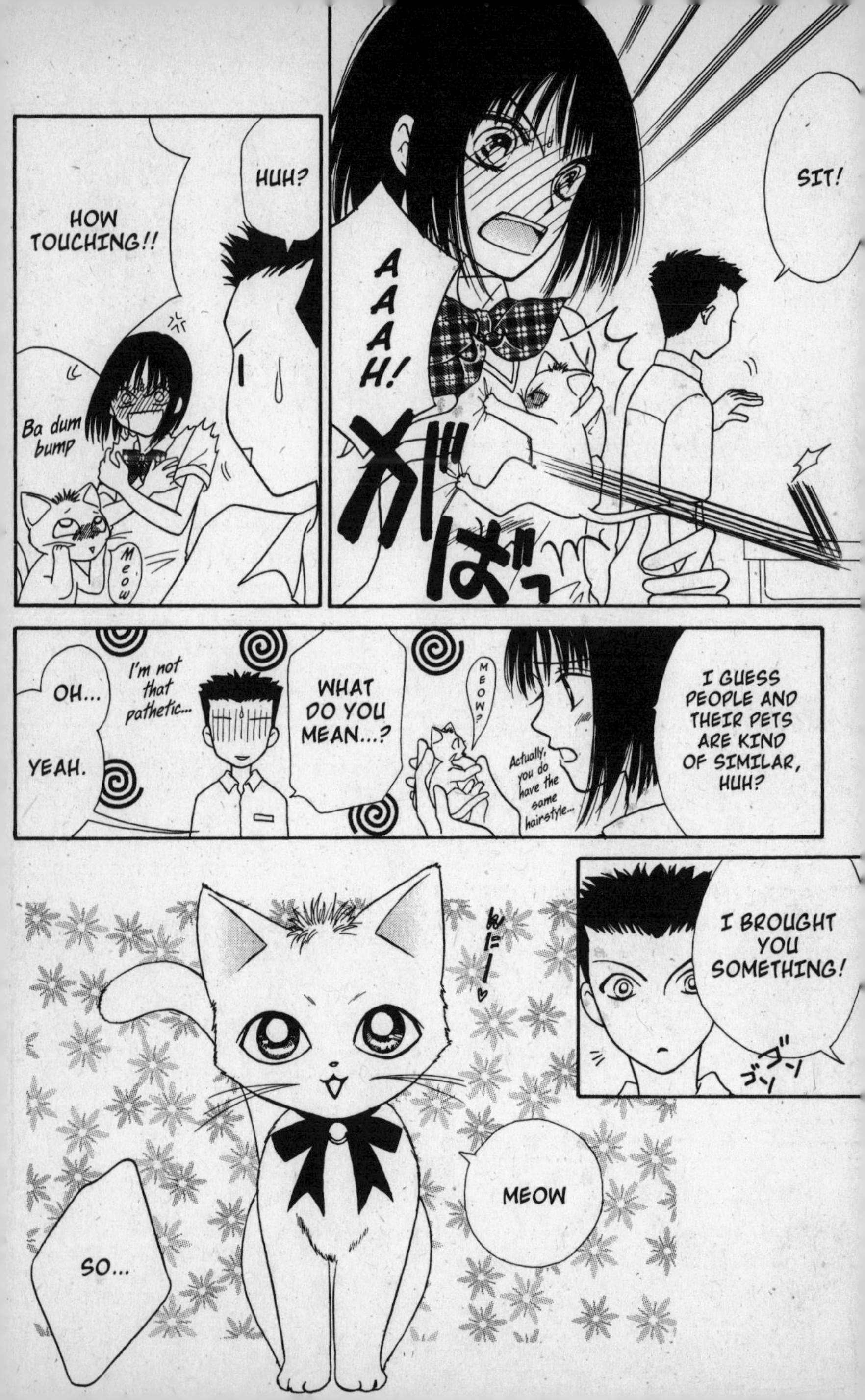
SIT!
AAAAH!
がばっ
HUH?
HOW TOUCHING!!
Ba dum bump
MEOW
I GUESS PEOPLE AND THEIR PETS ARE KIND OF SIMILAR, HUH?
Actually, you do have the same hairstyle...
MEOW?
WHAT DO YOU MEAN...?
I'm not that pathetic...
OH... YEAH.
I BROUGHT YOU SOMETHING!
ゴソゴソ
MEOW
SO...

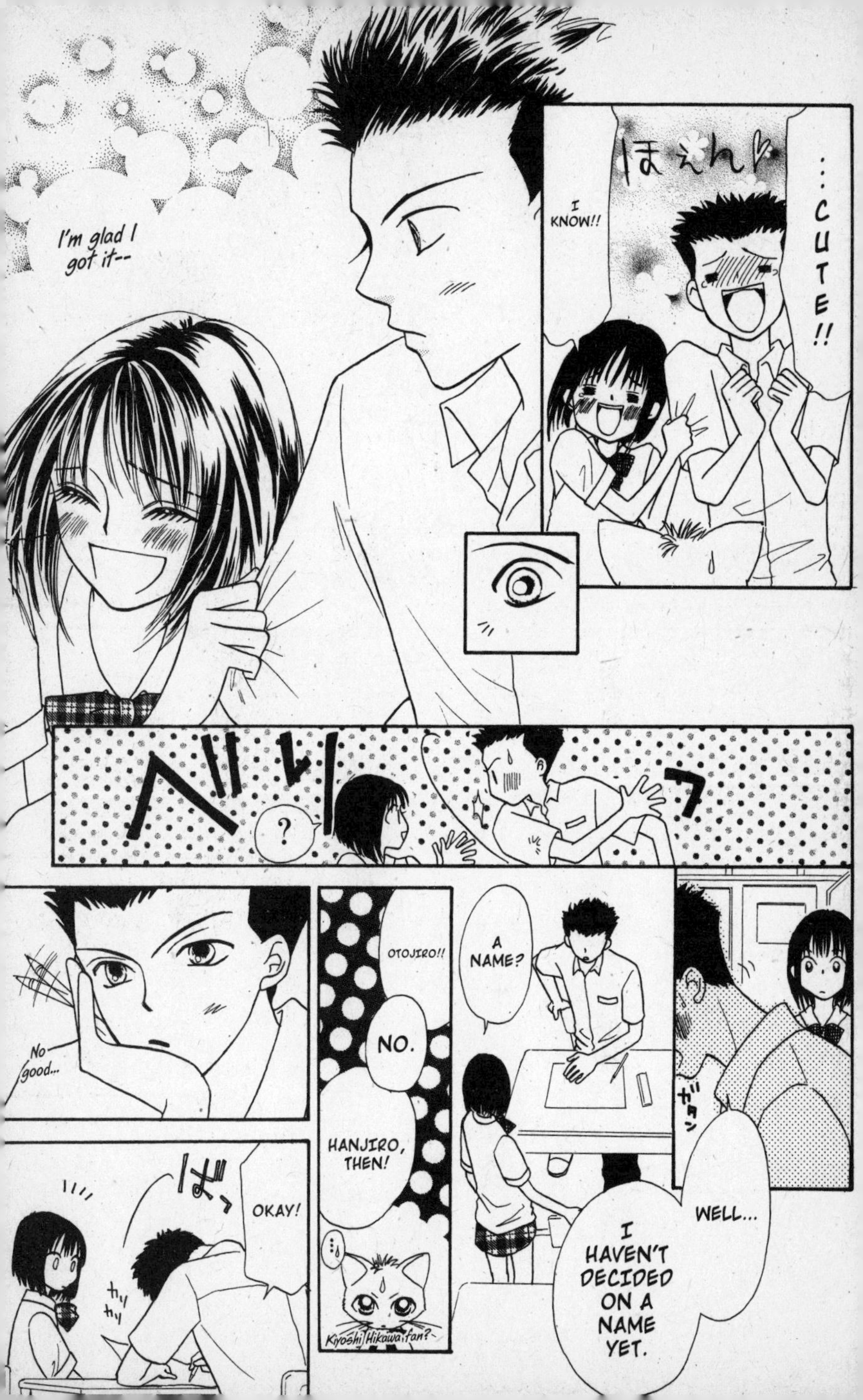
...CUTE!!
ほえん
I KNOW!!
I'm glad I got it--
?
ガタン
WELL...
I HAVEN'T DECIDED ON A NAME YET.
A NAME?
OTOJIRO!!
NO.
HANJIRO, THEN!
Kiyoshi Hikawa fan?
No good...
ぱっ
OKAY!
カリ カリ

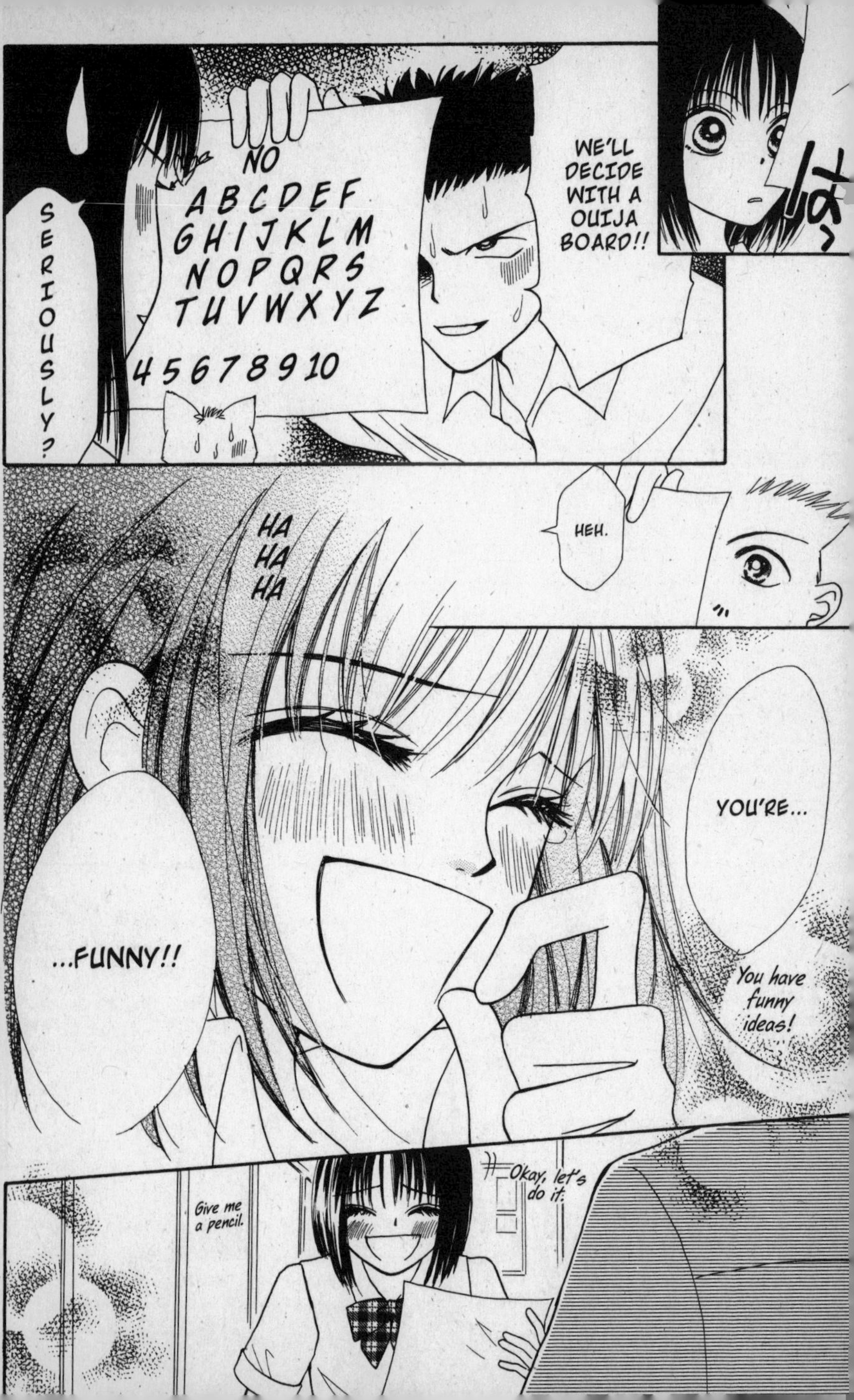
はっ
WE'LL DECIDE WITH A OUIJA BOARD!!
NO
A B C D E F
G H I J K L M
N O P Q R S
T U V W X Y Z
4 5 6 7 8 9 10
SERIOUSLY?
HEH.
HA HA HA
YOU'RE...
...FUNNY!!
You have funny ideas!
Okay, let's do it.
Give me a pencil.

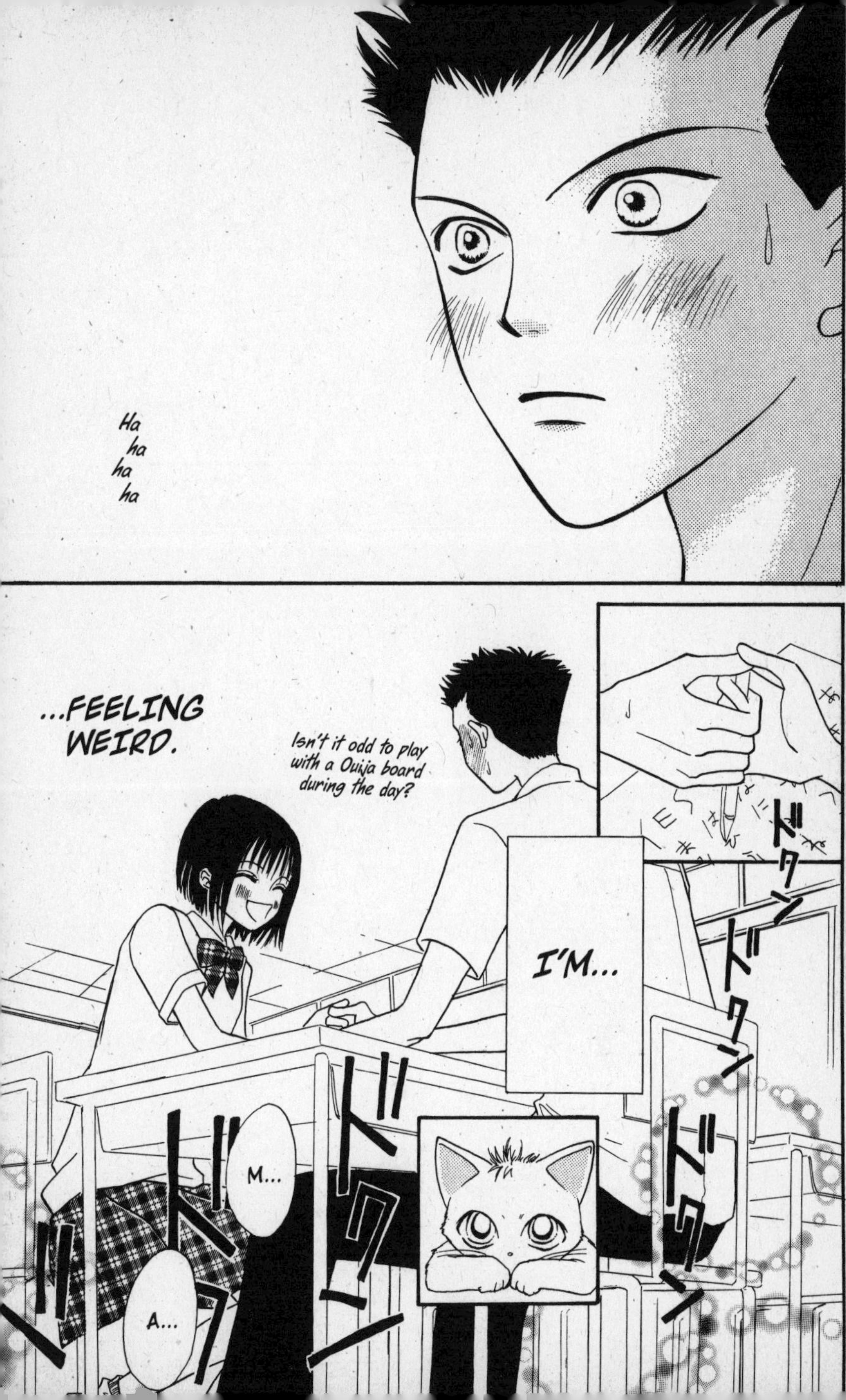
Ha ha ha ha
Isn't it odd to play with a Ouija board during the day?
...FEELING WEIRD.
I'M...
M...
A...

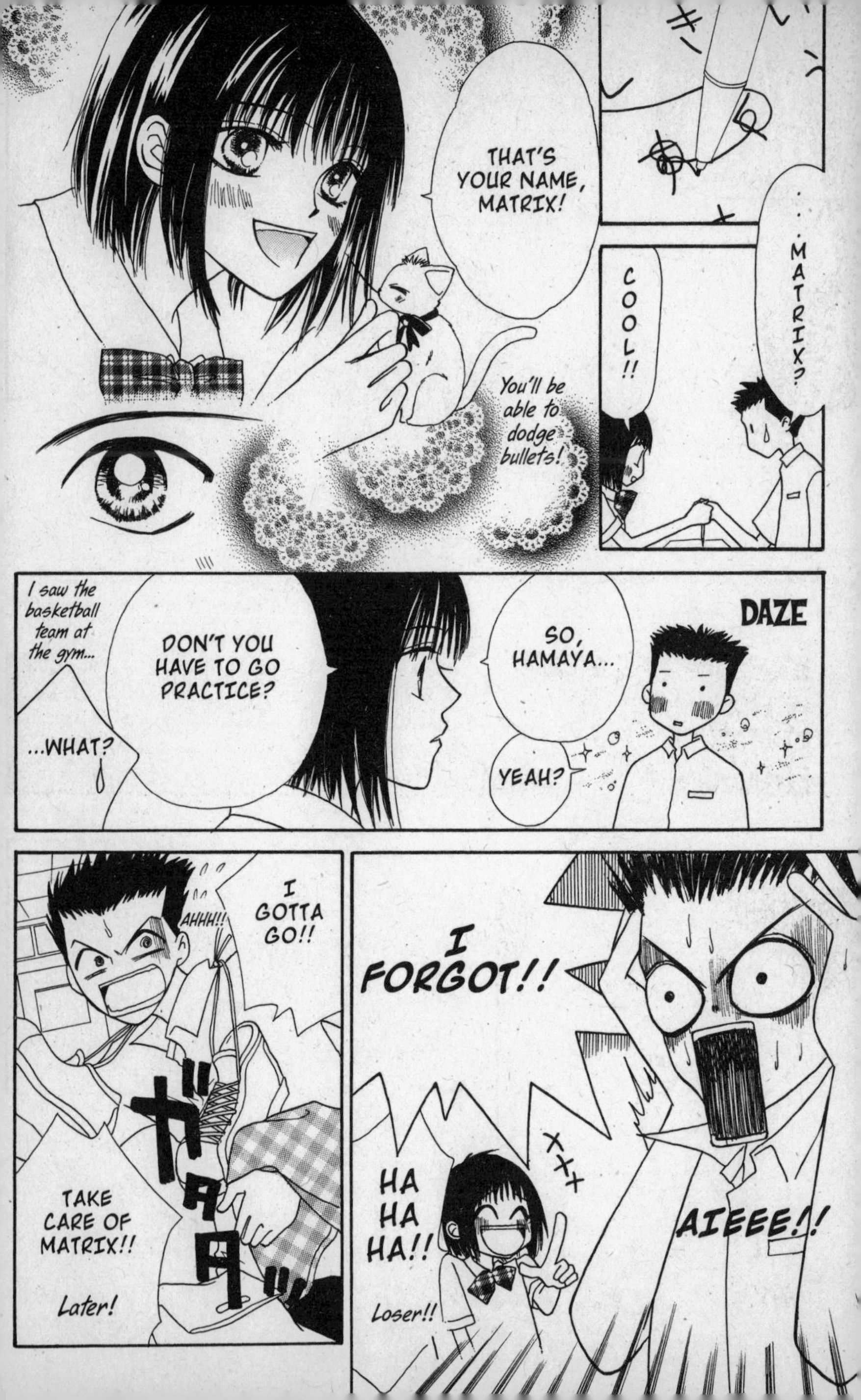
...MATRIX?
COOL!!
THAT'S YOUR NAME, MATRIX!
You'll be able to dodge bullets!
DAZE
SO, HAMAYA...
YEAH?
DON'T YOU HAVE TO GO PRACTICE?
I saw the basketball team at the gym...
...WHAT?
I FORGOT!!
AIEEE!!
HA HA HA!!
Loser!!
I GOTTA GO!!
AHHH!!
TAKE CARE OF MATRIX!!
Later!

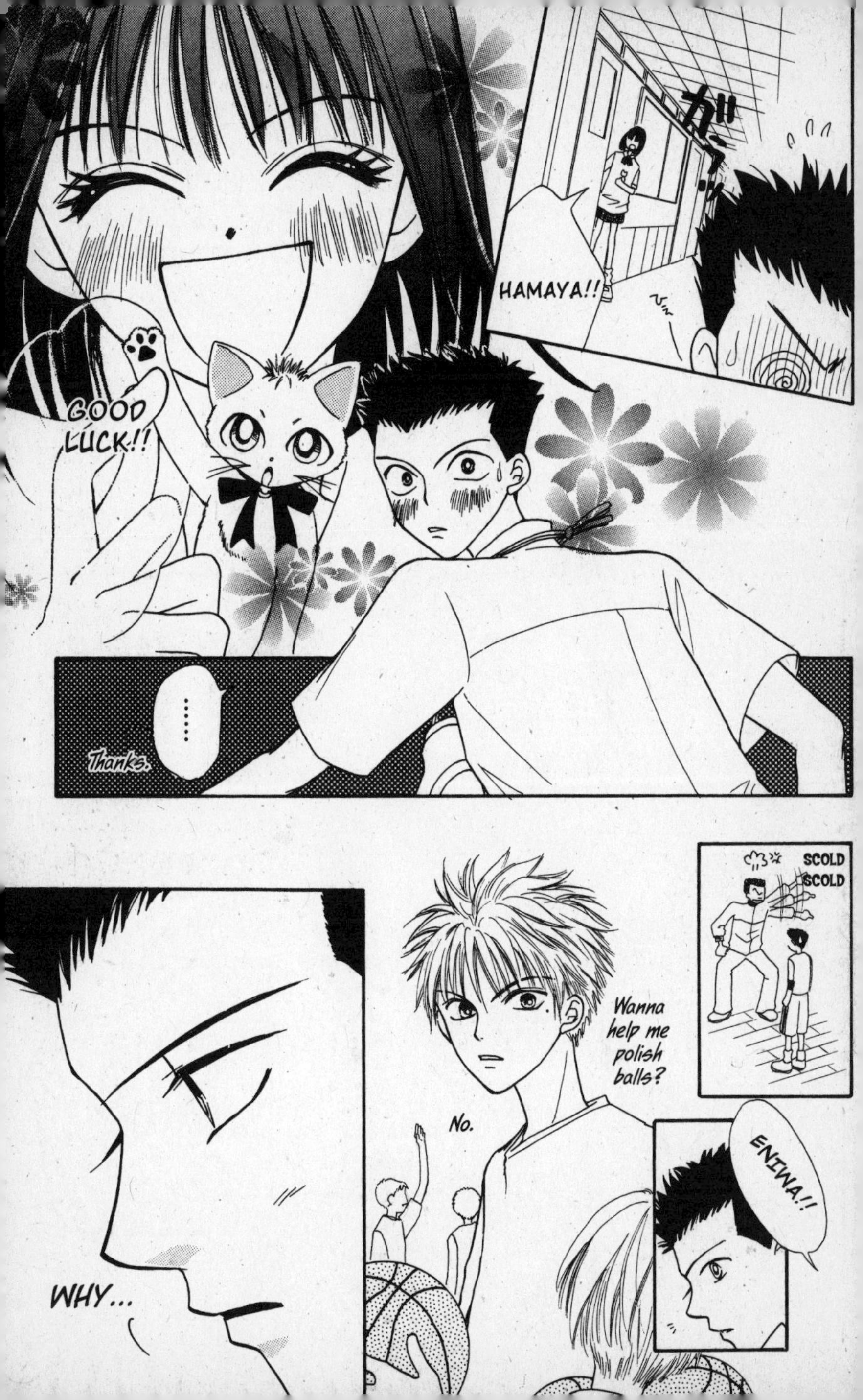
HAMAYA!!
GOOD LUCK!!
......
Thanks.
SCOLD
SCOLD
ENIWA!!
Wanna help me polish balls?
No.
WHY...

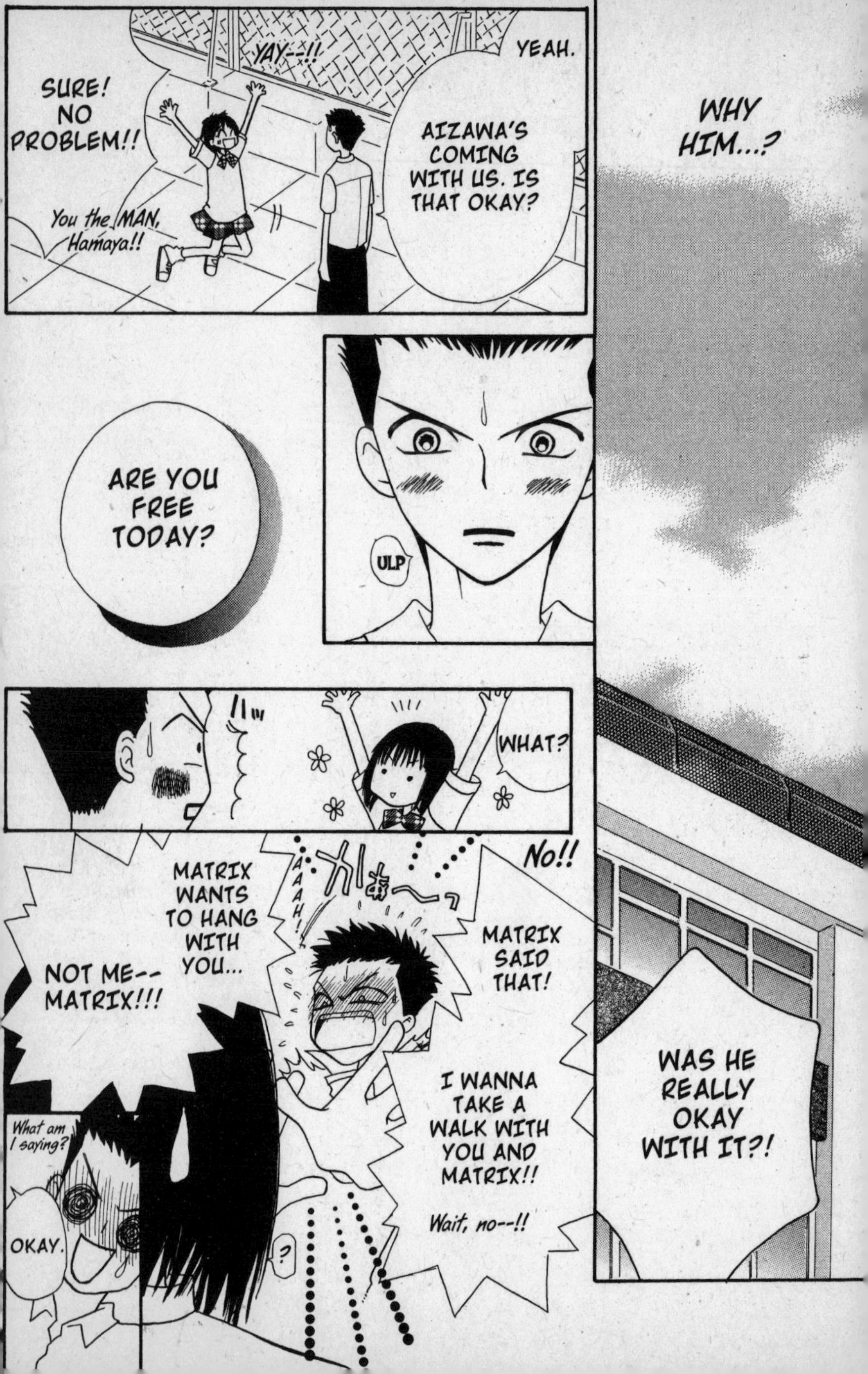
WHY HIM...?
WAS HE REALLY OKAY WITH IT?!
YEAH.
AIZAWA'S COMING WITH US. IS THAT OKAY?
YAY--!!
SURE! NO PROBLEM!!
You the MAN, Hamaya!!
ULP
ARE YOU FREE TODAY?
WHAT?
No!!
MATRIX SAID THAT!
MATRIX WANTS TO HANG WITH YOU...
AAAAH!
NOT ME--MATRIX!!!
I WANNA TAKE A WALK WITH YOU AND MATRIX!!
Wait, no--!!
?
What am I saying?
OKAY.

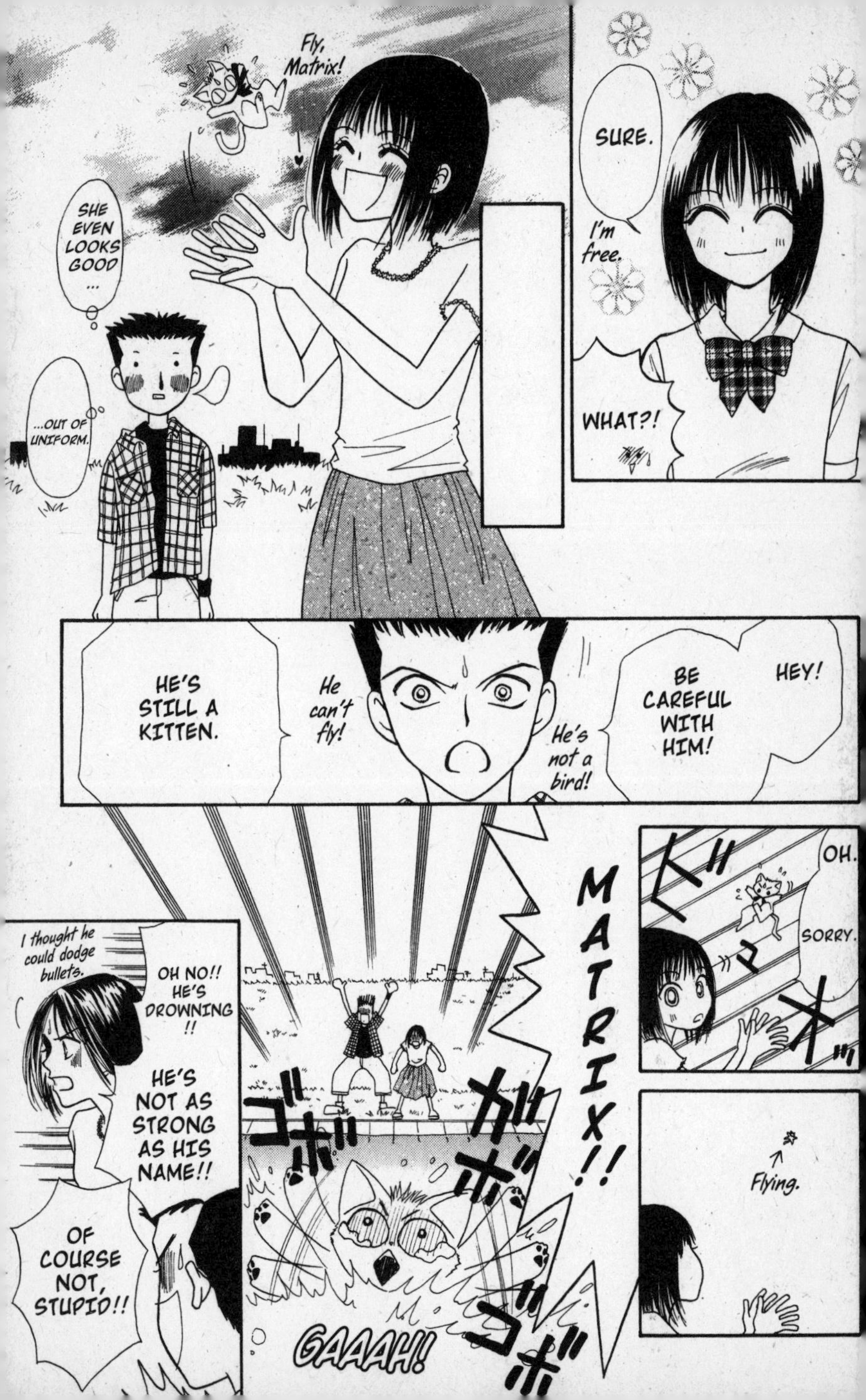
SURE.
I'm free.
WHAT?!
Fly, Matrix!
SHE EVEN LOOKS GOOD ...
...OUT OF UNIFORM.
HEY!
BE CAREFUL WITH HIM!
He's not a bird!
He can't fly!
HE'S STILL A KITTEN.
OH.
SORRY.
Flying.
MATRIX!!
GAAAH!
I thought he could dodge bullets.
OH NO!! HE'S DROWNING !!
HE'S NOT AS STRONG AS HIS NAME!!
OF COURSE NOT, STUPID!!

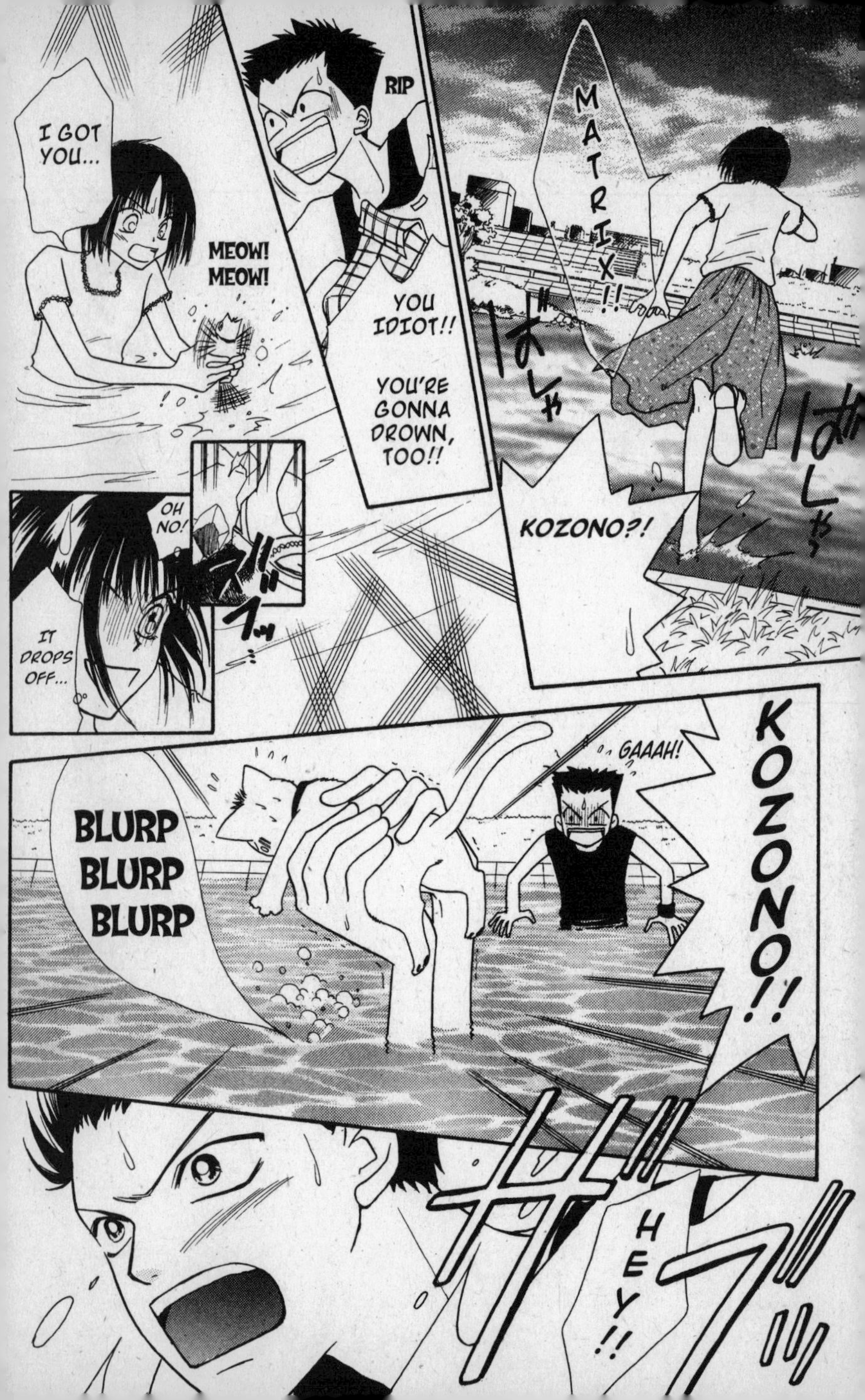
MATRIX!!
KOZONO?!
RIP
YOU IDIOT!!
YOU'RE GONNA DROWN, TOO!!
I GOT YOU...
MEOW! MEOW!
OH NO!
IT DROPS OFF...
KOZONO!!
GAAAH!
BLURP BLURP BLURP
HEY!!

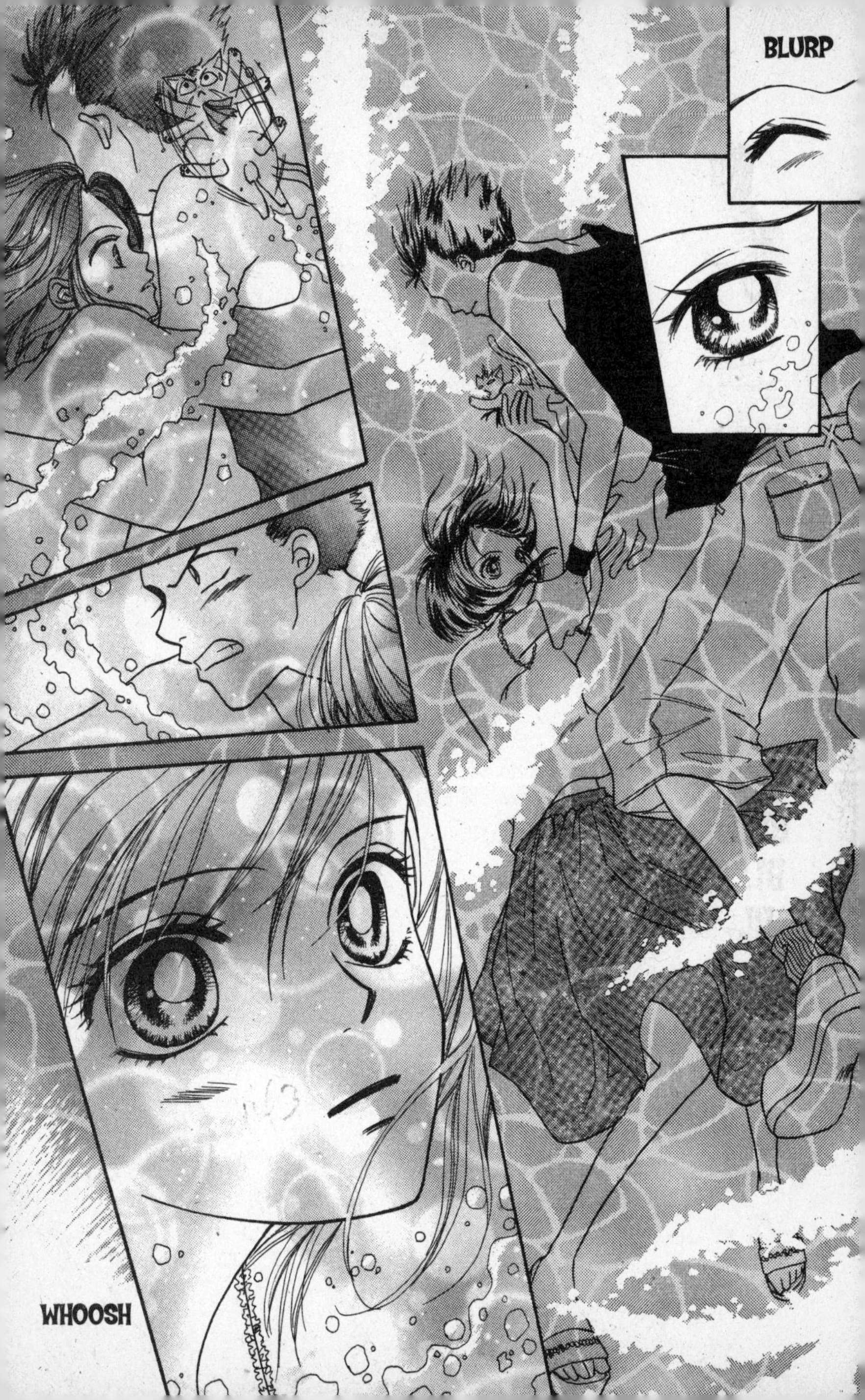
BLURP
WHOOSH

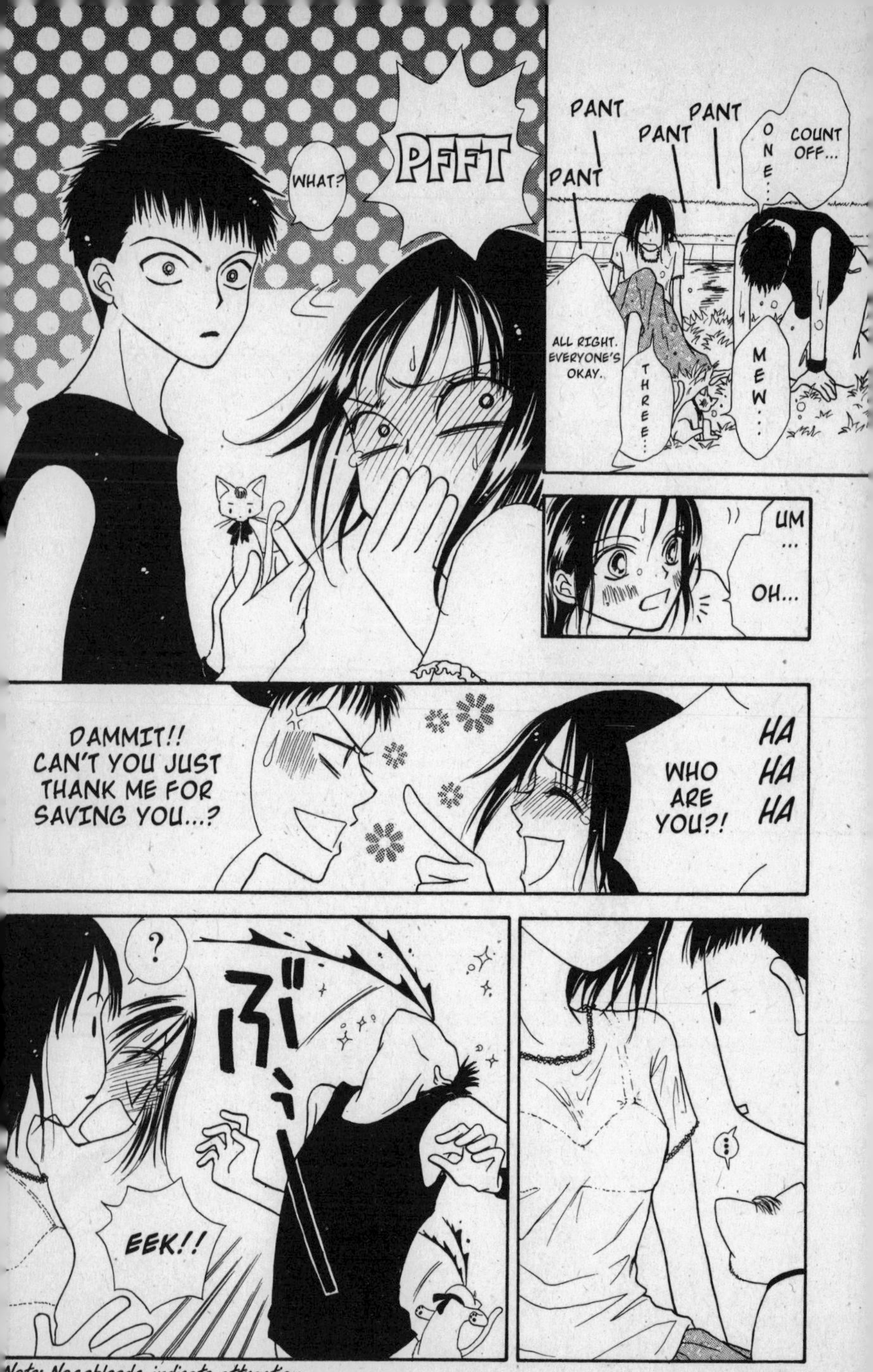
COUNT OFF...
ONE...
PANT
PANT
PANT
PANT
MEW...
THREE...
ALL RIGHT. EVERYONE'S OKAY.
UM ... OH...
PFFT
WHAT?
HA HA HA
WHO ARE YOU?!
DAMMIT!! CAN'T YOU JUST THANK ME FOR SAVING YOU...?
...
?
ぶー
EEK!!

*Note: Nosebleeds indicate attraction.*

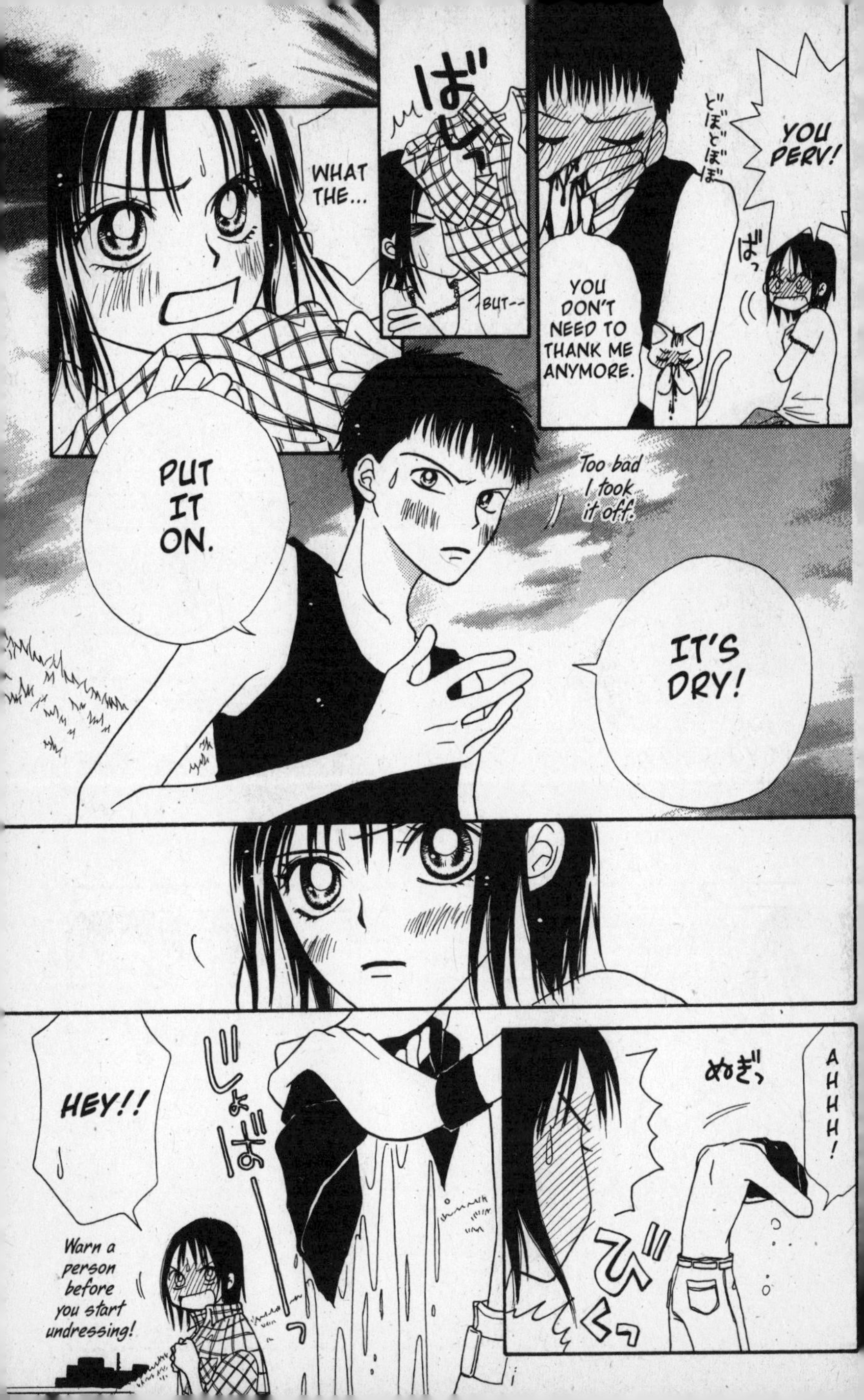
YOU PERV!
どぼどぼ
ばっ
YOU DON'T NEED TO THANK ME ANYMORE.
ばじっ
BUT--
WHAT THE...
IT'S DRY!
Too bad I took it off.
PUT IT ON.
AHHH!
ぬぎっ
びくっ
じょぼー
HEY!!
Warn a person before you start undressing!

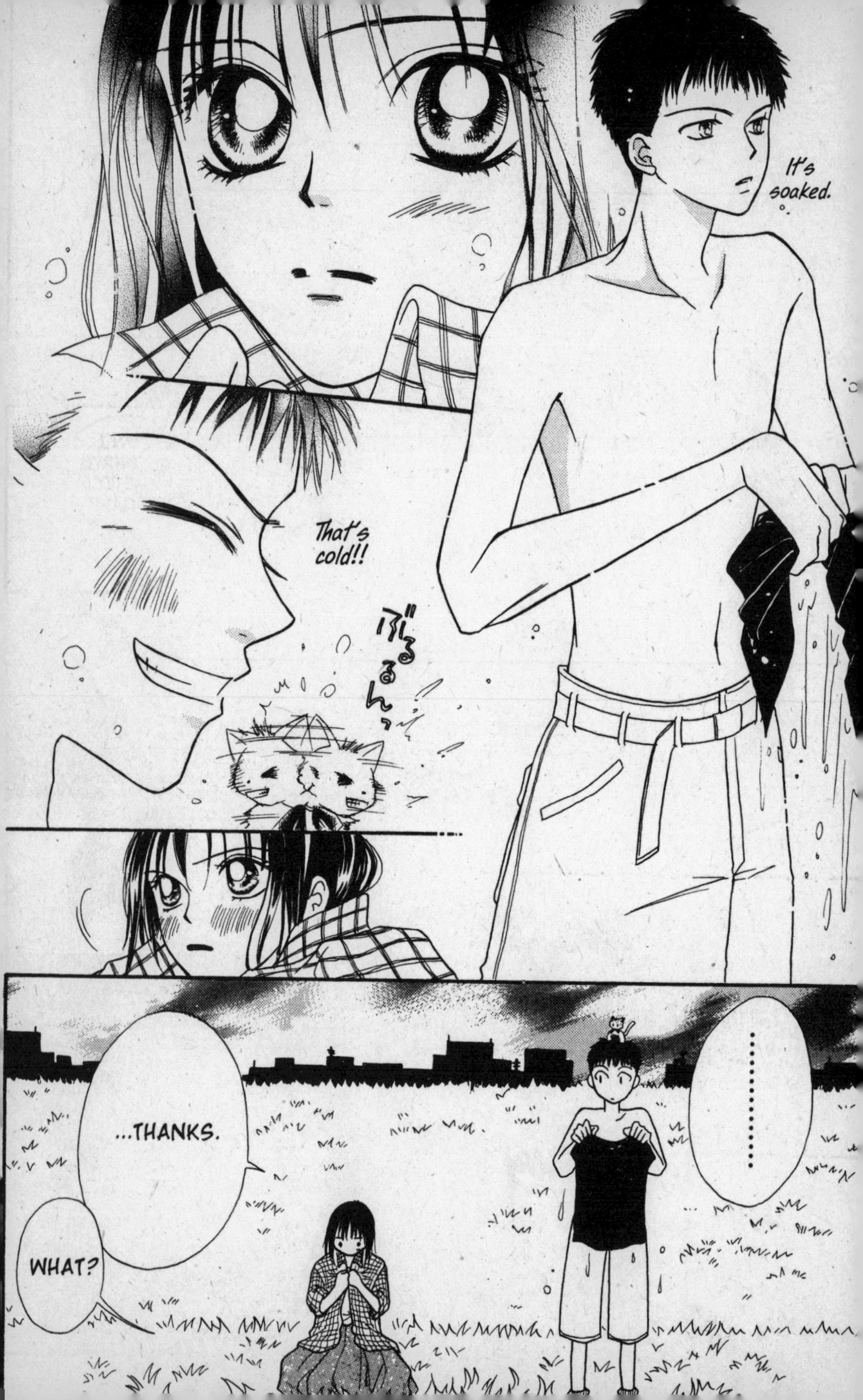
It's soaked.
That's cold!!
ぶるるん
……
...THANKS.
WHAT?

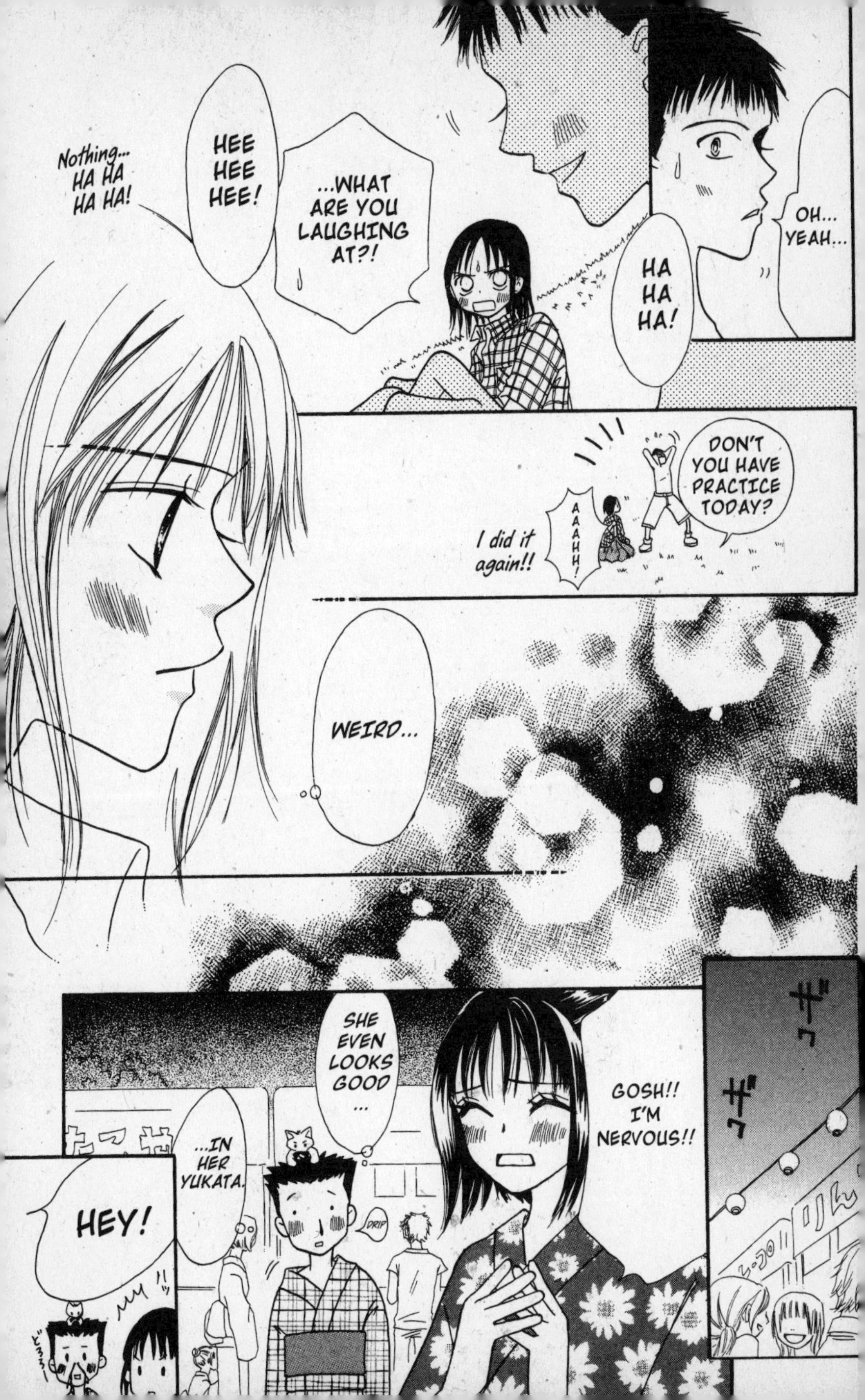
OH... YEAH...
HA HA HA!
...WHAT ARE YOU LAUGHING AT?!
HEE HEE HEE!
Nothing... HA HA HA HA!
DON'T YOU HAVE PRACTICE TODAY?
AAAHH!
I did it again!!
WEIRD...
GOSH!! I'M NERVOUS!!
SHE EVEN LOOKS GOOD ...
...IN HER YUKATA.
DRIP
HEY!

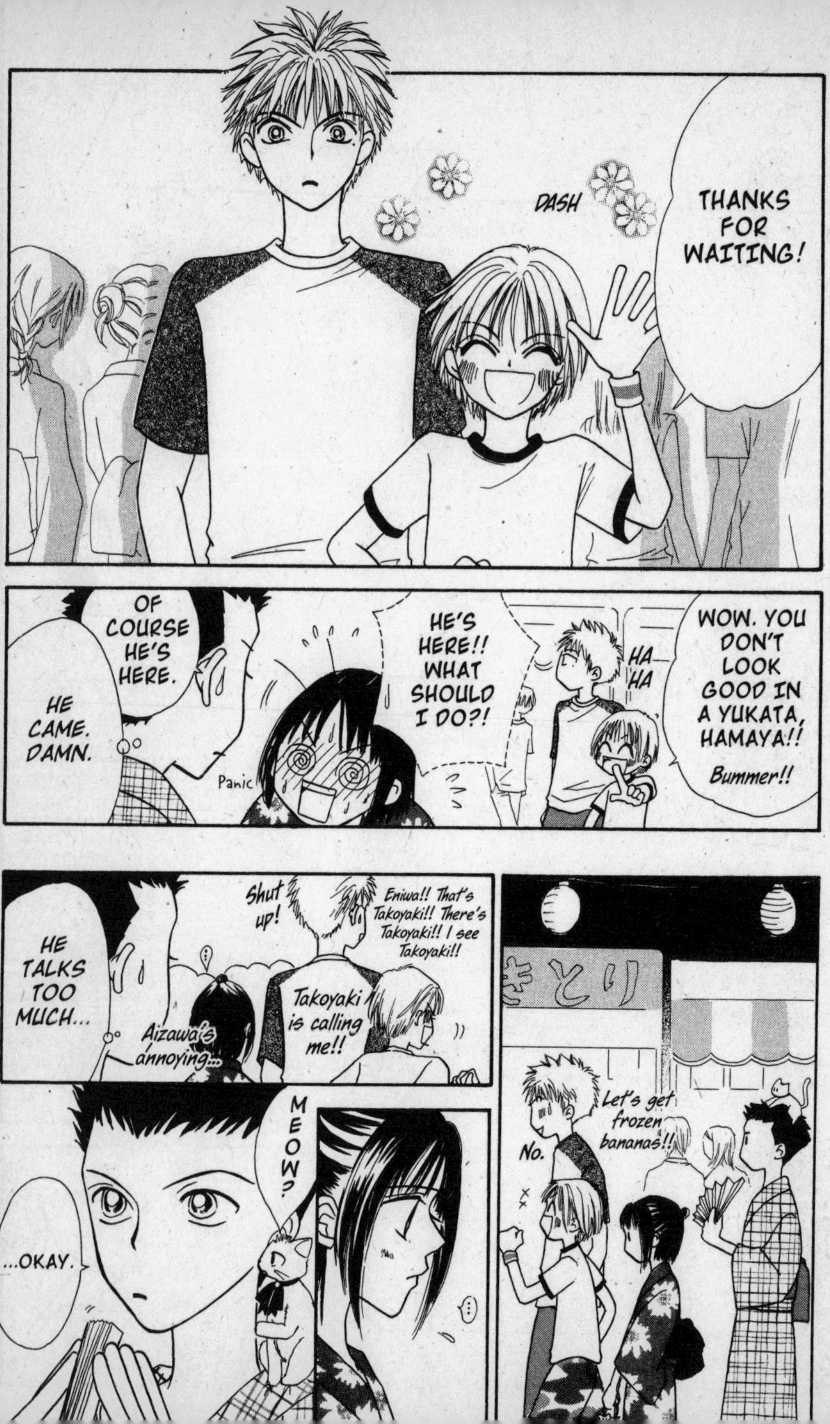
THANKS FOR WAITING!
DASH
WOW. YOU DON'T LOOK GOOD IN A YUKATA, HAMAYA!!
Bummer!!
HA HA
HE'S HERE!! WHAT SHOULD I DO?!
Panic
OF COURSE HE'S HERE.
HE CAME. DAMN.
きとり
Let's get frozen bananas!!
No.
Eniwa!! That's Takoyaki!! There's Takoyaki!! I see Takoyaki!!
Shut up!
Takoyaki is calling me!!
HE TALKS TOO MUCH...
Aizawa's annoying...
MEOW?
...
...OKAY.

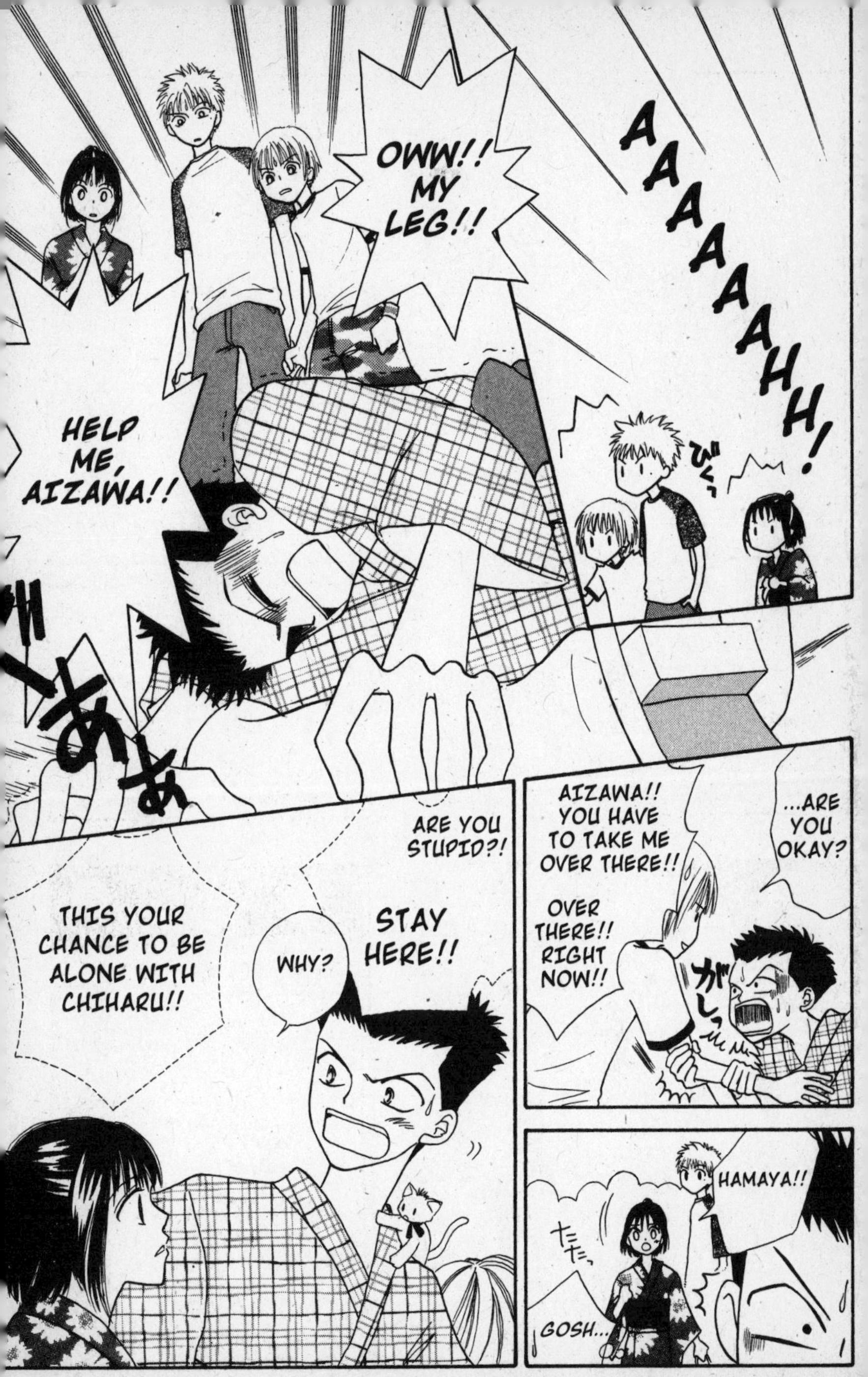
AAAAAAAHH!
びくっ
OWW!! MY LEG!!
HELP ME, AIZAWA!!
...ARE YOU OKAY?
AIZAWA!! YOU HAVE TO TAKE ME OVER THERE!!
OVER THERE!! RIGHT NOW!!
がしっ
HAMAYA!!
たたっ
GOSH...
ARE YOU STUPID?!
STAY HERE!!
WHY?
THIS YOUR CHANCE TO BE ALONE WITH CHIHARU!!

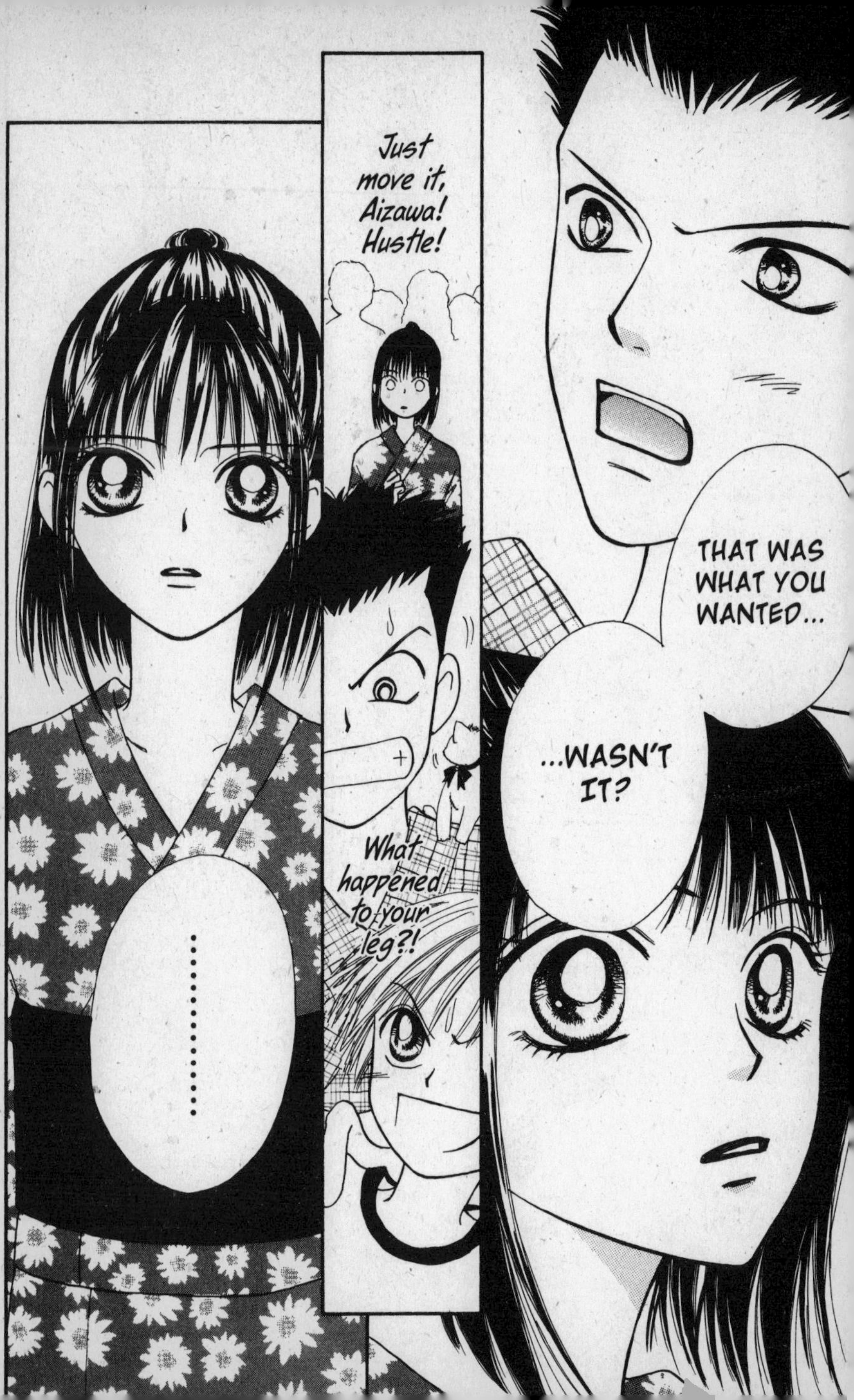
THAT WAS WHAT YOU WANTED...
...WASN'T IT?
Just move it, Aizawa! Hustle!
What happened to your leg?!
........

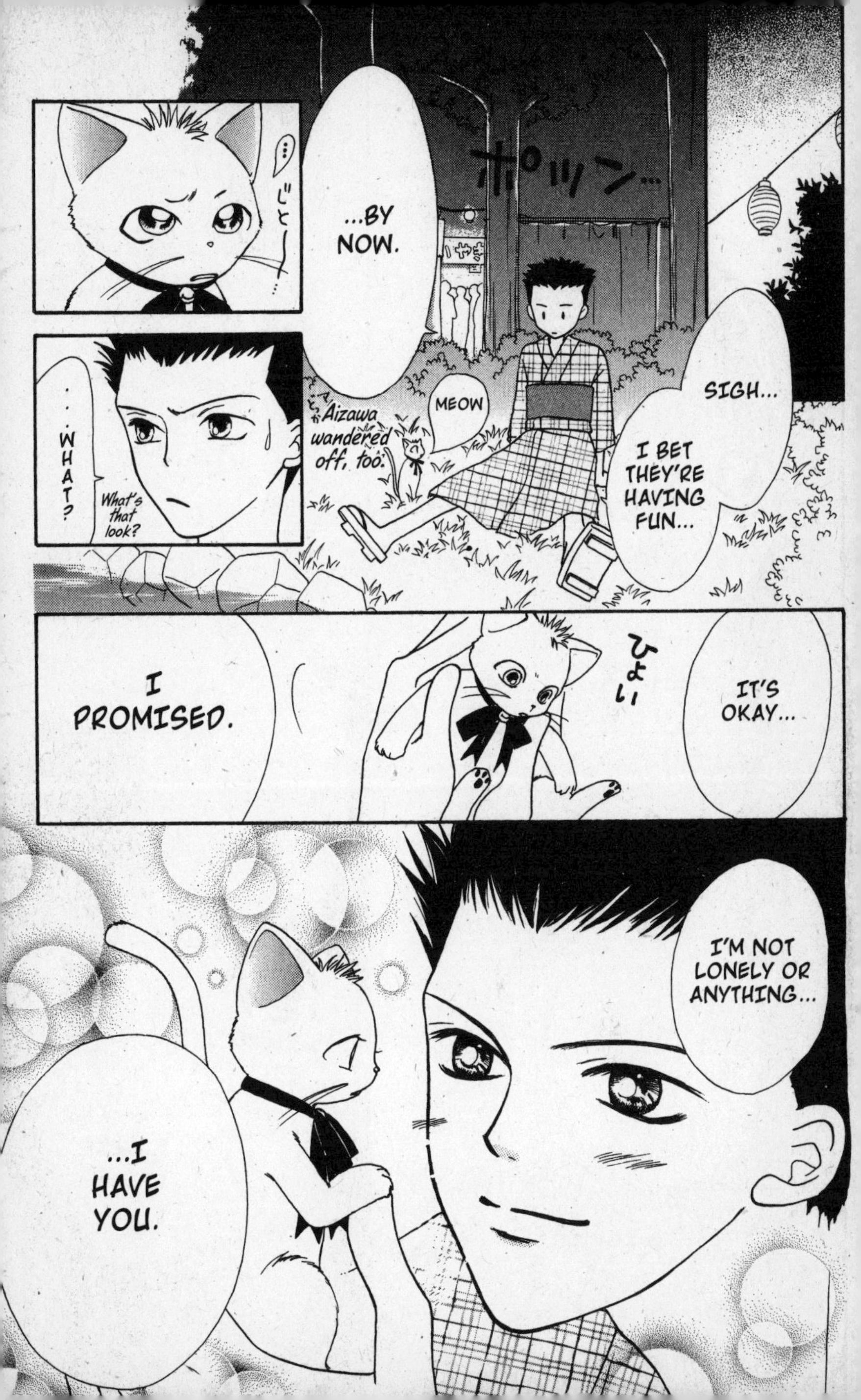
SIGH...
I BET THEY'RE HAVING FUN...
...BY NOW.
ポツン…
MEOW
Aizawa wandered off, too.
...
じと—
...WHAT?
What's that look?
IT'S OKAY...
ひょい
I PROMISED.
I'M NOT LONELY OR ANYTHING...
...I HAVE YOU.

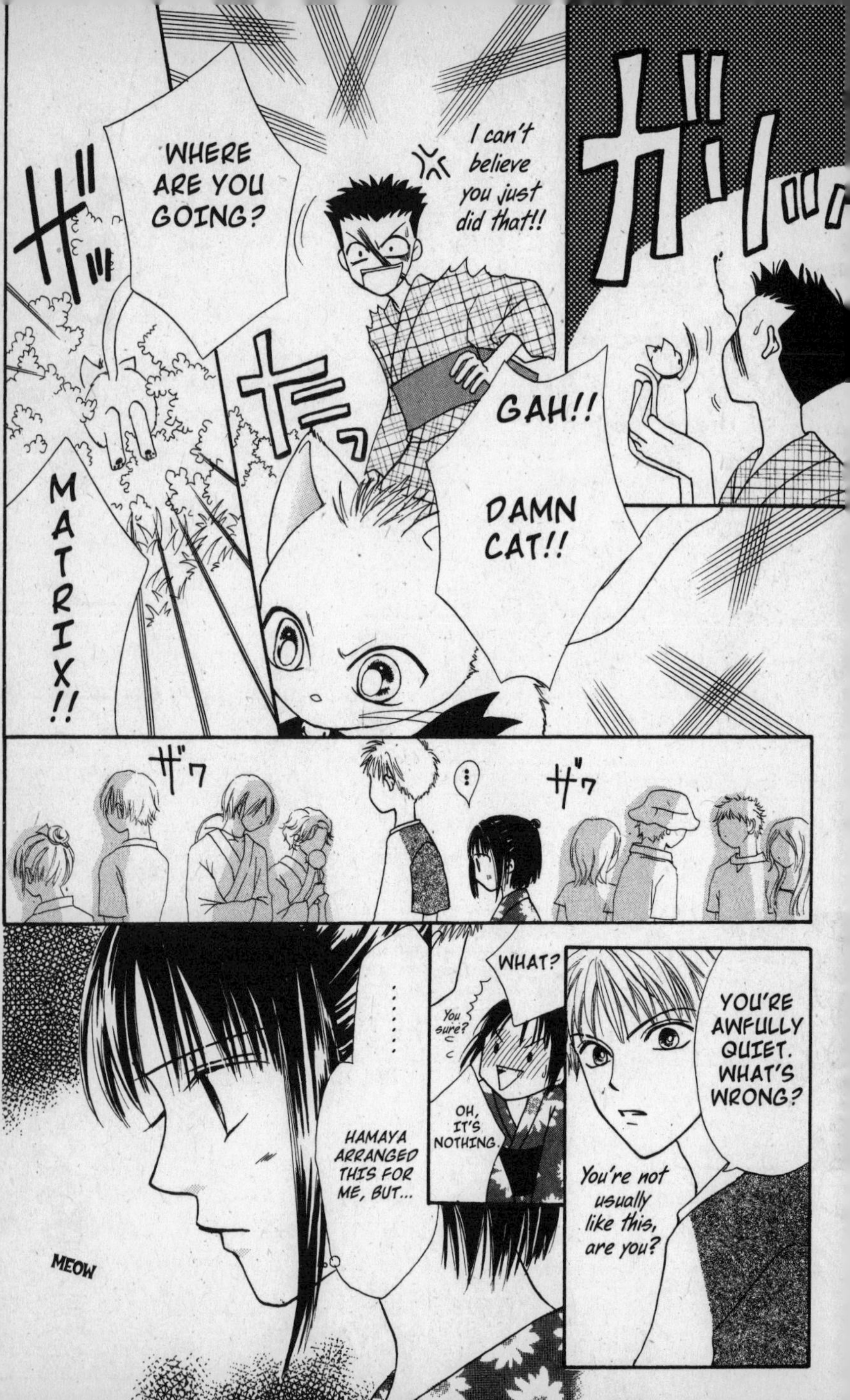
GAH!!
DAMN CAT!!
I can't believe you just did that!!
WHERE ARE YOU GOING?
ザッ
MATRIX!!
ザワ
...
ザワ
YOU'RE AWFULLY QUIET. WHAT'S WRONG?
You're not usually like this, are you?
WHAT?
You sure?
OH, IT'S NOTHING.
......
HAMAYA ARRANGED THIS FOR ME, BUT...
MEOW

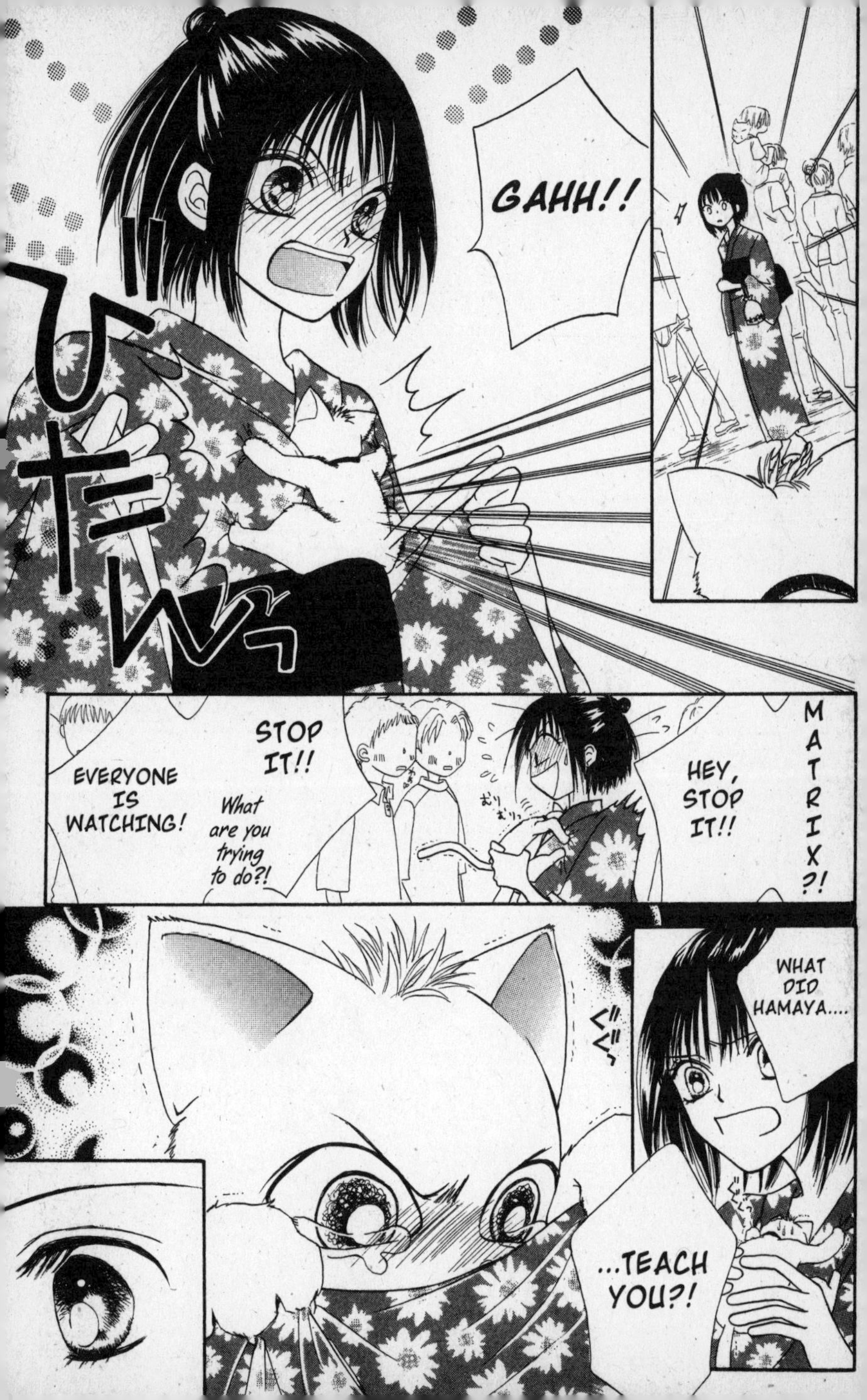
GAHH!!
MATRIX?!
HEY, STOP IT!!
STOP IT!!
What are you trying to do?!
EVERYONE IS WATCHING!
WHAT DID HAMAYA....
...TEACH YOU?!

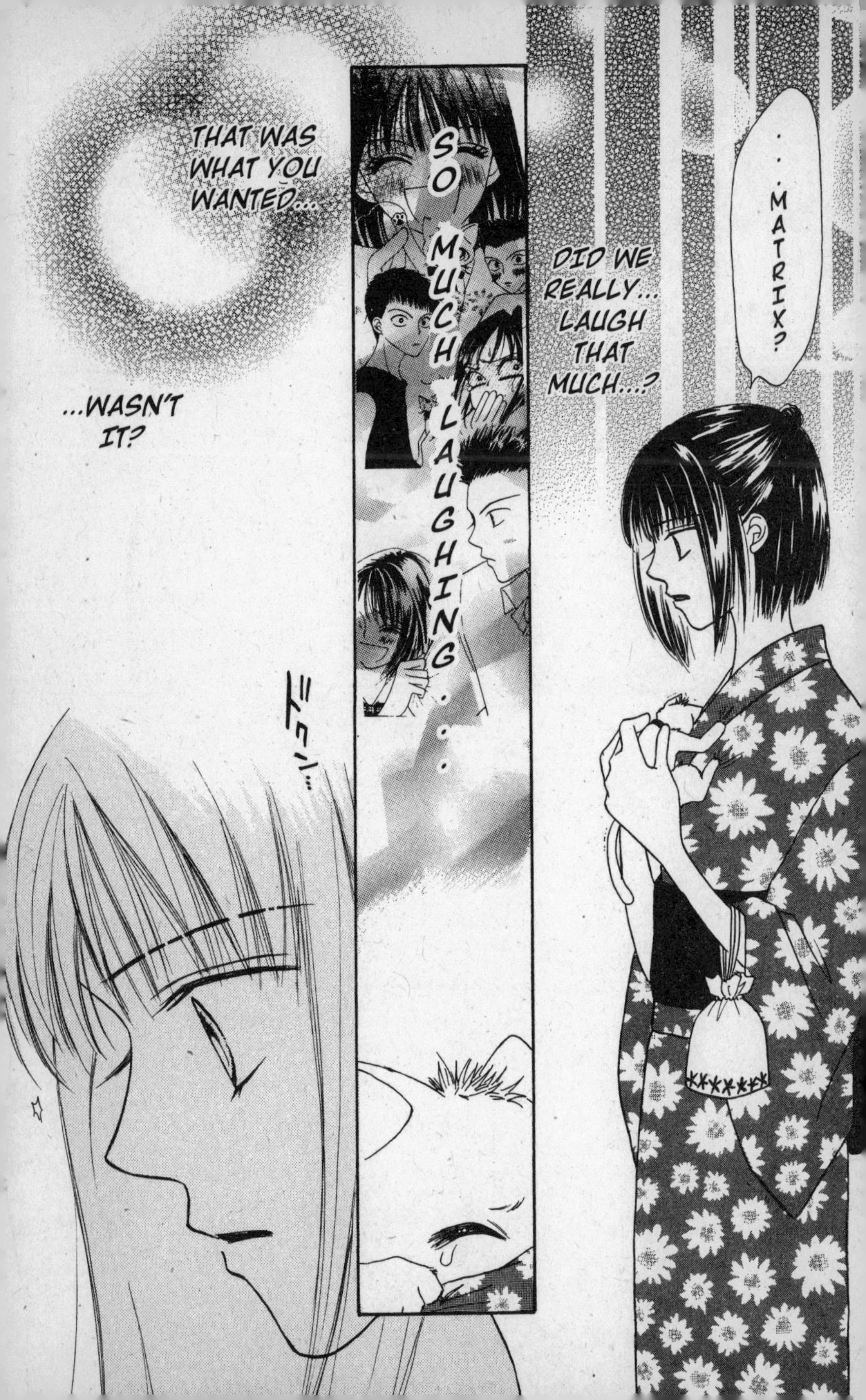
...MATRIX?
DID WE REALLY... LAUGH THAT MUCH...?
SO MUCH LAUGHING...
THAT WAS WHAT YOU WANTED...
...WASN'T IT?

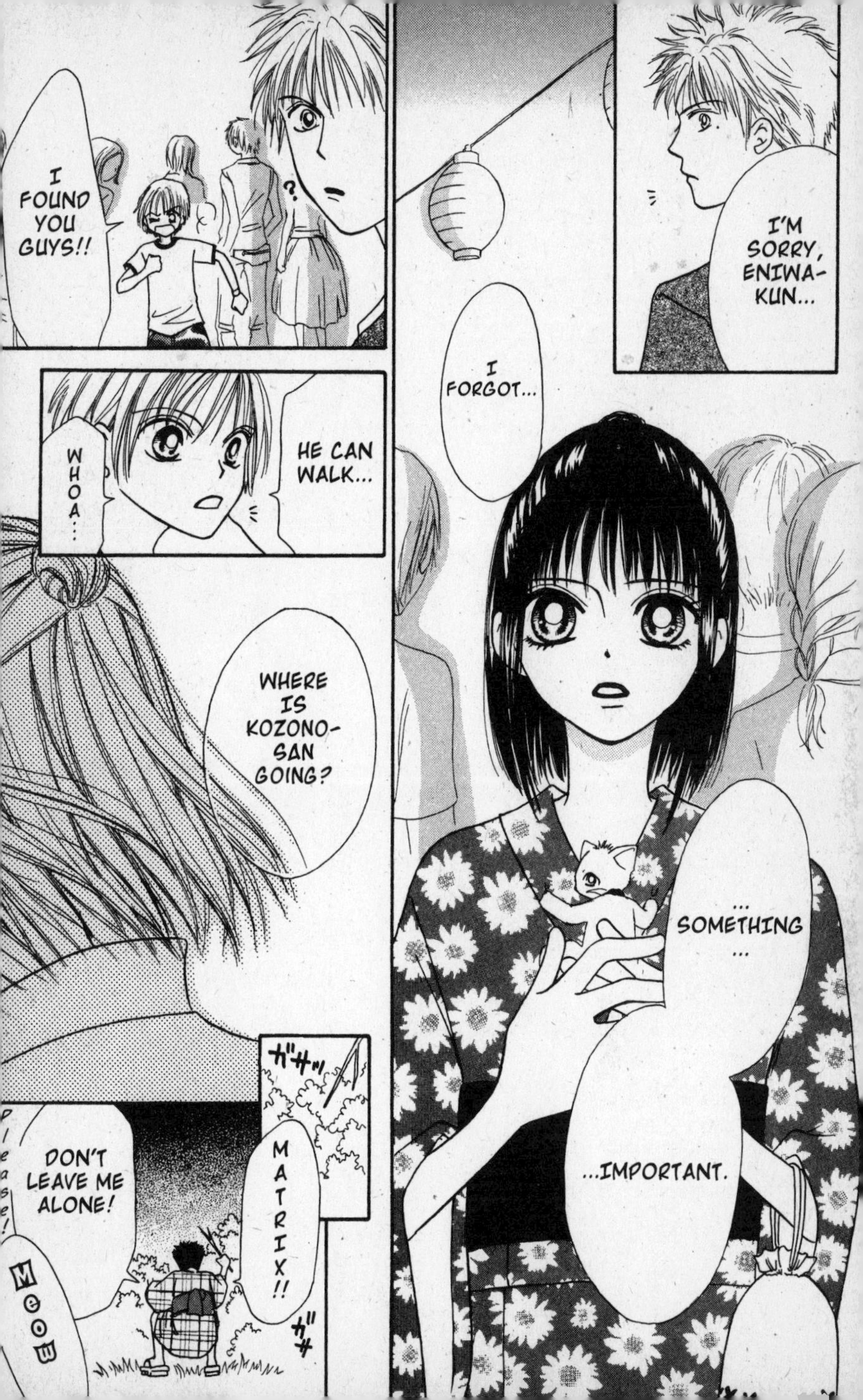

I'M SORRY, ENIWA-KUN...
I FORGOT...
...SOMETHING...
...IMPORTANT.
I FOUND YOU GUYS!!
HE CAN WALK...
WHOA...
WHERE IS KOZONO-SAN GOING?
ガサッ
MATRIX!!
ガサ
DON'T LEAVE ME ALONE!
Please!
Meow

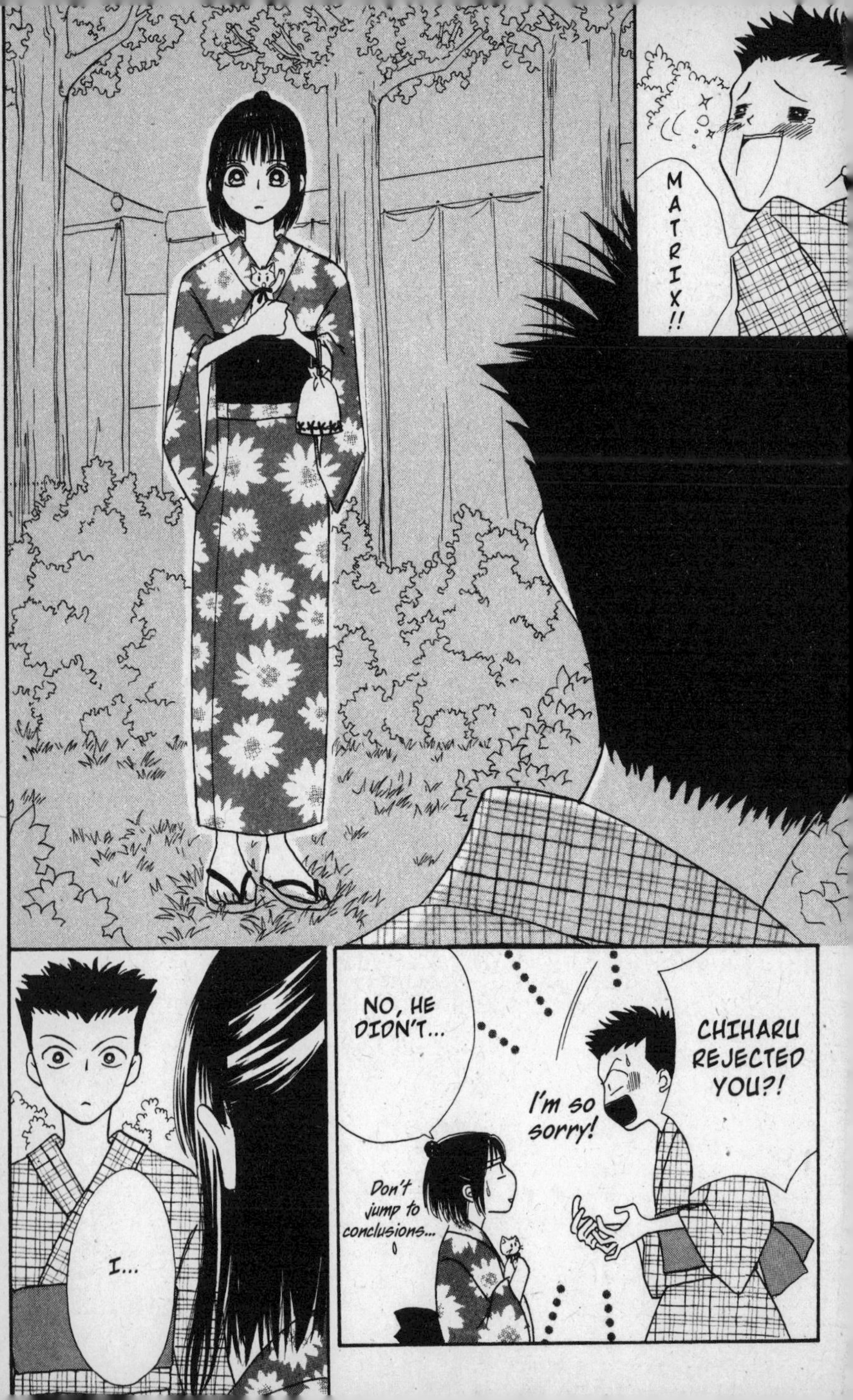
MATRIX!!
CHIHARU REJECTED YOU?!
I'm so sorry!
NO, HE DIDN'T...
Don't jump to conclusions...
I...

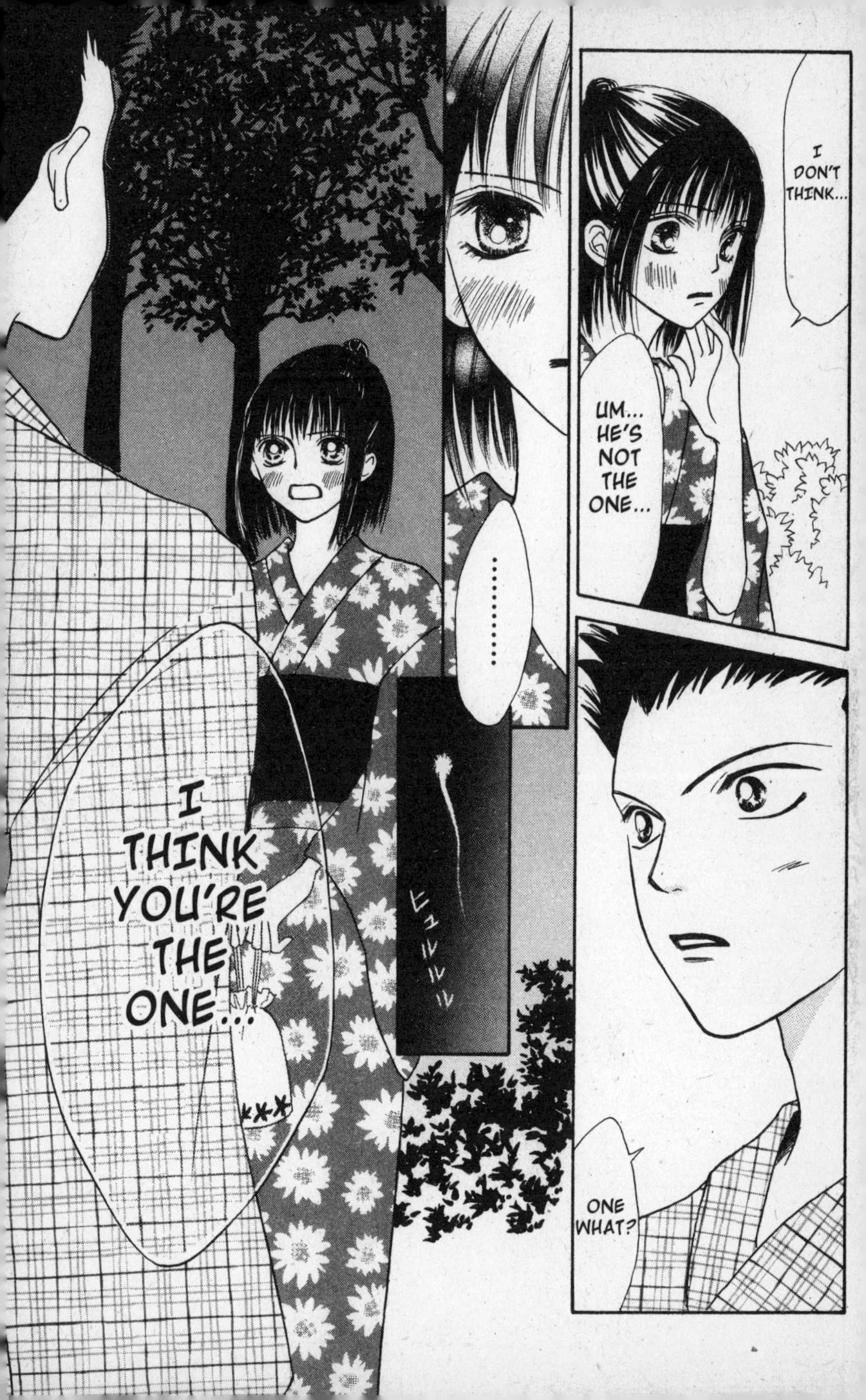
I DON'T THINK...
UM... HE'S NOT THE ONE...
ONE WHAT?
......
ヒュルルル
I THINK YOU'RE THE ONE...

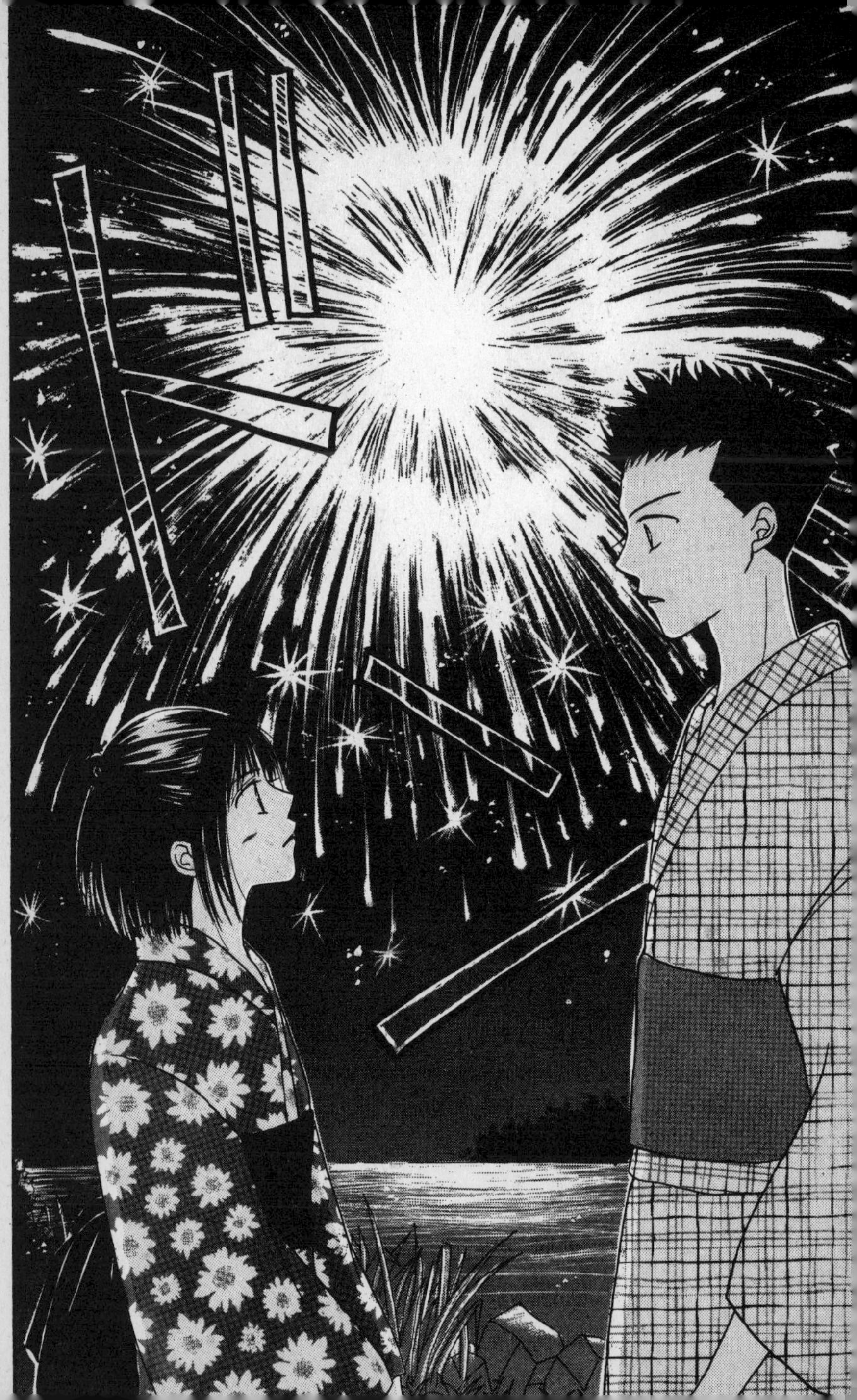

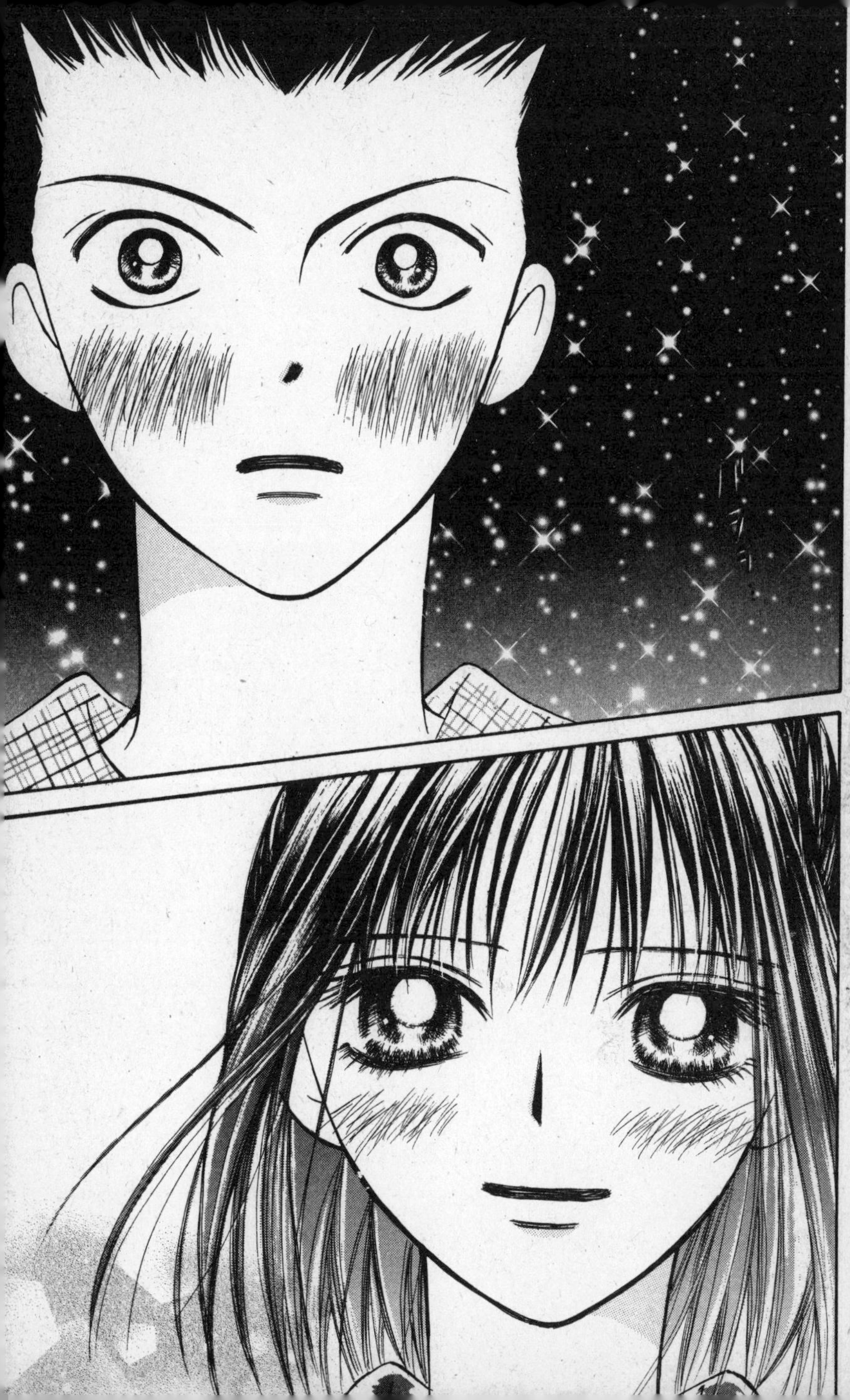

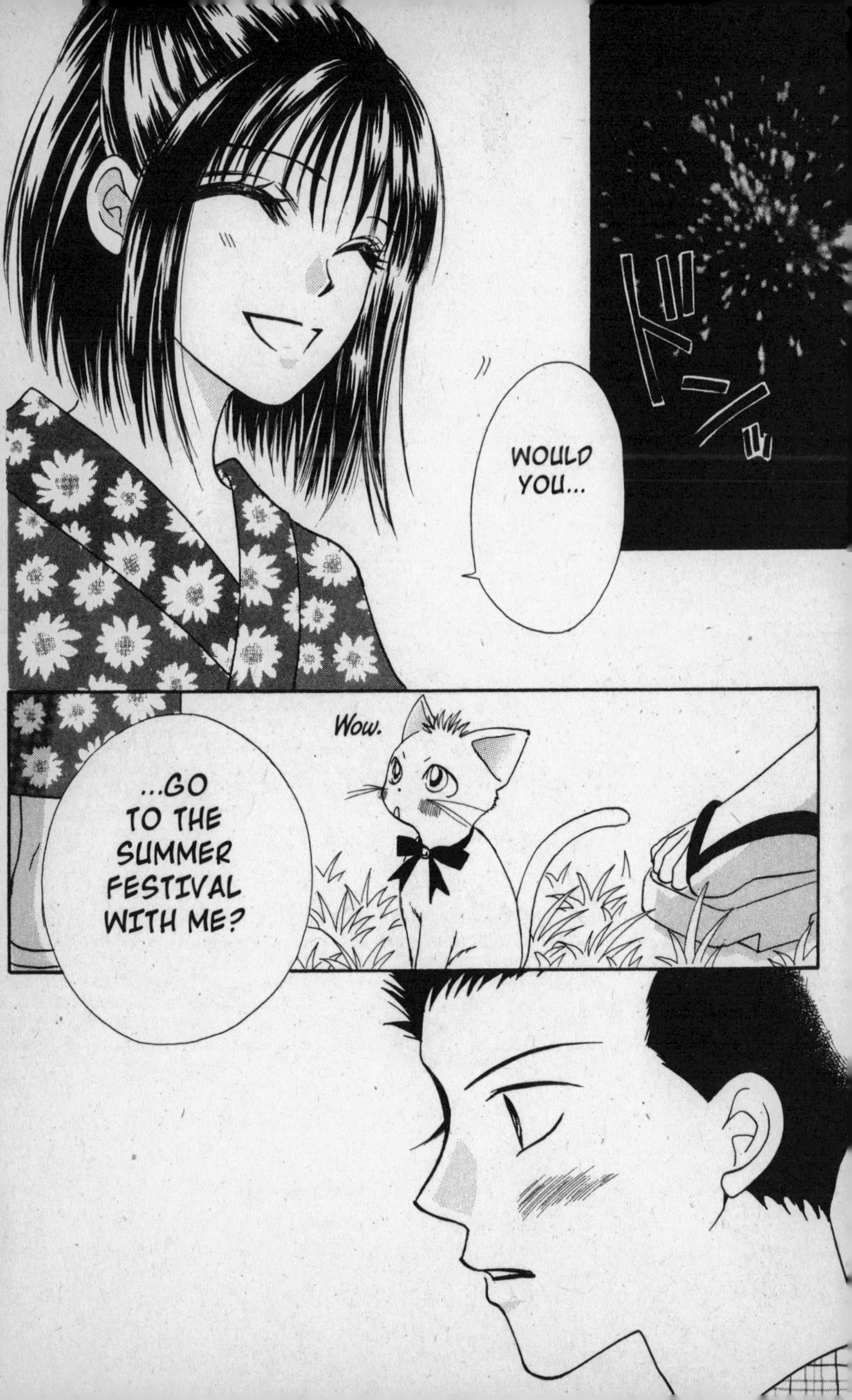
ドーン
WOULD YOU...
Wow.
...GO TO THE SUMMER FESTIVAL WITH ME?

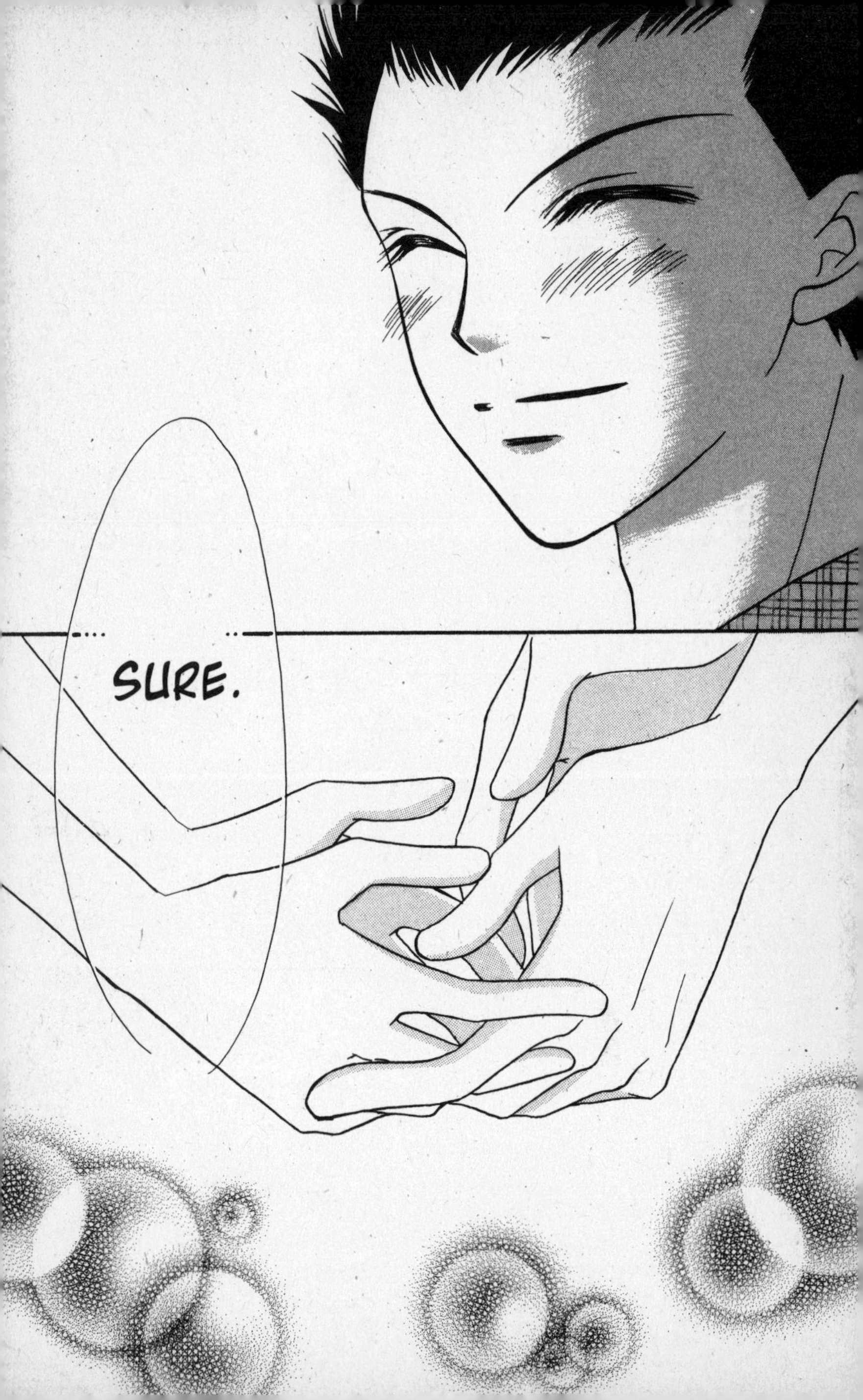

......SURE.

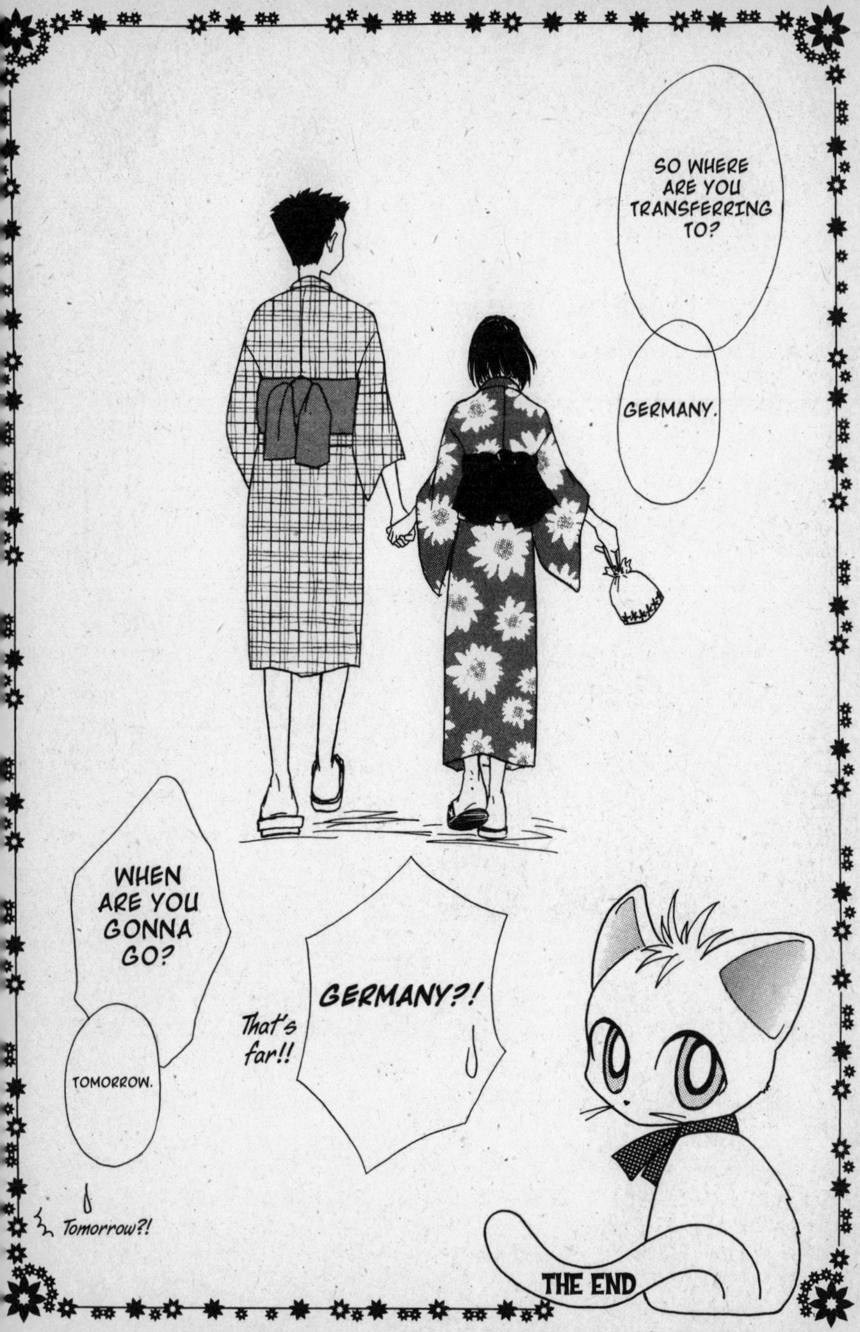
SO WHERE ARE YOU TRANSFERRING TO?
GERMANY.
GERMANY?!
That's far!!
WHEN ARE YOU GONNA GO?
TOMORROW.
Tomorrow?!
THE END

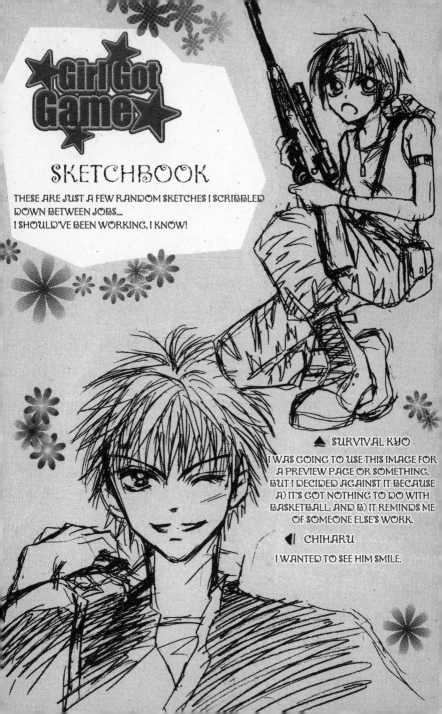

# Girl Got Game

## SKETCHBOOK

THESE ARE JUST A FEW RANDOM SKETCHES I SCRIBBLED DOWN BETWEEN JOBS....
I SHOULD'VE BEEN WORKING, I KNOW!

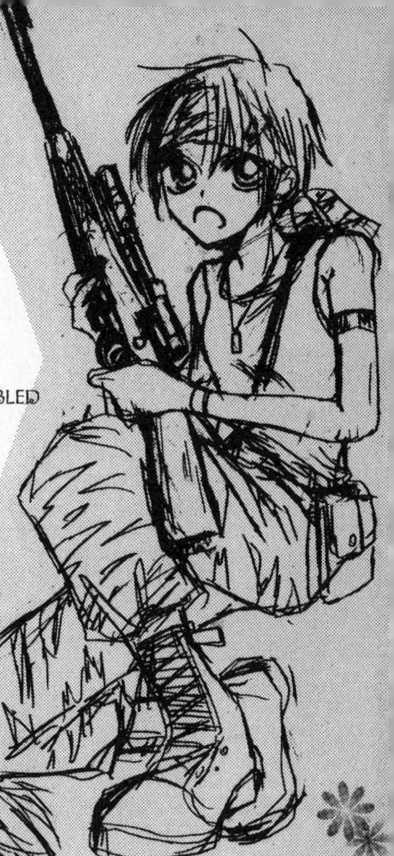

▲ SURVIVAL KYO

I WAS GOING TO USE THIS IMAGE FOR A PREVIEW PAGE OR SOMETHING, BUT I DECIDED AGAINST IT BECAUSE A) IT'S GOT NOTHING TO DO WITH BASKETBALL; AND B) IT REMINDS ME OF SOMEONE ELSE'S WORK.

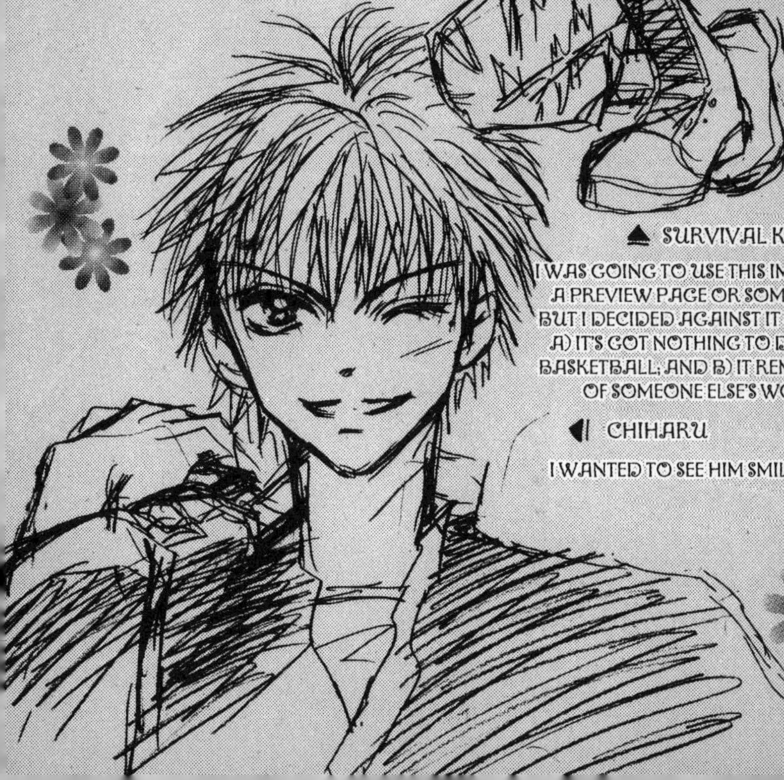

◄ CHIHARU

I WANTED TO SEE HIM SMILE.

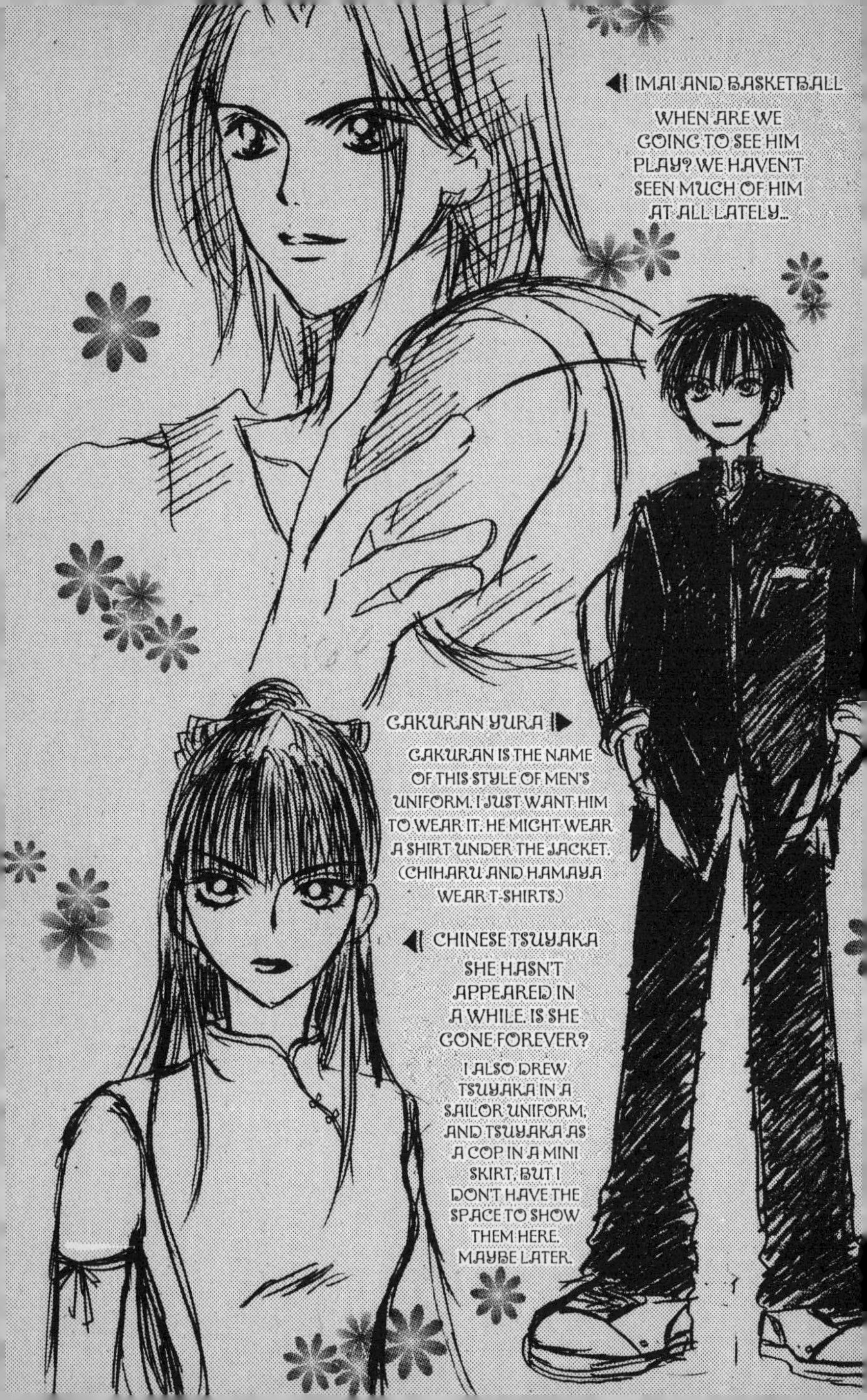
IMAI AND BASKETBALL
WHEN ARE WE GOING TO SEE HIM PLAY? WE HAVEN'T SEEN MUCH OF HIM AT ALL LATELY...
GAKURAN YURA
GAKURAN IS THE NAME OF THIS STYLE OF MEN'S UNIFORM. I JUST WANT HIM TO WEAR IT. HE MIGHT WEAR A SHIRT UNDER THE JACKET. (CHIHARU AND HAMAYA WEAR T-SHIRTS.)
CHINESE TSUYAKA
SHE HASN'T APPEARED IN A WHILE. IS SHE GONE FOREVER?
I ALSO DREW TSUYAKA IN A SAILOR UNIFORM, AND TSUYAKA AS A COP IN A MINI SKIRT, BUT I DON'T HAVE THE SPACE TO SHOW THEM HERE. MAYBE LATER.

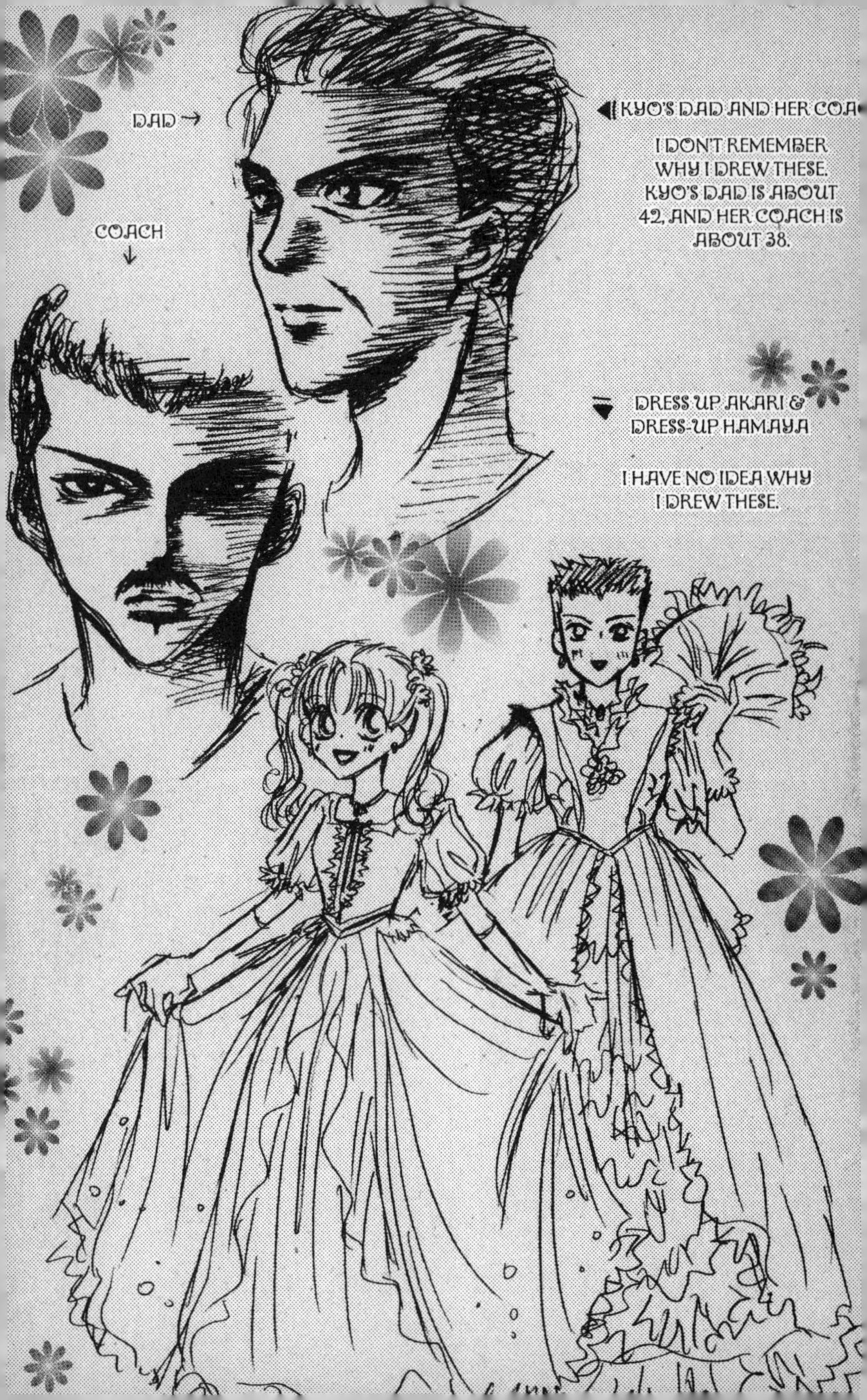
DAD →
COACH ↓
KYO'S DAD AND HER COA
I DON'T REMEMBER WHY I DREW THESE. KYO'S DAD IS ABOUT 42, AND HER COACH IS ABOUT 38.
DRESS-UP AKARI & DRESS-UP HAMAYA
I HAVE NO IDEA WHY I DREW THESE.

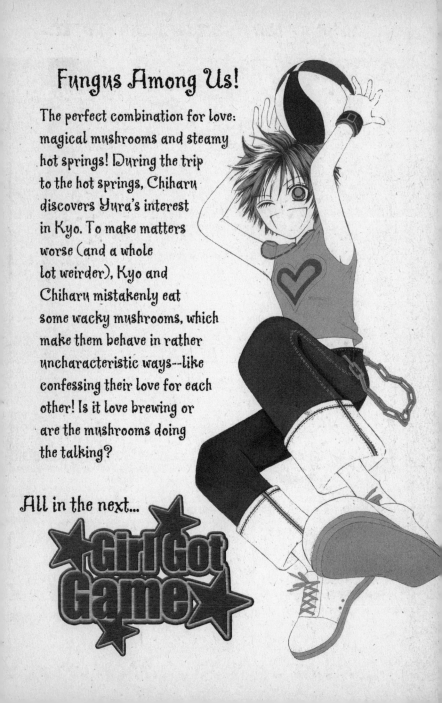

# Fungus Among Us!

The perfect combination for love: magical mushrooms and steamy hot springs! During the trip to the hot springs, Chiharu discovers Yura's interest in Kyo. To make matters worse (and a whole lot weirder), Kyo and Chiharu mistakenly eat some wacky mushrooms, which make them behave in rather uncharacteristic ways--like confessing their love for each other! Is it love brewing or are the mushrooms doing the talking?

All in the next...

★Girl Got Game★

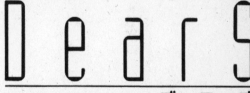

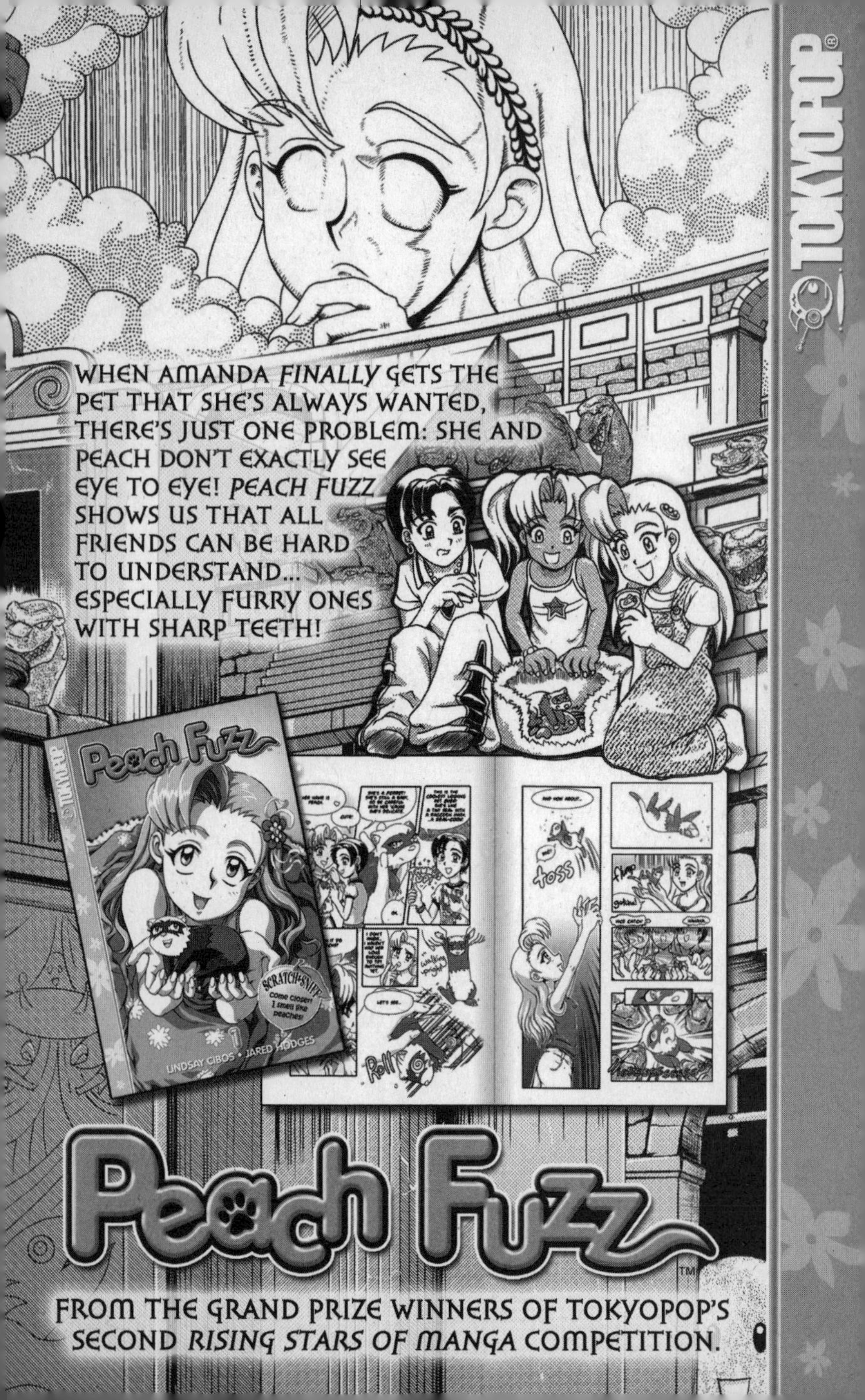
TOKYOPOP®
WHEN AMANDA *FINALLY* GETS THE PET THAT SHE'S ALWAYS WANTED, THERE'S JUST ONE PROBLEM: SHE AND PEACH DON'T EXACTLY SEE EYE TO EYE! *PEACH FUZZ* SHOWS US THAT ALL FRIENDS CAN BE HARD TO UNDERSTAND... ESPECIALLY FURRY ONES WITH SHARP TEETH!
Peach Fuzz
TOKYOPOP
SCRATCH & SNIFF
Come closer! I smell like peaches!
1
LINDSAY CIBOS • JARED HODGES
toss
Roll
Peach Fuzz
TM
FROM THE GRAND PRIZE WINNERS OF TOKYOPOP'S SECOND *RISING STARS OF MANGA* COMPETITION.

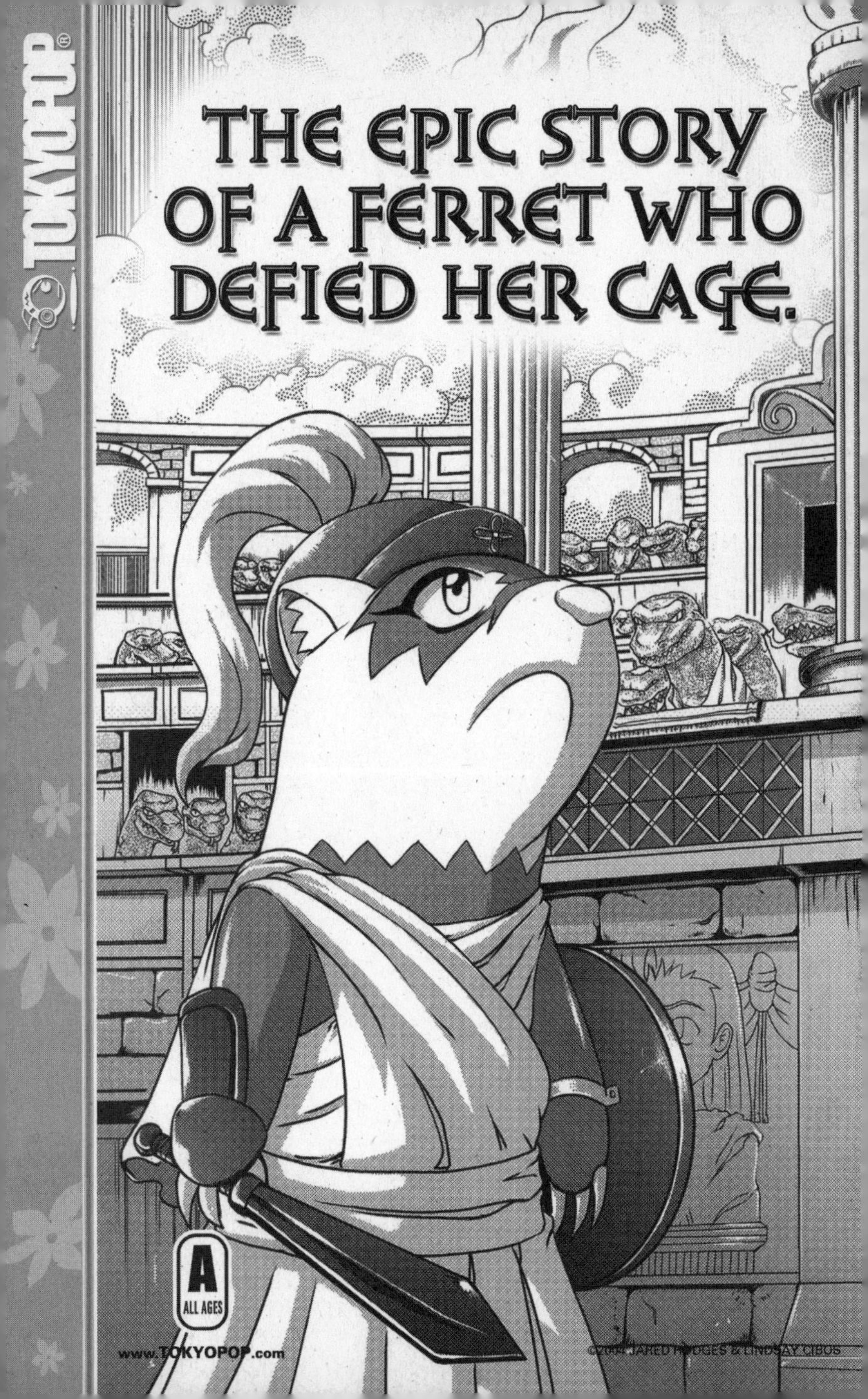
TOKYOPOP
THE EPIC STORY OF A FERRET WHO DEFIED HER CAGE.
A
ALL AGES
www.TOKYOPOP.com
©2004 JARED HODGES & LINDSAY CIBOS

# ALSO AVAILABLE FROM  TOKYOPOP®

**You want it? We got it!
A full range of TOKYOPOP
products are available now at:
www.TOKYOPOP.com/shop**

09.21.04T

# ALSO AVAILABLE FROM 🐱 TOKYOPOP®

## MANGA

.HACK//LEGEND OF THE TWILIGHT
@LARGE
ABENOBASHI: MAGICAL SHOPPING ARCADE
A.I. LOVE YOU
AI YORI AOSHI
ALICHINO
ANGELIC LAYER
ARM OF KANNON
BABY BIRTH
BATTLE ROYALE
BATTLE VIXENS
BOYS BE...
BRAIN POWERED
BRIGADOON
B'TX
CANDIDATE FOR GODDESS, THE
CARDCAPTOR SAKURA
CARDCAPTOR SAKURA - MASTER OF THE CLOW
CHOBITS
CHRONICLES OF THE CURSED SWORD
CLAMP SCHOOL DETECTIVES
CLOVER
COMIC PARTY
CONFIDENTIAL CONFESSIONS
CORRECTOR YUI
COWBOY BEBOP
COWBOY BEBOP: SHOOTING STAR
CRAZY LOVE STORY
CRESCENT MOON
CROSS
CULDCEPT
CYBORG 009
D•N•ANGEL
DEARS
DEMON DIARY
DEMON ORORON, THE
DEUS VITAE
DIABOLO
DIGIMON
DIGIMON TAMERS
DIGIMON ZERO TWO
DOLL
DRAGON HUNTER
DRAGON KNIGHTS
DRAGON VOICE
DREAM SAGA
DUKLYON: CLAMP SCHOOL DEFENDERS
EERIE QUEERIE!
ERICA SAKURAZAWA: COLLECTED WORKS
ET CETERA
ETERNITY
EVIL'S RETURN
FAERIES' LANDING
FAKE
FLCL
FLOWER OF THE DEEP SLEEP
FORBIDDEN DANCE
FRUITS BASKET

G GUNDAM
GATEKEEPERS
GETBACKERS
GIRL GOT GAME
GRAVITATION
GTO
GUNDAM SEED ASTRAY
GUNDAM WING
GUNDAM WING: BATTLEFIELD OF PACIFISTS
GUNDAM WING: ENDLESS WALTZ
GUNDAM WING: THE LAST OUTPOST (G-UNIT)
HANDS OFF!
HAPPY MANIA
HARLEM BEAT
HYPER RUNE
I.N.V.U.
IMMORTAL RAIN
INITIAL D
INSTANT TEEN: JUST ADD NUTS
ISLAND
JING: KING OF BANDITS
JING: KING OF BANDITS - TWILIGHT TALES
JULINE
KARE KANO
KILL ME, KISS ME
KINDAICHI CASE FILES, THE
KING OF HELL
KODOCHA: SANA'S STAGE
LAMENT OF THE LAMB
LEGAL DRUG
LEGEND OF CHUN HYANG, THE
LES BIJOUX
LOVE HINA
LOVE OR MONEY
LUPIN III
LUPIN III: WORLD'S MOST WANTED
MAGIC KNIGHT RAYEARTH I
MAGIC KNIGHT RAYEARTH II
MAHOROMATIC: AUTOMATIC MAIDEN
MAN OF MANY FACES
MARMALADE BOY
MARS
MARS: HORSE WITH NO NAME
MINK
MIRACLE GIRLS
MIYUKI-CHAN IN WONDERLAND
MODEL
MOURYOU KIDEN: LEGEND OF THE NYMPH
NECK AND NECK
ONE
ONE I LOVE, THE
PARADISE KISS
PARASYTE
PASSION FRUIT
PEACH FUZZ
PEACH GIRL
PEACH GIRL: CHANGE OF HEART
PET SHOP OF HORRORS
PITA-TEN
PLANET LADDER

09.21.04T

# STOP!

## This is the back of the book.
## You wouldn't want to spoil a great ending!

This book is printed "manga-style," in the authentic Japanese right-to-left format. Since none of the artwork has been flipped or altered, readers get to experience the story just as the creator intended. You've been asking for it, so TOKYOPOP® delivered: authentic, hot-off-the-press, and far more fun!

# DIRECTIONS

If this is your first time reading manga-style, here's a quick guide to help you understand how it works.

It's easy... just start in the top right panel and follow the numbers. Have fun, and look for more 100% authentic manga from TOKYOPOP®!

1
2
3
4
5
6
7
8
9
10

100% AUTHENTIC MANGA
品質第一公式商品